JOSEPH PRIESTLEY

and

ENGLISH UNITARIANISM *in* AMERICA

JOSEPH PRIESTLEY

and

English Unitarianism *in* America

J. D. BOWERS

The Pennsylvania State University Press
University Park, Pennsylvania

LIBRARY OF CONGRESS CATALOGING-IN-PUBLICATION DATA

Bowers, J. D.
Joseph Priestley and English Unitarianism in America / J. D. Bowers.
p.   cm.
Includes bibliographical references and index.
ISBN-13: 987-0-271-02951-9 (cloth : alk. paper)
ISBN-10: 0-271-02951-X (cloth : alk. paper)
1. Priestley, Joseph, 1733–1804.
2. Unitarianism—United States—History—18th century.
3. United States—Church history—18th century.
4. Unitarianism—United States–History—19th century.
5. United States—Church history–19th century.
I. Title.

BX9869.P8B69 2007
289.1092–dc22
2006100016

The Pennsylvania State University Press
is a member of the Association of American University Presses.

CONTENTS

ILLUSTRATIONS

ACKNOWLEDGMENTS

As John Demos asked in *The Unredeemed Captive*, where does the story begin? This book has its origins in my childhood, growing up in Northumberland just four blocks from the Joseph Priestley House. It took on a new dimension and importance in graduate school, when Paul Lucas encouraged me to seek both personal meaning and intellectual challenge in local history. Over the ensuing decade I found both, and owe Paul a debt of gratitude that I can never repay. Though he died before it came into its present form, this book is nonetheless a product of his tutelage and generous spirit, though its flaws should not be cast upon his memory.

All historians understand the significant role that others play in bringing their work to light. Ms. Andrea Bashore and Dr. Bill Richardson, the current and former site directors of the Priestley House, consistently provided knowledge, a place to work, and the resources to facilitate this project. Both also became friends. Bernard Sheehan graciously agreed to shepherd me through my graduate studies and provide the necessary guidance and prodding when it seemed as if the dissertation might never be completed. Stephen Stein, whose work has shaped my own interests, taught me more than he realizes about the role of religion in American history and society (though he too should not be blamed for any oversights or errors). Michael Grossberg, Marianne Wokeck, and R. David Edmunds were also patient stewards and gave substantive advice that has only improved this project. I would also like to thank Conrad Wright, who provided me with substantial assistance on theological particulars (though we may still disagree and I might not have learned as much as he had hoped) by helping me draw the parallels and distinctions between Socinians and the New England liberals. Mark McGarvie helped me rethink and restructure the presentation of some ideas. Len Smith's careful reading of the manuscript also led to additional insights, corrections, and a stronger argument.

There are many other colleagues who have helped me clarify and strengthen my arguments, including Charlie Barbour, Patricia Bonomi, Rita Cooley, Than Healy, David Kyvig, William Pencak, and Josh Reppun.

Many others contributed to the research process. Roy Goodman and the staffs of the American Philosophical Society, the Library of Congress, the Northumberland County Historical Society, Dickinson College, and the Historical Society of Pennsylvania provided endless hours of assistance in locating materials, discussing new areas for investigation, and providing access to their collections. The Information Delivery Services staff of Founders Library at Northern Illinois University, especially Ron Barshinger, was instrumental and expeditious in locating and obtaining many sources and dealing with the multitude of requests. Fran O'Donnell, curator of Archives and Manuscripts at the Andover-Harvard Theological Library, also deserves a very special mention for her many efforts and continued interest in the project. Without her guidance and support the archival work behind this would have been incomplete. I am also grateful for the support of Tricia Pyne at the Archdiocese of Baltimore Archives; Reverend Andrew Hill of Edinburgh, Scotland, for his tireless efforts to promote Unitarian scholarship on the other side of the Atlantic; Frank Haas of the Harrisburg Unitarian Church; the late William Weston of Priestley Chapel; Dufour Woolfley, who shared with me his research on Northumberland; and the Reverend John Morgan, who took over Priestley's pulpit in the 1980s and brought Unitarianism, though with a vastly different theology, back to Northumberland.

Peter Potter, former editor-in-chief at Penn State Press, and the anonymous readers of the original manuscript also deserve special mention for their efforts. Peter was most patient with a certain professor whose obligations exceed his time, while both of the readers provided me with the kind of comments that were evidence of their careful and close reading of the work and which were eminently helpful in bringing the book to its present form.

The Friends of the Joseph Priestley House has generously funded numerous research trips over the years and, most recently, provided publication support. The History Department and the Office of the Dean of the College of Liberal Arts and Sciences at Northern Illinois University also provided generous research and publication assistance, without which this book would never have been completed. Indiana University (both the College of Arts and Sciences and the Graduate School) provided seed funds in the early stages of my research through the Arts & Sciences Outstanding Teacher/Scholar Fellowship and the Graduate Student Research Award. Additional funding from the National Society of the Colonial Dames of America, Indiana Chapter, provided assistance for photocopying and research expenses. Finally, the National Endowment for the Humanities, whose sponsorship of a multiyear project at the Priestley House allowed me to interact with exceptional colleagues and to gain greater insight to Joseph Priestley and his religion, provided essential financial and intellectual assistance. Through the grant I met Derek Davenport, Jenny Graham, Roy Olofson, and Michael Payne. They were generous with their time, suggestions, and support, even as they were forced to tolerate the presence of a young graduate student who did not think that Priestley's chemistry was the most important aspect of his life.

Some of the ideas and arguments in this work were presented as conference papers to the Organization of American Historians, the Society for Historians of the Early American Republic, the Pennsylvania Historical Association, the Conference of the Indiana University Museum Studies Group, and the American Chemical Society, History Division. Portions were also delivered at the annual meeting of the Friends of the Joseph Priestley House, before the members and public at the Northumberland County Historical Society, and the students and faculty of Messiah College. I am grateful for the feedback from numerous participants, audience members, and panelists at those conferences and presentations and thank them for allowing me to present my work.

I also want to thank several former students—their interest in my intellectual endeavors and influence on my teaching demand such justice. They listened to my stories and gave me the kind of encouragement that comes with youthful optimism, and many of them became wonderful friends. Wendy DeGorter, Melinda Delis, Cesi DeQuesada, Roy Esaki, Lauren Esposo, Blaine Saito, and Garrette Silverman all continue to share their lives with me and remain connected in ways that I could only have dreamed of when I started teaching. I also have fond memories of Beth Bless, Benay Brotman, Camden Burton, Kee Campbell, Kanoe Lum, and Bess Smith.

My family has earned the final acknowledgment. They gave me strength, a healthy dose of humility, financial support, the connections to Northumberland, and a passion for history—though they often viewed the latter as a personality quirk. They gave their time so that I could release myself from other obligations in order to research, travel, and write. My wife, Kristy Wilson Bowers, has listened to endless arguments about Unitarianism, has endured countless tours of the Priestley House with great humor, and has made great sacrifices.

Through it all she has been my greatest supporter and deserves my deepest gratitude. She has also given me two very beautiful and delightful daughters. It is to her and my daughters, Caroline and Julia, that this work is dedicated.

ABBREVIATIONS

ABA	Archdiocese of Baltimore Archives
AHTL	Andover-Harvard Theological Library, Cambridge
APS	American Philosophical Society, Philadelphia
AUA	American Unitarian Association
AUA (AHTL)	AUA collection at AHTL
	bMS 193/4. AUA. Circular book, 1825–31.
	bMS 496. AUA. President, Samuel Atkins Eliot, Records and correspondence, 1900–1927.
	bMS 571. AUA. Secretary, Correspondence (Letterbooks), 1822–1902.
	bMS 01446. Unitarian Universalist Association. Inactive minister files, 1825–1999.
	bMS 11092. AUA. Secretary, Central Administrative Subject Files, 1851–1962.
	bMS 11180. AUA. Charles Graves, "An Adventure of Faith," a history of the AUA, 1825–1925.
	bMS 14018. AUA. General Publications, 1829–1961 (with gaps).
DC	Dickinson College, Waidner-Spahr Library Archives and Special Collections, Carlisle, Pennsylvania
HSP	Historical Society of Pennsylvania, Philadelphia
JPH	Joseph Priestley House and Museum, Pennsylvania Historical and Museum Commission, Northumberland
LOC	Library of Congress, Rare Books and Manuscripts Division, Washington, D.C.
LCP	Library Company of Philadelphia
MLTS	Meadville Lombard Theological School Archives, Chicago
PSU	The Pennsylvania State University, University Libraries, Rare Book and Manuscript Division, University Park

Works   *Theological and Miscellaneous Works of Joseph Priestley, LLD, FRSD*. Edited by John Towill Rutt. London: R. Hunter, 1832.

INTRODUCTION

"In my opinion, those who are usually called Socinians (who consider Christ as being a mere man) are the only body of Christians who are properly entitled to the appellation of Unitarians," declared Joseph Priestley, the English Unitarian minister, in his 1786 treatise *An History of Early Opinions concerning Jesus Christ*. He simultaneously rejected all other theological expositions of belief in the unity of God, specifically noting that those who believed in the preexistence of Christ, the belief that Jesus was coeternal with God, and yet not God, "can have no claim to the appellation of an *Unitarian*," and thereby set into motion a theological dispute over Unitarian religious identity and religious practice that would linger for more than a century and involve Unitarians on both sides of the Atlantic.[1]

The doctrine of one God, for which English Unitarians were named, centered on the belief that there was no coexistent Christ, only the human prophet Jesus (which sometimes led people to call them Humanists or Humanitarians), and that the Holy Spirit was equally unscriptural.[2] Though Priestley and others called their theological system and loose confederation of believers Socinian, the term was not completely accurate. The English Unitarians of the eighteenth century, who considered Priestley to be their leading theologian, were not in complete agreement with Faustus Socinus, the sixteenth-century divine who had been responsible for codifying the doctrines of what became the Minor Reformed Church of Poland in his work *Bibliotheca Fratrum Polonorum*. While the English accepted Socinus's rejection of Christ's divinity and promotion of the use of reason in scriptural analysis, they were not as open to some of his other rationalistic justifications of faith.

Nonetheless, English Unitarians took the name on the grounds that it identified them with the single most important aspect of unitarian

---

1. Priestley, *An History of Early Opinions concerning Jesus Christ*, in *Works*, 6:48.
2. Price, *Sermons on the Christian Doctrine*, 37 and 105.

thought and cast them into the religious landscape of England as reformers. The principles of rationalism and historical progress held by the Unitarians taught that as time passed old errors were corrected and previously unknowable truths were revealed. The most important of these old errors and new truths concerned what Priestley had come to identify as the historical corruptions of true Christianity—acceptance of Jesus as Christ, the notion of Jesus' coeternal existence with God, his preexistence in the world, and the Holy Spirit—all formed in centuries when believers were prone to misinterpret both oral and written testimony. Contrary to what such positions might indicate and how their opponents categorized them, Unitarians also professed an acceptance of Christian evidences, historical and spiritual, compatible with prevailing Protestant beliefs, as well as being in agreement with them that God embodied human attributes. Most Unitarians also accepted the Arminian view of the doctrines of free will, resistible grace, and universal atonement. It was on such matters as universal atonement, the accepted notions of grace, and the existence of a corporeal soul (a later variant of Unitarianism would even question the soul's very existence) remaining with the body until the time of the resurrection that the Unitarians were in disagreement with the Calvinists. Most Protestants, however, would have found the Unitarian belief that salvation was universal and their acceptance of the final resurrection as a literal event to be a familiar, if not fully acceptable belief.[3]

Guided by this set of religious principles, Priestley, along with Theophilus Lindsey, initiated the transformation of Unitarianism in England, later formalized by Robert Aspland and Thomas Belsham, into an acknowledged and avowed denomination. But his religious principles, coupled with his challenges to the established political and social views brought him into conflict with those who controlled England's religious and political establishments. He was forced to flee, opting in 1794 to come to the United States, bringing with him his religious principles and his desire to spread the Unitarian beliefs.[4] For a decade Priestley served as the inspiration and leading force in the spread of Unitarianism in America and the formation of numerous societies that followed his teachings on congregational formation, the education of youth, lay preaching, and espousing one's faith in the presence of opposition from (and to) both the Protestant majority and a competing liberal faction. Fortunate to have been preceded by

---

3. Belsham, *American Unitarianism*, 10.
4. Conkin, *American Originals*, 57.

the dissemination of his writings and itinerant English Unitarians, Priestley's arrival was the capstone in a process of transatlantic exchange that resulted in the formal emergence of Unitarianism in 1796 as yet another newcomer in the American religious landscape.

The collection of societies, some of which openly adopted the name "Unitarian," was quickly identified by its Socinian theology and the English influence. Priestley's efforts were the inspiration for at least a dozen congregations, mostly led and populated by English émigrés who were already present and waiting for viable leadership or who had come to escape oppression. Congregations of Unitarians, who directly attributed their existence to Priestley, were established in Maine, Massachusetts, New York, Vermont, Pennsylvania, Virginia, and Kentucky. Priestley's American sermons were well attended, attracting many non-Unitarians, as well as published and distributed throughout the country. Ministers of other congregations shared their pulpits with him and engaged him in theological discussions intended to reveal their mutual understandings. Unitarian beliefs were categorized as "a denial of the catholic doctrine of the Trinity, and an adherence to the literal sense of those passages of scripture which assert the unity of God and the humanity of Christ, who they think cannot lawfully be considered an object of religious worship," wrote James Mease. Widely known, but not universally accepted, these beliefs and the congregations who professed them became the accepted foundation of American Unitarianism.

But they did not occupy the liberal ground alone, and they were not the only group who professed the unitarian concept as part of their theology. As Mease further noted, Unitarians, "although agreed concerning the character of Christ as a man sent and approved of God, they are not unanimous as to his miraculous conception," and therein lie the seeds of the theological contest that would ensue as English Unitarianism confronted an already-extant American liberalism with unitarian leanings.[5] While there were many differences between the two beliefs, the major feature was that Priestley and many other English Unitarians believed that Jesus was never more than a man, had never ascended into heaven, and was a simple, yet special prophet of God. This was in contrast to the liberals, who professed that Jesus was of divine birth, had been taken into heaven and returned to earth with God's blessing, and was both human and divine.

Reaching back to the time of the Great Awakening, if not earlier, New England liberals (as they both called themselves and were labeled

5. Mease, *Picture of Philadelphia*, 217 and 221.

by their opponents) had increasingly come to accept the notion of a single God with a distinct, yet still divine Jesus—rejecting the fullness of the trinitarian conception of God the Father, Son, and Holy Ghost—and promoting human reason as a necessary instrument in *biblical* interpretation. However, while they believed that Christ was preexistent, combining their Arminian views with an Arian conception of Jesus, they were unwilling, and in most cases theologically incapable, of espousing the unitarian idea as their central, defining belief and thus remained ensconced within the Congregationalist tradition prominent throughout New England. Despite holding beliefs that coincided with Socinianism, the liberals adamantly denied any association with the English Unitarians, believing them to be both extremist and polemical. The Socinians felt that the two groups shared a natural connection, one that should have resulted not only in a common agenda but also a common religion. The Arians shied away from interaction with Socinians and were content to side-step the early fracas the latter had created with their open advocacy of Unitarianism. While Priestley and his followers put themselves into the public realm, the New England Arians were content to remain within the confines of congregationalism—liberal impulses were one thing, open declaration of beliefs others would consider heretical was another.[6]

Thus, while the English Unitarians were not simply free to grow unchecked and their development in America was challenged by established Protestant denominations and a lack of fellowship with the liberals, the various congregations were nonetheless able to achieve relative stability and develop institutional norms. Their views regarding religious rationality and theological dissent were the only ones openly denoted as Unitarian and offered the only presence with which the opponents of religious liberalism could contend. The forces of Christian apologists saw no reason, however, to confine themselves to splitting theological hairs when it came to repudiating the arguments and proclaiming the destructiveness of their opponents, freely conjoining the New England liberals with the professed Unitarians. As events would unravel, especially following the dispute in 1805 over religious authority at Harvard, known as the Unitarian controversy, the English Unitarians also attempted to call the liberals into their camp on the basis that they themselves had often passed through Arianism on

6. Ebenezer Gay espoused these thoughts in the Dudleian Lecture at Harvard in 1759 "Natural Religion as distinguished from Revealed," 5–7, 13. Only Charles Chauncy published writings during this period which asserted that faith was a product of reason and had an intellectual foundation.

their way to more Biblically consistent, logical Socinian belief. They were also quick to point out the growth in the number of Unitarian ministers and congregations throughout the nation, adding to their argument favoring association, not to mention that the liberals represented a potentially expansive base for the growth of a nationwide Unitarian denomination.

As the pressure on the New England liberals increased they began calling themselves "Liberal Christians" and sought to distinguish themselves from their Congregationalist brethren. In 1819, when they were finally ready to take further steps, the decades-old presence of Priestley's Unitarianism forced them to contend with its competing ideas and beliefs. In short, if the New England Arians were to claim the Unitarian name, as William Ellery Channing proposed in his sermon "Unitarian Christianity," they would only be able to do so by circumventing or eliminating preexisting Unitarian traditions.

The liberals' quest to establish a "distinct sect" created quite a stir in the religious community.[7] Their formal separation from the Congregationalists, predicated on the basis of their overwhelming numbers and legal decree, began to erode the English Unitarian identity and influence. Theirs was a new unitarian theology and identity, and they quickly relegated Socinianism to the periphery of American religion and fervently denounced all associations between themselves and the Unitarianism of old. In 1825, under the leadership of Channing they formed a ministerial association, known as the American Unitarian Association (AUA), and from that moment on, Channing and New England Unitarians of his ilk spent their entire ministerial and religious lives denouncing Priestley and his variant Unitarian theology. The "corporate development" of Unitarianism required the rejection of the original Unitarians and their beliefs if it was to succeed.[8] Though there was an occasional charitable comment that separated "Priestley the man" from "Priestley's beliefs" or that parsed the English theological system until the individual elements were found acceptable, conflict was the order of the day. The AUA sought exclusive claim to the name "Unitarian" and acceptance within the wider religious community on its own terms. Given the circumstances of the day and a continued desire to remain a part of the Christian community, it was left with little choice. Socinian belief included universal salvation and toleration, a literal view of the apocalypse, religious experimentalism,

7. Wright, "American Unitarianism in 1805," 2.
8. Stokes, *Church and State*, 1:720–21.

and humanistic visions of the soul. These ideas, derived from scientific and religious rationalism, were considered too extreme and were associated with the fringes of the standing order, a position that those who were coming out of Congregationalism fought to avoid. Likewise, Socinian theology served as a focal point of attack for other, competing religious groups who pointed to inconsistencies within the denomination's beliefs and the absurdity of rationalism.[9]

But there were those who, as Unitarianism confronted the changing religious realities of the American nineteenth-century, recognized that liberal religion was stronger when it was more inclusive. There were certain tenets of Priestley's theological system that were widely accepted and understood as representing the universal foundations of religious reform, rationalism, and liberalism. Priestley's advocacy of free inquiry was quite acceptable, since the very idea of unfettered discourse and investigation was what had attracted many liberals to the unitarian position in the first place. As Transcendentalism emerged among young Unitarians in the 1830s, and when Theodore Parker further transformed the faith in the 1840s, many Unitarians began to recognize that Priestley's theological system represented a potentially strong ally against the new, even more extreme humanism. While Priestley's ideas on the humanity of Jesus were rapidly becoming the acceptable stance with respect to the Trinity, Parker's movement away from a Christian and Bible-based faith were not. If Unitarians hoped to remain within the Christian community, as many did, and if they hoped to recapture the identity of their faith, Priestley's now seemingly benign rationalism was viewed as an acceptable, historical, and effective weapon against the new extremes of rationalism. By the late nineteenth century it was clear, Joseph Priestley and the English Unitarians were accepted back into the Unitarian continuum.

In fact, Priestley and English Unitarianism had never disappeared; they had only faded into the background for a time. They had been sustained by the emotional, financial, and intellectual support of the Unitarians in England. Small groups of American intellectuals, liberal thinkers, and elites, most of whom were English immigrants themselves, continued to profess Priestley's beliefs and teachings, and the flow of English Unitarian ministers, while never plentiful, was constant and produced some of America's most notable Unitarian clergymen of the period.

9. Conkin, *American Originals*, 65.

When viewed in light of its context and existence in the Atlantic world, a history of Unitarianism reveals new connections and a deeper internal conflict among like-minded believers, not to mention the growing rift between Americans and Britons. The English involvement in American Unitarianism was significant and lasting, even if that involvement was as a result of ceaseless efforts to reject it.[10] Although the Priestleyan version of Unitarianism never rivaled its successor in numbers of adherents or the extent to which it was tolerated by outsiders, its influence and initial successes in America were important. Priestley's presence gave others the courage to openly profess their unitarian leanings and eventually proclaim themselves denominational Unitarians. Just as Priestley was able to capitalize on earlier efforts to spread Unitarianism in America, the New England wing was able to capitalize on Priestley's efforts, even if they denied this link. Further testimony to Priestley's success was the fact that his Unitarianism buckled only under the pressure of the New England liberals' onslaught, not the pressures of the trinitarians. It was Channing's supporters, those who felt it necessary to shove Priestley's followers aside precisely because the latter represented a threat, who ended up erasing the English presence. Had Priestley and his followers failed, their legacy would have been easier to discredit.

It is doubtful if Channing and the later Unitarians could have succeeded without the earlier efforts of the Socinians to spread their religion. In fact, the New England Unitarians might not have even emerged as a separate entity had it not been for Priestley and his followers. It was the English Unitarians who pulled the New England liberals further from their orthodox heritage and engaged them in a debate over the substance and meaning of unitarian beliefs. This created a gulf between the Unitarians and the trinitarians that was later exploited and led to one of the most profound shifts in religious definition within any denomination in early national America. In the early years, Priestley and his followers attracted the wrath of trinitarian opposition, deflecting it away from the New England liberals, and thus shielded the unitarians hiding within Congregationalism. The English Unitarians also established the social and political message

10. For an introduction into the importance of considering religion in the context of the British Atlantic world, and justification for analysis based on a transatlantic framework, see Carla Gardina Pestana, "Religion," in Armitage and Braddick, *British Atlantic World*, 69–89. In the same work, see also Bernard Bailyn's preface and Braddick's introduction, especially xix, and 1–6.

of the religion through their efforts to create congregations, publish theological writings, and involve themselves in the nation's social issues, thus precluding the need for the New England Unitarians to stake out this ground once they formed themselves into the new denomination.

Throughout the Enlightenment America transformed many foreign ideas into distinctly American concepts.[11] Though New England Unitarians denied the influence of the English denomination's ideas on the development of their faith, the Unitarianism of Lindsey and Priestley was discernible in America almost immediately.[12] "America was more than a passive party, receiving and reflecting what had emanated from others. . . . In ways that are not altogether clear, the American people as a whole absorbed and adopted from Britain . . . some leading features of Enlightenment thinking."[13] The tradition of cross-cultural adoption and later adaptation has been a constant force throughout history, and we should not think of Americans as any different. Paul Conkin notes that "in no sense was doctrinal Unitarianism . . . a product of American reformers. And, to an extent rarely recognized by most Americans, neither doctrine [the humanity of Jesus and universal salvation] would be distinctive to those American Christians who adopted the labels 'Unitarian' or 'Universalist.'"[14] The ideas thought to be uniquely American were the product of a complex transatlantic process of intellectual and religious exchange. This exchange can be seen in the personal letters of interested parties on both sides of the ocean, in the libraries and bookshops of America, and through the connections that America retained with Europe in literary, scientific, and political concerns.

In an 1824 essay, F.W.P. Greenwood, the editor and chief correspondent of the *Unitarian Miscellany,* challenged William Ellery Channing's characterizations of Joseph Priestley in his ordination sermon at the installation of Ezra Stiles Gannett as Channing's associate pastor:

> We hold it our duty to remark, that we were not pleased with the manner in which the writer speaks of DR. PRIESTLEY. It is true that the merits of Unitarian Christianity are not indivisibly linked with the character of any one of its advocates; but it seems to us, that if there is one man to whom, more than to any other, Unitarians can look with confidence, and point

11. This process may have been, as several scholars have noted, the result of American exceptionalism. See Lerner, *Revolutions Revisited,* 14–21.

12. Conkin, *American Originals,* 57.

13. Lerner, *Revolutions Revisited,* 25.

14. Conkin, *American Originals,* 57.

with pride, as the honest, zealous, pious, unwearied, distinguished champion of their principles, Dr. Priestley is that man. If the orthodox see fit to revile him, and speak of him as an instance of the injurious tendency and influence of Unitarianism, we can only say, that we wish we had many more like him, to the objects of their calumny and misrepresentation, and of our pride. . . .

Dr. Priestley's character was full of the beauty of Christianity; and, unless our ideas of him are altogether erroneous, he was so far from being "constitutionally deficient in moral enthusiasm and deep feeling," that he rather seemed to overflow with those qualities, which had been poured into his constitution in double measure.[15]

Greenwood's sentiments echoed throughout the rest of the century, so that by its end, Joseph Priestley was once again recognized and celebrated as one of America's leading Unitarian protagonists.

Scholars today have continued to overlook Priestley, leaning toward a confined consideration that explores only his immediate impact or contrasts his efforts with later developments of denominational formation. In the classic study *Our Unitarian Heritage,* Earl Morse Wilbur notes that Unitarianism was a uniquely American faith, a position that has been carried across the breadth of scholarship and reiterated with increasing fervor so that by the late 1980s, even after the New England centric approach to American religion was called into question, it was succinctly reaffirmed by Conrad E. Wright, when he labeled Unitarianism "indigenous to New England."[16] David Robinson's somewhat tempered contention that "the story of the development of the denomination remains largely a New England affair," includes an acknowledgment that English Unitarianism was "not without its impact," though what that was remains unexplored save for its relationship to Jefferson's views.[17] Robert Schofield has labeled Priestley's years in America as his religious "anticlimax" and contends that his presence left no lasting impact on Unitarianism.[18] More recently Conrad Wright has written that "one suspects that there were many instances of Arians who . . . were actually as humanitarian in the Christology as Priestley had ever been,"

15. Greenwood, "Dr. Channing's Sermon," 208–11.
16. Wright, "Preface" in *American Unitarianism, 1805–1865,* viii.
17. Robinson, *Unitarians and Universalists,* 23.
18. See Schofield, *Enlightenment of Joseph Priestley,* 275, and *Enlightened Joseph Priestly,* 373–401.

but even still cautions that one must be "wary of exaggerating [Lindsey and Priestley's] contribution to it."[19] Likewise, Priestley's influence on the theological and denominational development of American Unitarianism remains virtually ignored. Even a visit to the Joseph Priestley House and Museum today, located in Northumberland, Pennsylvania, is likely to leave the visitor with a less-than-whole understanding of Priestley's religion and the role he played in the course of the nation's religious history.

This book seeks to restore Joseph Priestley and English Unitarianism to their proper and influential place in the history of the American denomination and to investigate the theoretical dimensions of early American religious denominations, using Unitarianism as a case study, through a combined focus on the theological, social, and political elements that shaped the formation of the nation's religious identities and groupings. Denominations have multiple manifestations, never just one, and the threshold for considering a group a viable denomination needs to be reconsidered. While Priestley and his followers clearly lacked the formal, institutionalized structures of a denomination, they lacked little else. For all intents and purposes, as this work will show, they were regarded, though not necessarily welcomed, as one of the multitude of religious denominations in the United States well before 1825. This book does not contend that English Unitarianism was more important than the variant that emerged out of New England, but it does seek to call into question the traditional, monolithic New England-centered study of American Unitarianism. The historical narrative of American Unitarianism is viewed by many as one that is settled and unchanging. Unitarianism, alone among the assortment of American religious denominations, has been viewed as the proprietary religion of New England. Most religious histories place the central focus on the denomination's transformation from New England Congregationalists into Unitarians, facilitated by a specific series of events that took place in and around Boston largely independent of any outside influence. This approach ignores several key developments and numerous important moments in the history of Unitarianism, when the matter of theology—its focus, language, and definition—was shaped by a multitude of influences, as John Allen Macaulay has recently pointed out in his study on Unitarianism in the American Antebellum South.[20] Simply put, "traditional" Unitarianism does not

---

19. Wright, "American Unitarianism in 1805," 15–16.
20. Macaulay, *Unitarianism in the Antebellum South.*

exist save in the minds of those who choose to ignore all other elements; the traditions which have emerged—in theology, fellowship, doctrine, and identity—are products of change and time, what one scholar has called "traditioning."[21] There is movement in all religious dispensations and early American Unitarianism was no exception. The history must reflect this movement and its myriad origins.

It is incorrect to argue that over the course of its two centuries of existence in the United States, Unitarianism simply grew out of an isolated and unchanging tradition. If one surveys the continuing history of Unitarianism (today known as Unitarian Universalism), one cannot help but see multiple threads of influence spanning its entire existence. Ideas about the reasonableness of Christianity, a leading tenet among Unitarians, were espoused by John Locke—whose writings were replete with references to religion and his nascent Socinian religious beliefs.[22] Locke's ideas were echoed, notably but not solely, by Charles Chauncy, one of the most influential religious figures in early New England and a significant figure in the development of New England's liberal tradition, the same tradition that later emerged as Unitarianism. The ideas and theology of English Unitarianism were equally influential. Unitarian itinerants in the 1780s, open adoption of the English Unitarian liturgy in the 1790s, and Joseph Priestley's decade-long personal efforts, supported by a host of others and carried on by supporters both in America and in England for years afterward, all attest to this fact. Finally, it is the later events in the development of Unitarianism, those developments between the 1830s and the 1890s, which clearly lay bare Unitarianism's ever-changing and unstable status, and gave rise to a full recognition of the totality of theological influences.

Some have argued that denominational history is no longer relevant, that it is too frequently grounded in hagiographic tendencies and that it lacks relevance to the wider scope of historical and religious study, not to mention the prevailing emphasis on analytical themes and categories. Denominational studies, note two scholars, are often dismissed because they are rooted in "the obvious" and result in historical accounts that "pale by contrast to the great issues" and thus evoke only

21. Heilman, *People of the Book*, 62–65. See also Alan Wolfe's discussion of the development of religion, especially the aspect of traditions, in *The Transformation of American Religion*, 97–126. Although Wolfe explores the contemporary religious scene, his applications can easily be evaluated in light of the historical background that is often overlooked by such recent sociological investigations.

22. Wallace, "Socinianism," especially 63, where Wallace quotes Jonathan Edwards who criticized Locke for being "all over Socinianized" in his views on atonement, redemption, and Christ's sacrifice.

"ambivalence . . . not worth the intellectual attention" invested.[23] Other scholars—including Henry Warner Bowden, William Hutchinson, Charles Long, and Nancy Ammerman—contest such views, noting that studies which investigate the multifaceted layers of denominational investment in American society can help shed light on the nation's long-standing theological traditions, social and religious organization, and cultural identity.[24] This study adopts a very similar view, going beyond traditional denominational history to document American Unitarianism's central role in the nation's broader theological discussions, its transatlantic context that stretched well past the conclusion of British rule in America, and the political-social issues that transcended religion and yet were such a part of the religious and intellectual milieu of the period.

This book seeks to pick up where Greenwood left off in 1824 and show cause for the inclusion of Priestley and his English theology as a significant part of the early story of American Unitarianism. By presenting the history of Unitarianism in America through the developments among the Socinian faction, something never before done in the historiography, it adds to the existing literature. With an emphasis on Socinianism and Priestley, much of the work will focus on Pennsylvania and other selected sites where both were physically present or prominent, with particular emphasis on the Northumberland congregation and its two most notable ministers, Priestley and a later successor, James Kay. Because this is a work that seeks to resurrect the ongoing conversation within American Unitarianism over the theology of Priestley, I have chosen, for the most part, to allow the individual and group actors to speak for themselves, more so than has been the trend in recent historiography, yet far less so than in the histories of old, which were full of complete transcriptions.

Despite assertions to the contrary, there were various significant theological ideas and religious groups that influenced early American Unitarianism and presented challenges to its development. This early period of conflict predated the internal Congregationalist dispute that many claim resulted in the declaration of Unitarianism. The competing entities and ideas continued to influence the denomination's direction even after the period of conflict had ended. These elements left a legacy that is discernible in the Unitarian religion today, even though

23. Russell E. Richey and Robert B. Mullin, "Introduction," in Mullin and Richey, *Reimagining Denominationalism*, 3–4, 6.

24. Nancy Ammerman, "Denominations: Who and What Are We Studying?" in Mullin and Richey, *Reimagining Denominationalism*, 111–13.

it is greatly altered. The absence of the early contests from the histories of the religion in America has led to an oversimplification of Unitarianism's past. The outcome of this oversimplification is a narrative that routinely presents the religion as a single entity at a time when the plurality of its views was a defining component of Unitarianism's strength in America, a strength provided from England. As Greenwood concluded, "In short, Dr. Priestley was as good as he was great. In our opinion, he is not a man to be disclaimed. . . . We regard his memory with a fond reverence; and every time we think of his remote and quiet grave by the banks of the Susquehanna, we feel tempted to make a pilgrimage there, and offer our thanksgivings to Heaven for the instructions and the life of such a man."[25]

25. Greenwood, "Dr. Channing's Sermon," 208–11.

ONE

English Socinianism:
Antecedent to American Unitarianism

The sacred Scriptures do not decide for us all questions of orthodoxy. They do not
answer the problems of science, of philosophy, or history. They do not cover the
whole ground of theology. There are important matters in which Christian religion
enters into the spheres of science, philosophy, and history where the divine revelation given in these departments of knowledge is either presupposed by the sacred
Scriptures, or else has been left by them for mankind to investigate and use in successive constructions of Christian theology, which have gone on since the apostolic
age and which will continue until the end of the world.

—CHARLES BRIGGS, *The Authority of Holy Scripture*

When Theophilus Lindsey and Joseph Priestley established the first
avowed English Unitarian congregation and opened the Essex Street
Chapel in 1774, over two hundred people attended Lindsey's dedication sermon, filling the make-shift pews and spilling out into the
street.[1] Those in attendance heard Lindsey's explication of Unitarian
theology as well as admonitions on how Unitarians were to position
themselves in relation to the Anglican establishment. The text for
Lindsey's sermon was taken from Ephesians 3:4, "Endeavoring to keep
the unity of the Spirit in the bond of peace," an entreaty to pursue a

---

1. The first chapel, opened April 17, 1774, was an auction room converted into a
place of worship. It could seat three hundred people. It was outfitted by subscription, most
of which was donated at the behest of Priestley and Richard Price. No doubt Benjamin
Franklin's appearance at the opening dedication of the chapel also had some bearing
on the group's success in raising funds as well as the numbers of people present at the
opening service. If Franklin ever donated any money to the cause, it has not been
recorded. But if he gave so much to Whitefield, how much might he have given to a group
with whom he had a greater fellowship? Franklin would, in fact, continue to inquire about
the status and success of the chapel, as he did in a letter dated August 21, 1784. (See
Franklin, *Writings,* 1102–3.) In any event, the sum total of all donated funds must have
been substantial for within four years the group purchased Essex House, on the same
street, and a proper chapel was built on the site and dedicated on March 29, 1778. See
Lindsey, *Historical View,* 474–75.

common association outside the established church and to maintain Christian virtues in the face of opposition. He further elucidated the tenets of Unitarian theology again drawing from the Bible, by paraphrasing Ephesians 4:4–6. There is, he said, "One Lord, one faith, one baptism, one God and Father of all, who is above all, and through all, and in you all . . . One body . . . One Spirit, one rule of faith, and one Lord Jesus Christ . . . himself subordinate to, and receiving all his powers from the One God and Father of all."[2] The opening and closing prayers, not originally planned for publication, echoed many of Lindsey's comments, urging the congregants to open their hearts to the wisdom of God, acknowledge the role and importance of Jesus as a prophet, preserve them from blind zeal, and adopt a "divine temper" in their pursuits of daily life and religious liberty.

The significance of the occasion was not to be measured simply by the number of people in attendance, or the expressions of a unitarian-based theology, or even that dissenters had opened a chapel despite the prevailing legal and religious restrictions against doing so. Rather, the event was notable for the simple fact that the doctrine of God's divine unity, unitarianism, had moved beyond its existence as a singular theological idea to become the cornerstone of an emergent denomination and the foundation of a developed theological system. Though neither Priestley nor Lindsey could be assured of the lasting contributions and significance of the occasion, what they set out to accomplish eventually changed the course of religion on both sides of the Atlantic Ocean and "occasion[ed] a new era in the history of religion."[3] Within four years the congregation was able to build a proper chapel, developing into one of the most notable dissenter chapels in England over the next twenty years. As the congregation grew and progressed, so too did English Unitarian theology. Together Priestley and Lindsey designed a liturgy, which was inspired by and drawn from the writings of Samuel Clarke and Dr. Isaac Watts, to include their preferred order and practices of worship; espoused a distinct denominational identity built around the central belief that they, though unitarian in belief, remained well ensconced in the Christian faith and were, with only a few notable exceptions, still in fellowship with other Christians; and articulated a clear theology, beginning with the idea of God's singularity, but also including a staunch belief in the authority of Scripture, honoring Jesus for his divinely appointed role (while denying his eternal existence and

2. Lindsey, *Sermon . . . April 17, 1774*, 8.
3. Priestley, *Autobiography*, 98.

asserting his humanity), and a continued acceptance of God's future promises of salvation and a day of judgment. For the better part of two decades this transformation of unitarianism into a denominational identity and as part of a broader belief system was effected within England, eventually finding its way into the United States by the middle of the 1780s and with renewed intensity and prominence in the 1790s and beyond.

In order to understand Unitarianism's eventual development in the United States, however, attention must first be focused on the developments in England that preceded and followed from the formation of the Essex Street Chapel. It was there, in the Strand, that the theology, practice, and formal recognition of Unitarianism were first made publicly known.

English Unitarian Beliefs

Unitarianism is traceable back into antiquity and the questions it poses and the theological issues it wrestles with are almost as old as Christianity itself. Much of Unitarian theology was derived from the ministry of Jesus and revelations provided by the Gospels; Unitarians often quoted Jesus as the source of their theological belief in the unity of God, citing his own statements about his humanity. The Unitarians also derived many of their ideas from the first three centuries of Jesus' disciples. According to the interpretations of the Gospels offered by rationalist, liberal thinkers, the apostles followed the teachings of Jesus exactly as they had received them, and considered heretical any notion of Christ's divinity.[4] The doctrine of the Trinity was formalized by the fourth century as a result of the application of Greek philosophy to matters of Christian theology.[5] But Unitarians, especially those who were well-versed in Priestley's theological tracts, decried the Trinity, arguing that previous theologians, the apostles, and even Jesus himself had held that there was no entity equal to God and that any mention of Jesus or the Holy Spirit (which was more problematic) must acknowledge that they were below God.

4. Wilbur, *History of Unitarianism*, 1:185–208.

5. For an overview of the influence of rationalism throughout religious history, see Pelikan, *Christian Tradition*, especially volumes 4, *Reformation of Church and Dogma (1300–1700)*, and 5, *Christian Doctrine and Modern Culture (since 1700)*. For commentary specifically related to the doctrines associated with Christ, including unitarian views, see Pelikan, *Jesus Through the Centuries*, 59–101.

The Reformation was an important era in the development of Unitarianism. The leading figures of unitarian thought were Lelio Sozzini and his nephew, Fausto (Faustus Socinus), who were prominent in the Italian and Polish liberal religious movements during the Radical Reformation. They challenged the divinity of Christ and condemned the failure of church authorities to use reason when interpreting scripture, for which they suffered public reprisal and attack. Faustus's major role in the promulgation of unitarian doctrine was in the "unification of various tendencies in the movement: antitrinitarian, ditheistic, tritheistic; a question of adoration and non-adoration of Christ; the problem of negation of civil authority and negation of participation in civil life; justification of faith against rationalistic and antireligious views." Although the English Unitarians did not adopt the ideas of Faustus in every detail, he was, nevertheless, a significant inspiration to them in their endeavors along similar lines.[6]

Other figures who helped push a reform agenda that facilitated Unitarianism's emergence included Michael Servetus in Spain; Ulrich Zwingli and Heinrich Bullinger in Switzerland; Desiderius Erasmus in Holland; and eventually Giacomo Contio in England.[7] Each of these figures sought to reform the doctrines and institutional practices of Catholicism, and in their scriptural commentaries each betrays a growing unease with the doctrine of the Trinity and many of the mystical elements of religious belief. The Enlightenment idea of religion, which held that religious belief was a tool to be used to address the spiritual needs of the people, stemmed from the changes in practice that emerged during the Reformation. Many new groups emerged, some totally outside the established churches and others as splinter groups within them, and, like the Unitarians, they used reason to assess the value of any given theological tenet. As Priestley put it in 1794, the Trinity was not a rational doctrine—that "*three divine persons constituting one God* is, strictly speaking, an *absurdity,* or *contradiction.*"[8] Although they were heavily grounded in the ideas of their own era, the English Unitarians of the eighteenth century had inherited a great deal from the theologians of the sixteenth.

The earliest arrival of unitarianism into England is often traced to Reginald Peacock, bishop of St. Asaph, who had adopted the idea from

6. For the life and complete theology of Faustus and his uncle, see Hillar, "Laelius and Faustus Socini," 12. For more on the Radical Reformation and the emergence of Unitarianism, see Williams, *Radical Reformation.*

7. Wilbur, *History of Unitarianism,* 2:16–98.

8. Priestley, *General View* (1794), 4.

like-minded religious thinkers on the European continent in the fifteenth century. The evidence for this is limited, especially if one allows that Peacock was routinely accused of holding beliefs that contradicted what he actually preached or published. The attribution, however, shows that even one who was intent on remaining solidly within the dogmatic spectrum of the established church was prone to question even the most unyielding tenets of the Trinity. No matter who was the first to bring the idea into England, and this may never be known, it is undeniable that the idea spread among several key religious clerics and simultaneously was considered one of the most troubling of heresies. Adherents endured increasingly harsh repression even though they remained firmly ensconced within their original religious framework in all other ways. Despite attempts to root out the heresy, at the time of Anglicanism's founding under Henry VIII, unitarian belief was so widespread that it engendered a new wave of zealous response, forcing unitarian believers to endure more than a century of repression, censorship, executions, and harassment.[9]

The status of Unitarians was especially tenuous. It was one thing for Anglicans to accept the presence of Methodists or Baptists, who disagreed with Anglicans in relatively minor ways, and quite another to extend that toleration to a group that dismissed Christ's divinity altogether. English Unitarians had the additional burden of being held in suspicion by orthodox Presbyterians, other dissenters, and Catholics, who regarded the Unitarians' combination of heterodoxy and extreme rationalism as both heresy and as a significant threat to their own well-being. Many feared that the Anglican Church or the English government would use the Unitarians as an excuse to eliminate all religious dissent.[10]

The contest over the Trinity was substantial, though not always conducted as a direct challenge to church teachings or authority. Isaac Newton and John Locke were both unitarian in their leanings; John Biddle, who preached in the first half of the seventeenth century, is considered by many to be the first openly unitarian minister. All three men advocated, with varying degrees of openness, the use of reason in religion and the ability to hold views that challenged traditional or

9. Lindsey's account, although slanted toward a sympathetic view of Unitarian progress, is corroborated in its facts and the extent of persecution by other, non-Unitarian-leaning sources. See Lindsey, *Vindiciae Priestleianae*, 446–66.

10. During the Interregnum, when dissenters were allowed to flourish, Unitarians were not included. John Biddle, one of the most well-known unitarian believers of the era was jailed and left to die in prison even after the Restoration. See Toulmin, *Review of the Life*, 109ff.

"orthodox" theology on the grounds that the church rarely spoke with one, consistent voice on such matters.[11] A virtual civil war over the issue of the Trinity and the presence of Socinian ideas broke out in the late 1600s in England with accusations of heresy on one side and of superstition on the other prominent in print and ringing from the pulpits throughout the nation.[12]

In the late 1690s, as a result of the increased prominence of these antitrinitarian views, the English minister Jonathan Edwards launched a sustained attack against John Locke's use of reason in scriptural interpretation and Socinianism. His was among the first of many such attacks against the unitarian dissenters, who had yet to declare themselves outside the parameters of the Church. Edwards noted that it was "absolutely necessary, to make one a Member of the Christian Church, to believe a Trinity in the Unity in the Godhead."[13] As he noted in *Socinianism Unmask'd*, this idea was but the "*One Article of Christian Faith necessarily to be believ'd to make a man a Christian.*"[14] Edwards's ideas, and even his phrasing, particularly his warnings against the seduction of Socinianism, were often adopted verbatim in the writings and sermons of American ministers. He likewise accused Socinianism of making common cause with Judaism and other non-Christian faiths to propagate atheism.[15] Not surprisingly, these words were echoed time and again by those who followed in Edwards's footsteps, and Edwards's ideas went on to form the core of the American rejections of Socinian and unitarian beliefs.

More important than just his phrasing or the tone of his writing was the example that Edwards set by his method of argument. Well aware that there was a multitude of unitarians who were in communion with the church, who themselves made a distinction between their beliefs and the wider, foreign-inspired Socinian beliefs, Edwards sought to link the two in order to defeat them on the basis of their commonalities. There was, he wrote, no distinction between the English and foreign Socinians who shared "a Principle constantly asserted and maintain'd by the generality of them, and upon all occasions insisted upon," despite their ever shifting arguments on other matters of theological

---

11. See John Locke, *Reasonableness of Christianity*, and Isaac Newton, *Historical Account*.

12. For an excellent account of the emergence of Socinianism and disputes surrounding the presence of the unitarian idea in England during the seventeenth century, see McLachlan, *Socinianism in Seventeenth-century England*, 317–35.

13. Edwards, *Some Thoughts*, 106–7.

14. Edwards, *Socinianism Unmask'd*, viii–ix.

15. See Edwards, *Some Thoughts*, 75, 105–6.

significance.[16] The trinitarians of New England adopted Edwards's tactic of making a connection between divergent groups in order to expose and drive out the unitarian believers of their region. When they later linked the unitarians of New England to Priestley and the Unitarianism of the Middle Atlantic states, they were responsible for establishing the foundations of confusion over the complex and distinct beliefs that were held by different groups who converged on the topic of their belief in the singularity of God.

The contentious discourse over the unitarian heresy had been current for more than a century. As unitarianism was bolstered by the influence of rationalism as embodied in the Enlightenment and persisted within the theological constructs of most Protestant denominations, the number of adherents increased. Slowly these ideas about Christ, the relationship of God to humanity, and the mysteries of the Gospel wound their way into the belief systems of Englishmen who applied them with a latitudinarian bent, even among Presbyterians and Anglicans, many of whom revised their beliefs as well as their preaching. Priestley, Lindsey, Thomas Belsham, and even the Anglican Samuel Clarke, author of *Scripture Doctrine of the Trinity* (1712), became the spiritual inheritors of this debate and the doctrine of divine unity. The most significant difference was that Priestley and Lindsey, unlike many of their English and continental European Sabellian-Socinian-Unitarian forefathers (save those in Poland and Transylvania), felt it necessary to reside in both figurative and religious terms outside the confines of the established Church of England.

English Religious Dissent and Legal Toleration

The formation of the Essex Street society was the culmination of a prolonged conflict between unitarian-leaning dissenters and the established Catholic and Anglican Churches in England, each in turn. For centuries the doctrine of divine unity had been considered one of the greatest heresies; those who espoused it were often persecuted. Beginning with the ascension of Elizabeth I to the throne in 1558, Anglicanism had become the national religion of England, codified over time in the Acts of Uniformity, Supremacy, and Blasphemy and in the Thirty-Nine Articles. Following the Interregnum, Charles II and his successors, most notably William III and Mary II, reasserted and reaffirmed Anglicanism's

16. Ibid., 69 and 67–69.

position. Although these later monarchs granted dissenters limited legal recognition, under terms spelled out in numerous legislative acts, non-Anglicans were still historically discriminated against in matters of theology, civil discourse, economics, and institutional development.

There were other impediments to denominational formation. As dissenters against the Church of England, unitarian believers were in direct violation of laws and customs as codified in the Reform and Test Acts of the early 1700s. Even after the laws restricting the rights of dissenters were repealed, many still felt their effects, as the legacy of intolerance did not wane quickly.[17] One of the most prominent laws that remained in force throughout the 1700s was the Ordinance for the Punishing of Blasphemies and Heresies of May 2, 1648, a law often called the "Draconian Law" because its prescribed punishment was death. Although the punishment was rarely inflicted, the law remained the basis for legal trials and additional restrictive acts. Later revisions, conceding the unreasonable nature of the punishment, allowed considerable leeway in enforcement. This often resulted in uneven application of the law from region to region, against particular dissenting ideas, or according to shifts in social and political opinion.

Notable, however, was the fact that the belief in God's unity was consistently persecuted, and among all dissenters unitarians often suffered the worst punishments. They especially felt the brunt of the 1689 Act of Toleration, which permitted religious dissenters the freedom to worship, minister, and teach their ideas, as well as construct their own houses of worship, so "that the Occasions of Differences and mutual Animosities may be removed,"[18] but expressly excluded both Roman Catholics and "anti-Trinitarians." The act simultaneously prohibited dissenters from holding important civil and military positions and denied them access to the universities. Dissenters were permitted to worship separately and to reject the Book of Common Prayer, no small concessions, yet the term "church" was reserved for Anglican houses of worship, forcing dissenters to use the lesser term of "chapel," and dissenters were still required to pay taxes to support the Anglican Church. It is important to note, however, that while the Act gave relief to some, unitarians were officially excluded from its provisions and therefore still subject to penalties. There was no active effort by the

17. Not until 1813 was the Act to Relieve Persons Who Impugn the Doctrine of the Holy Trinity passed that freed them, officially, from any legal repercussions. The *Test Acts*, which remained in effect until 1829, also excluded Unitarians from most political offices.

18. "Message from the King, that He will support the Protestant Religion;—recommending Toleration for the Dissenters," *House of Lords Journal*, vol. 14, April 20, 1689.

Anglican hierarchy, however, to actively seek out and excommunicate unitarian believers. As a result, early English unitarians managed to quietly exist within the church, holding their convictions as long as they held their tongues. Perhaps it would have been futile to even attempt to ferret out such believers, as rationalism was not something that could easily be identified, let alone stamped out. Such an uneasy accommodation lasted for only a brief period.

Dissenters came under greater scrutiny following a perceived increase in their numbers and a growing body of literature that supported their beliefs. In 1698 Parliament passed the Act for the More Effectual Suppressing of Blasphemy and Profaneness, which stripped offenders of their civil rights. The act originally included the word "atheism" in its title and defined offenders as anyone who preached or espoused a version of Christianity that stood contrary to the faith as defined by the leaders of the Church of England.[19] Once again some provision was made for certain groups of nonconformists, but antitrinitarians were not among them. Unitarians and certain other religious dissenters were not well situated legally. These new regulations placed them in an increasingly precarious situation, where they remained until the middle of the eighteenth century.[20]

Laws proscribing individual beliefs had only limited efficacy, especially because British subjects were often reluctant to punish citizens for ideas they themselves felt were a matter of individual conscience, no matter how erroneous or illegal.[21] Though fewer dissenters were targeted than might have otherwise been the case, the overall impact on those few who were attacked was far more noticeable. Accordingly, more significant although less-codified efforts were made against the corporate efforts of dissenters. Simply put, there were no obligations to assist religious dissenters in their collective quest to flourish. "Religious undesirables" were more often subjected to public persecution, harassment, and physical abuse than to punishment under the law. A court putting a dissenter in prison did not have the same social impact as a mob putting dissenters' homes and chapels to the torch. Such was the case several years later during the Birmingham Riot of 1791 when the businesses, private dwellings, and chapels belonging to Priestley and his fellow dissenters were all destroyed while the law looked on.[22]

---

19. "Atheism, & c. to suppress, Bill," *House of Lords Journal*, vol. 16, February 24, 1698.

20. McLachlan, *Socinianism in Seventeenth-century England*, 252–56, 285–86.

21. See Jacob, *Lay People*, 1–32.

22. The riots in Birmingham were sparked by the prevailing political sentiments of the day and a celebration of the second anniversary of the fall of the Bastille. But the mob

Nowhere were these developments as revealing as in Coventry, the economic and cultural capital of the Warwickshire region. Coventry had a long history of resistance against the religious establishment, both Catholic and Anglican. Over time the Presbyterians gained the strongest foothold in the city and surrounding countryside and were joined by single congregations of General Baptists (who established the city's first, regular congregation of nonconformists), Particular Baptists, Quakers, and Congregationalists, all of whom grew under the protections of several Declarations of Indulgence.[23] Sometime in the 1730s and 1740s the membership of Coventry's Presbyterian Great Meeting found itself sliding into unitarianism, and as a result many of the members began attending the Vicar Lane Independent Chapel. Vicar Lane, which attracted dissenters from other beliefs as well, was aided in its movement into unitarianism by a like-minded shift in theology at Smithford Street Chapel.[24] Nevertheless, unitarianism in England was growing quite substantially; so great was the movement that by 1750, the Crown rarely used its own laws to enforce the religious establishment. The government found it much too troublesome to seek out, prosecute, and place dissenters in prison. "Unitarianism discreetly practiced brought nothing more than nominal disapproval and occasional survelliance," notes Lowell Blaisdell.[25]

The sufferings endured in England were great indeed, but they had the opposite effect intended by the authorities. In terms of the larger religious community and prevailing belief systems, unitarianism was still largely restricted to a small cadre of thinkers and their small flocks of supporters. Despite the prominence of many believers and the voluminous collection of writings they produced on the subject, unitarians had failed to move the establishment toward their version of rationalism and were unable to gather other dissenting groups to their cause. As a small yet very visible part of the English dissenting minority, unitarians also embraced many principles that defined the swiftly changing political and social character of the nation; instead of leading many away from religious dissent, persecution only strengthened the convictions of those who found the established church and its association with the government wanting. The end result was a profound and lasting separation

---

that destroyed Priestley's house, laboratory, and chapel and a second dissenting chapel was as much motivated by religious tensions as political. See Miller's preface to Priestley, *Political Writings*, xv–xxii.

23. Stephens, *History*, 3:373–77.

24. See ibid., 375–77, and Kerrison, "Coventry and the Municipal Corps," 223–24, 257.

25. Lowell Blaisdell, in Baylen and Gossman, *Biographical Dictionary*, 1:292.

between the Church of England and almost ten percent of the nation's religious believers. Emboldened by their growing numbers and strength in the face of adversity, several unitarian believers stepped forward to transform the collection of rational ideas into the beginnings of a denomination. But one has to keep this whole English movement in perspective; even as late as the 1760s, unitarians were not yet certain whether or not they could create a denomination of their own, given rationalism's lack of appeal among the common people and their own aversion to proselytizing. Nonetheless, it is clear that these early efforts and the emergence of the Essex Street society determined the substance of the denomination that later emerged.

But the general movement toward unitarianism was recognized and its theological ideas were well known. While the potential for failure was still significant, the time seemed right and the convictions of the men who held these ideas would not let them delay any longer in making their case in a more public forum. Even though Socinian theology had been present in England since the late sixteenth century, it was still marginalized and regarded with suspicion. Unitarian believers were keenly aware of the dangers that lay behind an open profession of the doctrine of divine unity and the even greater challenges that would confront a denomination built around such tenets. Foremost among those who choose to meet such challenges headfirst were the Anglican minister Theophilus Lindsey and the zealous dissenting minister, Joseph Priestley.

A Little Sect by Itself . . . Some Peculiar Tenets of Its Own

Theophilus Lindsey was a religious pioneer and the unequivocal founder of Unitarianism in England. Although Priestley and Richard Price were more influential in defining Unitarian theology, it was Lindsey, Cambridge-educated and an ordained Anglican priest, who established Unitarian practice and applied its tenets to practical denominational affairs. Lindsey's conversion to Unitarianism followed a circuitous path and took more than a decade to fully complete. Well before he had officially renounced his ecclesiastical position within the Church of England, Lindsey had come to accept some basic tenets of religious dissent—the supremacy of rationalism and reason in scriptural interpretation and the belief that the state had no role in matters of faith and conscience.

Lindsey was ordained an Anglican deacon in 1746; a year later he was ordained as a priest and assigned to Kirby Whiske, Yorkshire, as rector, where he remained for seven years. He was then made a vicar, and for the next twenty years he served congregations in Dorset and Yorkshire. His promising career in the church was curtailed by his increasing doubts about the Trinity. While ministering in Dorsetshire, in the late 1750s, he first questioned the Trinity, but such were his doubts that he did not consider himself to be in a state of opposition to the Thirty-Nine Articles, which all Anglicans professed, or the Acts of Uniformity.[26] During his subsequent service as vicar of Catterick Chapel, Yorkshire, to which he was appointed in 1763, his doubts turned into convictions. After studying the epistles of St. Paul and the words of the apostles—"the original Christians"—he publicly denounced the doctrine of the Trinity.[27] As a vicar in the Church of England he was required by law to subscribe to the belief in the Trinity; nonetheless, he delayed severing his association with the church for three years. He continued to hope that the process of reform, already under way through challenges being made from many other quarters of English society, might allow him to remain in the Anglican fold. Lindsey's leadership in the failed Feathers Tavern petition, in which he and others sought relief from compulsory subscription to the Articles of Incorporation and an absolute acceptance of Anglican tenets, led him to conclude that the quest for internal reform was premature. Lindsey had long complained about disputes among divines, their abuse of each other, and the strange equivocations to which the Articles reduced them. As a result, he "grasped at [the petition] as one last straw, and went into the movement with great earnestness . . . determined that if the petition failed he would resign."[28]

It was at this juncture, in 1769, that Lindsey first met Joseph Priestley, a well-known dissenter and theologian. Lindsey turned to Priestley for assistance in matters of conscience and in so doing began a lifelong friendship. Priestley cautioned Lindsey against resigning: "At first I was not forward to encourage him in it, but rather advised him to make what alteration he thought proper in the offices of the church, and leave it to his superiors to dismiss him if they chose."[29] Instead, Priestley, usually derided by opponents for being one who thoughtlessly "attacked the orthodox and repulsed the incredulous," suggested that Lindsey

26. The Thirty-Nine Articles (1563) derived from the Forty-two Articles (1553) and the Acts of Uniformity (1549 and 1552). All of these laws constrained religious belief and practice in England.

27. Belsham, *Memoirs*, 13.

28. Wilbur, *Our Unitarian Heritage*, 262–78. See also Lindsey, *Apology*, 220–22, 1–2.

29. Priestley, *Memoirs*, in *Works*, vol. 1, pt. 1, p. 82.

should merely modify his use of the prayer book, as so many other nonconforming ministers were then doing.[30] Out of conscience, however, Lindsey could not bring himself to publicly represent, even tacitly, what he privately rejected. Even if he was able to alter the liturgy, amend the order of service, or omit the creeds from the services entirely, "to act otherwise, and to compel to an outward religious profession, when there is no inward approbation and willingness, is to violate the most sacred rights of conscience," he remarked in his opening sermon at Essex Street several years later.[31] In 1773, after a decade of deliberation Lindsey openly professed his belief in the unitarian doctrine. "Learned Christians have indeed coined a new language of their own quite unknown to our Lord and his Apostles, and have called God *Trinity, a Trinity in Unity that is to be worshipped;* which is obviously departing from the simplicity of the gospel, and is at best making a plain thing obscure," he wrote, defending his rejection of key Anglican tenets.[32] Still, Priestley cautioned Lindsey not to take further and even more drastic measures.

Against such advice Lindsey resigned, preaching his farewell sermon on November 28, 1773, in which he detailed his objections to the liturgy on both theological and personal grounds. "Your minister, by reading it, makes it his own," he told his parishioners of the liturgy and his reasons for no longer being willing to make accommodations for his views.[33] The Catterick parish register provides only a hint to his objections against Anglican teachings, simply denoting "principle of conscience" as his reason for separation.[34]

Lindsey elaborated on his objections in his *Apology on Resigning the Vicarage of Catterick,* in which he cited the specific, and most objectionable, beliefs leading to his resignation as the Trinity and the unyielding opposition to any latitudinarian bent on subscription. He could not, he wrote, support views that were "directly contrary to the mind of Christ, and condemned by him," even if these same views were held by his parishioners.[35] The publication of his *Apology* sparked a host of both critical and laudatory responses from leading clerical and governmental

30. G. Cuvier, "Obituary of Joseph Priestley," *Aurora and General Advertiser* (Philadelphia), January 23, 1808, 3.

31. Lindsey, *Sermon . . . March 29, 1778,* 7.

32. Lindsey, *Apology,* 10.

33. Lindsey, *Farewell Address,* 11.

34. Belsham, *Memoirs,* 21.

35. Theophilus Lindsey, quoted in Belsham's 1820 edition of his memoirs. Lindsey felt compelled to write a reply to his detractors and admirers both, issuing *A Sequel to the Apology,* in which he gave his clearest defense of his actions. In these, and two subsequent

officials. Those who criticized him charged that he had secretly harbored these ideas all along and had misled his parishioners and church leaders for decades.[36] Supporters, including Priestley, now accepted Lindsey's "better judgment" in resigning and, despite their hopes for his ability to serve as a leading voice of Anglican reform from within, praised his ethical decision while they simultaneously lamented that he had abandoned a promising ecclesiastical career.[37] Other Anglicans followed in Lindsey's wake, including John Disney, though not as many as he had hoped. For his part, Disney, the vicar of Swinderby and a relative of Lindsey by marriage, resigned in 1782. He quite literally followed Lindsey's path out of the church by rejecting the liturgy and moving to London in 1782, and became the first secretary of the Unitarian Society for Promoting the Knowledge of the Scriptures. In the following year, owing to growing demands on Lindsey, Disney became the associate minister at the Essex Street Chapel and eventually took it over when Lindsey resigned in 1793.[38]

Lindsey and Priestley each recognized the vital role that the other played in accomplishing their common objectives; yet each was equally aware that their theological positions were not always harmonious. For his part, Lindsey considered Priestley to be the catalyst. "Dr. Priestley is indefatigable in his endeavours, and to him, Dr. Price, and other friends of theirs will it be owing that the matter is brought to bear at last," he wrote in regards to the establishment of the Essex Street Chapel.[39] It was Priestley's standing among dissenters that earned him such regard from the Anglican convert. But Lindsey was an equal catalyst in his own right and provided the central foundations of Unitarian worship and practices. Nowhere was this more evident than in his publication of *A Liturgy, Altered from that of the Church of England, to Suit Unitarian Doctrine,* a work specifically written for use at Essex Street and copied for wider distribution. As the backbone of all subsequent Unitarian worship, this new liturgy highlighted the Unitarians' central objections to the Church of England through its omissions and alterations.[40]

---

writings published in 1779 and 1781, Lindsey defended denominational Unitarians as practicing Christians.

36. Belsham, *Memoirs,* 21ff.

37. Joseph Priestley, as quoted in Stephen and Lee, *Dictionary of National Biography,* 360.

38. Andrews, *Unitarian Radicalism,* 46–47.

39. Theophilus Lindsey to William Turner, February 9, 1774, in *Letters of Theophilus Lindsey,* 21.

40. Lindsey, *Apology,* 210. Though the point of worship was the central element of his concern, he spent considerable effort detailing the biblical passages that justified the unity

Beginning with Samuel Clarke's already extant, amended version of the liturgy, which omitted all references to the Trinity, Lindsey added a few emendations of his own. First, he clarified the role of scriptural authority—the belief that the authority of the Old and New Testaments was not to be doubted. Second, he eliminated references to all historical corruptions, which established the primacy of revelation over all subsequently developed doctrines.[41] Finally, bringing himself into concert with Priestley, he put forward an absolute rejection of the halfway position on Christ's divinity that had been adopted by those known as Arians. The Socinian view of Christ was coming to the forefront of Unitarian belief in England.

In 1783, Priestley added his own contribution to the new religious society. Building on Lindsey's ideas, Priestley wrote a practical manual to assist the Unitarians in their congregational and later denominational growth. His *Forms of Prayer, and Other Offices for the Use of Unitarian Societies* helped to establish Unitarian patterns of worship, institutional structure, and accepted norms.[42] Lindsey not only recognized such efforts for their efficacy, but also for their influence on shaping the group's future. "I must confess myself daily inclining towards Socinianism. I cannot resist the force of Dr. Priestley's reasoning," wrote Lindsey as he reflected on a subsequent edition of the *Liturgy* and the prevailing Socinian theology among an ever-growing body of adherents.[43] For his part, Priestley noted that the two men shared "an entire concurrence in every thing that we thought to be for the interest of Christianity."[44] Together the two also resolved to bring to fruition a corrected and rational version of the Bible, an effort that they saw as a perpetual work in progress. They even obtained commitments from several other leading dissenters and outlined a timetable for the initial draft's completion. The advancement of the work, based upon a return to the ancient texts and original Christian practices, was later interrupted by the riots of 1791 during which many of Priestley's notes for his portion of the edition were destroyed and subsequently slowed even further by

---

of God, citing John 4:23, 24; 5:18–19, 22–23; 6:57; 7:16; 8:28–29; 9:4; 10:17–18, 24–30, 33, 37; 11:40–42; 12:49; 13:16, 20; 14:1, 16, 28, 31; 15:8, 10; 16:5, 23; 17:3; Acts 1:24; 4:24, 29; 5:56 and 1 Corinthians 8:6. These verses became the stock passages cited by subsequent defenders of the faith, including Priestley and were the foundation of both men's writings.

41. See ibid., chaps. 1 and 9.

42. Priestley, *Forms of Prayer.*

43. Theophilus Lindsey to William Tayleur, June 26, 1788, in Lindsey, *Letters of Theophilus Lindsey*, 126; Belsham, *Memoirs*, 235

44. Priestley, *Autobiography*, 97.

his migration to the United States and Lindsey's retirement. Thus, the work was never completed according to plan.[45]

At the same time that Priestley put forward his *Forms of Prayer,* Lindsey traced the lineage and extolled the potential of Unitarianism in his *Historical View of the State of the Unitarian Doctrines and Worship.*[46] He held that Unitarians were uniquely positioned among their theological brethren: only they offered a system of religious belief that was inoffensive to other Christians. Lindsey noted that Unitarians welcomed all Christians into their services through their profession of worship to God and God alone, and their acknowledgment of Christ as prophet. But Christians could not reciprocate as a consequence of their idolatrous worship of the Trinity and the two additional gods it represented. While trinitarian Christians saw Unitarians as blasphemers who rejected the mystery of the Trinity and the divinity of Jesus, Lindsey cast blame for the rift between the two groups back upon the accusers, who, he argued, refused to see Unitarians as members of a long tradition of Christian reformers. He condemned the trinitarian practice of denouncing those who sought theological reform as un-Christian and questioned the strength of the Anglican faith. Ironically, Lindsey argued, such intolerant behavior, historically and in the present, had "contributed much to the spreading of the Unitarian doctrine."[47] In subsequent theological works Lindsey refined the Unitarian doctrines, adding changes suggested by Priestley, and gave new expression to the growing body of Unitarian ideas. Part mainstream Protestantism and part rationalist dissent, derived from the historical as well as contemporary manifestations, English Unitarian thought thus embodied the rejection of the Trinity, denial of Christ's divinity, open subscription, religious toleration, a belief in the resurrection, a materialistic conception of the soul, and biblical rationalism, as well as ideas that were held in accord with other Christians, including biblical revelation, the moral conduct and divine mission of Christ, and restoration of the uncorrupted church.

After nearly two decades leading the Unitarians Lindsey retired from active preaching. In his farewell sermon he exhorted the people

45. Joseph Priestley to Theophilus Lindsey, October 28 and November 27, 1787, in *Works,* vol. 1, pt. 1, pp. 419–21; Priestley, *A Proposal for Correcting the English Translation of the Scriptures,* in *Works,* vol. 17, app. 5, p. 531, and also app. 6, pp. 532–33. Priestley originally presented the idea for this Bible in 1784. See also Brooks, "Priestley's Plan." Although the work envisioned never materialized as such, Priestley published portions of it in his *Notes on All the Books of Scripture* and in Belsham's anonymously published *Improved Version Upon the Bias of Archbishop Newcome's New Translation.*

46. See Lindsey, *Two Dissertations.*

47. Lindsey, *Apology,* 15.

to carry on the work he and Priestley had started in order to ensure that the foundations of Unitarianism and its tenets would carry on. "It is my ardent wish now, to impress upon you with a sense of the importance of the principle by which we distinguish ourselves from other Christians, and of the obligations which it lays upon us to the practice of piety, integrity, benevolence, and all virtue," he wrote, and further reminded them to practice universal tolerance and continue their defense of the core unitarian beliefs.[48]

To trace Priestley's progress to Unitarianism one must begin with the Calvinism of his youth and a childhood filled with rebellion against the established church. Sarah Keighley, an aunt who raised him from age nine until his departure for his studies at Daventry, welcomed ministers of all beliefs at her dinner table and encouraged her nephew to engage their ideas and think for himself, for which Priestley was eternally grateful. By his early teens he had moved into Arminianism, and shortly thereafter into Arianism. This ultimately led to his transformation, by 1768, into a Socinian, swayed by his reading of Dr. Lardner's *Letter on the Logos,* which he remained until his death.

While at Daventry, where he studied from 1751 to 1755, Priestley came under the influence of John Walker, the man who led him, as he later remarked, forever "astray from the paths of orthodoxy."[49] Although it was not published until 1774, Priestley first outlined his religious thinking in *Institutes of Natural and Revealed Religion,* written while he was enrolled at Daventry. The *Institutes* established two important elements of Priestley's Unitarian faith: the importance of scripture as the "only *proper authority in matters of faith,*" and the rejection of a corrupting and antiscriptural religious establishment in favor of the more "*rational and liberal sentiments*" of God.[50] Although his religious ideas were grounded in scripture, Priestley did not accept all passages of the Bible as equal. He believed that many historical interpretations of scripture were erroneous and had led to the corruption of true Christianity over the centuries (a point that he expanded upon in later works) and that these corruptions were often integrated into subsequent translations or new versions of the Bible. He was particularly contemptuous of Anglicanism because of its connections with the political authority of the Crown and Parliament; no denomination, he argued, should depend upon government for its very existence.

48. Lindsey, *Discourse.*

49. Joseph Priestley as quoted in *Universal Theological Magazine,* April 1804, 172, in Manuscripts, JPH, Research File no. 2.

50. Priestley, *Institutes of Natural and Revealed Religion,* ix and iii; italics in original.

"Respect a *parliamentary king,* and cheerfully pay all *parliamentary taxes,* but . . . have nothing to do with a *parliamentary religion,* or a *parliamentary God,*" he exhorted, echoing the often paraphrased parable "render unto Caesar." God alone ruled over matters of faith.[51]

Priestley began his ministerial career in the 1750s in Suffolk and Cheshire, where he preached to congregations with liberal leanings though they were not as liberal as he would have preferred. At Needham Market (Suffolk), he succeeded a Presbyterian minister and was assisted in his annual salary by the London Presbyterians, presumably an indication of their acceptance of his universal, Christian message. It was while ministering at Needham Market that Priestley first indicated that he was, unequivocally, an Arian.[52] From Needham Market he moved on to Nantwich, where he was praised by the congregation for his liberal spirit and concern for all Christians. In 1767, Priestley became the minister of the Mill Hill Chapel in Leeds, from which he resigned six years later, citing a lack of liberalness among parishioners, to take a position as the personal assistant to Lord Shelburne. But it was while he was in Leeds that Priestley announced his conversion to Socinianism, stemming from his reading of Nathaniel Lardner's writings.[53]

Priestley returned to the ministry in 1780, taking over the New Meeting in Birmingham. Following the 1791 riots, which destroyed his home and chapel in Birmingham, he was asked to preach in the Amersham Chapel, a congregation of not-so-staunch Calvinists, where he also found support from local Methodists. From Amersham he moved onto his final post in England, to spend three years at the Gravel Pit Chapel in Hackney, a restructured congregation gathered from the membership of several congregations—some members left following the departure of Richard Price, whom Priestley replaced, and others joined as a result of Priestley's election. Priestley resigned this position in 1794 upon his departure for the United States.[54]

51. Ibid., ix–x.

52. Priestley, *Memoirs,* in *Works,* vol. 1, pt. 1, p. 30.

53. Priestley wrote that he had read Dr. Lardner's *Letter on the Logos* (fully titled, *A Letter to Lord Viscount Barrington (written in the year 1730) concerning the Question, Whether the Logos supplied the Place of a Human Soul in the Person of Jesus Christ*). See *Works,* vol. 1, pt. 1, p. 69.

54. It has often been asserted that Priestley's political activities and religious views were the primary cause for the 1791 riots. Such was not the case, as attested by the willingness of many people throughout England to welcome Priestley to their pulpits. The riots, although they did attack the home, laboratory, and meetinghouse of Priestley in the first hours, were a reaction to suspected liberal ideas and connections with France. Though Priestley had an open fondness for France and its Revolution, he was less outspoken than his associates. Birmingham was a fairly riotous place during that period. According to Dent, *Old and New Birmingham,* riots occurred in the city in the years 1791, 1793, 1810, 1813, 1816, and 1837.

These were the years of his greatest activity in theological matters and the years in which he endured the greatest opposition. One of his works, *A History of the Corruptions of Christianity,* written in 1782, was officially banned and burned in England in 1785. As a result, Priestley spent the remainder of the decade embroiled in a public battle with the Reverend Samuel Horsley, archdeacon of St. Alban's, who denounced the work as heresy. Priestley's status as a heretic was assured with his pronouncement that Anglicanism was "not a *progressive* religion, but a *progressive* reformation of a corrupted religion," and his subsequent overture to help its adherents release themselves from Anglicanism's troubled past.[55]

Taking advantage of this prolonged controversy to keep his ideas before the public, Priestley published his *History of the Early Opinions concerning Jesus Christ,* which Thomas Belsham, who was himself an avowed protégé of Priestley and successor to Disney at Essex Street, labeled "the most curious and valuable of all Dr. Priestley's works." Belsham, in paraphrasing Priestley's ideas, presented one of the most concise formulations of the historical foundations of unitarian thought and the belief that the apostles were themselves Socinian (as defined by Priestley and Belsham) in their unitarian beliefs.

> [The] great body of Christians, both Jews and Heathens, for the first three centuries, were strenuous advocates for the proper unity of God, and that they zealously opposed the Gnostic, the platonic, and the arian doctrines as they were successively introduced. . . . No person of reflection can for a moment, maintain that the apostles believed, and distinctly taught, the pre-existence and divinity of their master, and that the great mass of their converts were unbelievers in their testimony.[56]

Thus, the Trinity was idolatry, Jesus was a mere prophet, corruptions were repulsed by the earliest Christians, the virgin birth was ascriptural, and the doctrine of the atonement was contrived over centuries of theological errors. The message of *Early Opinions* was so influential that William Christie called it the "lasting monument of [Priestley's] genius and literary industry."[57]

55. Priestley, *History of the Corruptions of Christianity,* x.
56. Belsham, *Vindication,* 97, 88–89.
57. Christie, *Speech,* 11.

Early Opinions went further than a mere historical examination, however. In conjunction with his rejection of Jesus' divinity, historically and biblically, Priestley went on to set down the reach of beliefs for a proper Unitarian. Such a believer was antitrinitarian, materialist, universalist, humanist, moralist, rationalist, restorationist, and reformist. Furthermore, a Unitarian also believed that the doctrine of everlasting and predetermined punishment for sin was a corruption of both God's laws and writings. Finally, a Unitarian rejected any and all embellishment on the nature of God. Thus, Priestly wrote, the Arian idea that he himself once held, was both illogical and untrue, an error even more egregious than a belief in the Trinity, given that Arianism was "destitute of support in the scriptures, in reason, and in history."[58] Although many of his theological views were considered quite radical, Priestley actually retained an orthodox view on several theological questions, especially those of church polity and the need for religious rationalism. It was in the foundations of rationalism that he found his mechanism for unfettered inquiry. Priestley's path to Socinianism was enmeshed in an atmosphere of religious instability—theological adaptations, congregational schisms, and a growing confidence among dissenters of all stripes.

Priestley's materialism, it was noted, rejected the idea of any solid and fixed concept of the soul and suggested that the soul remained on earth with the body in its ethereal state until the time of the resurrection. This was actually not materialism as it was then defined, but rather misnamed and misunderstood as such by both Priestley's detractors and some of his more fervent yet misinformed supporters.[59] He first expressed his ideas about the existence of the spirit and the soul in *Disquisitions Relating to Matter and Spirit,* published in 1777, which provoked considerable opposition and brought him into the public spotlight. His beliefs regarding the soul can easily be discerned from the epitaph he had placed on his tombstone in Northumberland more than twenty-five years later. "Return unto thy rest, O my soul, for the Lord hath dealt bountifully with thee. I will lay me down in peace and sleep till I awake in the morning of the resurrection."[60] Priestley's doctrine of "soul sleep" was based on the belief that the soul, which was not something one could physically identify, would remain in a

58. Priestley, *An History of Early Opinions concerning Jesus Christ,* vol. 1, in *Works,* vol. 6, p. 15.

59. See Belsham, *Vindication,* 103–4, and also Priestley, *Disquisitions,* 17.

60. Inscription on Joseph Priestley's Tombstone, Riverview Cemetery, Northumberland, Pennsylvania; transcribed by the author.

state of stasis within the body until the resurrection and the final ascension into heaven. This was one of Priestley's more unorthodox beliefs, and he often found himself forced to explain its logical inconsistencies as well as address the challenges of those who demanded he explain how a physical soul continued to exist after death, despite his repeated denials that he considered the soul to be physical. One such opponent, the Welsh poet David Davis, penned an alternative epitaph for Priestley, offering a caricature of Priestley's beliefs and mocking him: "Here lies at rest, / In oaken chest, / Together packed most neatly, / The bones and brains, / Flesh, blood and veins, / And soul of Dr. Priestley."[61] Despite all efforts to the contrary Priestley was never able to completely distance himself or his religious beliefs from the pejorative labels that came to him through the popular press and his opponents concerning his beliefs on the nature of the soul.

Once Lindsey had fully joined with Priestley, he set out to ensure that the ideas were given a full hearing, most notably in a series of lectures delivered to the students of Oxford and Cambridge, entitled *Vindiciae Priestleianae*. Published in two volumes in 1788, the lectures were based on a compilation of "eighteen hundred passages from the early ecclesiastical writers, all of which, in [Priestley's] estimation, tend in one way or another, to confirm the Unitarianism of the great body of unlearned Christians in the primitive ages," and served as a corrective to "the corruption of the true doctrine concerning Jesus Christ."[62] Lindsey's orations detailed many of Priestley's historical and philosophical beliefs on Moses' lack of divine inspiration, the defects of St. Paul's reasoning, the sleep of the soul and body at death, early Christian monotheism, and his opinion that the doctrine of the immaculate conception was a misguided fallacy. Lindsey further defended Priestley against charges of extreme rationalism to the point of having no fixed creed.[63] Priestley was not a deist, and opposed the extreme views of Jefferson and Franklin as strongly as he did the corruptions of the orthodox religions.

Over the course of sixty years Priestley held five different ministerial appointments and preached to the congregations of at least another nine churches. These congregations ranged widely across the spectrum of dissenting beliefs then current in England and at least one was still within the Anglican fold; all of them fully understood, though

61. David Davis, quoted in Cox, "Nonconformist Joseph Priestley," 60.
62. Belsham, *Vindication*, 91, and Lindsey, *Vindiciae Priestleianae*, 2:144.
63. Lindsey, *Vindiciae Priestleianae*, 1:71.

they did not always completely agree with, his views.[64] The presentation and progression of Priestley's theological ideas is an important factor in the development of Unitarianism, both in England and as it emerged in America. His was a theological quest that was never finished and his path to doctrinal Unitarianism took almost forty years to complete; he had "passed through three religions before he determined to teach any," wrote one chronicler of him many years later.[65] He questioned his own ideas, admitted his own errors, and searched for deeper truths his entire life. In sum Priestley's theological thoughts centered on the rejection of Protestant orthodoxy's most important theological positions. He denounced the Trinity as untenable and specifically denied any evidence for the Holy Spirit. He detested the concepts of original sin and the atonement as misunderstandings and corruptions of man's relationship to God. He likewise rejected the virgin birth as a contrived theological fallacy. His views on materialism—the corporeal soul and its resurrection at the time of the second coming—were further rejections of Calvinist interpretations of the end times. Biblical inerrancy, a topic which Priestley approached with subtle distinctions, was most often, when employed by the Protestant majority, an error of reasoning or a misapplication of scripture. He further rejected most of Protestantism's notions of apostolic Christianity, citing their ahistorical development and misinterpreted reason as the cause of centuries of errant beliefs and practices. Finally, underlying all of his efforts, was his staunch support for free inquiry in all matters religious. Far too often, he held, the inherent problems within and among the various Protestant and other prominent established denominations were to be found in their efforts to suppress unfettered examination and exploration.

Anglicanism and Socinianism

Despite Adam Smith's assertion that Anglicans, after two centuries of establishment, had "become altogether incapable of making any vigorous exertion in defense even of their own establishment . . . [or] any vigorous defense against any new sect which chose to attack its doctrine or discipline," even when forced to accept an ever increasing presence of dissenters in religious affairs, the Church of England remained very

---

64. G. Cuvier, "Obituary of Joseph Priestley," 3. Priestley began life as a Presbyterian, then became an Arian, and finally moved into Socinianism.

65. Smith, *Wealth of Nations*, bk. 5, chap. 1, pt. 3, art. 3.

adept at staving off the forces of religious nonconformity.[66] Unitarianism was, until the passage of the Unitarian Relief Bill in 1813, one of its principal targets.

The Church of England capitalized on the prevailing sense of disdain for Socinianism to attack its proponents both in the press and from the pulpit. Many of the earliest attacks were directed against John Knowles, the known "asserter of the Socinian errors" whom, it seems, had established a Socinian ministry in the 1670s, one of just two that were then in existence in London. These were not independent churches, but rather meetinghouses led by known Socinian ministers which attracted a wide variety of worshippers. At the time, Socinianism was present only in "small coteries of people inside and outside the Church of England . . . where one or another preacher, Churchmen or Independent, could lead them, propound a new view of Christian doctrine, and exhibit a wider tolerance in matters of faith than that normally allowed."[67] Despite official neglect and erratic enforcement of the laws, dissenters were reluctant to properly organize and were daily reminded of their tenuous position in English society. "Infinite, my brethren, have been the mischiefs that have arisen to religion from compulsory payment of tithes, or any other *dues*, as they are called, for the maintenance of the clergy, and other religious purposes," Priestley noted in a speech given to supporters at Hackney's New College in 1791. "This country, beyond any other, groans under the unnatural oppression, and religion itself more particularly suffers by it."[68] In fact, Nathaniel Lardner, the author of *Letter on the Logos*, the work Priestley credited with his own conversion from Arianism to Socinianism, had published anonymously to avoid retribution from both the civil authorities and private citizens—in vain, as it turned out.[69]

Beginning in the early 1770s and lasting for nearly four decades, numerous tracts were published and reprinted decrying the unscriptural, hyperrational, and offensive aspects of Priestley's theology. Timed

66. McLachlan, *Socinianism in Seventeenth-century England,* 252 and 285–86. McLachlan notes the existence of numerous Socinian "circles" throughout England as a result of seventeenth-century inroads made by believers in the unitarian idea. These groups existed in Cheltenham, Gloucestershire, London, and elsewhere, but were not independent or dissenter churches. See also pp. 252–56.

67. Priestley, *Proper Objects of Education,* 8–9.

68. Priestley, *Letters to Dr. Horsley,* iv–v. Lardner had not only published without attribution, but he also delayed publishing the work for almost thirty years, having penned *Letter on the Logos* in 1730.

69. Macgowan, *Socinianism brought to the test.* Macgowan's tract was republished in 1805 and 1822 by W. Baynes of London, years that coincided with or followed close upon major developments in Unitarianism, especially in the United States.

to respond to or coincide with key developments in the public profession of Unitarianism, these writings challenged the historical and
religious foundations upon which Priestley and Lindsey based their
emerging faith. They denounced the anti-Calvinistic elements but
also, more important, took them to task for their lack of regard for
tenets which were central to Anglicanism. Edwards's writings against
Locke were just the first of many by notable English ministers that
would take Socinianism to task. One opponent, the Scotsman John
Macgowan, minister of London's Devonshire Square church from 1767
until his death in 1780, went so far as to challenge Priestley's conception
of a fully human Jesus by asserting that "if Jesus Christ is not a divine
person, the Mohammedan is, in all respects, preferable to the Christian
religion."[70] Macgowan's satirical piece, *The Arians' and Socinians' Monitor,*
was a harsh characterization of Socinian thought and a detailed
defense of Calvinist belief. In it, a former pupil of a famed Socinian
minister dreams that he has encountered his deceased tutor while on
an evening stroll. The tutor, never mentioned by name, has ascended
from the depths of hell to warn his former pupil of the dangers and
damnation that await Socinians in the afterlife. "Oh that I had never
been born! Oh that I had never been a deceiver! . . . Alas! A preacher,
a false preacher, endureth a double hell!" The pupil awakes the next
morning to find his world still intact, but the visions of the previous
night lead him to "utterly cast off all Arian and Socinian errors and
embrace the orthodox faith, which I had despised the day before" and
take on a new name in order to proclaim his visions to the world, to be
known, henceforth as "ANTISOCINUS."[71]

Even Unitarianism's more genteel opponents took its adherents to
task. William Jones of Nayland, who, like Priestley, was a Fellow of the
Royal Society, was a fervent opponent of what he considered "non-
scriptural religious beliefs," leading him to reject unitarianism and
present a staunch defense of Christian orthodoxy.[72] Jones considered
the very existence of the Essex Street congregation an affront to the
standing religious order of the nation and the commonly accepted
principles of faith and piety. Jones's "Preservative against the Publications Dispersed by Modern Socinians" attacks Priestley on the grounds
that he is both impious and absurd. Jones was joined by a multitude of

---

70. Macgowan, *Infernal Conference,* 653–76.
71. Ibid., 676.
72. Jones, *Catholic Doctrine,* 11.

other defenders of Anglicanism, including Francis Randolph, who accused Priestley and the Socinians of scriptural revisionism.[73]

Perhaps the most notable critic of Priestley and Lindsey was John Wesley's Methodist associate and anointed successor, John William Fletcher (de la Flechere), the one-time minister of Madeley parish in Shropshire. Wesley, in his sermon on the death of Fletcher, praised him for his oratorical eloquence and devotion to his parishioners, as well as his grasp of complex theological matters, expressed through "the purity of the language . . . the strength and clearness of the argument, [and] the mildness and sweetness of the spirit which breathes throughout the whole."[74] No reactionary, Fletcher, simultaneously called for reforms within Anglicanism while chastising those dissenters, specifically Unitarians, who adhered to unconditional rationalism. Fletcher denounced Priestley's antitrinitarianism as "most unreasonable and unscriptural," declaring that "all the prophetic Books of the Old Testament contain strong *hints*, or express declarations of the Messiah's Divinity."[75] Like William Jones, Fletcher considered Priestley's theological beliefs incongruous at best, and their implications concerning the apostles abhorrent: "St. *Paul* has for many Ages been looked up to with Respect, as an *Apostle*, as a *Christian*, as a *Scholar*, and as a man of *Genius* and *Parts*. But this new Socinian Doctrine, still more adventurous than the old, dares to strip him of his Honour in all these Respects. It degrades him as an *Apostle*, for it denies that he wrote by inspiration; as a *Christian*, for it makes him an Idolater; and an Encourager of Idolatry."[76] It was further unclear to Fletcher how Priestley and Lindsey could claim to be Christian when they rejected the divinity of Christ. In Fletcher's view, the view that was held by the vast majority of Englishmen of all denominations, the idea of a merely human Christ was blasphemous and lacking in common sense.[77] Joseph Benson, who originally occupied the pulpit in Birmingham that was later held by Priestley, echoed Fletcher's attacks. Benson examined Priestley's arguments and found portions of them irrational and lacking scriptural support. In his opinion, there could be no reason for an apostolic association, no possibility of grace, and no meaning in the Crucifixion, if Jesus were mere man.[78]

---

73. Jones, "Preservative," 223–47; Randolph, *Scriptural Revision of Socinian Arguments*.
74. Wesley, *Death of the Rev. Mr. John Fletcher.*
75. Fletcher, *Socinianism unscriptural*, Letter IV, 3–6, 27.
76. Ibid., iv.
77. See Fletcher, *Vindication.*
78. Benson, *Demonstration*, 121–24.

Fig. 1　*The Mystical Divine* by Annabel Scratch [Samuel Collings], British engraving. Reproduced by Margaret Aydelotte, Chemical Heritage Foundations Collections. Published by permission from the Chemical Heritage Foundation, Philadelphia.

There were, however, those in England who advocated church reform and included toleration of dissenters as a part of their overall program. Richard Watson, whose ideas for reform were sweeping in scope, was one of the most noted and vocal proponents of religious latitude. "Want of genuine moderation towards those who differ from us in religious opinions, seems to be the most unaccountable thing in the world," wrote Watson in the introduction to *A Collection of Theological Tracts*. "What is that to you?" he asked of those who sought to chastise and condemn dissenters. "To his own master he standeth or falleth; his wrong judgment may affect his own salvation, it cannot affect yours."[79] Other prominent members of England's political and religious leadership—including John Jebb, Gilbert Wakefield, Samuel Parr, and William Paley—followed suit. While some were more tolerant of Unitarians than others, all held the same basic idea that toleration was not a danger to church or state. Their position, while not popular with the English government or the hierarchy of the Church of England, was nonetheless gaining ground and within a half century would result in the passage of acts that would ease the barriers erected against dissenters.[80]

Priestley and Lindsey were the inheritors of the achievements of their predecessors as well as the extensive baggage that accompanied religious dissent. English Unitarianism emerged amid a long-standing discourse over the Trinity. The particular combination of anti-Trinitarian theology and a rejection of the religious establishment was a necessary and vital part of the Unitarian quest for religious truth. "Some persons dislike controversy, as leading to a *diversity of opinions*," wrote Priestley, but it was also "only a temporary inconvenience. It is the only way to arrive at a permanent and useful uniformity, which it is sure to bring about at last."[81] Thus, while Unitarians were not unique in their break from the Church of England, they were among the first to do so avowing a theology outside the boundaries of what the established church could tolerate. Yet Priestley and Lindsey both denied their separation from Christianity, and each spent as much time trying to establish Unitarians' credentials as members of the Christian tradition and allaying the fears of other Christians by highlighting their reverence for Jesus' role as a prophet, as they did espousing their theological ideas. Unitarianism, both men argued in sermons and pamphlets, represented the joining of many historical and religious ideas, gathering together the teachings of John Biddle, John Locke, and Thomas Firmin, along with several important pre-Nicaean thinkers, and shared many theological commonalities with trinitarian Christians. To minimize the potential affront presented by the primacy with which they regarded the doctrine of a single divinity, they repeatedly called themselves Unitarian Christians.[82]

79. Watson, *Theological Tracts,* 1:xi–xii.

80. For more background on the relationship between Crown and society in matters of religion, see Robbins, *Eighteenth-century Commonwealthman.*

81. Priestley, *Free Inquiry,* in *Works,* 15:78.

82. See Lindsey, *Apology* and *Sermon . . . April 17, 1774.* The writings that Lindsey and Priestley most often referred to as part of the unitarian legacy in England included Biddle's *Apostolical and true* and Locke's *Reasonableness of Christianity* and *Paraphrase and notes on the Epistle of St. Paul to the Galatians.*

By the early 1770s, as revealed in their letters, Priestley and Lindsey had come to a common understanding of Unitarian doctrine and eventually a shared vision for the development of an open and avowed Unitarian congregation.[83] While both men had attempted to lead existing congregations down the path of theological discovery, their success was not to come until they joined forces to establish a newly gathered group dedicated to this purpose. From their chapel on Essex Street in London, the two men could survey the religious landscape of England and consider both their religious predecessors and progeny. "We owe lasting obligations to those, who in times of great corruption of the truth, and in the midst of dangers and difficult trials have stood up for it. Others are thereby excited and encouraged, and the work of finishing what they so happily began, is made easier and safer for those that come after them," reflected Lindsey in his *Historical View of the State of Unitarian Doctrine and Worship* in 1783.[84]

The foundation of the Essex Street congregation under the leadership of these two men marks the birth of English Unitarianism as an institution and the beginning of major conflict with the prevailing dissenter and established churches. Although they still lacked a formal denominational structure, the group of religious liberals known commonly as Unitarians did band together under the auspices of the Unitarian Society for Promoting Christian Knowledge and the Practice of Virtue by the Distribution of Books in 1791. This society served as the precursor to the later Unitarian Fund and the Association for Protecting the Civil Rights of Unitarians and thus the rise of Robert Aspland, through his *Monthly Repository* and *Christian Reformer,* and eventually the formation of the British and Foreign Unitarian Association in 1825. This earlier vision—with its developed theology, worship practices, its rejection of religious exclusivity, continuously refined ideas, and the establishment of formal organizational structures—was the vision that was later imported into the United States as the central beliefs among the followers of the first avowed Unitarian societies in the new nation.

83. See Lindsey, *Historical View,* 473–76. For Priestley's earlier views on the subject, see Priestley's pseudonymous *Free Address to the Protestant Dissenters, as Such.*
84. Lindsey, *Historical View,* 442.

TWO

The Socinian Migration and the Founding of American Unitarianism

> Having been educated in the strictest principles of Calvinism, and having from
> my early years had a serious turn of mind . . . I was very sincere and zealous in my
> belief of the doctrine of the trinity . . . and was as much shocked on hearing of
> any who denied the divinity of Christ (thinking it to be nothing less than impiety
> and blasphemy) as any of my opponents can be now. I therefore truly feel
> for them, and most sincerely excuse them.
>
> —JOSEPH PRIESTLEY, *Letters to Dr. Horsley*

In 1786, just three years after his installation as minister of the East
(or Second) Church in Salem, Massachusetts, the Reverend William
Bentley remarked that "Dr. Priestley's short tracts [give] a good statement of the simple doctrines of Christianity," and he became, as a
result, an open and avowed Unitarian.[1] At the time, Bentley had been
engaged in a thoughtful reading of Priestley's *Appeal to the Serious and
Candid Professors of Christianity*, a work that had been given to him a few
years earlier by the English Unitarian itinerant minister, William Hazlitt.

Bentley's Socinian leanings were acceptable to his congregation
and shared by his close friend James Freeman, the minister of King's
Chapel in Boston. The East Church congregants, consisting mostly of
merchants and seafarers who came into frequent contact with English
influences, were liberal in thought and supported their minister's
conversion—they heartily approved of Freeman's guest sermons while
Bentley was away in 1783 and would again approve of the two men's
formal pulpit exchange in 1790. Bentley was an active proselytizer and
did not keep his acceptance of Socinianism quiet, recommending
Priestley's writings to others and sermonizing on its other tenets. "In
religion Priestley's smaller tracts are all you may want to know of the
simple doctrines of Christianity. Your own good heart will supply the

---

1. Cooke, *Unitarianism in America*, 71.

rules for practice. Priestley, on inquiry, will recommend the liberty of thinking for yourself," he wrote to one parishioner.[2] Bentley especially favored unfettered religious inquiry and diversity, which resulted in tolerance for ideas and a willingness to allow them free expression. Consequently, when Catholics arrived in Salem in the middle 1790s, Bentley openly welcomed them and defended their right to worship.

Bentley's congregation was quite receptive to Priestley's Socinianism.[3] They and Bentley sponsored the 1785 Salem publication of Priestley's catechism as well as subsequent editions that appeared in the late 1790s.[4] In 1791, Bentley set aside a period of each service, immediately preceding his sermon, to offer commentary on the scriptures, openly espousing English Socinian ideas, noting that these beliefs were now "less frightful" than they had been owing to Socinianism's steady and increasing presence in America.[5] In the course of several commentaries, Bentley explored, successively, the Athanasian, Arian, and Unitarian "hypotheses," dismissing the half-divine status espoused by Arians and giving full weight to the ideas of Priestley, to show that Jesus was not even partially divine and to conclude otherwise, he asserted, "is not a true reading" of the scriptures.[6] In his understanding and acceptance of Unitarianism on these terms and the recognition of the importance of the distinction between Arian and Socinian beliefs, Bentley was not alone. As a result the English Unitarian influence and presence in America grew; all that was missing was the presence of a permanent leader around whom the movement could coalesce.

That leader soon appeared when Joseph Priestley arrived in the United States aboard the *Samson*, which dropped anchor in New York harbor on June 4, 1794. He cleared customs the following day in the company of his family and a small group of English companions. Henry Wansey, a close friend, was halfway through a personal tour of America and was on hand to welcome him. According to Wansey, Priestley's disembarkation was "in as private a manner as possible," as he had wished. Yet his arrival "was soon known through the city, and next morning the principal inhabitants of New York came to pay their

2. William Bentley, quoted in Eliot, *Heralds of a Liberal Faith*, 150.

3. Bentley, *Diary*, 1:19, 111.

4. Priestley, *Catechism for Children and Young Persons*. This work is cited in Crook, *Bibliography*, 10. Crook gives the location of the earliest copy as the library of Dr. J. F. Fulton, New Haven, Connecticut.

5. Belsham, *Memoirs*, 187.

6. See especially Bentley's *Admitted the Unitarian attitude* and *Church of God*, AUA (AHTL), bMS 01446/12; Eliot, *Heralds of a Liberal Faith*, 151; William Bentley, quoted in Eliot, *Heralds of a Liberal Faith*, 151.

respects and congratulations. . . . No man in any public capacity could be received with more respect than he was."[7]

Priestley arrived in the United States full of optimism concerning the prospects for the spread of Unitarianism and brought with him the lessons he had learned as an English dissenter. His sanguinity came from what he knew about the religious situation in America, especially in comparison with England. In England dissenters made up less than ten percent of the population, and despite some legal toleration they remained the targets of repression; given the circumstances which led to his own departure, many considered Priestley to be among the most persecuted. All dissenters in England evoked, though some said provoked, both explicit and tacit resistance to their practices and the spread of their beliefs. For Priestley, the history and legacy of religious nonconformity in America bode well for the reception of another dissenting tradition. In a land where almost two-thirds of the population held some claim to the legacy of Protestant dissent, Priestley felt that immigration would allow him and his followers to free themselves from the rebukes of the English establishment. In America, the state assured religious pluralism under democratic principles, leading Priestley and his supporters to believe that Unitarianism, under the leadership of a prominent figure such as himself, would complement the American dissenting heritage. "The greatest difficulty," noted Priestley in dismissing a potential lack of toleration as a problem in America, instead "arises from the indifference of liberal-minded men here to religion in general; they are so much occupied with commerce and politics. One man of proper spirit would be sufficient to establish a solid Unitarian interest, and I am persuaded it will be done soon."[8] Attracted by the liberalism and rationalism of the English Unitarians, educated American Christians read their writings, debated their ideas, and showed significant interest in their efforts to form avowed Unitarian congregations.

The Liberal Congregationalists

Although the initial efforts by Lindsey and Priestley to unite and institutionalize disparate unitarian thought and dissenter worship practices

---

7. Wansey, *Journal*, 85.

8. Joseph Priestley to Theophilus Lindsey, June 15, 1794, in *Works*, vol. 1, pt. 2, p. 257. On the role of dissent and pluralism in American religion during the era of the New Republic, see Ferguson, *American Enlightenment*, 45; Lambert, *Founding Fathers*, 207–64; and Hutchinson, *Religious Pluralism in America*, 11–58.

took place in England, the effects were felt in America. But this was not always positive and was often met with more disdain than acceptance, finding a formidable, albeit unexpected opponent in the liberal wing of New England Congregationalists, who did not reject all of the principles and values of English Unitarianism, but found themselves at theological odds with Priestley and Lindsey in several key elements of belief.

The unitarian idea that had emerged in America by 1700 was a product of Arminian, rationalist, and Arian-based antitrinitarian influences. Conrad Wright calls the adherents to this unique strain of belief, alternately, Arminians, liberals, and "the liberal movement," and clearly notes that they were not to be known (and fervently denied any identification as) Unitarians until the late second and early third decades of the nineteenth century.[9] Because they believed that Christ was not consubstantial with God, yet was of God and fully divine, they were able to remain within the congregational superstructure of the New England churches.

Unitarianism was slow to fully work its way into the belief systems of a liberal wing of New England Congregationalists wary of the complex arguments used to defend the Trinity. The liberals first emerged out of opposition to the growing tide of emotionalism so prominent in the Great Awakening, an opposition led by the venerable Charles Chauncy and Jonathan Mayhew, both of whom found inspiration in Ebenezer Gay.[10] Chauncy's 1742 sermon, "Enthusiasm Described and Caution'd Against," is considered the harbinger of New England Unitarianism. Chauncy put forth "a positive set of ideas . . . a commitment to logic and reasoning in theology, a Biblicism that was strict but demanded critical and historical analysis, and an overriding concern for moral aspiration as the focal point of the Christian religion."[11] Chauncy also believed that human beings were inherently good (rejecting total depravity), held a more humanistic conception of God, and preached that the Trinity could not be justified by a rational reading of the scriptures. A cadre of ministers and laity who found the revivals an insufficient response to the crises that plagued their religion rallied around these ideas.[12]

Although the liberals were certainly aware of Priestley and his fellow English believers, the events in America led them on a slightly different path, tempered by their internal challenges, disputes, and conditions. If they drew anything from England, it came through the works of

---

9. Wright, *Beginnings*, 3–10.
10. Ahlstrom and Carey, *American Reformation*, 22.
11. Robinson, *Unitarians and the Universalists*, 9.
12. Ahlstrom and Carey, *American Reformation*, 5–6.

Samuel Clarke and Richard Price. In fact, at the time of the Revolution, the religious writings of Richard Price were widely circulated and could be found side by side with the works of Priestley, competing for the attention of the faithful.[13] Both Clarke and Price accepted that Christ and the Holy Spirit were subordinate to God, but elevated Christ to his divine status because of his preexistence to humanity. In his work *The scripture-doctrine of the Trinity: wherein every text in the New Testament relating to that doctrine is distinctly considered* (1712) Clarke argued that "the Father alone is self-existent, underived, unoriginated, independent," while Jesus was "proceeding from God . . . begotten . . . derived from the Father, he declares the *Father* to be the *One* true Eternal *God* from whom alone that Divinity of the Son is derived."[14] These ideas, like the Socinian position of Christ's mere humanity, were justified on their historical and rational basis.

Unconvinced by the convoluted arguments supporting the doctrine of the Trinity, the liberals adopted a simple and direct approach to faith and practice. Their ideas were conditioned by religious inquiry into the nature of God, religious competition within the Congregationalist tradition, and conflict with several emerging rivals, including the Methodist and Baptist faiths. They quietly adopted theological unitarianism, based on a literal reading of the Bible, mostly from the Gospel of John, Acts, and 1 Corinthians. As a result they were able to remain within their original congregations, becoming a faction within the tradition "remembered less for specific tenets than for a gradual shift of emphasis . . . and an opposition to enthusiastical religion."[15] Their limited rationalism, confined to the unity of God, permitted them to adopt unitarianism but not change their entire worship or belief system, and they retained many more of the traditional notions of Puritan and Congregationalist theology than they rejected. Thus unitarians in America remained in the shadows, content to occupy a place within the dominant religion of New England, and there they remained until 1819, drifting ever so slowly, yet not avowedly, toward their own identity, ultimately, as Unitarians. In the meantime, English Socinianism arrived, fully avowed as Unitarians, and claimed the mantle as such in the American religious landscape. While English dissent and Unitarianism did little to shape the overall liberal theology emerging in New England, it was not entirely disconnected, as Conrad Wright and

---

13. Thomas, *Honest Mind*, 202.
14. Clarke, *The scripture-doctrine of the Trinity*, in *The Works*, 4:123, 126–27.
15. Ahlstrom and Carey, *American Reformation*, 23.

others have claimed—Earl Morse Wilbur going so far as to call Unitarianism "indigenous" to America—nor was it devoid of influence. As we shall see, there was clearly a broadly defined religious society present in America calling itself Unitarian by 1800, and widely acknowledged as such, which would remain influential and a focal point for the entire nineteenth century. It is to this initial group, often glossed over in the history of American Unitarianism in a few brief sentences, that we now turn.

The English Unitarian Migration Begins

William Hazlitt, a member of Priestley's English circle, was among the first to personally bring English Unitarianism to the United States, traveling to the new nation as an itinerant minister in 1783. From his very early years, Hazlitt had been exposed to some of the more modern and rational ideas of the age. While a student at the University of Glasgow, Hazlitt read Priestley's writings and befriended the soon-to-be-famous Adam Smith. In their writings Hazlitt discovered similar thoughts about the state of monopolies (be they religious, economic, or political) expressed in similar terms. Smith predicted that religious competition "might in time probably reduce the doctrine of the greater part of [all sects and established religions] to that pure and rational religion, free from every mixture of absurdity, imposture, or fanaticism, such as wise men have in all ages of the world wished to see established"; and Priestley asserted that "whatever is true and right will finally prevail, that is, . . . rational Christianity will, in due time, be the religion of the whole world. In the prophetical language of our Savior, he will draw all men unto him."[16] Not surprisingly, Hazlitt praised both men and adopted a personal and religious worldview based on their theories, rejecting the Scottish Presbyterianism of his youth, finding it insufficient for his spiritual and intellectual needs. Like Lindsey, he resigned from his ministerial post and took up the mantle of a dissenter.

Hazlitt arrived in Philadelphia eager to spread the faith, and remained there for fifteen months, guest preaching and supporting the publication of Unitarian religious pamphlets. He delivered a course of lectures at

---

16. Smith argued in favor of religious competition using the same line of analysis that he did for matters of economic competition; he called the established religion "dangerous and troublesome." Only when pluralism reigned, he noted, would a nation prosper in religious matters. See Smith, *Wealth of Nations*, bk. 5, chap. 1, art. 3. See also Joseph Priestley, *A General History of the Christian Church*, in *Works*, 10:534.

Philadelphia College titled "Evidences of Christianity," which was well received by the leading intellectuals in the city. He also traveled to several of the more populous towns in the interior, including Carlisle, although in those regions he was often met with "all the zeal of orthodox indignation."[17] When he likewise failed to attract a substantial following in Philadelphia, he turned to the dissemination of several of Priestley's writings, the most prominent of which was *An Appeal to the Serious and Candid Professors of Christianity*, a concise thirty-three page explication of Unitarianism for the layperson.[18] The publication included sections on the proper use of reason in religion, the relationship of humanity to God, the rejection of original sin, the humanistic views of Christ, and a dismissal of the atonement. This American edition also included an appendix on the heresy trial of Mr. E. Elwall as a testimony to orthodox opposition and the struggles that might befall Unitarian adherents. Its frontispiece included an excerpt from 1 Corinthians and 1 Timothy, "To us there is one God, the FATHER, and one Mediator, the MAN CHRIST JESUS," to refute any claims that Unitarians were not Christians, and the preface further expounded upon the importance of the Gospels to the Unitarians and the support they drew from biblical passages for their ideas.[19] Hazlitt later carried *An Appeal* with him to New England and gave copies of it to Bentley and other supporters for circulation there.[20] Another work distributed by Hazlitt was Priestley's *General View of the Arguments for the Unity of God*, which Priestley himself considered the seminal explanation of the most central Unitarian doctrine, and had encouraged Hazlitt to consider in his efforts to propagate Unitarianism. Although this work was slow to circulate, it soon gained the acclaim of a growing public in Philadelphia and brought Priestley to the attention of the very people Hazlitt most wanted to reach.[21]

17. Benjamin Rush to Charles Nisbet, June 1, 1784, in Miller, *Memoir,* 116.

18. The publication and sale of the work was announced in *The Pennsylvania Gazette,* May 19, 1784. It was offered for sale at the price of "one third of a dollar, *with considerable allowance to those who buy Quantities to give away.*"

19. Priestley, *An Appeal to the Serious and Candid Professors of Christianity,* iii.

20. Only one secondary source, William Sprague, D.D., ed., *Annals of the American Pulpit,* mentions, by name, any of Priestley's writings that were edited and distributed by Hazlitt. Sprague calls it "An Appeal to the Pious and Candid Professors of Christianity" (vol. 8, p. xi). Interestingly enough, Crook's *Bibliography of Joseph Priestley* lists nothing published in America between 1783 and 1787. There were several tracts of Priestley's on political matters published during the years directly preceding and during the American Revolution, but no works appear again until 1793. Crook must not have been aware of Hazlitt's efforts and somehow must have overlooked the presence of these early religious tracts in the collections of the American Philosophical Society.

21. Joseph Priestley to Theophilus Lindsey, June 24, 1794, in Belsham, *Memoirs,* 414. See also Priestley, *General View* (1784).

While the publication of these works was a success in terms of their distribution and widespread impact on the ideas and preaching of ministers and laity throughout the nation, it did not earn Hazlitt what he most desired—a permanent ministerial position and congregation in Philadelphia. For all of his strengths, one of Hazlitt's significant weaknesses was his personality, which many found aggressive and irritating. Even his most ardent supporter, Priestley himself, who was inclined to be charitable when it came to explaining Hazlitt's struggles later remarked that "Mr. H was the most imprudent of men, and did apparently much harm here."[22] This, coupled with an inability to clearly articulate the broad expanse and depth of the English Unitarian tenets, led to failure when it came to his ultimate goal.

Failing in Philadelphia, Hazlitt decided to try his luck in Boston, but his reception there was no more promising than it had been in the nation's capital. Even among most of those who were inclined toward unitarianism, as many Bostonians claimed to be, Hazlitt's adherence to Socinian ideas led to a rather cool reception by the ministers and congregations. He had fully expected English Unitarian belief to flourish in New England and believed that it remained dormant for want of the right figure to lead it. He found them "already Arians . . . yet generally afraid to avow their sentiments."[23] Much of this optimism was the result of the remarkable reception given the reprinting of Thomas Emlyn's 1702 work, *A Humble Inquiry into the Scripture Account of Jesus Christ*. The work was antitrinitarian in the broadest possible sense.[24] Of Jesus, Emlyn wrote, "I *credit* [him] as my great *teacher;* whom I desire to *admire* and love as my gracious endeared *benefactor,* beyond father and mother, or friends, & c. whom I reverence as my *Lord* and ruler, and solemnly *expect* as my final glorious *judge,* who is to come in his own, and in his Father's glory," but secondary to God.[25] Theologically, Emlyn's work straddled the Arian-Socinian divide and did not completely satisfy either. Although Hazlitt considered this work as the foundation for the future of Socinianism in America, the tract's popularity among the liberals in New England was not an appropriate measure of English Unitarianism's potential success.

Nonetheless, a small group of ministers and independent congregations welcomed Hazlitt into their midst, foremost among them was Freeman of King's Chapel and Salem's Bentley. Hazlitt's association

22. Belsham, *Memoirs,* 414.
23. Conkin, *American Originals,* 65.
24. Emlyn, *Humble Enquiry,* iv.
25. Ibid., 49; italics in original.

with Freeman (the two met for the first time on May 15, 1784) helped the latter push King's Chapel toward an open rejection of the Trinity.[26] Over the course of almost three years, Hazlitt preached throughout central and eastern Massachusetts, in the frontier regions of Maine, and at a few churches in Boston.[27] The congregations that welcomed him were more willing to confess unitarian beliefs despite the overwhelmingly conservative, trinitarian majority and were among the most theologically tolerant in New England, with a membership that was predominantly of English heritage. The reluctance of these congregations to consider their beliefs sufficient cause to break with the standing order was for the want of a leading figure, a role Hazlitt seemed at first to fulfill. But his presence also exposed the budding differences that were later to erupt in a full-scale conflict between the central tenets of the English Unitarians and the New England liberals. The Socinianism of the English Unitarians "set [Hazlitt] apart from the Boston liberals who held an Arian Christology and wanted to maintain their distance from the Unitarianism of Joseph Priestley."[28] While few congregations changed their professions or adopted Unitarian-leaning doctrines while he was among them, many gave him credit for being the spark. "Before Mr. Hazlitt came to Boston, the trinitarian doxology was almost universally used. That honest good man prevailed upon several respectable ministers to omit it," wrote James Freeman. "Since his departure, the number of those who repeat only scriptural doxologies has greatly increased, so that there are now many churches in which the worship is strictly Unitarian."[29] Even still, the success was limited; apart from his association with a small group of like-minded ministers, Hazlitt remained an outsider, an Englishman in American New England whose desire to effect an association of American unitarians and liberals with the nascent English denomination went unfulfilled. In 1787 Hazlitt gave up and returned home.

Although he failed to achieve his personal ambitions and was unable to establish a Unitarian congregation with direct connections to the Unitarians of England, the central core of Socinian ideas caught hold. Americans, who were once totally unaware of the English actions, were slowly introduced to this emerging denomination. When Priestley arrived in America seven years later, he found the congregations prepared by

---

26. Robinson, *Unitarians and Universalists*, 259.

27. Hazlitt preached in Salem, Plymouth, Barnstable, Bristol, Weymouth, and Dorchester, in the frontier churches of Saco and Portland, and at King's Chapel in Boston.

28. Robinson, *Unitarians and Universalists*, 259.

29. James Freeman to Theophilus Lindsey, June 1789, in Belsham, *Memoirs*, 179n.

Hazlitt actively reading English Unitarian religious tracts and still engaged in discussions over the Unitarian theology, sufficiently hungry for a leader to direct their efforts.

English Unitarianism survived in Pennsylvania, despite Hazlitt's departure, owing to a renewed flow of English immigrants to Philadelphia and Pennsylvania's backcountry.[30] Many of them came, as John Vaughan and William Hazlitt had, seeking the opportunities afforded by political freedom and economic development, and they constituted the last great wave of British migrants.[31]

Vaughan, a former student of Priestley's, came in 1782 with letters of introduction from Benjamin Franklin. Working in collaboration with Hazlitt, he did much to spread Socinian beliefs via Priestley's writings, especially among the more educated elite of the capital city. William Furness, the famous Unitarian minister of the nineteenth century, who became, for all intents, the first settled minister of the Unitarian Church in Philadelphia, once described Vaughan as "prompt and zealous in furthering the interests of the infant church," a man who "shrunk not from bearing the unfashionable name of a Unitarian. . . . He never obtruded his faith on those who differed from him. . . . By forgetting doctrinal distinctions, he made others forget, despite their sectarianism, that he was a heretic. And yet he did not permit his faith to be denounced. He was always ready with a reason to answer the ignorant and the bigoted."[32]

In 1784 Vaughan presented several copies of Priestley's works, many bearing his signature, to the American Philosophical Society library. Among these were Priestley's *Letter to a layman, on the subject of Rev. Mr. Lindsey's proposal for a reformed English church, upon the plan of the late Dr. Samuel Clarke* and the aforementioned *A scripture catechism: consisting of a series of questions, with references to the scriptures instead of answers,* a revised

30. In 1786 there were 66,925 taxpayers in Pennsylvania. If taxpayers represented between one-fifth and one-sixth of the total population then the 1786 population of the state was 368,087. For Philadelphia County there were 9,392 taxpayers, resulting in an estimated population of 51,656 residents. In Northumberland County there were 2,166 taxpayers, thus approximately 11,913 residents. The 1790 Federal Census records a total population for the state of 434,373. Philadelphia's population increased to 57,044 and Northumberland County's rose to 17,147. By 1800, the state's population was 602,545, Philadelphia's was 81,009 and Northumberland's was 21,098. See Purvis, *Revolutionary America,* 124–25, 155, and 158–59, for population statistics. Most of these increases were due to British immigration. See Baseler, *"Asylum for Mankind,"* 190–309, for the details on English immigration to America during the immediate post-Revolutionary period.

31. McFarlane, *The British in the Americas,* 288–93.

32. Furness, *John Vaughan,* 11. After twenty-nine years without a permanent minister, the Philadelphia society invited Furness to take over in 1825, and he served for fifty years, until 1875.

version of his first catechism and the catechism that was included in the liturgical revisions at King's Chapel.[33] Other publications given by Vaughan to the society included works on philosophical necessity, forms of family prayer (which was to play a large role in the life of American Unitarians), and the ministry of Jesus. Vaughan continued this practice throughout his life, including the donation of Belsham's edited 1815 *Tracts in controversy with Bishop Horsley . . . to which is annexed, an appendix, containing a review of the controversy, in four letters to the bishops . . . never before published,* a work that recalled the original controversies that launched Priestley's espousal and subsequent defenses of Unitarianism and which reignited a discussion of Priestley's influence a full decade past his death.

King's Chapel, Boston

King's Chapel was the first established congregation to turn toward English Unitarianism. During the American Revolution, the congregation found itself in the midst of a crisis: the presence of a large number of loyalists with substantial social and economic ties to England, the loss of many members to the war itself, the absence of a permanent minister, and the conjoining of worship with a neighboring church were all determining factors in the outcome of the chapel's postwar transition. As a remedy to one of these missing elements, in September 1782 the wardens of the church invited young James Freeman, a twenty-three-year-old Harvard graduate, to "officiate for the Proprietors of the Chapel in the capacity of a reader for six months," a position that Freeman felt would be for life.[34]

Shortly after his appointment, Freeman began to express reservations about the Trinity but also had equally compelling reservations about expressing such beliefs publicly.[35] Freeman was acutely disappointed in the "concealment practiced about the Trinity" by his fellow ministers, and he considered their partial justifications of Jesus' divinity to be "poor shifts" of theological argumentation.[36] Soon thereafter he offered to

33. Priestley, *Letter to a layman;* Priestley, *A scripture catechism.*

34. Foote, *James Freeman and King's Chapel,* 6–7.

35. Freeman loved to relate the story of Byles's statement. Once, when Freeman was walking with Dr. John Clarke, they came upon Mather Byles. Byles, taking Freeman by the arm stated, "Now we have the whole Bible here. I am the Old Testament, you, Mr. Clarke, are the New Testament, and as for Mr. Freeman, he is the Apocrypha." For the account of this story, see Sprague, *Annals of the American Pulpit,* 8:170.

36. Foote, *James Freeman and King's Chapel,* 17.

resign his post but was persuaded by several liberal-minded parishioners to make his case openly before the church members. In a series of sermons that revealed the fullness of his beliefs and the path he followed to arrive at them, the first of which was given November 14, 1784, Freeman justified his rejection of the Trinity. "*There is one God, and one Mediator between God and man, the man, Christ Jesus. There is but one God, the Father, and one Lord Jesus Christ.* In both these passages, Jesus Christ is plainly distinguished from God," he wrote to his father in an account of his sermons.[37] The congregation generously permitted Freeman, still officially a "reader," nearly three years to outline his positions and to deliberate the matter themselves. Finally, on June 19, 1785, the congregation voted to omit references to the Trinity from their doctrines and accepted Freeman's changes to their liturgy, as well as the use of selections from Priestley's catechism, as amended by Freeman, for instructing the youth of the congregation; these changes lasted over fifty years.[38] The newly combined liturgy and catechism was printed by the end of the year. *A Liturgy, collected Principally from the Book of Common Prayer,* based on "several of Mr. Lindsey's amendments . . . adopted entire," introduced what the congregation now held to be "doxologies from the pure word of God." It held fast to the often repeated notion that its order of service was now "such, as no Christian, it is supposed, can take offense at." Thus they expressed and formalized the practice and beliefs of English Socinianism in America.[39] Lindsey, Priestley, Hazlitt, and fellow English Unitarian, Dr. Richard Price, applauded this outcome of Freeman's efforts, and their approval was an important step. "The Liturgy of our church was during a long time unpopular. But your approbation [has] . . . raised it in esteem," wrote Freeman, noting that "it now seems to be acknowledged that the book cannot be very absurd which is praised by gentlemen of such great learning and abilities, who have been so long known and so justly admired in this country."[40]

Coinciding with Hazlitt's departure and the publication of the new liturgy, the congregation encouraged Freeman in his quest for ordination as an Episcopal minister. This, however, forced a showdown with the Congregationalist hierarchy and established traditions. When Samuel Provoost, the first Episcopal bishop of New York, refused to

37. Ibid., 17; italics in original.
38. Foote, *Annals of King's Chapel,* 457–58.
39. Freeman, *Liturgy,* 2.
40. James Freeman to Theophilus Lindsey, July 7, 1786, in Belsham, *Memoirs,* 178n. See also Jeremy, *Henry Wansey and His American Journal,* 59–60n.

ordain Freeman because of his Unitarian beliefs, the potential conflict seemed forestalled. But the congregation decided to ordain him on their own authority.[41] The right to ordain a minister without approval from the local ministerial association had been an issue among the Boston liberals for many years. Although in principle it was permissible under Congregationalist practices, it was generally not viewed favorably. This particular cause was bolstered by the long-standing English Unitarian practice which justified lay ordination in biblical terms, as expressed by Hazlitt during his American sojourn. The Englishman's views were so prominent in the transition to Unitarian beliefs that some have claimed that Hazlitt, more so than Freeman, was responsible for what many have called "the first Episcopal church in New England [to become] the first Unitarian Church in the New World."[42] Freeman also relied on such justifications as found in Lindsey's *Vindiciae Priestleianae*, writing to Lindsey of the congregation's successful transition and acknowledging the role played by the English Unitarians. "If any prejudice remained upon the minds of my people . . . what you say in your book, the *Vindiciae Priestleianae*, would effectively remove them. But they are already cured of all prepossessions of that nature."[43]

King's Chapel was moving in a new direction. Their decision to disassociate from those neighboring congregations which had expressed disapproval of their new direction was a clear indication of English Unitarianism's influence. "Although Freeman was a pioneer of Unitarianism in Boston, his views were outside the mainstream liberalism of Charles Chauncy, Joseph Stevens Buckminster, and William Ellery Channing, the [later] founders of American Unitarianism," writes one prominent Unitarian historian.[44] That Freeman was proposing to minister to a denomination professing a congregational polity while holding an Episcopal ordination and professing Unitarian theology reflects the complex character of the early history of American Unitarianism. Indeed, the situation itself pointed to the complex machinations of the early American unitarians. Freeman's connection with the English Unitarian movement, not to mention his influential relationship

41. The most complete account of this matter can be found in Greenwood, *History of King's Chapel in Boston*, 183–85.

42. Sprague, *Annals of the American Pulpit*, 8:165. For the entry on James Freeman, see 162–76. See also Foote, *James Freeman and King's Chapel*, in which the author accepts the views of William Carew Hazlitt, who said that it was his grandfather who was the "founder" to which Foote adds "there may be a grain of truth in this statement" (p. 10).

43. James Freeman to Theophilus Lindsey, October 15, 1788, in Foote, *James Freeman and King's Chapel*, 27.

44. Robinson, *Unitarians and Universalists*, 259.

with Hazlitt, "set him apart from the Boston liberals who held an Arian Christology and wanted to maintain their distance from the Unitarianism of Joseph Priestley."[45] Freeman spoke openly of his relationship to the English leaders and used his sermons to trace his own theological development back to Socinus. He and several others who both supported his efforts and accepted a close relationship with the English movement were not shy about their opinions or in expressing their beliefs.

Freeman was routinely invited to exchange pulpits, a sign of the degree of acceptance of a minister's views, with Jeremy Belknap of Long Lane and Joseph Eckley, pastor of Boston's Old South, two prominent mainstream ministers, the former of whom was known to consider the ideas of Socinus both illogical and incorrect.[46] Eckley and his congregation invited Freeman to exchange pulpits following the latter's open profession of Unitarianism. Eckley himself denied the supreme deity of Christ, thus only leaning toward Arianism, but his decision to exchange pulpits with Freeman demonstrated that he had no issue with the latter's rationalism or the ideas of the English Unitarians.

When Priestley's ideas met with resistance in the United States, Freeman picked up where Hazlitt had left off and became the leading force behind the publication of both *Discourses on the Evidence of Revealed Religion* and the controversial *History of the Corruptions of Christianity*. He also donated several copies of Priestley's theological works to the Harvard College library.[47] Still, his congregation was not as quick to accept either the title or all the tenets of English Unitarianism. Despite Freeman's excitement and the freedom of congregations to act as they wished, they remained very close to their heritage and doctrines, and their journey into Unitarianism proceeded very slowly, something which pained Freeman. "I wish the work was more worthy of your approbation," he wrote to Lindsey. "I can only say that I endeavoured to make it so by attempting to introduce your Liturgy entire. But the people of the chapel were not ripe for so great a change. Perhaps in some future day, when their minds become more enlightened, they may consent to a further alteration."[48]

---

45. Ibid., 260.

46. Belknap, in defense of his views of the Trinity, wrote that should "any be stigmatized with the name either of SOCINIANISM or ARIANISM, appears to me perfectly uncandid and unjust," to which he added, "Certain is it that Socinians reject such kind of language and disavow the notion of a Trinity in any form; not now to say any thing of the *atonement*, which they universally deny, but which those I am defending as strenuously maintain." See Sprague, *Annals of the American Pulpit*, 8:81.

47. Conkin, *American Originals*, 65.

48. Freeman to Lindsey, July 7, 1786, in Belsham, *Memoirs*, 178n.

Modern scholars of Unitarianism have questioned Freeman's link to the English Unitarians on the basis of his reluctance to follow Hazlitt in support of Emlyn's writings and their publication in New England. They claim that he was in concert with the liberals who rejected Priestley and the English influence.[49] But the joint efforts of Freeman and Hazlitt prove just the opposite. Hazlitt's brief presence notwithstanding, he was the first in this country to accept the Unitarian name and to "defend the doctrine" by upholding the ideas that transcended a simple rejection of the Trinity.[50] Freeman's promotion of the ideas of the English Unitarian movement gave Priestley and Lindsey a substantial presence, if not influence, in the direction of American religious affairs among those who would be categorized as dissenters in any other nation. In fact, by the turn of the century Freeman was fully in Priestley's camp, so much so that the publication of a work that denounced the ideas of English Unitarianism led him to withdraw his support of its distribution. Instead, Freeman put his efforts, as had Hazlitt, toward the publication of writings that challenged the prevailing trinitarian beliefs as well as the prevailing Arian orientation of the liberal faction.

The Spread of English Unitarianism

Others followed in Freeman's wake, giving rise to a significant segment of leading Congregationalist ministers who now turned to the English Unitarians for support. Two Salem ministers, John Prince of First Church and Thomas Barnard of North Church, both became Socinians and had allowed Hazlitt into their pulpits when he visited and frequently exchanged ministerial duties with Bentley.[51] Meanwhile Abiel Abbott of Haverhill used the English Unitarian influence as a means to separate from the Congregationalist juggernaut, while not becoming a Socinian himself. The list does not stop there, for the English Unitarian impulse reached out into the United States from Maine to Kentucky.

Thomas Barnard declared his Unitarian views from his pulpit and in his discourse with his parishioners. It was said that Barnard "practice[d] a uniform hospitality to various opinions, and was disposed to judge

49. See Cooke, *Unitarianism in America,* 69–72, and Robinson, *Unitarians and the Universalists,* 25–33.
50. Sprague, *Annals of the American Pulpit,* 8:169.
51. Ibid., 156.

men by the standards of their character rather than of creed. He demanded freedom for all." He was also outspoken in his views; once, when challenged by a parishioner, "Dr. Barnard, I have never heard you preach a sermon upon the Trinity," Barnard emphatically replied, "And you never will."[52] Barnard and his congregation steadily shifted toward an English-influenced theological position and dismissed Arianism in the process. By the 1790s, they were almost wholly in agreement with the English Unitarian movement. Under Barnard's leadership this particular congregation spent more than two decades in concert with the Unitarianism of Priestley.

Likewise, the Reverend John Prince of Salem's First Church read the writings of the English Unitarians and filled his library with heavily anno-tated copies. "For a half-century he was in constant correspondence with the principal London booksellers, and he accumulated a large collection of rare and valuable theological works." These included the complete collection of Priestley's writings, several revisions of Lindsey's most important works, and several on Socinian theology. Prince had read them all and incorporated their ideas into his preaching; Barnard followed his lead. Like others who had accepted Priestley's ideas, Prince was far more tolerant than most New England ministers. He discussed Priestley with his parishioners and allowed John Murray, the Univer-salist preacher who had also adopted God's singularity, to preach from the pulpit of First Church as early as 1787.[53]

Even among those who did not directly and wholly follow Priestley and the English Unitarians into Socinianism, thus not accepting the particular strain of liberal theology put forth by the English movement, there was little question that there was still substantial transatlantic influence. The most notable element of this influence was the call to openly declare one's unitarian sentiments and to make them the corner-stone of one's religious identity, something that was seen as problematic by many liberals, given the growing acceptance and association of the term "unitarian" with the English movement.

In 1796 Abiel Abbott announced to his congregation at Haverhill that his unitarian convictions were solidly entrenched; but he was equally adamant that he was no Socinian. "The process by which he was led to a change of some of his former opinions," noted one of Abbott's followers in a compilation of his sermons, "was, first, a doubt of their reality, from their apparent inconsistency with what he esteemed the

52. Eliot, *Heralds of a Liberal Faith*, 133 and 142.
53. Batchelor, *Social Equilibrium*, 262.

plain doctrines of Christianity."[54] Even though Abbott did not become a Socinian, his views were shaped by Priestley's writings, and it was clear that he had broken with the liberals as a result of the English Unitarian influence. When Abbott left Haverhill, there was no shortage of suitors for his subsequent employment. He entertained offers to serve as the president of Bowdoin College and from two congregations, the religious societies of Beverly and Brattle Street in Boston, both of which were fully aware of his unitarian leanings and public pronouncements.

Though many of the churches did not openly declare their beliefs until after Priestley arrived, for those that did the process often began before 1794. In 1802, the Pilgrim Church of Plymouth, Massachusetts, which had been founded in 1620 with the arrival of the first settlers, entered into the Unitarian fellowship. But the congregation had changed its liturgical practices following a series of sermons by Hazlitt in 1784 and an examination of the writings he distributed. Within a few years, twenty other churches followed their example. It was reported that the counties of Plymouth, Barnstable, and Bristol, home to the descendents of many of the first settlers, were also coming under the influence of ministers who denounced the Trinity and favored the establishment of Unitarian societies in these places.[55] Unitarian congregations also formed in Portland and Saco under the leadership of two ministers who acknowledged their conversion as a result of English Unitarianism. Thomas Oxnard of Portland and Samuel Thacher in Saco were avowed Socinians. Oxnard began his conversion in 1792 while still an Episcopal minister. He first attempted a moderate reform of the liturgy, but when that embroiled the congregation in controversy, he and his supporters withdrew and formed their own Unitarian society.[56] "I cannot express to you the avidity with which these Unitarian publications are sought after," Oxnard wrote to James Freeman. "Our friends here are clearly convinced that the Unitarian doctrine will soon become the prevailing opinion in this country. . . . Three years ago I did not know a single Unitarian in this part of the country besides myself: and now, entirely from the various publications you have furnished, a decent society might be collected from this and the neighboring towns."[57] His new Unitarian society met in a local schoolhouse and formed a separate church from the Episcopal minority with

54. S. Everett, *Sermons*, xiii.
55. Belsham, *Memoirs*, 187–88.
56. Wilbur, *Our Unitarian Heritage*, 400. See also Wilbur, *History of Unitarianism*, 8:394–95.
57. Thomas Oxnard to James Freeman, November 1788, in Belsham, *Memoirs*, 183–84. Oxnard continues, "When you write again to Mr. Lindsey, you may assure him in the most

whom they had once shared communion. But following Oxnard's death in 1799, the new meeting collapsed, and the cause of Socinianism suffered a major loss.[58]

According to William Wells, Samuel Thacher was "an excellent man and most zealous Unitarian."[59] Thacher had been swayed toward English Unitarianism while at Harvard during the 1791–92 academic year. He was an avid reader of Priestley's writings, which Lindsey had donated to the school library, and which, according to the library's records were read by a great number of the students.[60] Almost immediately he obtained a settled position in the Maine territory, where he then led a group of Saco residents, among them the Honorable George Thatcher, a member of Congress from the district of Maine and later a judge on the Supreme Court of Massachusetts, in the formation of a Unitarian society. This conversion, wrote one of Lindsey's frequent correspondents, was "an event peculiarly favorable to the progress of Unitarianism in this country." Thatcher was characterized as being "untrammeled by the tenets of sects and fond of polemics . . . a believer in the Christian faith and a devout member of a Christian Church."[61] By 1794, the Saco Unitarians took up a subscription to build a church, forming the Second Religious Society of Saco-Biddeford the following year. Just two years later, as a culminating moment, one that was inspired by Priestley's arrival in America and their long-standing connection with English Unitarianism, the congregation incorporated.[62] Given their location on the frontier, the prospects for this society were promising. "What favours this expectation is that one of the ministers of the town, a very liberal and enlightened man, is upon very good terms with the Unitarian Society, and is not disposed to discountenance them. In sentiment, he professes to be a Sabellian," wrote one of Lindsey's many American correspondents. Such optimism was furthered by the fact that "there is less appearance of religion in the province of Maine than in any other part of New England," leaving the door wide open for all religious groups, so that "a number of Unitarians possessing

---

positive terms that his and Dr. Priestley's publications have had, and probably will have, great effects in this part of the country; which I am sure must afford him great satisfaction."

58. Wilbur, *History of Unitarianism*, 2:395. Wilbur notes that many of the members returned to the Episcopal church and some went into the First Parish, which later became Unitarian, owing much to their presence.

59. William Wells to Thomas Belsham, in Belsham, *Memoirs*, 401.

60. Cooke, *Unitarianism in America*, 79.

61. "Letters of Joseph Priestley," *Proceedings of the Massachusetts Historical Society* 19 (June 1886): 13.

62. Belsham, *Memoirs*, 184–86.

that purity of morals for which they are generally distinguished will have a great effect, not only in diffusing rational sentiments, but also in reforming the practice of their fellow citizens."[63] It was a sentiment that was echoed time and time again in the coming years.

William Wells was an English Unitarian who, like Priestley, came to America fleeing the persecution and social tensions following the Birmingham riots. Wells and his family disembarked in Boston on June 12, 1793, but moved farther north and settled in Brattleboro, Vermont, where Wells lived until his death in 1827. Within a few years he was invited to become the pastor of a fledgling Unitarian society in the town but declined, though he in fact performed the functions of the position for over twenty years. "As a preacher, he laid little stress upon the differences among Protestants. He had his own opinions, but he thought that the real religion—the religion of the heart and of the life—was the one thing which was necessary. He was ardent and unshaken in his zeal for the right of private judgment, and would never subject himself to or aid in imposing upon others any creed or article of faith."[64] According to both his son and the Reverend Samuel Willard, Wells was an Arian. If he harbored any deeper thoughts, he kept them closely concealed. Wells did not search beyond "Unitarianism in the technical sense of the word," for he was able to sustain his beliefs with the most ease "without searching very deeply into those hidden things which he considered as belonging to God and not to man."[65] Even so, there is room to suspect that Wells did in fact harbor deeper unitarian sentiments. His son could only say that his father "in early life, believed much according to the sentiments of Dr. Samuel Clarke—but considerably modified during the last half of his life."[66] More important, Wells saw heresy in behavior and not in theological opinion.

The extent to which English Unitarianism and its prevailing Socinian theology permeated the American religious landscape prior to 1800

63. Letter to Theophilus Lindsey from unknown, quoted in Belsham, *Memoirs*, 185–86. Thatcher's supposed "Sabellian" stance puts him fully into concert with the English Unitarianism of Lindsey and Priestley. Sabellius was the bishop of Ptolemais during the Arian controversy of the third century and established the idea of subordination of the Son to the Father, clearly distinguishing between the two through a reference to the Logos and the Creator of the Logos. They further taught that the Word and the Holy Spirit were functions of God, not coequals. English Unitarianism used Sabellianism to promote humanitarian Christology as well as dismiss Arianism.

64. Eliot, *Heralds of a Liberal Faith*, 68–69n.

65. Samuel Willard to William Sprague, in Sprague, *Annals of the American Pulpit*, 8:260–61.

66. William Wells Jr. to William Sprague, in Sprague, *Annals of the American Pulpit*, 8:258.

can be measured in multiple ways—acceptance, degree of toleration, and opposition. Together, the aforementioned ministers and their congregations represented a significant movement in the history of American religion. While they did not institutionalize, their efforts nonetheless resulted in making Unitarianism an established, known, and prominent presence in the United States. English Unitarianism had been transplanted through an increasingly familiar transatlantic process of itinerancy, distribution of tracts, and the emergence of native adherents along with settled ministers. Likewise, it also experienced opposition.

American Anti-Unitarianism

As one might expect, given that English Unitarianism challenged the most central tenet of Protestant Christianity, Jesus' divinity, the opposition was quite substantial, checking Unitarianism's acceptance and growth. But the extent and degree of opposition is in itself evidence of the far-reaching influence (or at least the fear of its reach) of Socinianism in the United States and the influence of Priestley's disciples.

One of the most notable early opponents was Joseph Bellamy. Bellamy, a one-time student of Jonathan Edwards and long-standing minister of the First Church of Christ (Congregational) in Bethlehem, Connecticut, encouraged his students and parishioners to read the works of the opponents of Christianity in order to counter their arguments and correct their falsehoods. One of the foremost opponents, as identified by Bellamy, was Joseph Priestley. Several years before Priestley's arrival, Bellamy drafted a response to Priestley's *Letters to the Members of the New Church, signified by the new Jerusalem in the Revelations*. Later, as he continued his quest to bolster his Puritan-inherited faith against the extremism of rationalism (as well as the excesses of emotionalism), Bellamy defended the trinitarian stance against Priestley's humanistic conception of Jesus, what he called a "mere empty, dry, lifeless notion of God in the head."[67]

Charles H. Wharton, one of the leading Episcopalians in the United States, also gave voice to the growing concerns over the presence of Priestley's Unitarianism. Wharton, who was born a Catholic in St. Mary's County, Maryland, was educated at several Catholic schools in Europe, and in 1772 became a priest. While serving in Worcester, England,

67. Bellamy, *Jesus Christ the only God.*

Wharton undertook his own intense investigation of the scriptural basis for the teachings of the church. Though the accepted wisdom on rationalism and the rejection of the Trinity intrigued him, he did not turn away from his belief in Christ's divinity. On the contrary, his acceptance of the teachings of Jesus and the apostles was only strengthened. But the church's solid rejection of historic rationalist impulses in favor of its own development over the centuries weakened his convictions in its teachings and authority, leading him to leave the church. As a result he became a Protestant, returned to America, and became the Episcopal minister of Immanuel Church in New Castle, Delaware, where he spent many years refining his religious views. He is said to have remarked to a fellow minister, "Oh my dear friend, the Cross, the Cross, is all. What should we be without the Cross? The Lamb of God—*He* taketh away the sins of the world. The blood of Jesus Christ—*that* cleanseth from all sin!"

Wharton was the ideal figure to challenge the growing threat of Unitarianism. Wharton was familiar with his foe and the effects of the widespread publication of Priestley's ideas, was an elected member of the American Philosophical Society in 1786, the year after Priestley's election, and had access to the writings of Priestley donated to the society by John Vaughan.[68] In his *Short and Candid Enquiry Into the Proofs of Christ's Divinity* Wharton first challenged the growth and development of Unitarianism, even before Priestley had set sail for America, as based on an unsubstantiated reading of the Bible and contrived theology.[69] Wharton later wrote *Opinions Concerning Jesus Christ* in response to Priestley's *History of the Corruptions of Christianity,* a direct attack on orthodox religion, and a *History of the Early Opinions Concerning Jesus Christ,* in which Priestley argued that the Trinity was not scriptural. Unlike other opponents of Priestley, Wharton valued the "philosophic and inquisitive spirit of the times" and found the process of debate "laudable" despite his contempt for Priestley's rejection of "the most received doctrines of Christianity." Wharton dismissed Priestley's ideas that the original Christians (the apostles) rejected Christ's divinity and preexistence. In Wharton's reading of the Gospels Jesus clearly claimed to be on an equal level with God. "He is in me and I am in he," Wharton quoted from the scriptures. Furthermore, Wharton noted, theological mistakes made in the past were not, as Priestley

68. Rev. George W. Doane, "Charles Henry Wharton, D.D., 1784–1833," in Sprague, *Annals of the American Pulpit,* 5:132.

69. Wharton, *Enquiry.* The full title—*A Short and Candid Enquiry Into the Proofs of Christ's Divinity*—demonstrates the acceptance of English Unitarian ideas as those then under investigation.

claimed, errors in revelation per se but rather resulted from the need for piecemeal revelation because of the ignorance of those to whom the original Christians preached.[70]

Wharton's challenge provoked a great deal of opposition to Priestley from all corners of the country and sparked further disagreement in England. Bellamy expressed this hostility in his pamphlet *Jesus Christ the only God*, which defended the fundamental doctrine of Christianity against the errors of both the Arians and the Socinians. He exposed the weakness of rationalism's arguments not only on the unity of God but also on the association of the divinity with humanity and salvation. Finally, he attacked the scriptural readings proffered by Unitarians to justify their views.[71]

In contrast to Wharton and Bellamy, whose opposition not only rejected the theology of the Unitarians but also denied their claims to rationalism and humanism, there were those who accepted the general principles advocated by the English Unitarians but rejected their specific tenets. Theological tolerance, rationalism, and tentative acceptance of the unitarian idea were all hallmarks of the New England liberal movement. The growth of rationalism had little outward impact on the Congregationalists, just as reason and revelation commingled in the Episcopal, Methodist, Jewish, and even Catholic religious traditions.[72] To these opponents, the unitarian belief, without all of the other theological adjustments made by the Socinians, was viewed as nothing out of the ordinary, an idea within acceptable boundaries of religious inquiry and experimentalism. The majority of those who professed God's divine unity did so according to an Arminian-influenced Arian conception, holding that Jesus was both man and divine and remained within the established religious traditions. These believers were in no rush to make their tenets an object of debate. They were, however, quite aware of the competing ideas offered by Priestley and the Socinians, owing both to their presence in the curriculums of their academies as well as their historical foundations and the extent to which they continued to be discussed as challenges to their own beliefs and those of the trinitarians. For these adherents, however, the time had not yet come for them to avow the unitarian idea as something worthy of elevation or to identify themselves with a religious tradition as "radical" as that of the English Unitarians.

70. Ibid., 2–3.
71. Bellamy, *Jesus Christ the only God*.
72. Ferguson, *American Enlightenment*, 44–79.

As has been shown, there was also a growing minority who were not only familiar with the doctrines of the English Unitarians but who also accepted them. English Unitarianism offered a theology that fit well with the democratic orientations of American Christianity at the time, especially the claim that it simplified key aspects of religious belief and returned to the original tenets of Christianity.[73] By 1794, America was already imbued with the core principles and ideas espoused by the English Unitarians. English immigrants and home-grown liberal preachers professed the faith as practiced in England by the Essex Street Society and published in the religious tracts and liturgies of Lindsey and Priestley. Socinian-based Unitarianism was found in their libraries, was preached from their pulpits, and achieved recognition in the new nation. Through the exchange of peoples and ideas English Unitarianism grew among a select group of believers from New England through the Middle Atlantic states and even into the South and the expanding frontier. English Unitarianism, it seemed, was on the verge of thriving in America, if not institutionally or numerically then at least in the spread of its ideas. Though few in number and only partially organized, all they seemed to require was an acknowledged and established leader to help their movement take root and achieve their objectives. One of the most significant challenges this group would face, however, was contending with the two-pronged opposition.

The Emigration of Joseph Priestley

While Unitarian proponents were optimistic about its future because of the prevalence of religious liberty in the wake of the Enlightenment, the threat Priestley's ideas posed to existing American religious groups loomed large in the late 1780s and early 1790s, as the writings of the critics confirm. But it seemed that the opponents were winning and the movement was never able to materialize as a concerted body of believers able to enter into the mainstream, let alone actually challenge the standing denominations. With the arrival of Priestley, however, all that was going to change and the stage was set for a religious conflict that was transatlantic in scope and sustained over several decades.[74]

73. See Hatch, *Democratization of American Christianity*. Hatch argues that American Christianity became increasingly democratic and tolerant as the nation developed and consequently the multitude of denominations began to appeal to larger cross-sections of the population.
74. Kloppenberg, "Virtues of Liberalism," 12.

Wharton's fear over the growing presence of the "Unitarian Doctrine" in America attests to the extent to which Unitarianism had made inroads into the nation, both as a part of the emergent English-inspired movement and more quietly among adherents to more orthodox denominations. Likewise, Bellamy's writing bears witness to the depth of opposition in England, as manifested in the Birmingham riots. Wharton's publications were intended to call the trinitarians to action and make them aware of the need for sustained vigilance against the growing tide of rationalism "when the Unitarian writers are making so many proselytes in America." At the same time Bellamy connected all religious liberals together, regardless of their particular tenets, and exposed the fundamental errors of both the Arians and Socinians.[75]

Unitarian beliefs as promulgated not only included denial of the Trinity, but also doubts about the divinity of Christ, and the rejection of limited salvation, and doubted the true nature of the historical church. "None of the liberals were, technically Unitarians . . . almost all the leading founders of the unitarian movement in America were more nearly Arians than true Unitarians," leaving the door wide open for the English Unitarian movement and its influence.[76] Both "liberal Christians" and the more orthodox believers of all faiths—including Congregationalists, Methodists, and Presbyterians—were clear in their definition of Unitarianism and their mutual rejection of it. The liberals did not want the Unitarian label despite their own concerns about the Trinity and their conversations about their own beliefs revolved around many other issues besides the divinity of Jesus.

All that remained for English Unitarianism to emerge as an important player on the religious scene was a spark. Upon arriving in America Priestley sought out like-minded believers, providing that necessary spark. It was a task he relished; he made it clear that he intended to pursue his religious work even if that meant challenging the standing order. "I can truly say that I always considered the office of a Christian minister as the most honourable of any upon earth, and in the studies proper to it, I always took the greatest pleasure," he wrote in his memoirs. He arrived in America with every intention of following "my still more favourite pursuit, the propagation of Unitarianism," and despite the struggles of those who were already moving in that direction, he was nonetheless optimistic and emboldened by the opportunity.[77]

75. Wharton, *Enquiry,* 4; Bellamy, *Jesus Christ the Only God,* 118–19.
76. Conkin, *American Originals,* 65, 58.
77. Priestley, *Memoirs,* 92, 132.

New York City provided an opportunity for Priestley to begin, though his efforts there were short-lived. The state had disestablished Anglicanism in the Revolutionary era, and its resulting constitution affirmed that religion was a matter of personal conscience. Pluralism was further codified in 1784, and as a result the city and state had become home to many new and developing religious groups. The city's position as a gateway into America and a jumping-off point for its frontier assured a steady flow of new immigrants. Indeed, the city was home to a large and influential English immigrant community. In 1790 New York State's population was over 50 percent English in origin, third overall behind Pennsylvania and Virginia; the city itself was 42 percent English.[78] Many in the city's English community, including some of the more prominent members, were or became followers of English Unitarianism.[79]

Jedediah Chapman addressed the topic of New York's vibrant pluralism in a sermon delivered at the 1788 annual meeting of the New York and Philadelphia Presbyterian Synod. Chapman was known for being more tolerant of denominational differences than other Presbyterian ministers and sought to downplay the tensions that many regarded as a central feature of pluralism. The most important facet of pluralism was not religious competition, he noted to his fellow ministers, but rather the common theological foundations and the shared denominational interests. If all of the groups would focus on the commonality of their beliefs, they would all thrive; but if they all attack each other, he argued, each is irreparably harmed.[80] Chapman's views prevailed, at least for a time, among a select yet prominent group of congregations; the late 1780s and early 1790s have been characterized as a period of "cooperation or at least peaceful coexistence" among the various Protestant groups in New York resulting in a noticeable and "growing commitment to the principle of religious equality."[81]

However, despite professing the ideals of tolerance and religious equality and extending them to the growing body of religious liberals, as well as to Jews and Catholics, New York's religious community found it more and more difficult to reconcile this attitude with doctrine. Religious pluralism "involved for [New Yorkers] an acceptance or an acknowledgement of the validity of contrasting religious beliefs," but the "majority remained solidly convinced that it alone held the truth

78. Purvis, "European Ancestry," 98.
79. Kring, *Liberals Among the Orthodox*, 24.
80. Chapman, "Synodical Discourse."
81. Pointer, *Protestant Pluralism*, 118, 142.

and all other claims to the contrary were pernicious falsehoods."[82] The practice of pluralism did not equal the practice of toleration, as the various denominations freely attacked one another. In the eyes of most Christians, not all religions had to be tolerated, only some, and very few believers felt the need to include every religious variation within the pluralist collective; Unitarianism was particularly vulnerable under these terms.

Indeed, just a few months before Priestley's arrival, a Unitarian society was formed in the city under the leadership of an English layman by the name of John Butler. Butler gathered the society following his delivery of a series of lectures on rational Christianity and Unitarian liturgical practice. His efforts attracted a sizable following within the immigrant, English community and provoked the ire of the city's trinitarian clergy. The press played a role in the propagation of his ideas and the reaction from non-Unitarians. In an edition of the *Daily Advertiser* Butler decried the attacks upon him and publicly demanded that the ministers of other denominations who denounced his theology as a threat to the social and religious order of the city respect the presence of Unitarian believers in their midst as a consequence of the law and Christian principle. Undaunted by their refusal and the lack of ministerial support, Butler called upon "the Friends of Free Inquiry" to join him at the continuation of his lecture series in February.[83] The attendance at these lectures, which examined the unity of God, exceeded even Butler's expectations and resulted in the formation of the First Unitarian Society of New York.

The group of avowed Unitarians was in its infancy when Priestley arrived and sought to capitalize on his presence to strengthen their fellowship and push for acceptance. They hoped that their declaration of principles would convince Priestley to serve as their minister. Certainly, many of them reasoned, a man of his stature could help them navigate the complex paths of rational theology and inclusion in a nominally pluralist society. Priestley himself reaffirmed such beliefs. "I am fully persuaded an Unitarian minister, of prudence and good sense, might do very well here. If I were here a Sunday or two more I would make a beginning, and I intend to return for this purpose. One man of proper spirit would be sufficient to establish a solid Unitarian interest; and I am persuaded it will soon be done."[84] Henry Wansey

---

82. Ibid., 143–44.
83. *The Daily Advertiser,* vol. 10, January 24, 1794 (no. 2789) and February 7, 1794 (no. 2802), LOC Newspapers Division.
84. Joseph Priestley to Theophilus Lindsey, June 15, 1794, in Belsham, *Memoirs,* 410–11.

similarly noted the promising developments of the First Unitarian Society and was the most optimistic among those who viewed Priestley as the necessary catalyst to ensure the group's longevity. The evening events of June 12, 1794, seemed to confirm Wansey's confidence, when he and Priestley dined with the Episcopal bishop of New York, Samuel Provoost, who was well known for his views favoring tolerance.[85] Provoost's willingness to attend a public dinner with Priestley was all that Wansey required to proclaim it as an omen for the future of Unitarianism in America: "I could not help remarking, that I was seated between the Bishop and Dr. Priestley, the seat of war in England, but of peace and civility here. (No loaves and fishes in the way)."[86]

Wansey's predictions were overly sanguine. Even though Priestley's presence helped promote Unitarian ideas within liberal religious circles, it also exacerbated underlying tensions and emboldened the opposition, thus bringing the group under greater suspicion. Many trinitarians, particularly among the Episcopalian and Methodist congregations, viewed Butler's challenge as an isolated action and unlikely to succeed; but Priestley's involvement presented a potentially different outcome. His success in England convinced them of the dangers to come if he were allowed to preach unchecked. The trinitarian clergy quickly gathered their forces and unleashed a torrent of opposition. Ministerial courtesies were the first elements to fall. "The preachers, though all civil to me, look upon me with dread, and none of them has asked me to preach in their pulpits," Priestley wrote to Lindsey.[87] Within weeks the situation had taken a turn for the worse. The few anti-Unitarian tracts begun in the wake of Butler's efforts were hastily amended and republished. The trinitarian ministers, fearing Priestley, now undertook to act in concert to prepare an onslaught of writings in response to his presence.[88]

Several ministers used the occasion of Trinity Sunday, on June 15, to preach "universally in support of that doctrine" and invoked the teachings of Samuel Clarke to reaffirm the Trinity. Clarke's *Collection of the Promises of Scripture* was then in wide circulation. Proving that both

---

85. George B. Rapelye, writing to William Sprague, called Provoost "thoroughly versed in Ecclesiastical history and Church Polity," and says that he, like Priestley, read the Bible in many languages including Greek, Hebrew, and Latin. "Though Dr. Provoost had probably little sympathy with the views and feelings of most other denominations of Christians, his general courtesy was never affected by any considerations merely denominational." Sprague, *Annals of the American Pulpit*, 5:244–45.

86. Wansey, *Journal*, 127.

87. Priestley to Lindsey, June 15, 1794, in Belsham, *Memoirs*, 410–11.

88. Wansey, *Journal*, 127.

sides could draw upon Clarke for their inspiration, the anti-Unitarians heralded Clarke's argument that the scriptures promised salvation through the various manifestations of the Trinity.[89] Multiple ministers declared, in unison, that "the cause of [Priestley's] troubles was his ignorance of the nature of the Deity" and his misrepresentation of Clarke, who had clearly warned against Socinianism.[90] Clarke himself had reasoned, they claimed, that "they who are not careful to maintain these personal Characters and Distinctions . . . to avoid the Errors of the Arians, . . . in reality take away their very existence, and so fall unawares into Sabellianism (which is the same with Socinianism)."[91] Principles of legal tolerance and religious equality notwithstanding, the city's ministerial leaders were not going to allow Unitarianism into their midst without resistance. Their actions went beyond simple criticism or theological opinion, and were directed toward denying Unitarianism a presence.

The brevity of Priestley's stay in the city, his decision to continue on to Philadelphia, and his failure to return to assist them in the dissemination of their ideas severely hurt the society. Despite a promising beginning, the group was unable to meet the challenges of institutionalization and the lack of a settled minister in a city full of already established denominations opposing them. Few liberal believers actively came forward to join, and the congregation was disbanded by the end of the year and disappeared from the public record. Despite its rapid growth into one of the three largest urban and commercial centers in the young nation, New York would remain without a Unitarian congregation until the 1820s.

New York's loss was Pennsylvania's gain, at least for the supporters of religious liberalism, and the optimism that was generated in others in response to his presence in the former was rewarded in the latter. While historians have argued that the two states were more often similar in their religious perspectives than different—especially when it came to matters of religious competition and freedom—such was not the case for those groups on the fringes.[92] Priestley's arrival in Philadelphia stimulated more interest than opposition, especially among the large English population and the influential intellectual circles comprised of

---

89. Samuel Clarke, *A Collection of the Promises of Scripture,* in *The Works,* vol. 4.

90. Wansey, *Journal,* 128.

91. Clarke, *The scripture-doctrine of the Trinity,* in *The Works,* 4:148–49.

92. Bonomi, *Under the Cope of Heaven,* xiv. Bonomi argues for the similarity of the two states as part of a larger regional identity. As this study will show, there were complexities underneath any prevailing idea of a regional similarity.

political and civic leaders. There were also preexisting groups, including the Universalists, who had helped pave the way, and as a result, Priestley experienced his greatest successes in Pennsylvania. Though he never gathered the numbers boasted of by others, his leadership led to the formation of the first lasting and openly Unitarian congregations in the United States. These congregations became an important part of the religious community and managed to survive in the face of great opposition. The Pennsylvania groups were joined by other congregations throughout the country, and together, between 1796 and 1819, were the sole adherents to Unitarianism, openly and avowedly, in America.

Philadelphia in 1794 had more than thirty-two thousand residents and was the social, intellectual, and economic capital of the nation.[93] The city boasted a vibrant culture, a flourishing manufacturing sector, and had become a leading center of science. Both the city and its surrounding state populations were ethnically and religiously diverse and dominated by immigrant groups. The diversity resulted in cooperation among German, English, Scots-Irish, French, and other groups. Although not always in complete harmony in matters of public concern, their cooperation opened a prospect for future growth.[94] Pennsylvania's religious vitality matched the intensity of its political economy. Its ethnic divisions defined its religious variety: Scots-Irish Presbyterians, English Anglicans, German Lutherans, German pietists, English Quakers, and even Catholics. Newer religious groups included the Presbyterians, Baptists, Methodists, and a number of black churches, all of which found a safe haven. "It was in this province that all these groups experienced the difficulties and discovered the possibilities for fruitful coexistence that American democracy was to offer. Within the borders of no other state was so much American church history anticipated or enacted."[95] By 1810 this fruitful coexistence had created forty-one different religious places of worship belonging to twenty different faiths within Philadelphia. The Quakers, who had once dominated civil and religious society, were still influential, as were the Episcopalians, Presbyterians, Methodists, and Baptists. Each of them had multiple congregations within the city, and each controlled a great deal of Philadelphia's civic and religious life. But the Swedish Lutherans, Free Quakers, Moravians,

93. In 1794 Philadelphia had 32,983 residents. For general population and census figures, see Greene and Harrington, *American Population*. See also Bureau of the Census, *Century of Population Growth*, 9, 11, and 13.

94. Ireland, *Religion, Ethnicity, and Politics*, 273. See also Emma Lapsansky, "Building Democratic Communities: 1800–1850," in Miller and Pencak, *Pennsylvania*, 153–202.

95. Ahlstrom, *Religious History*, 212–13.

German Reformed, Catholics, Lutherans, Universalists, and Jews were also represented, legally tolerated, and widely respected, if not always privately accepted.[96] Thus it is easy to understand how Priestley was led to declare that in Pennsylvania "everything was ripe for the propagation of Unitarianism."[97]

This is not to say that Priestley and his followers were free from any opposition. As in New York the Pennsylvania opposition was lined up against Unitarianism several years before Priestley's arrival. Charles Wharton's attack on Socinian Unitarianism was only a preview of what Priestley would have to endure. In January 1793, the *Pennsylvania Gazette* advertised a tract written by Samuel Wetherill Jr. written in reply to Priestley's *Appeal to the Serious and Candid Professors of Christianity*, and Lewis Nicolas's scriptural exploration of Christ's divinity, which ascribed to Priestley ideas that he had never endorsed. Wetherill's *Divinity of Jesus Christ proved* attacked the Socinian conception of Christ's humanity and challenged Priestley's membership in the Christian community.[98] Opponents cared little for the rhetorical maneuverings of Priestley and consistently attacked his ideas by linking them to greater evils and impugning his less conventional ideas, elevating them to a status in his system of beliefs that was not conveyed in his own writings.[99] Wetherill's tract resulted in an almost permanent rift between the Unitarians and the Quaker majority in Philadelphia. Although the Quakers themselves were out of favor as a result of their long history of political and religious repression, the attack helped to further the adversarial relationship between Unitarianism and the other denominations.

As word of Priestley's arrival spread, the Reverend William Rogers of the Second Street Baptist Church in Philadelphia fearfully warned his congregation to "Beware, for a Priestley has entered the land! Oh,

---

96. Mease, *Picture of Philadelphia*, 216–21. On the matter of acceptance, see Ireland, *Religion, Ethnicity, and Politics*, who argues that the Pennsylvania political majority had "resisted social and cultural pluralism, been uncomfortable with political ambiguity, defined citizenship in normative terms, favored a theistic, Trinitarian Christian orthodoxy and remained intolerant of those who disagreed with them" (273).

97. Priestley to Lindsey, September 14, 1794, in *Works*, 2:274.

98. Wetherill, *The divinity of Jesus Christ proved*. See also Wetherill, *History of the Religious Society of Friends*, 41–42.

99. Wetherill, who was a leader of the Society of Free Quakers, held his own peculiar religious ideas—he linked religious moral intentions to the wider issues of society and sought the creation of a religious society open to all beliefs and practices. These ideas earned him the reputation of an infidel within the dominant religious community. His writings also served a personal purpose in that they attacked those who were even more extreme in their views and thus deflected the accusations against him. See Brock, *Pioneers of the Peaceable Kingdom*, 191–94, and Bauman, *For the Reputation of Truth*, 167–68.

Lamb of God! How would they pluck thee from thy throne!"[100] Rogers was not alone in warning the public of the impending threat Priestley represented to trinitarianism, Christianity, and religion in general. Abraham Beach, the senior associate pastor at Trinity Church in Philadelphia, copied the New York ministry by preaching against Priestley on Trinity Sunday.[101] These efforts were not lost on Priestley. "With respect to religion, things are exactly in the same state here as in New York. Nobody asks me to preach, and I hear there is much jealousy and dread of me."[102] Two years later he recounted the efforts of the opposition by noting the doubts that they raised about his standing in the religious community. "I could not help suspecting, either that I was not in a Christian country or that I was not considered as a Christian in it. . . . Not doubting, however, but that I was among Christians, for I attended public worship in various places and found it to be Christian, I necessarily concluded, that I was not myself considered as a Christian, or one that was deserving of the name."[103]

But the effect of having such strong opposition was not entirely negative. "On the whole I am not sorry for the circumstance, as it offends many who have, on this account, the greater desire to hear me; so that I have little doubt but that I shall form a respectable Unitarian society in this place," wrote Priestley in one of his more optimistic moments. As for men like Rogers, Priestley also understood that his decree was likely to backfire, given that liberal-minded individuals often held little regard for ministerial authority. "The alarm of danger of Unitarianism has been sounded so long, that it has ceased to be terrific to many; and I stand so well with the country in other respects, that I dare say I shall have a fair and candid hearing."[104] In fact, the reaction against Rogers was severe and swift. He was rebuked in the public press for his comments, and within a matter of days he issued an apology from the pulpit in which he acknowledged the lack of Christian charity in his comments.[105] Furthermore, in the course of rejecting Unitarianism the opposition simultaneously exposed the rational foundations of its theology to the attention of the general population. Contrary to their intentions, the oversimplifications and unjust characterizations used by trinitarians to denounce the English

100. Bakewell, "Some Particulars," 393.
101. Kring, *Liberals Among the Orthodox*, 23.
102. Priestley to Lindsey, June 24, 1794, in Belsham, *Memoirs*, 413.
103. Priestley, *Unitarianism Explained and Defended*, 2.
104. Priestley to Lindsey, June 24, 1794, in Belsham, *Memoirs*, 413.
105. Bakewell, "Some Particulars," 394.

Unitarian theology—its espousal of religious primitivism, liberal individ-
ualism, its distance from deism, and its place in the heritage of English
religious dissent—gave Unitarianism a wider acceptance than it would
have otherwise obtained. The opposition's hostility certainly contributed
to the quiet reception given to Priestley's ideas in Philadelphia. During
the next twenty years, of significance for this story, it also contributed
to the reluctance of the New England liberals to be more open in their
declarations of belief.

Priestley in Philadelphia

Rising to the challenge, Priestley took it upon himself to deliver several
sermons refuting the misrepresentations and clarifying the principles
of Unitarianism, thereby demonstrating "the real *use* and genuine
spirit of this religion, and therefore why it is of so much importance as
to be worth contending for."[106] Subsequently published in 1794 and
1796, these sermons served as the foundation for the development of
the nation's first openly Unitarian congregations.

The first sermon, delivered immediately upon his arrival in Pennsylvania, *A General View of the Arguments for the Unity of God; and against the
divinity and preexistence of Christ,* defined the basic elements of Unitarian
theology and practice and staked out the liberal ground for the Socinian
position. Its concise formulation was reworked from an earlier English
sermon and represented the accumulated wisdom of Priestley's ministerial career. Priestley's purpose in publishing *Arguments for the Unity
of God* was to ascertain "a just idea of the place and value" of "the proper
Unitarian doctrine" (in contrast to Arianism) among the American
people. He utilized a three-pronged attack—reason, scripture, and
history—to counter both the trinitarian and Arian positions. Priestley
argued that Unitarians, as followers of the scriptural teachings of Christ,
who proclaimed his own humanity, were the true Christians. "It was
never denied that the proper Unitarian doctrine existed in the time
of the apostles; and I think it evident, that it was the faith of the bulk
of Christians . . . for two or three centuries after Christ," he argued.
Arianism was as much a corruption of the original Christian idea
and subsequent rational deductions as trinitarianism. His view that
Arianism was "destitute of all support," stemmed from his belief that it
was constructed through intricate machinations that defied reasoning

---

106. Priestley, *Unitarianism Explained and Defended,* iii.

and thereby separated him and his followers from the liberal Congregationalists.[107] The simplicity of his reasoning and the depth of his conviction impressed those who had heard it, and *Arguments for the Unity of God* was so well received that it sold out within weeks.

This success contributed to the favorable reception of his second publication, *Unitarianism Explained and Defended*. Delivered from the pulpit of Elhanan Winchester's Universalist Church, this sermon appealed to a wide audience and was seen by the public as a summary of the Unitarian plea to be seen as Christians. The primary audience, however, was the growing body of Unitarians in the city of Philadelphia. As a follow-up to *Discourses on the Evidences of Revealed Religion*, a series of sermons delivered the previous year, this sermon, later published as a pamphlet, was both a theological treatise and an instructional guide. *Discourses* laid out Priestley's advice for the organization and institutionalization of Unitarian societies in the absence of a denominational body and further instructed unitarian believers on matters of securing and spreading their faith. The reaction to this sermon was twofold: it served as the inspiration for the official formation of the First Unitarian Society of Philadelphia, the first such avowed organization in the nation, and it also provided a focal point for Unitarian opposition. It was a monumental event and turning point in the history of American Unitarianism. From this point forward, when Americans referred to the progress of Unitarianism in America, its beliefs, leading figures, and the spread of its ideas, or expressed their fears about its presence, their references centered on the elements presented in this sermon and always included reference, positive or negative, to Priestley and Socinian Unitarianism.

Aware that his ideas provoked significant opposition, Priestley tried to conciliate those who considered him a heretic and sought to associate his principles with those of the trinitarians, citing their common history rather than their differing theologies. This was an attempt on his part to elevate the Unitarian theology above the sectarian fray and establish religious reciprocity. In this way he hoped to avoid the confrontations that had led to attacks against his beliefs and driven him out of England; Priestley truly believed that sectarian strife undermined the common goals of Christianity and gave non-Christians a potent weapon in their critique. His message, however, was often lost in the presentation. Priestley's style of argumentation only alienated many potential advocates, and his manner of writing, though based on a desire for

107. Priestley, *General View* (1794), 1, 23.

"mutual candour" between opposing forces, was often viewed as vitriolic and condescending.[108]

Priestley's detailed chronicle of Unitarian views on the divine mission of Christ, the authority God granted to him as a prophet, the doctrine of the resurrection, and the state of salvation was offered as the basis for reconciliation between Unitarianism and Protestant Christianity. In all of his sermons, writings, and correspondence, Priestley insisted that Unitarians were Christians, and he never passed up the chance to make his point, and he often argued that one of the most important attributes of Unitarianism was that "their devotional services are such as any other Christians may join in."[109]

Priestley's arrival in the United States was a momentous event for liberal religious thinkers and their ideals. His presence served as a catalyst to the nascent Unitarian movement, which had struggled to establish itself over the previous twenty years. He arrived at a time when religion in general was resurgent, when the American people were once more focused on matters of faith, and when the laws of the newly formed nation promoted religious freedom in the name of civil liberty. These factors resulted in the emergence of new religious groups which found the changed religious atmosphere conducive to their quest for reform and renewal. They considered their ideas to be driving the intensity of the quest for religious truth that marked the era. They used religious writings and sermons to establish their positions, mark their progress, and ascertain future possibilities. They also set out to prove that groups who advocated free inquiry and religious pluralism would ultimately succeed and become the majority among all denominations.[110]

108. Priestley, *Unitarianism Explained and Defended*, iv.
109. Ibid., iv–v.
110. Moore, *Religious Outsiders*, iv.

THREE

Joseph Priestley and Unitarianism in Philadelphia

Let those then, who have a just zeal for their Christian and Unitarian
principles confer together, and may it please God that a small
beginning may lead to a great and valuable end.

—JOSEPH PRIESTLEY, *Unitarianism Explained and Defended*

"In standing forth . . . by forming yourselves into a society professedly
Unitarian, in a part of the world in which no such thing existed before,"
Priestley told Philadelphia's assembled Unitarians in March 1797, their
actions were "reminiscent of the truly glorious conduct of the primitive
Christians." But more remained to be done, and the group had to
remain on guard and steel themselves for the inevitable onslaught of
attacks. He reminded them of their further obligation to act as the
original Christians had, to remain "mindful only of their obligation to
confess their Lord before men, [and] nobly disregard all calumny."[1]

Even though Priestley never settled among the Philadelphia Unitarians, only visiting on occasion for varied periods of time, and twice
declined their request to become their permanent and settled minister,
he remained their spiritual leader. Indeed, Philadelphia was where most
of his American religious work took place and was first expounded to
the nation's citizenry. Only when he stepped forward, in an admittedly
partial manner, were the Philadelphia believers willing and able to
step forward to openly declare their principles and present themselves
as an organized society. Just as in England, where Priestley played an
instrumental but by no means solitary role in the formation of Unitarianism, so too did he play that role in the United States. In fact, it
was his stature in the English Unitarian movement that gave him the
necessary influence to carry forth in the United States.

Through example and oratory, Priestley guided the Philadelphians
in their quest to formulate their own society and profess their views in

1. Priestley, *Address to the Unitarian Congregation at Philadelphia*, 5.

a way that would assure them of public and private autonomy. In rejecting the two requests of John Vaughan, a former student of Priestley's who made the offers on behalf of his fellow believers, Priestley was cognizant of the need for Unitarianism to transcend any one person. "America itself must find the man, as in due time I doubt not will be the case," he had written to Vaughan from England on the occasion of the first request.[2] While he made himself available to them once he arrived in the United States, he was adamant in his refusal to formally accept a settled position in the city, citing his preference to remain more removed in both principle and practice and pushed for a system of broad lay leadership.[3] Priestley's efforts, stemming from his experience in England, were designed to keep Unitarians focused on establishing, explaining, and defending Unitarianism's presence in positive and meaningful terms. First, he sought to lay the theological and liturgical groundwork for Unitarian congregations, with or without a settled minister, by formalizing their religious rites, outlining a congregation's structure, promoting lay leadership, and delineating the patterns of worship. Second, he helped outline a series of explanations and defenses of Unitarianism for the purpose of confronting the seemingly endless line of critics—both those in the trinitarian majority and those who were liberal but not Socinian in temperament. Only then, he believed, would Unitarianism be able to claim a position among the established American, Protestant, Christian, reformed tradition as just one denomination among many.

While his efforts and influence were not limited to Philadelphia, it was here, slowly and steadily, that his impact on American religion and Unitarianism was primarily established. While New England liberals were preoccupied with their own efforts to determine their theological and institutional attachment to those already established within the tenets and practices of Congregationalism, Priestley, Vaughan, and the myriad others involved directly and indirectly in the Philadelphia society

2. Joseph Priestley to John Vaughan, October 27, 1791, Priestley Papers, APS.
3. Priestley tried from the outset to recruit fellow ministers from England. He repeatedly asked Belsham and Lindsey to make the journey. For the first of these exchanges, see Priestley to Lindsey, June 15, 1794, and Priestley to Belsham, June 16, 1794, and August 27, 1794, in *Works*, vol. 1, pt. 2, pp. 255, 260, 271–72. Joshua Toulmin, father of Harry, and John Millar, son of the noted professor, were also among those Priestley hoped would immigrate to the United States and settle near him. He also made repeated attempts to persuade Harry Toulmin to relocate from Kentucky to Pennsylvania. See Priestley to Theophilus Lindsey, February 10, 1795, and July 12, 1795, in *Works*, vol. 1, pt. 2, pp. 295, 312. Millar actually traveled to the United States in 1795 but died before he could establish himself. See "John Millar," in Stephen and Lee, *Dictionary of National Biography*.

openly and unequivocally professed their beliefs as separate and distinct, leading to the formation of the nation's first avowed Unitarian congregation, united in sentiment and resolute in their objectives. They quickly found support among other like-minded groups who helped ensure their status under the law, professed an affinity for their religious views, and assisted them in the construction of their own chapel. Others aligned with them as fellow dissenters, though often not sharing the same religious convictions, and found affinity based on their common, base, Christian principles. As a result of these actions, Americans quickly came to identify Unitarianism with Priestley and his Philadelphia brethren, for better or worse.

Such openness led to substantial opposition as well. Detractors were not deterred by the society's formal organization and engaged in substantial efforts to counter any progress. They stepped up their efforts against the unitarian heresy by publishing an even greater number of tracts in defense of the Trinity. Ministers also increased the frequency and tone of their anti-Unitarian rhetoric. For their part, the New England liberals also joined in the opposition, citing the potential for misinterpretation and misassociation, fearing that they would be erroneously saddled with the baggage of Socinian beliefs and decrying the extremism that they identified as a characteristic of the transatlantic import.

All told, it was clear that what was emerging in Philadelphia was the result of an ongoing series of developments in the American religious landscape and that there were now two distinct groups who held the unitarian belief in substantial regard. Priestley and the Philadelphia Unitarians were soon entrenched as a part of the American religious story.

The Society of Unitarian Christians of Philadelphia

The Philadelphia Unitarians' efforts to integrate themselves into the Christian fold began, first and foremost, through a formal organization of their society, which took place on August 21, 1796, when the members adopted the name "The Society of Unitarian Christians of Philadelphia" and wrote out a charter of membership. Priestley had helped to lay the groundwork several months earlier through a series of sermons, *Discourses on the Evidence of Revealed Religion*, delivered in the church of the Universalists throughout February, which was well received. The crowds in attendance "were so numerous that the house could not contain them, so that as many were obliged to stand as sit, and even the doorways were crowded with people," reported one commentator.[4] The professed Unitarian and congressman George Thatcher, who attended Priestley's lectures in the company of John Adams, Benjamin Rush, and several other members of the nation's elite, related his own pleasure in hearing Priestley. "He gave universal satisfaction," wrote Thatcher, and even effected a change in his listeners. "For as I turned in the street," Thatcher continued, "it seemed as if every tongue was engaged in speaking his praise, or answering the clergy of the City."[5] Priestley judged his own efforts successful as well, noting that "the congregations have always been numerous, and most respectable," and that it was "evident that I am heard with more attention than was given to me in any place before."[6]

Discourses established Priestley's reputation as an able minister of the gospel and elevated his religious esteem among many of the city's inhabitants. It also led to another round of publication for some of Priestley's tracts in defense of the divine unity.[7] Later Priestley was so convinced of his success that he was able to claim that "the violent prejudice that had been raised against me is overcome. Many of my hearers were those who were the most prejudiced, and great numbers such as never attended any public worship before." This latter claim quickly became one of Priestley's most frequent justifications for Unitarianism's place in America. Too many people had been turned away from the standing faiths as a result of their rigid stipulations and unforgiving tenets. Unitarianism, in particular the Socinian variant, did away with all of the various trappings and claimed to bring forward only the simple and direct elements of Christianity as Christ had offered them. His was a faith, so Priestley claimed, that actually brought people back to Christianity and reached out to those who were otherwise disaffected. "I daily hear of the great impression that my discourses make on those who were the most averse to everything relating to religion."[8] As word of his efforts spread, numerous invitations to preach, something

4. Ware, *Views of Christian Truth*, lix.

5. George Thatcher to James Freeman, February 14, 1796, *Proceedings of the Massachusetts Historical Society*, series 2, 3 (June 1886): 39–40.

6. Joseph Priestley to Theophilus Lindsey, April 8, 1796, in *Works*, vol. 1, pt. 2, p. 336.

7. See Benjamin Rush to Griffith Evans, March 4, 1796, in Rush, *Letters*, 773. See also Joseph Priestley to Theophilus Lindsey, June 15, 1794, in Belsham, *Memoirs*, 412. Predictably, *Discourses* created great controversy when Priestley dedicated it to John Adams, who summarily rejected the dedication because he considered it dangerous to his political future and personal religious standing in New England. See Donald D'Elia, "Joseph Priestley and His American Contemporaries," in Schwartz and McEvoy, *Motion Toward Perfection*, 237–50.

8. Priestley to Lindsey, April 8, 1796, in *Works*, vol. 1, pt. 2, p. 336.

that had been earlier denied to him, were extended to Priestley for such places as New York, Princeton, Boston, Charlottesville, and Lexington, Kentucky, where his friend and fellow Unitarian Harry Toulmin had migrated.[9] Although he declined almost all of these invitations on the grounds that they were not convenient to the circumstances of his residence and family, they indicated growing, and at least tacit, acceptance of Unitarianism among a wide array of people and places in America.

Priestley's arrival and multiple, serialized sermons caused enough of a stir in the hearts and minds of Philadelphia's liberal English immigrant community that a series of discussions, begun two years earlier, on the prospect for gathering a Unitarian congregation were finally formalized into a plan of action. The initial meeting included fourteen representatives, and a follow-up meeting included another seven, so that by the end of the summer of 1796 there were twenty-one names in the society's book of records. By the end of the first full year of existence another nineteen names were added, including some of the most prominent citizens of the city. Surprisingly, among those not involved was John Vaughan, who did not officially join until after the society was firmly established.[10] For his part, Priestley was in attendance at these meetings as his travels and other obligations permitted. United in purpose and direction, the group went forward with great optimism. "Indeed my coming hither promises to be of much more service to our cause than I had imagined," but he did not expect miracles. "Time is necessary," he wrote to Lindsey, if the harvest was to be abundant.[11] These feelings of purpose and future prospects led Priestley to formally join the society on January 8, 1797, when he traveled from

9. Priestley was a rather frequent guest in the pulpits of other dissenting congregations in England. He welcomed Robert Robinson, an eminent Baptist clergyman to preach for him in Birmingham, and he was invited to preach in several Presbyterian chapels. In England the dissenter label bound many of these groups together in ways that did not seem to occur in America. For reports of Priestley's British pulpit exchanges, see *The Pennsylvania Gazette*, October 13, 1790. For general reference to these invitations, see Wansey, *Journal*, 127–28, and Priestley, *Unitarianism Explained and Defended*, in *Works*, 15:274, 278, 304. For specific references to the invitations to preach in Boston, see Wansey, *Journal*, 52, 89n. John Adams sent Priestley a letter of welcome upon his arrival in America and suggested Priestley settle in Boston, where he would find himself well received. James Freeman also wrote to Priestley and encouraged him to visit Boston. Thomas Jefferson's entreaties for Priestley to settle in Charlottesville are a well-known aspect of their correspondence. See Jefferson to Tench Coxe, May 1, 1794, and Jefferson to Joseph Priestley, January 18, 1800, in Jefferson, *Writings*, 1014, 1069–72. The invitation to preach in Kentucky was part of the correspondence between Harry Toulmin and Priestley. See Priestley to Theophilus Lindsey, August 24, 1794, Priestley Papers, APS.

10. Geffen, *Philadelphia Unitarianism*, 31–55.

11. Priestley to Lindsey, June 15, 1794, in Belsham, *Memoirs*, 412.

Northumberland to Philadelphia to deliver a second series of sermons on the Unitarian cause.[12]

As in England the new society took the Unitarian name, though not without some consideration for its potential impact on their efforts. "When persons form themselves into societies, so as to be distinguishable from others, they never fail to get some *particular name,* either assumed by themselves, or imposed by others. This is necessary in order to make them the subject of conversation," Priestley had earlier written concerning denominational appellations.[13] He and his followers were confident that their efforts would quickly address and correct any pejorative connotations and mistaken notions about their theology and practices. Although the term was theologically descriptive and a point of pride among the adherents, they adopted it advisedly, given that the unitarian label "bore a great weight of odium" and provided their opponents with a ready-made and simple focal point for their attacks.[14]

The unique religious history and development of the former Quaker colony, however, is what provided the foundation of the new society's optimism. Pennsylvania's religious community was universally lauded for its "principle of universal charity, and truly Christian spirit of harmony, on religious subjects toward each other."[15] J. William Frost notes that this spirit of tolerance produced a "distinctive pattern of religious liberty" within Philadelphia and the surrounding hinterlands of the state.[16] Pennsylvania's religious liberty originated with the proprietary founder William Penn, a Quaker. Incorporating the principle of toleration into the 1682 *Charter of Liberties and Frame of Government,* Penn declared "that all persons living in this province, who confess and acknowledge the one Almighty and eternal God, to be the Creator, Upholder and Ruler of the world; and that hold themselves obliged in conscience to live peaceable and justly in civil society, shall, in no ways, be molested or prejudiced for their religious persuasion, or practice, in matters of faith and worship."[17] This principle was repeated, almost verbatim, in the more famous Act for Freedom of Conscience issued in December 1682

12. See Geffen, *Philadelphia Unitarianism,* Appendix B, 257.

13. Priestley, *General View* (1794), 23–24. This work was a significant sermon in his quest to have all religions given the right of "free inquiry."

14. Geffen, *Philadelphia Unitarianism,* 33–34.

15. Mease, *Picture of Philadelphia,* 221–22.

16. Frost, *A Perfect Freedom,* vii–viii.

17. William Penn, *Charter of Liberties and Frame of Government of the Province of Pennsylvania in America,* article 35, May 5, 1682.

and reaffirmed in the Pennsylvania Constitutions of 1776 and 1790.[18] Although Pennsylvania endured several governmental changes—rule by a Proprietor, governance by a revolutionary assembly, a government founded on the principles of a commonwealth within the Confederation, and finally as part of the federal arrangement of the new nation—it continued to uphold "liberty of conscience . . . without any alteration, inviolably forever," on matters of religion, as Penn commanded at the outset.[19]

By 1790 disestablishment was the law in most states.[20] But in practice, an establishment still held sway as the dominant denominations resisted competition and acted as though they were entitled to special privileges, resulting in a complex and often unprincipled struggle that alternated between cordial and hostile extremes. Nowhere was this more apparent than in Philadelphia and the Pennsylvania backwoods where religious groups routinely attacked each other's theological tenets and practices. Laws upholding pluralism assured that these attacks were never officially condoned, but they were no less vehement and numerous. Furthermore, given the highly emotional nature of Christianity at the turn of the nineteenth century the legal and social constructs of toleration were rarely extended to non-Christians with atheists and Jews among the most frequently singled-out. Though guarantors of freedom and liberty, the state constitution and the colonial heritage upon which it was based created an overtly Christian commonwealth. Groups that the self-appointed establishment considered

18. The Pennsylvania Constitution of 1790 in article 9, section 3, repeats the 1776 Pennsylvania Constitution's *Declaration of the Rights of the Inhabitants of the State of Pennsylvania*, section 2, almost verbatim. The 1790 passage, though briefer than its predecessor, conveyed the same rights and sustained the legacy of the state's founding ideals: "That all men have a natural and indefeasible right to worship Almighty God according to the dictates of their own consciences; that no man can of right be compelled to attend, erect, or support any place of worship, or to maintain any ministry, against his consent; that no human authority can, in any case whatever control or interfere with the rights of conscience; and that no preference shall ever be given, by law, to any religious establishment or modes of worship."

19. William Penn, *Charter of Liberties and Frame of Government of the Province of Pennsylvania in America*, preface, May 5, 1682.

20. Nine of the original thirteen states ensured religious disestablishment by 1790. Three—Rhode Island, Pennsylvania, and Delaware—never recognized an established faith. Six—New York, Maryland, Virginia, North Carolina, South Carolina, and Georgia—recognized the Anglican Church. New York, Maryland and North Carolina had set aside that recognition in their state constitutions by 1778. The remaining three did so through legislation. Only the New England states of Connecticut, Massachusetts, New Hampshire, and the district of Maine (which continued its status as the northern district of Massachusetts until 1820), retained a religious establishment past 1800—all of them Congregationalist.

threats to its power were also excluded from the guarantees of liberty, despite the fact that many of these groups professed to be Christian. Although the suspicion and contempt were officially removed from public considerations by law, opposition to such groups was no less prevalent than if it had been legalized,[21] as exemplified by the ample "ambiguities and inconsistencies" identified by Frost in his examination of the shifting nature of the application of religious policies and principles in the face of more immediate, temporal needs. Philosophical ideals often gave way when faced with religious competition and open dissent, forcing the Unitarians to endure a more concerted and open resistance to their presence than a simple reading of the legislation and rhetoric of the day might otherwise reveal.[22]

Unitarianism was confronted with this reality. Though their opponents most often characterized them according to their commonalities with the rationalist extremes of atheism and deism, Priestley's sustained response was to champion Unitarianism's foundations in the earliest history of Christianity and structure Unitarian identity around its role as Christian reform movement. In his brief tract *A General View of the Arguments for the Unity of God* Priestley listed fourteen "maxims of historical criticism" that were essential to the formation of "the proper unitarian doctrine" and by which others could also judge the veracity of his ideas. The proper Unitarian doctrine, including Christ's humanity, was biblically derived and "existed in the time of the apostles; and I think it evident, that it was the faith of the bulk of Christians."[23] Priestley often repeated this claim as a central point in his efforts to convince trinitarians of the error in their critiques. Even though Priestley and others did not consider Unitarianism a proselytizing religion, he connected his ideas with the long-standing Christian effort to convert both Jews and Muslims, claiming that unitarianism removed their objections to Christianity. The vision of a singular God fit well with the Jewish belief that the messiah had yet to appear and also complemented the Muslim belief that there were prophets who came after Jesus, thereby rejecting the latter as the son of God. Priestley frequently denounced many of the beliefs and practices of the non-Christian traditions, but nonetheless offered the quest for a universal fellowship as a justification for Unitarianism. Such efforts were the cornerstone of Priestley's conviction that

21. Stephen Botein, "Religious Dimensions of the Early American State," in Beeman, Botein, and Carter, *Beyond Confederation*, 318–19. See also McGarvie, *One Nation Under Law*, 21–31.

22. Frost, *A Perfect Freedom*, vii–viii.

23. Priestley, *General View* (1794), 21.

all religions, despite their corruptions and errors, were essentially linked at the most basic levels.[24] While this accorded Priestley some respect, many notable American religious and political leaders who themselves agreed with Priestley more than they disagreed with him, were nonetheless careful to limit their personal expression and exposure in support of him.

The tolerance and bigotry with which the ministerial and lay members of competing denominations greeted Priestley shaped his efforts to establish Unitarianism in America. The congregation and its spiritual leader were often forced to adapt to their new circumstances out of need rather than conviction. This reality led them to contest the notion of toleration, which they held out as a "degrading idea." The very fact that they had to be tolerated meant that the true spirit of Christian charity and liberty were missing from the general perception of the Unitarians and the reception given to them upon their formal declaration of religious sentiments. In its place the Unitarians hoped that the American churches would ensure, "to every individual, the free and uninterrupted exercise of the dearest right with which his Maker has invested him"—unrestricted religious liberty.[25] Religious liberty was not something that needed codification; it was the natural state of Christ's grace. To restrict it and confine it by superimposing a sense of tolerance violated the precepts of Christ.

Making the Cause Respectable

Once formally organized, the Unitarians stopped using Elhanan Winchester's Universalist chapel for worship, not wishing to jeopardize his standing in the city, and obtained the use of the chapel on the campus of the University of Pennsylvania. The Board of Regents was generally sympathetic to Unitarian views, having previously offered Priestley the position of chemistry professor in full knowledge of his beliefs, and agreed to suspend their own rules and allow the group to use its facilities, even as they continued to prohibit the use of school property to all other outside organizations.

The initial members of the Philadelphia society were close associates of Priestley. Most prominent among them were William Russell, a former

24. See ibid., vii–ix.

25. "Observations. Explanatory of the foregoing Constitution," in *Constitution of the First Society of Unitarian Christians*, 14.

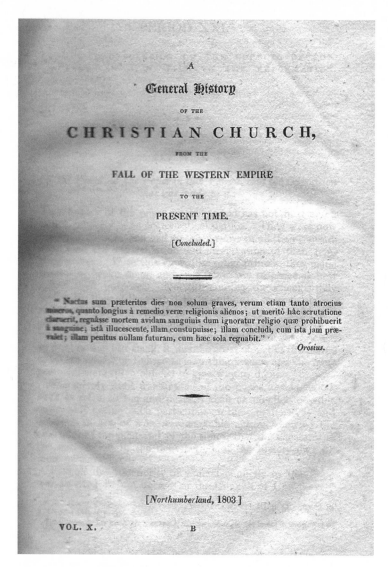

A

General History

OF THE

CHRISTIAN CHURCH,

FROM THE

FALL OF THE WESTERN EMPIRE

TO THE

PRESENT TIME.

[*Concluded.*]

" Nactus sum præteritos dies non solum graves, verum etiam tanto atrocius miseros, quanto longius à remedio veræ religionis aliènos; ut meritò hâc scrutatione claruerit, regnâsse mortem avidam sanguinis dum ignoratur religio quæ prohibuerit à sanguine; istâ illucescente, illam constupuisse; illam concludi, cum ista jam prævalet; illam penitus nullam futuram, cum hæc sola regnabit."
Orosius.

[*Northumberland*, 1803]

VOL. X.   B

Fig. 2   Title page, Joseph Priestley, *A General History of the Christian Church, from the Fall of the Western Empire to the Present Time [Concluded],* vol. 3 (Northumberland, Pa.: John Binns, 1803). Published by permission from the Joseph Priestly House and the Pennsylvania Historical and Museum Commission, Northumberland and Harrisburg.

manufacturer from Birmingham; Ralph Eddowes, a merchant who spent most of his American life in nearby Chester, and who had been a student of Priestley's at Warrington Academy; and several other former students, including the printer Joseph Gales, James Taylor, and John Vaughan, who like Eddowes had been a student of Priestley's at Warrington

Academy, along with his brother Benjamin. Vaughan's connections with Priestley transcended their mutual faith: Vaughan had assisted Priestley in making the arrangements for his emigration and had set up Priestley's finances in America so he could live in the style that he had been accustomed to in England. Furthermore, he served as the treasurer of the American Philosophical Society, to which they both belonged. William Russell shared not just a friendship with Priestley but also a common experience, for he too had lost his house in the Birmingham riots of 1791. Russell also determined to flee to America, but en route his ship was captured by a French frigate, which sailed back to Europe and landed him in France. His arrival in the United States was therefore delayed until 1795. Gales also arrived almost a full year after Priestley, docking in Philadelphia on July 30, 1795, where he remained until 1799 as the publisher of the *Independent Gazetteer,* a paper that often sided with Jefferson. Together, these men became the most prominent figures within Philadelphia Unitarianism.[26]

Priestley and his fellow English Unitarians moved among Philadelphia's high society. Charles Willson Peale, whose eclectic, renaissance interests surpassed even Priestley's, gave him a ticket good for a year's admission to his museum and supported financially the Unitarians' efforts to formalize their society.[27] Benjamin Rush, who was a vocal yet scholarly opponent of Unitarianism, found frequent occasion to interact with Priestley, owing to their common affinity for scientific investigation, and acknowledged their right to exist even in the face of their extreme errors. It was Priestley's presence that assured the society respect among the citizenry and made "the cause of religion more respectable, as not declining, but inviting discussion." Of the Unitarians, it was noted, "many who do not openly join them respect them."[28]

But their tight-knit membership and acceptance by the elite did not assure them of a smooth transition. The society was immediately confronted with the challenges inherent in constructing a formal congregation. Although Priestley's experiences in England served them well in this regard, they encountered a collective and concerted opposition, who viewed a formal Unitarian presence as a much greater threat, if that was even possible, than the simple existence of their ideas informally held. A series of actions intended to derail the Unitarian efforts was

26. See Macaulay, *Unitarianism in the Antebellum South,* 18–19. When Gales moved to North Carolina in 1799, he took the lead in a movement to establish Unitarianism within that state as well.

27. Brigham, *Public Culture,* 7.

28. Joseph Priestley to Theophilus Lindsey, April 3, 1797, in *Works,* 2:375.

begun. Trinitarian ministers regaled their congregations with tales of Unitarian transgressions, assumed dangers, and the destruction that awaited them should a Unitarian congregation persist. They issued detailed rebuttals to the writings of Priestley and other Unitarian authors accusing them of undermining the religious and moral order of American society, oftentimes without having even read them, and defended their own established Protestantism. Accusations that Unitarians were anti-Christian had lasting implications and were at the core of the attacks directed at Priestly by William Cobbett, who labeled him a deist, atheist, anti-Christian, and anti-American.[29] But Cobbett mostly confined his attacks to the political and social realms of Priestley's support for the French Revolution, his alien status, and his antiauthoritarian writings; the religious attacks came from other corners of American society.

The most vehement opposition came from the Reverend Charles Nisbet, a Scottish Presbyterian who had come to the United States during the Revolution. Nisbet had earned his degree from Princeton and was almost immediately elevated to the presidency of the newly formed Dickinson College, owing to his association with one of its founders, Benjamin Rush. Nisbet's particular interest in confronting Priestley, whom he called "our own distinguished Savans," stemmed from several sources, including their common residency in Pennsylvania's interior, the latter living just sixty miles upriver, their dramatic political differences, and Priestley's efforts to establish a competing college in Northumberland. Yet each was secondary to Nisbet's real animus toward English Unitarianism. He rejected Priestley's "*spirit of free inquiry,* which has been so prominent, and which indeed has been carried almost to madness." As a religious conservative, Nisbet detested the very idea of continuous revelation or biblical interpretation as well as the new experimentalism. In this regard Priestley served as a convenient focal point for his critiques. "The present age, in the progress of decrepitude, is busy in vamping up old publications, and reviving old exploded errors, such as Atheism, Socinianism, and what seems to be the last stage of delirium, the indifference to all opinions in religion." In particular he denounced Priestley's convictions on the materialism of the soul and his adherence to the "established creed" of the "equality of the opinions of one God, twenty Gods, or no God."[30]

There were plenty of others who wished to counter the growth of Unitarianism, including Tristam Burges, who later went on to great

29. Cobbett, *Observations.*
30. Miller, *Memoir,* 268–69, 114–16.

fame as a congressman from Rhode Island. Burges found the rejection of Christ's divinity to be untenable and was not about to allow organized Unitarianism to go unchallenged. In his published letters addressing Priestley, Burges took issue with the idea that Socinianism existed side by side with trinitarianism as two parts of the same Christian whole.[31] Most trinitarians found such commentary offensive. Many, like Jonathan Edwards Jr., considered the justifications used in favor of Unitarian rationalism or any "philosophical religion" as destructive of the social and political order and an "abuse and perversion" of the Christian faith. Edwards made it clear that no self-respecting Christian considered the Unitarians' theology, which permitted open religious services and a universal fellowship, a virtue. To Edwards and his fellow Protestant ministers, Priestley's claim that "every man is *a christian* who believes the divine mission of Christ, and consequently the truth of his religion" was the greatest of many errors perpetrated by Unitarians.[32] In fact, trinitarians found their clearly circumscribed theology a comfort and a cushion against the perils of rationalist excess; their faith formed the bulwark of their efforts to sustain themselves in times of conflict, social liberalism, and religious pluralism. Clearly, Priestley's pluralistic views represented the most extreme version of pluralism against which most trinitarians aligned themselves.[33]

Another opponent emerged as the result of a dispute carried out in a series of open letters and writings between Priestley and Dr. William Linn. Linn was one in a long line of Presbyterian opponents, and a minister who was regarded as "an elegant scholar, and a very popular and eloquent preacher . . . of great prudence and piety."[34] In an effort to discredit Priestley, Linn originated a rumor that Priestley had, upon his arrival in America, changed his views on the person of Christ.[35] Linn had significant cause to try and undermine the expansion of English Unitarianism into the United States. American Presbyterians would have been more familiar with Socinianism than Arianism and would have found no barrier to recognizing the Socinians when forced to deal with them under the terms of religious pluralism. The drive among Presbyterians for strict subscription to the 1720 Pacific Act abroad was

31. Burges, *Extracts*, 2–4, 112. The errors in spelling of both "Burges" and "Priestley" were part of the original tract.

32. Priestley, "The Importance of Free Inquiry," in *Discourses on Various Subjects*, 376.

33. Edwards, *Necessity*, 11–15. Edwards's sermon was just one of many that attacked Priestley's ideas as destructive of the state, let alone Christianity.

34. Rush to Nisbet, June 1, 1784, in Miller, *Memoir*, 116.

35. Anderson, "William Linn," 391.

mirrored by the American quest for the Adopting Act in later years. The dissension over the Pacific Act led many in the losing minority to drift into Socinianism.[36] Linn sought to ensure that whatever alliances and affinity Priestley and the Presbyterians may have shared in England were clearly not going be reproduced by American Presbyterians.

The society held to the Socinian belief—a rejection of Christ's divinity while calling themselves Christians—so that it was easy for opponents to misconstrue their theology to suit their own needs or, as was often the case, misread the theology in light of their own preconceived notions. Either way, the group was forced to cautiously define itself in light of the opposition. It was a challenging position to be in, as noted by the social commentator Senex, who in an open letter to Priestley warned the Unitarians about those who might assume "that because you had written and preached in favor of the unity of the Deity, you, therefore, (with them) were adverse to the principles of Christianity inculcated in the sermon of Jesus Christ."[37] In truth, such an "alliance" was hardly the cause for trinitarian opposition, but it certainly added fuel to the fire and was often cited in support of their already preexisting contempt. Such was the case with the Quakers, who, Priestley became aware, cited the two groups' religious commonalities, as revealed in his *Continuation of the Letter to the Philosophers and Politicians of France* with "great avidity." And yet, he lamented, "they have no knowledge at all of the proper evidence of Christianity, or the doctrines of it."[38] Pennsylvania's fervent trinitarians were all too happy to seize upon a potential link between Quakerism and Unitarianism, the former having long been seen as a rejection of all things religiously proper and Christian.

In an effort to make a unitarian-trinitarian association more acceptable, Priestley set out to detail mutual historical and Christian foundations. Priestley's belief in Unitarianism's theological connections with "other" Christian denominations was made apparent in his *History of the Corruptions of Christianity*. In this four-volume work he claimed that his efforts to rid the Christian faith of its accumulated errors were intended to bring all human beings together under God, as Christ himself had intended. Most notable among the groups with whom he sought affiliation, despite such vocal opposition from Linn, were the Presbyterians, with whom Priestley had once been affiliated in England.

---

36. Hodge, *Constitutional History*, 136–56.
37. Wansey, *Journal*, 86.
38. Ware, *Views of Christian Truth*, lvii.

In fact, he had passed through Presbyterianism and its tenets on his way to becoming a Unitarian and had been an avid reader of the London editions of the American Jonathan Dickinson, particularly *The Reasonableness of Christianity*, who like Priestley had been influenced by Locke and Clarke.[39] His desires for an open relationship with American Protestants also extended to the Baptists and Methodists. He noted that the view of God's unlimited foreknowledge, espoused by the American Baptists in their 1742 Philadelphia Confession of Faith, was similar to that espoused by Socinians even if the Baptists did not share most of the Socinian implications of such a view.[40] But Priestley was also interested in getting beyond the theological connections. Baptists and Methodists in particular had proven successful in transferring their denomination from England to America, something to which Priestley aspired.[41]

The Methodists and their denominational wrangling served as a focal point of Priestley's writings on this matter. Formed into a regular church in 1784, at the Christmas Conference, the American Methodists modeled themselves on the Methodists of England.[42] Priestley had the advantage of witnessing this process in England before his departure for America and followed the American developments with great interest once he was settled on the Pennsylvania frontier. Although there was an eventual break between the Methodists of England and those of America, at the time of Priestley's residency in America the Anglo-American connection was still strong as the British continued to insist on continuities of practice and belief between the two countries. This was ensured by the constant stream of ministers from England. Furthermore, although fissures developed within Methodism, a cohesiveness of purpose and belief nevertheless existed among its followers.[43] It was this cohesiveness that appealed to Priestley, and he tried, mostly in vain, to establish it among the Unitarians in the hope that the multiple fissures that existed among unitarian believers, between New England liberals and his own followers in the Middle Atlantic states and the

---

39. Holifield, *Theology in America*, 94.

40. See George and George, *Baptist Confessions, Covenant, and Catechisms*.

41. See William Allum to Rev. William Richards, June 6, 1794, Papers of William Richards, MS, APS; Joseph Priestley to Theophilus Lindsey, June 24, 1794, in *Works*, vol. 1, pt. 2, pp. 264ff.; Priestley to Lindsey, October 16, 1794, in ibid., 275–78; and Priestley to Lindsey, no date, in ibid., 303–4.

42. This included their models of authority, forms of ordination, and worship practices.

43. For information on the spread and development of the Methodists, particularly in the Middle Atlantic region, see Andrews, *Methodists and Revolutionary America*.

South, could be overcome.[44] He found little to emulate in the circuit-riding efforts of the Methodists. In particular he denounced their practice of accepting members into the faith before they had learned the tenets as unconducive to a rationalist-based faith whose theology required years of study and an ability to support it against the attacks of the trinitarian majority. Nevertheless, the ability of the Methodists to spread their faith, draw inspiration and support from their English brethren, and thread their way into the complex social and religious setting of America impressed him greatly.

Priestley also held the Baptists up as a model of integration and success in America. Without an educated clergy they fought valiantly against domination by the Episcopalian and Congregationalist churches. Priestley identified and befriended a kindred spirit in William Rogers, a prominent Baptist minister in Philadelphia. Through his relationship with Rogers he was able to fend off many of the most abusive challenges by other ministers of the same denomination. Although he did not convert any of them to his faith, Priestley and Rogers found common cause in their charitable works and in their efforts to sustain their denominations in a hostile environment.[45] As with the Methodists, he also found some affinity in the Baptists' ability to produce ministers who were more concerned with the needs of the people rather than the needs of the pulpit.[46] Over the course of his residency in America, Priestley would come to pattern many of his actions after the behaviors of these "fellow" Christian denominations, a facet that later became a central concern of those who most closely followed Priestley's footsteps.

Politicizing the Faith

"You will, I doubt not, show that there is no danger whatever to any state from [religious] liberty, as enjoyed by Unitarians, any more than by any other denomination of Christians, by your being equally the friends of peace and good order, and by the exercise of meekness and

---

44. See Priestley, *Address to the Unitarian Congregation at Philadelphia*, 7–8, 18–19, and 22–23.

45. A well-known story about Priestley paying a visit to Rogers and encountering another Baptist minister who did not know him and yet came to admire his religious views *before* finding out his name is repeated in several sources. See Wansey, *Journey*, 84–97, and Priestley to Lindsey, June 24, 1794, in *Works*, vol. 1, pt. 2, pp. 264ff.

46. Priestley, *Letters to the Inhabitants of Northumberland*, vol. 1, Letter VII, "Of my Religion," 38–43.

candor towards those who differ from you," Priestley declared in his first sermon to the newly formed society.[47] It was a sermon that echoed the Unitarian history of confrontation in England and predicted a similar challenge in America. Priestley first set out to define Unitarian theology as Christian and professed that he and his fellow believers held to "all that is most essential" in common with Anglicans, Quakers, Baptists, and Congregationalists. The subtle theological differences were not what mattered most, he noted. "For whatever they may think concerning the person of Christ, all Christians believe the divinity of his mission, the reality of his miracles, of his death, resurrection, and ascension. None of them have any doubt with respect to his second coming, to raise the dead, to judge the world, and to give every man according to his works, in a future state of existence."[48] These ideas were almost identical to those that had been expressed on the opening of the Essex Street chapel and were to form the core of Unitarian expressions and action in America.

But the formal transition into an open and avowed religious congregation heightened the opposition's awareness of their English ties—both personal and religious—and the religious debate quickly took on a nationalistic tone. Though Priestley and the Unitarians mostly tried to remain above the fray, separating their religious ideas from the implications and associations with other facets of American society, they found that their place in America was challenged not only on religious grounds but also on political, social, and ethnic ones.[49]

Outside the religious realm, their greatest vulnerability stemmed from their status as immigrants, making the Unitarians, many of whom were English or Irish resident aliens, the objects of both scorn and suspicion. Such suspicion was fed, in part, by Unitarianism's appeal mainly to these outsiders, and most Americans were unwilling to tolerate an intrusion into their domestic affairs by individuals who remained "strangers" in both civic and religious terms.[50] The English

47. Priestley, *Address to the Unitarian Congregation at Philadelphia*, 8.
48. Ibid., 9.
49. Priestley to Dr. John S. Mitchell, January 8, 1803, in *Tracts by and about Dr. Joseph Priestley* (1804), 433, LOC. Priestley wrote, "as to the chaplainship to Congress, I should not think of it. They have my best wishes, and prayers too, without any salary" or official position.
50. In *Discourses on the Evidence of Revealed Religion*, the series of sermons delivered in 1796 and dedicated to John Adams, Priestley noted that he chose to live in America as a "stranger" or non-naturalized immigrant (vi–vii). Throughout his time in America, Priestley never did take U.S. citizenship, though he wavered on the matter more than once. The social and legal status of immigrants occupied Priestley's personal life as well as his religious life and formed a central part of his perspective on the American political economy.

nationality and background of many of the Pennsylvania Unitarians was a major factor influencing their reception. They were distrusted by other immigrant groups for the ease with which they entered into the upper levels of American society and considered suspect by those "native" Americans who were concerned about continued ties to England.[51]

Immigration was a contentious issue in the early national period, primarily over the type rather than the numbers or origins of people who were coming. "Transatlantic radicals" seemed to come from many different nationalities, varying classes, and with vastly different ideas about the nation's political and social direction. Although mostly welcome during the crisis of the Revolution, these same influences now threatened the desire for a return to stability that so clearly pervaded the American character of the early national period. Americans became very insular and sought to protect their achievements from potentially destructive forces, so easily identified as European in origin and extreme in thought. Americans, it was felt, had solved their only issue of the era through a war reluctantly entered into. But Europeans, as evidenced by continued warfare and the extremism of the French Revolution, were unable to control themselves and limit the impulse for change.[52] Priestley and the Unitarians were caught in the middle of this issue.

Many viewed their immigrant and alien status with disdain. When young William Bakewell, who lived and worshipped with Priestley in Northumberland from 1795 to 1797, returned to Philadelphia, he was confronted by trinitarians over his Unitarian associations. In one conversation Bakewell was told that "the Doctor did not put on respectability enough, but made himself familiar with the lower orders, and had preached a discourse for the benefit of the Emigrant Society."[53] But Charles Willson Peale did not suffer the same kind of contempt for his association with immigrant causes. According to one historian, "Peale's position as officer of the Philadelphia Emigrant Society promoted his image as benevolent protector of the less fortunate."[54] Priestley and Peale, who were friends, owing to their mutual membership in the American Philosophical Society and interests in science, were regarded in completely different ways on the same issue.

---

51. Daniels, *Coming to America*, 115–18. Daniels argues that there was no contention during this period, at least in relation to the excessive tension and hostility later. But evidence clearly shows that the Unitarians and other English, non-Christian religious groups were targeted for both their religious beliefs and nationality.

52. Durey, *Transatlantic Radicals*.

53. Bakewell, "Some Particulars," 567.

54. Brigham, *Public Culture*, 86.

When immigrants were seen as a problem, but not particularly a threat, involvement in the cause was acceptable. But when Priestley, an immigrant, became involved he was seen not only as an outsider on American affairs but also as someone who might be able to take advantage of the situation to benefit his own cause.

Priestley's sermon on immigration, though regarded by detractors as a sign of his intent to meddle in political affairs and to promote the causes of the lower orders, was an important document in the development of Unitarian social thought in America. It was also an attempt to clearly establish Unitarians within the nation's religious landscape on the basis of their regard for Christian charity. "Receive them, with equal humanity, the *persecuted* of every description. Let your object be simply their *distress* and not political principles of any kind; and indulge no fear, jealousy, or suspicion" of immigrants, he implored of his American audience.[55] It was a statement that could have been directly tied to the situation of the Unitarians. But Priestley saw an even deeper, more basic need to call for Christian and civil treatment of immigrants, for theirs was a condition not determined by choice, as was religious belief, but by circumstance.[56]

Such views quickly earned him the enmity of both William Cobbett and Noah Webster. Cobbett, an Englishman himself, noted that immigrants like Priestley, with all of their distasteful political and religious principles possessed "a popular prejudice against his [own] country" and that "a man of all countries is a man of no country . . . never [to] be either *trusted* or *respected*."[57] For his part, Webster believed that all immigrants, regardless of class, culture, or ethnicity threatened "a stable republic" and represented "the causes of decline." He found immigrants to be "factious men who, accustomed to quarrel with the unjust laws of their own countries, do not lay aside their opposition here, although the same evils are acknowledged not to exist." Although he did not entirely rule out immigrants as participants in American society, Webster noted that the country would be "as prosperous and much more happy if no European should set foot on our shores."[58]

55. Priestley, *Case of the Poor Emigrants Recommended*, 26; italics in original.

56. This section is derived from a paper presented to the Society for Historians of the Early Republic (1996) and the Pennsylvania Historical Society (1995). I am grateful to William Pencak, Paul Conkin, and Barbara Oberg for their comments and suggestions.

57. Cobbett ("Peter Porcupine"), *Observations*, 45, 19.

58. Noah Webster to Joseph Priestley, January 20, 1800, in Webster, *Letters*, 214–15. See also Noah Webster, *Ten Letters to Joseph Priestley in Answer to His Letters to the Inhabitants of Northumberland* (New Haven: Read and Morse, 1800).

Priestley repeatedly challenged the hostility with which many Americans regarded immigrants by infusing his religious values into his social commentary and attacking the nativist impulses. "Of what importance is it where I was born, or whence I came," he challenged his opponents. "Here I am. Here is my family. Here is my property and everything else that can attach a man to any place." Not content with establishing his own affections, Priestley turned the anti-immigrant arguments on their head. It is far more likely, he noted, that an immigrant would "have a real attachment to a country, and the government of it, to which I came *voluntarily* and from a preference to them to any other, as if I had been a native, and consequently had no other choice in the case."[59] Lest there be any doubt about the religious foundations of his views, he took the text of his speech from Exodus 23:9, "Thou shalt not oppress a stranger, for ye know the heart of a stranger," and Deuteronomy 10:19, "Love ye, therefore, the stranger. For ye were strangers." Both spoke of the central concerns that Priestley had over the lack of American tolerance.[60] He felt that of all nations, America was the land of immigrants and should respect the fact that its very foundations were laid on the backs of immigrants. "If not yourselves, yet your fathers, or not very remote ancestors, were also strangers, and not in a distant country, in this very country in which we are now met," he reminded the American people. Welcoming the most recent immigrants into America was a religious as much as a social or political matter. "The sight of their distress softens the heart and excites to acts of kindness in others, which strengthens the principles of benevolence" and by extension strengthened the moral compass of America.[61]

Priestley's advocacy for the Philadelphia Emigrant Society gained a great deal of attention and led to calls for the formation of similar organizations throughout the country. His message was held in high regard by the nation's leading political figures for its rejection of charity solely based on monetary handouts, noting that such gifts "would soon defeat the object of the charity." Instead, the society provided relief in the form of food, medical assistance, information, and employment services to recent arrivals. Its goal was to provide the new nation with a way to welcome the needed labor without straining

59. Priestley, *Letters to the Inhabitants of Northumberland*, vol. 1, Letter I, "Of My Situation as an Alien," 3–4.

60. Priestley, *Case of the Poor Emigrants Recommended*, i.

61. Ibid., 7, 10.

its limited resources.[62] The whole idea of charity was an idea endowed by the Creator. "We should, therefore, behave to one another . . . as brethren . . . brethren in affliction, difficulty, and trials," he preached. And it was up to those with more to "*give* out of what they can well spare *to him that needeth.*" This was the divine plan, to make men "the instruments of this discipline for the improvement of men."[63] In this manner Priestley implored his fellow Unitarians to act as models of Christian virtue, to lead the way in the support for the immigrants. He was well aware that as an English immigrant, with financial backing and social standing as a minister (even if he was a minister of a dissenting group), his status was less precarious than that of the artisans of the lower middle and working classes, but his convictions were no less intense as a result. Charity and immigrant relief became a central component of the Philadelphia society as its members became leading supporters of the Philadelphia Emigrant Society and its later counterpart, the Pennsylvania Society for the Promotion of Public Economy.[64]

Despite his status as an alien, Priestley was nominated for, and received votes in the balloting for the chaplain of the United States Senate in 1802. Out of seventeen votes cast, two went to Priestley, who lost the position to the Reverend Dr. Edward Gantt and finished third behind Alexander Thomas McCormick, both Episcopalians.[65] Gantt, a native of Maryland, was ordained a minister in England in 1770 and upon his return served as the rector of All Hallows Parish in Worcester County, Maryland. His stature as a minister of the Episcopal Church was such that he was elected to the position of Senate chaplain twice, serving from 1801 to 1804 and again from 1805 to 1806. The resolution introducing Priestley's nomination noted that each chamber of

---

62. Ibid., 18, 13. These ideas were not new. Priestley believed that a small loan and substantial advice would be repaid to the benefactor and society by placing the immigrant into "a condition to provide for himself" (15). These views can be found in his earlier English sermon, *An Account of a Society for Encouraging the Industrious Poor,* in which he advocated an alternative to the poor laws and parish relief system of England in order to give a poor man "certain prospects of bettering his condition . . . [and] enable him to do more for himself" (3–4). He continued with such advice in his later work *Lectures on History and General Policy,* in which he noted the ability of such assistance to actually lead to more assistance for future generations as the original assistance was paid off or led to direct social benefits.

63. Ibid., 7–8.

64. Geffen, *Philadelphia Unitarianism,* 105–6.

65. U.S. Senate, *Journal,* 243–44. Gantt received ten votes and McCormick four. McCormick went on to serve as chaplain of the Senate from 1804 to 1805, between Gantt's two terms.

the Congress, House and Senate, had to appoint a minister of a different denomination presumably to avoid any further questions about the links between church and state. During the first years of the nineteenth century, while Episcopalians dominated the Senate's position, Presbyterians and Baptists dominated the House chaplaincy. Priestley's appearance on the ballot was, no doubt, a result of the prevailing attitudes and ideas brought forth by the Jefferson administration. More than likely, Representative Samuel Thatcher from Massachusetts, a sympathetic Federalist who held Priestley in high regard and had strong Unitarian leanings, promoted his candidacy outside the walls of the Senate chamber, but since no individual floor votes on the matter were recorded, there will never be any direct evidence to show who actually voted for Priestley.

Priestley's failure to win the post could have been the result of any number of factors—his religion, his explicit desire not to be considered, his British citizenship. The likeliest is his religion. So widespread was the animus toward Unitarians in the United States that no one who professed such views, let alone a Socinian, would serve as Senate chaplain until the appointment of Dr. Edward Everett Hale in 1903.[66]

Their immigrant condition was just one of the many reasons that the Unitarians were uncertain of their fate. But the views of the opposition were beyond their control and had to do with the rapidly changing social conditions of the young nation. It was clear to the Unitarians that the cold reception, combined with other obstacles to social and religious recognition, were problems that transcended purely religious concerns. Carole Shammas recently suggested that many social conflicts in the early urban centers of America had their origins in spatial limitations. The rate at which American cities were putting people into close contact with each other and at which these cities had to absorb new peoples and new ideas was both alarming and disconcerting.[67] For

66. The Reverend Charles Nisbet, the Scots-American Calvinist and president of Dickinson College, wrote to William Young on July 29, 1794, with great irony, that "they [Democratic-Republicans] can not with Decency avoid offering Dr. Priestley the Office of Chaplain, if such Office shall be thought proper to be continued, in an Age so enlightened as the present." See Charles Nisbet Correspondence with William Young, July 29, 1794, p. 3, Dickinson College Archives.

67. Shammas, "Space Problem," 509–10, 514. Shammas discusses all the accompanying social problems that resulted from increased numbers of people in areas that were relatively confined by geography or politics. She compares Philadelphia, New York, Baltimore, and Boston to give varying perspectives on the matter. Priestley, in fact, cited overcrowding and unhealthy conditions within Philadelphia as one of the major reasons that he chose not to live in the city and was anxious to settle to the north near his son's proposed development. It was also the reason he later turned down an offer to teach at the University of

the Unitarians this meant adopting some survival skills. Formalizing their association, finding a place of worship, and adopting a worship manual were all methods to facilitate their integration into a new society. Priestley's final verdict, delivered in a statement that crossed political and religious grounds was that American values should prevail. "Where there is perfect liberty . . . no principles can be dangerous."[68] Americans, however, were split on the matter.

A Church Within Itself

The development of the Philadelphia Unitarian society continued unabated following Priestley's death in 1804. Joseph Gales, in a historical account of the society, noted that the group never abandoned its quest for Christian worship, despite enduring some significant challenges.[69] The group lacked a settled minister, experienced delays in the construction of its chapel, and continued to suffer under the anti-immigrant and antirationalist movements of the early nineteenth century. Still they pushed on, supported by their beliefs and associations with the English Unitarians, and the growth of other non-evangelical denominations. Although Priestley's death left them without their leader, his legacy provided them with both a "moral influence" and "standing in society" that many in the wider Protestant community came to acknowledge.[70]

In their 1807 Constitution, a revision of their earlier charter documents, the Unitarians made two claims that sustained their assertion to membership in the Christian community. Both were based on the fundamental belief that "every Christian Society constitutes a complete Church within itself." First, they asserted the right "of judging for themselves in matters of religion, and of performing the social acts thereof in that form and manner which conscience dictates as most rational, decent and acceptable," otherwise known as religious liberty.

Pennsylvania. See *Autobiography of Joseph Priestley*, 133–35. Perhaps this was not such a bad decision on his part. In 1793 Philadelphia was the site of an epidemic outbreak of yellow fever that killed over four thousand people. The city suffered from a series of subsequent outbreaks in 1798, 1799, and 1802. See Powell, *Bring Out Your Dead*.

68. Priestley, *Case of the Poor Emigrants Recommended* 26. He repeated this statement in *Letters to the Inhabitants of Northumberland*, vol. 2, Letter VIII, 4, 7. He wrote "in all countries, and under every form of government, *opinions* of every kind and those of all persons, natives or aliens . . . should be perfectly free; because they can do no harm."

69. Eddowes, "Proceedings."

70. Baird, *Religion in the United States*, 613.

As a right upheld by the "excellent constitution" of the United States, their claim to religious liberty was the first point of their charter. Their second point reaffirmed their form of worship which they "addressed to the ONE GOD and FATHER of all, in the name of the *one mediator* JESUS CHRIST." Still, the "proper object of supreme adoration and worship is the *One living and true God the* Father." The document went on to address subsequent issues of institutional organization—including the election of a pastor, criteria for membership, rules for general meetings, selection of officers, and the process for amendments.[71] The group flourished under these rules, bolstered in their efforts by the respectability that a charter and regularly scheduled worship conveyed. Between 1807 and 1813, the group began to act as though they were but one congregation of an established denomination and settled into a routine existence. The young nation's shifting patterns of migration and growth meant that the Unitarians, like all other groups, gained new members and lost old ones. Philadelphia's denominations experienced similar growth, internal divisions, and changes to their institutional structure, all as a result of the changing demographics and the increasing popularity of evangelicalism.[72]

Being a church unto themselves with only a dozen or so other affiliated congregations throughout the country forced the society to develop and refine their beliefs and practices in relative isolation and endure the trials of such a process on their own. Priestley had always believed and preached that no Christian group required a regular minister to be a viable congregation or to celebrate the Lord's Supper. He acknowledged the prevalence of contrary opinions but dismissed them as being "superstitious" and representative of the "great prejudice" that prevailed when it came to defining a successful or viable religious society, especially in regard to those areas newly under settlement.[73] Reliance on a minister was an outdated and erroneous object of faith that had no place in a religion where God was the sole arbiter of what was proper and just. He laid out his entire approach in *Unitarianism Explained and Defended*. The course of action he proposed became the model for the Philadelphia and all other extant American Unitarian societies. Unitarians, he wrote, "should form themselves into societies . . . [with] a few persons, who, as in primitive time, may be

---

71. *Constitution of the First Society of Unitarian Christians*, Preliminary Declarations 1, 2 and 5; "Rules. I. Public Worship," pp. 3–5. For a discussion of the Constitution and its context, see Scharf and Westcott, *History of Philadelphia*, 2:1405.

72. Mease, *Picture of Philadelphia*, 11–18.

73. Priestley, *Unitarianism Explained and Defended*, viii.

called *elders*, to be chosen to direct their affairs; let them meet every Lord's day for public worship, when any compositions approved by the society may be read, and baptism and the Lord's supper administered." He continued to believe that a society could strive for a settled minister (something they would finally achieve some years later) but not if that effort kept them from their worship. "By no means let the important object of *public worship*, and the holding up to the view of the world Christian and Unitarian principles, be abandoned, or long suspended, for want of such a convenience."[74]

Revelation's importance to unitarian believers was set forth in Priestley's *Discourses Relating to the Evidences of Revealed Religion*, which delved deep into the biblical foundations of religious faith in order to assign meaning to belief in God. "The principles of religion are acknowledged to consist in the belief of the being, the perfections, and providence of God here, and of a future state of retribution hereafter," he noted. Such discussions of revealed religion were not limited to any one religion and were the most important way to stave off unbelief. "I could not make choice of any subjects more unexceptionable, or more useful, than of such as relate to the *evidences of revealed religion*, in an age abounding with unbelievers, many of whom have become so merely for want of better information."[75] This conviction led his followers to challenge nonbelivers and became a cornerstone of their religious activities in the United States.

There was also an overriding concern for morality, as exemplified by Jesus and as the focal point for all of Christianity. Priestley's *Importance and Extent of Free Inquiry in Matters of Religion* became the central text from which the society drew their thinking on morality and its foundations in religion. Belief was a simple fact of acceptance of the preaching of Jesus and the word of God. "What doth the Lord thy God require of thee, but to do justice, to love mercy, and to walk humbly with thy God?" asked Priestley of his followers. It was a simple matter; the values of God were clear, even if the messenger sometimes was not. According to Priestley, the two greatest influences on a man's behavior were his "belief in the righteous moral government of God, and a state of rewards and punishments hereafter," and in these two imperatives man could easily discern the path to righteousness and justice.[76]

The decision to operate under the direction of the laity—using Priestley's conceptions of revelation, morality, and reason—and in any

---

74. Ibid.
75. Priestley, *Discourses Relating to the Evidences of Revealed Religion*, 2, ix.
76. Priestley, *Free Inquiry*, 9 and 19.

available location was an important one for the Priestleyan Unitarians. It shaped their conceptions of interfaith relationships, institutionalization, social responsibility, and church polity. Unknown to them at the time, it was to be the pattern that governed their religious affairs for the next twenty-eight years, with only a brief interlude of seven months in 1807. This decision meant that the congregation was never guided solely in one theological direction. Instead it heard multiple perspectives, some of which were original to the members themselves while others were readings of published sermons of leading clergy. Priestley relished this conduct. "The Unitarian Society is in a most promising state, and the members of it attend with a kind of enthusiasm, and shew attachment to each other similar to that of the primitive Christians," he wrote. "It is better, I am satisfied, than any congregation with a regular minister." The depth of his satisfaction was evident in his description of a service he took part in. "The last Lord's-day I administered the Lord's Supper, and Mr. Eddowes baptized two children in a manner that affected and edified all who were present; the discourse and prayers all his own."[77]

The brief period in which the Philadelphia society did operate under the leadership of a called and settled minister can only be called troubled. William Christie arrived in the United States in 1795 as an avowed Socinian and follower of Priestley. "From a very early period of my life I was an admirer of the writings of Dr. Priestley, and not a little improved by several of his publications, which I purchased as they came from the press," he wrote. In particular Priestley's *Free Address to Protestant Dissenters, as Such* stood out as having had "an effect on my mind that I cannot easily describe." The two men then engaged in an exchange of letters that "induced me to become a preacher." He abandoned his career as a merchant and founded the Unitarian society at Montrose, the first Unitarian church in Scotland, in 1781 and served as its pastor for over a decade. "All that ever I did as Preacher . . . may be indirectly ascribed to Dr. Priestley as the cause," he later noted.[78] Always ambitious, Christie left Montrose for the more promising prospects of Glasgow where he assumed the ministry of another congregation. Following much soul searching, however, he left that congregation after less than a year and followed Priestley to America, going first to Winchester, Virginia, where he stayed only briefly, before moving to Northumberland in 1801 to be with Priestley.[79] He remained in Northumberland for

77. Priestley to Lindsey, April 3, 1797, in *Works*, 2:374–76.
78. Christie, *Speech*, 9, 9–10n.
79. *Monthly Repository* 6 (1811): 193–204; 7 (1812): 58, 19 (1824): 214n, 363. See also Wilbur, *History of Unitarianism*, 2:320. Christie appears in the Northumberland County tax

several years before moving first to Pottstown and then on to Philadelphia in 1807, where he assumed the ministerial post of the First Unitarian Society. Overshadowed by Priestley's productivity, Christie produced two highly regarded, though not often read works on Unitarianism, *Discourses on the Divine Unity* and *Sixteen Dissertations on the Divine Unity.* An able defender of the faith who matched Priestley's direct and sometimes blunt style, his *Discourses,* originally published in Scotland, proclaimed that a Unitarian was simply a thoughtful Christian interested in understanding the true meaning of the scriptures.[80]

His election to the Philadelphia ministerial post was a mistake for all parties concerned. Resigning the position after a short period of time, Christie cited differences of opinion over governance—he felt that his connections with Priestley should have given him almost absolute authority, but the congregation was reluctant to surrender its heritage of lay leadership—as the reason for his departure. The society's records reveal very little except that Christie went on to lead a breakaway group's formation into the city's second Unitarian congregation. This new society met twice every Sunday on North Sixth Street and was led by an elder and two deacons, with substantial guidance by Christie. But the members quickly fell away, as did the commitment of the leadership, when circumstances of removal, family considerations, and workload soon overwhelmed the small group. The Independent Society of Unitarian Christians, which formally emerged in September 1807, stopped meeting after less than a year and ceased to exist in May 1808. During his time in the city Christie published three small tracts concerning his relationship with each of the two Philadelphia societies. His *Remarks on the Constitution, framed by Three Leading Members, and lately Adopted by a Majority of the Society of Unitarian Christians, Who Assemble in Church Alley; &c.* detailed his objections to lay leadership when a settled minister was available. Christie held that Priestley had advocated the option of

---

record for 1802, though under the spelling of "Cristy." He owned a lot within the town limits and was taxed on the value of the real estate but paid no personal or occupational tax. Northumberland County Public Records, 1802 County Tax Collection, Sunbury, Pennsylvania, JPH Research File no. 2.

80. Christie's other writings include *An Essay on Ecclesiastical Establishments in Religion* (1791); *A Serious Address to the Inhabitants of Winchester, on the Unity of God, and Humanity of Christ, &c.* (1800); various articles in the *Winchester Gazette* (1800–1801), among them his *Farewell Address, Protest Against the Trinitarian Doctrine and Worship,* a defense of both Jefferson and Priestley against their many detractors; and "The Doctrine of the Scriptures Concerning God, Jesus Christ, and the Holy Spirit, Briefly Stated; and accompanied with Remarks on *Observation on the Divinity of Christ,* ascribed to Judge Rush," which appeared in the *Sunbury and Northumberland Gazette,* October 28, 1803.

lay leadership only in the absence of ministerial leadership, but that he had fully intended the group to find a minister and thus conduct themselves more like other Christian denominations.[81]

His final writing on the matter, *Dissertations on the Unity of God in the Person of the Father,* originally delivered as a sermon, related the history of his association with both congregations in Philadelphia and the reasons for the suspension of the meetings of the Independent Society. "Since my coming to reside in *this City,* I have engaged in public worship, and other religious services, with two different classes of men of the Unitarian denomination; and neither of these Societies have answered my expectations in all respects; though I had the satisfaction of parting with *a majority* of the members of *the Independent Society,* in an agreeable manner."[82] His departure from the original society was particularly hostile and something of a scandal, though the specifics were never revealed. Christie noted in the preface to his publication of the sermons that he held the full collection of papers concerning the formation and dissolution of the latter group, but was unsure if he would publish the details.[83]

Christie's *Dissertations on the Unity of God* was an astute theological defense of Unitarianism. It began with 1 Timothy 2:5. "For there is one God, and one mediator between God and men, the man Christ Jesus."[84] The dissertations, numbering sixteen, were drawn from Scripture, informed by reason, in response to objections, and applied to practical matters of worship. Perhaps the most important aspect of the collection was Christie's reply to Arian objections to the Socinian Unitarian beliefs. Well aware that the New England liberals were maligning the Philadelphia Unitarians as extremists, Christie sought to distinguish the various manifestations of Unitarianism. But he was adamant that the New England groups should acknowledge their close connection to the English denomination, a connection that was, he held, closer than their professed association with the Congregationalist Church. Not surprisingly, Christie's conclusion was that the most perfect form of Unitarianism was that embodied by Socinianism. His decision to end with an account of the beliefs of trinitarians and a dissection of their centuries-old errors was thus a bold strike in favor of bringing the liberal Christians to a full acceptance of Priestley's ideas.[85] Christie delivered his *Dissertations* to the Independent Society over a period of

81. Christie, *Remarks on the Constitution.*
82. Christie, *Dissertations on the Unity of God,* xxix.
83. Ibid., xxxi.
84. Ibid.
85. Ibid., 243–45.

months, beginning in November and lasting through February and published them soon thereafter. When he was done with this, he turned his attention to the prophecies of Daniel, which had been the focus in much of Priestley's final writings, and ended his preaching with the dissolution of the group.[86]

Little is known about Christie's subsequent career as a minister. Rumors had him preaching out west, attempting to gain a foothold among the growing number of Unitarians in Kentucky and other frontier locations.[87] Nothing can be substantiated. In the end, however, he wound up in New Jersey where he passed his last years in relative seclusion, having failed in his desire to become Priestley's successor in America. He died at the age of seventy-four on November 21, 1823, in Long Branch, New Jersey, at the home of his daughter, Mrs. William Renshaw. Of him, Jared Sparks wrote, "Few men have possessed the talent of expressing themselves with greater clearness and strength of language, than Mr. Christie." He was "a Christian from principle and conviction . . . in the habit of acknowledging God in all his ways, and of referring all his concerns to the Divine disposal; . . . he always maintained that the ways of heaven were just, and wise, and good."[88]

Priestley's Philadelphia Legacy

Once the crisis of separation had been weathered, most of the members of the Independent Society rejoined the original group and refocused on their rites of worship and institutionalization. They continued to express their commitment to open and universal communion, noting that "every person . . . shall be admitted to a participation of [the Lord's Supper], who maintains a serious and proper behavior." They asked for no declaration of creed, only that the person be moral. "If he *name the name of Christ, and depart from iniquity* it is sufficient for us. In other respects we judge no man."[89] Finally, they gave stated periods for the celebration of the Lord's Supper (being the first Sunday of February, April, June, August, October, and December, as well as when special circumstances warranted).[90]

86. Ibid., xxx.
87. *Monthly Repository* 6 (1811): 193–204; 19 (1824): 241n., 263.
88. Jared Sparks, "Obituary: William Christie," *Unitarian Miscellany and Christian Monitor* (Baltimore), December 1823, 152.
89. "Observations. Explanatory of the foregoing Constitution," in *Constitution of the First Society of Unitarian Christians,* 22.
90. "Rules. I. Public Worship," in *Constitution of the First Society of Unitarian Christians,* 5.

The model of the Lord's Supper as an exclusive tool was one that continued to trouble many Unitarians, as it had Priestley. The Universalist position on communion, that it was open to all and provided salvation to all, was far more acceptable than the restrictions placed upon it by trinitarians. It was this concept that had originally brought the Philadelphia society into a close association with the Universalists, which Priestley promoted.[91] The trinitarian creeds perverted communion, both in its intentions and divine inspiration; furthermore, orthodox restrictions only served to create false and meaningless barriers to religious tolerance. "Thrice happy should we be to see the day when Christians of every denomination (Friends, and Catholics not excepted) laying aside their present prejudices, should jointly devise a plan for making the Lord's Table a point of union instead of an engine of division," the group proclaimed in their founding document.[92]

The most promising connection with the Universalists centered on the two groups' complementary ideas of the relationship of God to humanity, the salvation of the soul, and the principles espoused by Christ. Unitarians accepted the Universalists' arguments against eternal damnation and permanent human depravity. For Priestley the connections ran even deeper. He had hoped to benefit from the Universalists' experiences as newcomers to the religious arena. Led by Elhanan Winchester, whose path to Universalism by way of the Congregationalist and Baptist denominations mirrored Priestley's path to Unitarianism, the Universalist society was formed in 1781 when Winchester's proclamations of universal salvation led to his ouster as a Baptist minister. Despite their standing outside traditional trinitarian circles, the Universalists were able to form a denomination with support from the broader religious society, and attain a level of respect among those with different theological ideas. Unitarianism's hopes were aligned with the path already followed by these fellow dissenters.

Though two centuries away from a formal association, the Unitarian-Universalist connection was one of substantial optimism. It was the Universalists who had given Priestley the unequivocal honor of delivering the dedication sermon for their new chapel and who opened the pulpit of their church to him on a routine basis when other churches rejected him. "They propose to leave it open to any sect of Christians three days in the week, but they want money to finish it. My friends think

91. Baird, *Religion in the United States*, 640. Baird cites a continued connection between the two based on "the moral influence of the doctrine of the Universalists."
92. "Observations. Explanatory of the foregoing Constitution," in *Constitution of the First Society of Unitarian Christians*, 23–24.

to furnish them with money, and engage the use of it for Sunday mornings. The society itself, I hear, intend to apply to me to open it; which I shall gladly do." The open chapel provided Priestley and the Unitarians with an edifice from which to proclaim their ideas on religious toleration and the ecumenical spirit. At the same time it gave him a pulpit from which to preach and issue his defenses of the Unitarian faith, something he did every morning while in residence in Philadelphia. His growing audience and the increased attention given to his ideas led him to declare that "a person with a proper spirit and prudence may do great things here. I find I have great advantages, and I hope to make good use of them."[93] Over time this association played a role in the development of both churches and helped the Unitarians overcome many obstacles placed in their way.

The connection between Winchester and Priestley was so strong that two decades after the latter's death, F.W.P. Greenwood, who had taken over the publication of the *Unitarian Miscellany* from Jared Sparks, thought it poignant to relate a story about Winchester's convictions regarding Socinians. When asked by a "narrow minded" person if Socinians could be saved, Winchester turned the question back on the inquirer and through the gentleman's own admissions that Socinians accepted Jesus as the Messiah and that they also accepted his resurrection, established a firm assent that Socinians, like all other Christians, could be saved. In the end, Winchester stated from the pulpit, "it is of little consequence what *my* opinion is on this subject, but I can give you the opinion of the Apostle Paul respecting persons who acknowledge that Jesus is the Christ, and who believe that God raised him from the dead." At this point he quoted Paul in Romans 10:9, which established the tests of Jesus' status and resurrection as the criteria for salvation, then, noted Winchester, "agreeably to the decision of Paul . . . provided their conduct correspond with their profession, they *shall* 'be saved.'"[94] Not only was Winchester demonstrating his liberal spirit, but he was also harking back to the theology of his friend and fellow Christian traveler, Priestley.

The Philadelphia Unitarian society also continued to uphold Priestley's advocacy of the instruction of youth in the proper beliefs and forms of worship. When Priestley had first addressed the newly formed congregation in 1797, he had instructed them to "attend to the religious

93. Priestley to Lindsey, June 24, 1794, in Belsham, *Memoirs*, 414; Priestley to Lindsey, February 15, 1796, in *Works*, vol. 1, pt. 2, pp. 333–34.

94. "Annecdotes of the late Rev. Elhanan Winchester," *The Unitarian Miscellany and Christian Monitor* (Baltimore), June 1824, 70–71.

instruction of your children. There is no church regularly constituted, and whose affairs are well conducted, in which there is not some express provision for catechizing the children belonging to it." He had admonished them to beware of "the lamentable effects of the want of it," which all too often resulted in "the ignorance and rudeness, I may add the profaneness, of too many children and young persons." The congregation followed his advice diligently. He had asked that they "appoint then out of your body those who are most able and willing to undertake the conduct of this business," and the group identified several congregants to take the lead in the religious education of their young worshippers.[95]

Ralph Eddowes, one of the members charged with the education of the youth, reaffirmed Priestley's teachings by delivering a sermon on the topic of the treatment of children. This sermon, delivered in 1809, stressed the link between religious education of the young and the religious principles of social obligation.[96] A year later the Unitarian society printed its own *Catechism for Youth*. Based partially on Priestley's 1791 Catechism, this version was much amended to include briefer answers and a simpler explanation of Unitarian theology.[97] Unlike the catechism found in other denominations of the period, theirs was not a series of indoctrination points. One of Priestley's former students noted that his teacher's educational objective was "to engage the students to examine and decide for themselves, uninfluenced by the sentiments of any other persons," something which carried over into the Unitarian ideas on religious instruction as well as secular teaching.[98]

As a result Eddowes became the primary lay religious leader among the Philadelphia Unitarians, eventually calling himself the minister *pro tem* of the society. While Priestley was alive, he often served in this de facto role for the congregation, gladly stepping aside during the former's extended stays in Philadelphia. It was Eddowes, however, who took the lead in Priestley's absence and who most likely led the charge against Christie's attempts to take over the group, and he continued to lead the society well into the nineteenth century. His leadership was a wise choice for the society as it continued to fight for social respectability; Eddowes was adamant in his efforts to adhere to Priestley's principles

---

95. Priestley, *Address to the Unitarian Congregation at Philadelphia*, 21.
96. Eddowes, *On the Early Treatment of Children*.
97. First Society of Unitarian Christians, *A Catechism for Youth*, in *Collection of Pieces and Tracts*.
98. A Daventry student, quoted in Huxley, "Joseph Priestley," in *Collected Essays*, 3:5.

of religious liberty and that the congregation continue to profess their Socinian tenets.

Eddowes's first test came in May 1808, immediately following Christie's departure, when the Reverend Archibald Alexander went before the Presbyterian General Assembly and warned of the dangers of Unitarianism. "From the signs of the time, I apprehend the danger to evangelical truth which will now arise, will be from two opposite points: from what is called *rational christianity,* and *enthusiasm.* . . . Most of those speculative men who were lately inclined to deism, will now fill the ranks of socinianism or Unitarianism, as they choose to denominate their religion. The errors of idolized reason are very dangerous, because they have for their abetters the learned and powerful of this world, and the influence of their example is very extensive."[99] Eddowes dutifully took Alexander to task when he delivered an address to the Unitarian society in which he rejected Alexander's claim that the Unitarian faith divested religion of its awe for the power and glory of God and of its ability to be interesting and beneficial to even the most common American. Eddowes asserted that Alexander, like so many before him, had misrepresented and misconstrued the elements of the Unitarian faith.

Two years later, Eddowes once again responded to attacks against Unitarianism. A note had appeared in the September 1810 *Christian's Magazine* that accused the Unitarians of subversively attempting to amend the Bible to make it conform to their "heresy." The note, with its thinly veiled references to Priestley, read:

> We invariably suspect these *amended Bibles,* which the Iscariot bands of professed Christianity are labouring, on both sides of the Atlantic, to thrust into the hands of the unlettered and the simple.*
>
> * There is a late, most audacious attempt to explain away the whole gospel of our Lord and Saviour Jesus Christ; absolutely stripping it, with the single exception of the doctrine of the resurrection, of every principle which makes it "glad tidings" to a sinner; substituting, in the room of "redemption by the blood of Christ," a barren mortality, little, if any better than that of the Pagans, who were "without Christ, without hope, and without God in the world;" (Eph. ii. 12.) and straining into the "cup of salvation" the distilled version of Socinian blasphemy. This fatal

99. First Society of Unitarian Christians, *Collection of Pieces and Tracts,* AUA (AHTL), bMS 14018.

draught is handed about with incessant assiduity, and put to the lips of the unthinking, that they may "sleep the sleep of death." All this under the modest and respectful guise of, "*an improved version of the New Testament.*" The precedent of such treachery was set long ago. Its author is "gone to his own place." But the "improved version" with its accompaniments, show that his treason has not perished with him. "Betray ye the Son of man with a kiss."[100]

Eddowes proved up to the task of refuting such a brazen attack. "It is very convenient to have a nickname to apply to those whom it is wished to run down and expose to public hatred," he wrote in reply. "'*Socinian blasphemy*' is a phrase so hackneyed that few, if any, will think of enquiring into its meaning," forcing Socinian adherents to fight against sweeping and unspecified bigotry. That Eddowes could still point to the overuse of a specific pejorative term is not surprising. The Socinian label was clearly still in use, still attached to the American Unitarian church and still used to identify Priestley's legacy. "The obscurity of the concluding lines as to the original author of the supposed treachery, who is said to be 'gone to his own place,' has, as you know, set many conjectures afloat. I am now inclined to think that Dr. Priestley is intended. If so, the writer will of course, wish to keep at the greatest possible distance from him in the other world, and will deprecate the idea of the Doctor's place being his—*mutatis mutandis,* this may probably be the case."[101] Eddowes, who was naturally more mild mannered than the tone of this letter suggests, was in this one instance drawn into a vituperative response as a result of the venomous implications and insinuations. There are, he noted, "perverse minds upon which" his normal manner would be useless and go unheeded, "but by judging them out of their own mouths and correcting them with their own rods."[102]

If such attacks were intended to drive English Unitarianism and the Americans who were linked to it into obscurity, they had exactly the opposite effect. Instead they led to an increased exchange of ideas, a strengthening of convictions, and a more developed transatlantic network of Unitarian societies. The publication, in 1810, of *A Collection of Pieces and Tracts, chiefly intended to establish the doctrine of the Unity*

100. Eddowes, *Remarks,* 3.
101. Ibid., 10–11.
102. Ibid.,12.

of God, and the salvation of sinners by his free grace in The Gospel, marks an important milestone in this quest. It included pieces written in England that defined the tenets of the faith and issued direct challenges to Protestants. It focused its commentary, in the form of letters to clergy, on issues of infidelity, Unitarian arguments for rejecting the doctrine of the Trinity, and attacks on trinitarian ideas of consubstantiation and transubstantiation, original sin, human depravity, and the salvation of sinners. It is clear from the scope of this work that the Unitarian discussion was far from settled. The Philadelphians were active in the promotion of their faith and in the quest to define the parameters of their beliefs, and so too were their English brethren. Their connection to England was still evident, and the events that were transpiring abroad remained crucial to their own definition of their faith. The English Unitarians continued to assist the Americans with financial support as well as donations of sermons, books, and other materials necessary for the operation of a congregation.[103]

Seven years following his sermon on free inquiry, Eddowes still invoked the same images and the same ideas. The Unitarians were holding their theological position amidst changing religious ideas and shifting beliefs within the liberal wing of the New England Congregationalists. He asked that the people of differing ideas and beliefs allow the Unitarians the freedom and latitude to worship as they saw fit. They had, he said, "a privilege and a right which we are happy in being able to assure ourselves will not and cannot be denied us—I mean, the sacred *right of conscience,* for the exercise of which, every individual is accountable only at the highest of all tribunals."[104]

On the topic of doctrinal requirements, Eddowes noted that "we have kept the constitution of our society free from all entangling and intricate questions of theology; we have prefaced it merely with such general principles as might be sufficient to obviate misrepresentation, and with respect to doctrine have only introduced a single restrictive article (confining religious homage to the Father only) which was necessary to secure to us such a worship as we sought for by separating ourselves from other christian societies." He noted that true Unitarians were different from the other liberal Christians in that they accepted their teachings openly. "But having thus placed ourselves in a conspicuous light before the public, we have given them the right to inquire

---

103. Charles Lean to John Vaughan, June 27, 1816, and James Taylor to John Vaughan, November 1, 1817, as cited in Geffen, *Philadelphia Unitarianism,* 91 and 111.

104. Eddowes, *Unity of God,* 7.

into and to know all our opinions," which he defined as the Unity of God, the worship of only God, and the humanity of Christ, along with full liberty of opinion. "Nor is there any of them we wish to conceal," he continued, "or which may not at one time or other be brought forward in our public discourses from this place."[105]

Because he felt secure in his religious principles, Eddowes could go a bit further than his predecessors in his attacks on trinitarianism. "What is there in the trinitarian doctrine that it should be maintained with such unabated, and often with such intemperate zeal?" he asked the congregation. It was a doctrine to be held in contempt, "for it has filled the christian world with discord and animosity . . . for there has been so much disputation among trinitarians themselves that their *scheme has assumed five or six different forms.*"[106] Eddowes firmly believed that it was far easier to accept the Socinian Unitarian views over the trinitarian. The latter required one to hold an inconsistent theology, while the former was consistent in all aspects.

In his conclusion Eddowes reviewed both the history and efforts of the Philadelphia congregation. "Our society was originally nothing more than the voluntary association of a few individuals for the worship of God according to their consciences; destitute of the aid of a person bearing the ministerial character; and without the means of procuring it by the offer of such a settlement as any one of liberal education and respectable abilities could with prudence accept." At this point he added a footnote, which referenced Priestley's efforts in 1795 and 1796 and the suspension of most activities from 1800 to 1807. "No alternative presented itself but to conduct the public services by means of the talents, such as they were, of those of us who could resolve upon placing ourselves in a situation so novel, and so entirely different from all our former pursuits." Then he added his appreciation to those citizens who helped them, as they had helped the Universalists, to construct their chapel, "persons from almost every religious persuasion."[107]

Set adrift, without benefit of a national association, they carried on as Priestley had wished, with their own sentiments and convictions to guide them. Their efforts were rewarded when, on January 7, 1813, the Commonwealth of Pennsylvania granted the society a charter of incorporation as the First Society of Unitarian Christians in the City of Philadelphia. The Charter harked back to the act of the Pennsylvania General Assembly, passed April 6, 1791, which had permitted the

105. Ibid., 13.
106. Ibid., 32; italics added.
107. Ibid., 35–37.

establishment of corporations of religious standing. It was a simple corporate charter detailing their relationship to the state and responsibilities as a corporate entity with property and title. The statement of "General Principles" was virtually identical to their earlier constitution in the wording and order in which it spelled out the ideas of their faith.[108] In the decade following this official change in status, membership in the group increased steadily, eventually peaking with more than fifty active adult males and their families and many more nonmembers and irregular attendees.[109]

The issuing of the state charter coincided with the completion of their meetinghouse between 1812 and 1813. Laid out in an octagonal shape, in sharp contrast to the cross-shaped architecture of other churches, the Unitarians sought to make a clear, physical statement about their faith. But the membership did not waiver from their origins and were adamant that the presence of a church building would not detract from their devotional intentions and existence as a congregation of the people.[110] Their ability to gather sufficient contributions and to attract additional members testified to their continued success. With only a membership of thirty on the record books at the time, the congregation still managed to gather contributions from more than 250 different subscribers, and they collected a total of $25,000 toward their building fund. The church was dedicated on February 14, 1813, at a service presided over by Eddowes, Vaughan, and Taylor. Eddowes delivered the dedication sermon. Their success proved to themselves and others that they were a viable group, whose influence and ideas transcended their numbers; but they were more than happy to report that their physical presence helped attract new members.

Eddowes's sermon reiterated the group's attachment to the Socinian theology of their English forebearers and repeated his earlier call for the recognition of free inquiry as a central tenet of all religious groups living under a democratic and enlightened government. In his address, *The right, duty and importance of free inquiry in matters of religion*, Eddowes defended human reason, understanding, and moral discernment as a matter of religious necessity. "The *obligation* is to *inquire*, to *investigate*; and if the result be different from what is so authoritatively laid down,

---

108. *Charter for the first society of Unitarian Christians in . . . Philadelphia.* The signatories were John Vaughan, Thomas Astley, James Taylor, William Turner, Ralph Eddowes, William H. Smith, Peter Boult, Samuel Darch, Josiah Evans, Thomas P. Jones, Ralph Eddowes, Jun., and John Eddowes.

109. Geffen, *Philadelphia Unitarianism*, 104.

110. Eddowes, *Unity of God*, 3.

instead of being *bound* to believe, we are bound to *reject;* otherwise instead of obeying the precept to prove *all things,* we prove *nothing,* and may for ought we know be blindly following blind guides."[111] He was adamant that Unitarians not impose their own sentiments upon other Christians, nor attach infallibility to their interpretations of scripture. His quest for mutual deference was an essential element of the Unitarians' success in establishing their presence. It allowed the American Unitarians to both maintain their English foundations, evoking their same language and ideas, and yet establish their place among the American Christians.[112]

The absence of Priestley did not result in a dearth of publications or in a decline in their public presence. Members of the congregation actively published their views, the success of which was a measure of their ability to situate themselves in the religious arena. A list of their works in print in 1814 (mostly through the publishing house of Thomas Dobson, No. 41, South Second Street) included the aforementioned *Collection of Pieces and Tracts;* a reprint of a writing in the *Tracts* titled *The Salvation of Sinners by the Free Grace of God;* their updated *Catechisms for Children and Youth;* their own compilation *A Selection of Sacred Poetry;* the dedication sermon of the chapel, *The Unity of God and the Worship that is due to HIM Alone* by Eddowes; *A Summary View of the New Testament Evidences;* and also copies of "an improved version" of the *New Testament.* Like the earlier works of Priestley, these writings sold out their original subscriptions, were collected by various libraries and colleges throughout the nation, and went through repeated printings. These writings were primarily for their own membership, but also served as a means of introducing the orthodox and uninitiated to their ideas.

By 1815 English Unitarianism was firmly established in Pennsylvania. Unlike their liberal New England counterparts, these rational believers who denied the Trinity did so openly, under the name "Unitarian." "The increased lenity in government and liberality in individuals which renders the profession of a different faith from the established one, no longer dangerous or degrading, is a most important advantage to all dissidents," wrote one British observer who was sympathetic to the group.[113] By 1825 the Unitarian meetinghouse was filled to capacity on Sundays, drawing both members and nonmembers alike to hear the services. It seemed as though Priestley and the Pennsylvania Unitarians

---

111. Eddowes, *The right, duty and importance of free inquiry,* 6–8, 12.
112. Ibid., 15–16.
113. Aikin, *Memoir of John Aikin,* 312.

who followed him had succeeded in their efforts. Though they often found themselves competing in a religious landscape dominated by Protestant trinitarians, significant enough to create sufficient obstacles to their development, the Unitarians managed to make their way through most of them to create a dynamic and lasting religious congregation with connections to like-minded believers elsewhere, who were also slowly taking on the name "Unitarian." "As we have no establishment to oppose, the same zeal which is felt in England cannot be expected in this country," James Freeman had once written of the prospects for Unitarianism. He warned that it would "make a rapid though not very visible progress."[114] But in Pennsylvania as well as in other areas where the presence of Congregationalism was not so dominant and historically oppressive to such liberal efforts of free inquiry and open identity, it was just the opposite of Freeman's prediction. The English Unitarians were making slow progress, but their efforts were quite visible.

114. Freeman to Lindsey, July 7, 1786, in Belsham, *Memoirs*, 183n.

FOUR

Unitarianism in Northumberland and the American Religious Frontier

In the course of my life I have held and defended opinions very different from those which I now hold at present. Now, if my obstinacy in retaining and defending opinions had been so great as my opponents represent it, why did it not long ago put a stop to all my changes, and fix me a Trinitarian, or an Arian? Let those who have given stronger proofs of their minds being open to conviction than mine has been, throw the first stone.

—JOSEPH PRIESTLEY, *Letters to Dr. Horsley*

In the early national era, the United States was a nation driven by "populations that were both increasing and in motion," which often corresponded with a "rising level of religious intensity."[1] Particularly in the interior, these two factors often converged to create new and dynamic religious groups. But it also meant instability and a situation potentially uncongenial to permanent clergy, church construction, or formal church governance and uncertain prospects for a congregation's growth and security.

Throughout the first two decades of the nation's existence Northumberland's religious community adhered to these patterns and was both vibrant and unsettled. Its location, on the border between the established cities to the east and the frontier to the west, contributed to this instability even as it surpassed many similar backcountry communities in the number of denominations present as well as the number of settled ministers. Though there were numerous denominations in the town and surrounding countryside, each was small forcing many to share worship space and ministers and sometimes even both. This close cooperation resulted in a community that was more tolerant of theological peculiarities than elsewhere, although a constantly changing

---

1. Bonomi, *Under the Cope of Heaven*, 8. Bonomi notes that this trend was in full swing prior to the Revolution, was interrupted by the war, and then regained momentum during the early republic.

membership and the scarcity of ministers sustained a sense of competition and suspicion. Consequently, longevity, the ability to connect with larger religious communities elsewhere, the retention of a minister, and a sizable and stable congregation became the measurements of success in Northumberland.

Northumberland's Unitarians, though often challenged and to varying degrees, were successful on all three accounts. Like their counterparts in Philadelphia they overcame opposition and other obstacles placed in their way to create a lasting and vital congregation. The pace of the Northumberland Unitarians' development was slow, and their efforts were tempered by local circumstances, but they never deviated from their quest to establish their ideas and presence as openly declared Unitarians. In concert with many of the members of his small congregation, Priestley continued his efforts to connect with other denominations, ensure the group's Christian standing, and establish Unitarian worship practices. Priestley's residency in Northumberland led to the formation of a congregation that still exists today, albeit with some interludes of inactivity in its past. Yet his efforts in the town went virtually unnoticed owing to Philadelphia's position as the nation's capital, which gave his efforts there more notoriety and greater stature.

In his decade of residency in Pennsylvania's interior, Priestley tackled the issues that confronted Unitarianism in the rest of the United States and England. But the interior also presented several unique circumstances, including a higher rate of infidelity, greater suspicion of immigrants, and less tolerance for political experimentalism. Thus Priestley often found his efforts in Northumberland directed toward imploring religious backsliders to return to the true Christian religion, educating the community and surrounding areas about the credible elements of a rational religion all the while keeping them well informed of its Christian principles, overriding the tone of emotionalism then prominent in other American religions, and overcoming the people's natural suspicions of foreigners. He also had the added task of exerting a continued influence on the course of Unitarian development elsewhere, in such places as New York, New England, the upper South, and in the frontier regions of Kentucky and Ohio, made all the more distant by the remoteness of his residency.

The early national period placed new pressures on all religions, established and developing, as privatization played out and the competition for souls increased (albeit there were more souls available). In the realm of American religion, where almost all of the religious believers were of a dissenting heritage, Priestley and the Unitarians found themselves challenged on their desire to share the Christian and Protestant labels, forced to the margins of religious society, and labeled heretics. From his position on the outside Priestley was nonetheless successful in solidifying the place of English Socinianism in America. By the end of his decade in residence Americans identified his views and practices as those of the Unitarian belief and worship system.

Pennsylvania's Interior Religious Society

Founded in 1772, Northumberland was slow to emerge as an established community and it was still relatively undeveloped when Priestley arrived in 1794. In an event known as the Big Runaway, the town had been abandoned during the Revolution when it was overrun by the British and their Native American allies. Resettlement did not occur until 1783–84, at which time the town's citizens reestablished their homes and businesses, petitioned the state and national legislatures for assistance, and began their lives anew. Over the next two decades Northumberland and towns in the vicinity, including Sunbury, Shamokin, and Selinsgrove, flourished as farming expanded, light manufacturing took on a new importance, and the nation spread west beyond the region, transforming it into part of the secured interior. The town finally incorporated in 1829 but by then had already seen its heyday come and go.

Influence over the town and the entire central Susquehanna River valley was divided. Economically, Northumberland County was tied to the Susquehanna and the towns that sat along its banks, stretching from its northern reaches in New York to its southern terminus at Havre de Grace, Maryland, and on to Baltimore, which exerted a great deal of influence over the development of the upriver communities. Politically, the town remained tied to Philadelphia and the state's government ensconced for the time being in the southeast corner. Many of the region's political concerns were quite different from those of the city, but by virtue of political boundaries the region was at the mercy of its political power, not unlike the divisions between east and west in most of the coastal states. This difference was most notable during the Whiskey Rebellion, when Northumberland was the site of public demonstrations against the government's taxation policies; though not as uproarious as the western districts of the state, the townsmen seized the local arsenal, constructed a liberty pole, and held off the law until informed of the impending arrival of Washington's military force, at which time they summarily disbanded. Not completely without influence, the region was the home of several key members of the early state government and thus had ties to the eastern establishment, a fact that was made more evident when Northumberland itself was under consideration to become the state capital, losing to Harrisburg in 1812, an undeveloped city fifty miles to the south.[2]

Northumberland's religious complexion was influenced by its connections with both regions, giving it a character of its own, as removed from each in practice as it was in distance. As the national and state populations moved west, so too did religious diversity. Like in Philadelphia, "there were the Presbyterians, the Covenanters, the Dutch of Holland and the Huguenots, all forms of Presbyterians, essentially the same in doctrine and form of government. Then too, the German Reformed and Lutheran, . . . [and the] English, of various faiths— Presbyterians, Methodist, Episcopalian. The continental strain was threefold—Lutheran, Reformed, and Catholic." All were represented in the region and in ever-increasing numbers.[3] Baltimore too played a role, sending missionaries from several denominations, most notably the Methodists and Catholics, who were able to establish a stable though small presence as their adherents and itinerant ministers streamed into the town.

From 1778 until well into the 1780s, though brimming with adherents of all beliefs, the prospects for religious success in the interior were uncertain. Even those denominations that had associated churches and connections in the urban centers found themselves in precarious circumstances. In the Pennsylvania backwoods, religion was often a secondary concern among the citizenry. The denominational groups were small and transitory, meeting in individual homes and lacking the necessary monetary and institutional support to sustain their efforts. Philip Fithian, one of the region's earliest itinerant ministers, noted that "there was not a settled pastor or a stated supply within the limits" of Northumberland County.[4] Much of this changed between the end of the war and Priestley's arrival.

---

2. Northumberland's brush with capital status was close. Though the rumors about the national capital were less grounded in real prospects, the town was officially nominated for consideration. Its prospects for becoming the state capital were far more certain and the town lost by only one vote in 1810, after eight years of consideration. See Gutelius, *Northumberland*, 18–19.

3. Finney, *History of the Chillisquaque Church*, 25.

4. Fithian, *Journal*, 34. Northumberland County, at its greatest extent in 1785, extended from the Lehigh to the Allegheny Rivers and stretched from the Cumberland, Dauphin, and Bedford County lines in the south to the New York state border in the north, occupying more than one-third of the entire land area of the state, the territory for

The first group to establish itself in the town was the Presbyterians, the people of the countryside "being chiefly of this persuasion."[5] Fithian had led the initial efforts and gathered in his wake a substantial number of followers as he preached in Northumberland, Sunbury, and Buffalo Crossroads. His activity was cut short, however, by the Big Runaway. The postwar effort was led by the Reverend Hugh Morrison, who was called to serve all three local congregations on a rotational basis; almost immediately, forty-eight members subscribed to his ministry, seventeen from Northumberland and eight from Sunbury. Morrison's efforts were aided in Northumberland by the erection of a log cabin chapel on Market Street, putting an end to the use of private homes; eventually each of the towns established a permanent congregation, with the Northumberland and Sunbury churches sharing a minister.[6] Theologically Morrison's Northumberland congregation was conservative and its rites were staid, causing one visitor to declare that he found them "in general very contracted, and [I] was surprised to find that they never used any of Dr. Watts' psalms or hymns, giving as a reason that he wavered in his sentiments toward the latter end of his life," a reflection of the people's religious attitudes.[7]

Morrison continued to serve as pastor in Northumberland until his death in 1804. Following a four-year hiatus, the Presbyterians called upon the Reverend Isaac Grier, and from that point forward their congregation was led, without lapse, by a settled minister. Grier continued to serve Sunbury and Northumberland but also added Shamokin and Hallowing Run to his ministerial circuit. Owing partly to Grier's success in Northumberland, a meeting was held in 1811 to establish a presbytery, consisting of five ministers and thirteen congregations with 884 members. Under the new administrative framework the Presbyterians continued to prosper and became the leading denomination in central Pennsylvania.[8]

The Methodists established themselves in Northumberland in 1791 at the behest of the Methodist Conference of Baltimore. The conference

---

twenty-eight later and different counties. Fithian's lament meant that there were no settled ministers over a territory that spanned an eight-day journey from end to end. Bell, *History of Northumberland County*, 142–49, 152ff., map.

    5. Wilkinson, "Mr. Davy's Diary," 259.

    6. Fithian, *Journal*, 34.

    7. Bakewell, "Some Particulars," 394.

    8. Miller, "The Presbytery of Northumberland," 63. The Presbyterians were the first religious group in the region to establish a formal, organized Sunday School on the first Sunday in April 1816. Finney, *History of the Chillisquaque Church*, 28–30. The Presbyterians numerically dominated Northumberland for over a century.

appointed two itinerant ministers, Richard Parratt and Lewis Browning, to spread the word throughout the region even though there was, at that time, no existing lay society. Sending itinerant ministers to establish congregations where none existed was a common practice for the Methodists. In fact, this was their contribution to the religious developments of the early national period. The few Methodists in Northumberland at the time worshipped in private, forcing Parratt and Browning to spend the better part of a decade bringing them together as an identifiable group. In 1819 the Methodists finally established a stable and lasting society of worshippers, who immediately built a proper house of worship.[9] The membership of Christ United Methodist Church in Northumberland included fellow believers from Sunbury until 1824, when the latter group secured the use of a public building for services, thus avoiding the need to cross the river each week.

The Lutheran and Episcopalian congregations also started out small, slowly built themselves into formal congregations, and eventually constructed churches. The Lutherans had an itinerant minister and a small congregation by 1772, the year of the town's founding, but the Revolution interrupted their efforts, and it was not until 1818 that they were substantial enough to build their own church. The congregation was still not as strong as many of the others in that they were obliged to share the church with both the German Reformed and Episcopalian congregations, and for a time they borrowed their minister from the Lutherans in Sunbury. Unlike most of the other religious groups in town the Lutheran congregation did not rival the strength or size of its counterpart across the river in Sunbury. Formed before the Revolution, Sunbury's congregation was large and prosperous enough to first propose a church structure in 1791. By 1793 the Reverend Christian Espich published a letter in Andrew Kennedy's *Sunbury and Northumberland Gazette*, to formalize plans for the Sunbury edifice, which was completed in 1805, and the membership grew as a result. So rapid was their expansion that in 1815 the congregation was able to purchase one of the first pipe organs in the entire backwoods, which when played for the first time attracted such a crowd that the floor collapsed, causing considerable damage.[10] For their part, the Reverend Elijah Plumber was the leading figure in the establishment of the Northumberland Episcopalian society. He was named rector to

9. For the role of the Methodists as the organizing impulse of revivalist religion in the early republic, see Mathews, "The Second Great Awakening," 34–36. See also Andrews, *Methodists and Revolutionary America*.

10. Bell, *History of Northumberland County,* 502.

the Episcopal parish in 1817 and from 1820 to 1823 he led both the Episcopalians and Lutherans. His death in 1823 put an end to the close relationship between the two groups and stymied the efforts of the Episcopalians. The congregation languished for the better part of two decades, and failed to secure a settled minister or make strides toward institutionalization. Only in 1847 were the Northumberland Episcopalians able to erect their first permanent church, which they dedicated to the memory of Plumber.

There were also identifiable groups of Baptists and Quakers. The Baptists first held regular services in the 1820s, and shared the church of the Presbyterians until they were finally organized in 1842 and able to build their own sometime later. Not much is known about the Quakers, except for reports of burials in a Quaker cemetery. Rueben Haines, one of the founders of Northumberland, as well as Mary and Harry Priestley, Joseph's wife and youngest son, were all buried there. The Haines family, whose religious sentiments leaned toward the Society of Friends, reportedly owned the cemetery.[11] Though a meeting is said to have existed and a meetinghouse built in the town, no record survives and subsequent histories do not mention the group.

The story of the German Reformed church in Northumberland differs from that of the other denominations. Although Germans were less than ten percent of the nation's population, they dominated in the Pennsylvania backwoods, numbering one third of the state's population.[12] The German Reform Synod was the dominant church throughout the Susquehanna Valley and the lower reaches of Northumberland County. Perhaps as a consequence of the legacy of dissent within German religious sects, the early history of the German Reformed Church in Pennsylvania was rife with struggles. The central issues were church organization and ministerial authority, both of which evoked strong reactions, one way or another, among the members. They were also concerned with their ability to influence alternative sectarian groups and the potential crisis of internal schisms. Foremost among this latter issue was the constant presence of competing groups as represented by the Wesleyan, Brethren, and Moravian churches.[13]

11. For summaries of the religious activities on all of the aforementioned denominations, see ibid., 538–44. On the Baptists and Quakers, see Bakewell, "Some Particulars," 394–96.

12. See Fogleman, *Hopeful Journeys,* 6–8 and 85. Fogleman notes that the German population was concentrated in the "Greater Pennsylvania" backcountry. Though the heaviest concentrations stopped just short of Northumberland County, the Germans were still the single largest ethnic group in the county and controlled its religious, economic, and political affairs.

13. Ibid., 100–126.

The relative weakness of the German Reform congregation was compounded by an intense competition with the Presbyterians. Nevertheless, the German Reformed believers were ecumenical toward other groups, especially those with whom they had closer ties. When the local Lutheran congregation gathered to build a structure in 1817, one member on the five-man building committee was a parishioner of the Reformed congregation. This experience was initially positive for both groups, who jointly secured the services of a minister in 1818, the Reverend Martin Bruner, who served the two congregations through a period of contention over the building of the church. Bruner was blamed for the fighting between the two groups and replaced by the Reverend E. Meyer from Danville, ten miles to the northeast. Bruner, however, was obviously the scapegoat. Meyer's resignation in 1839 resulted in both the Lutheran and the Reformed congregations disbanding, testifying to their overall weakness.

In Selinsgrove, ten miles south of Northumberland, a German Reformed congregation was established in 1794. This group traced its heritage to Row's Church in Salem, two miles west of Selinsgrove, formed in 1766, when Henry Melchior Mühlenberg is said to have preached to the original congregation. The Reverend George Geisweit led the newly formed group and ministered not only in town but also throughout the surrounding countryside to the west. By 1796, the population of Selinsgrove was only sixty-five people, with ten homes. Nevertheless, over the next thirty years, this small population maintained a much stronger and larger congregation than Northumberland. Geisweit served the Selinsgrove congregation until 1801, when the Reverend John Deitrich Adams replaced him. In the meantime the group joined forces with the Lutherans, and the combined group took up a subscription to erect the Sharon Union Lutheran and Reformed Church. This new congregation was led by Reverend Enderly until 1804, and from 1804 until 1819, was under the leadership of the Reverend John Herbst, the original minister of the Sunbury Lutherans.[14]

Catholics were also part of the religious community in Northumberland. When the town was laid out in 1772, several plots were reserved for the exclusive and perpetual use of religious denominations. The Catholics, owing to the traditional suspicions and animosity directed toward them by Protestants, more as a result of the English legacy of religious wars between the two groups than anything they had done in

14. Schnure, *Selinsgrove*, 41, 88–92. Selinsgrove always has been connected in commerce and other matters to Northumberland, Sunbury, and Lewisburg (then Derrstown).

America, were not included among the groups eligible to be given land.[15] Nevertheless, Father Keyzler, a Jesuit missionary, bought two conjoining plots in the town in November 1774. These lots were one of only five properties publicly owned by the Catholic Church in Pennsylvania before the Revolution.[16] As in the other religions, the efforts of the Catholics were postponed by the war and only proceeded slowly following the town's resettlement. The planned church was never built, but the title to the plots was passed on to Father Molyneaux, who subsequently traveled the region's mission circuit and was the first priest known to have ministered to Catholic settlers in this area. He was followed, for a brief time, by Father deBarth, who traveled to the missions in Sunbury and Chillisquaque, presumably visiting the Catholics in Northumberland as well.

In response to appeals from the local German and Irish Catholics, Bishop John Carroll sent the Franciscan priest, Father Patrick Longeran, to Sunbury. From there he moved across the river, and beginning in early 1796, for one year, Longeran resided in the house next to Joseph Priestley, who was then living with his son until his own house was complete. Over the course of his stay, Longeran wrote three reports to Carroll about his efforts to further Catholicism in the Pennsylvania backwoods. He found only one Catholic family living in Northumberland, nine living in nearby Montandon, and an unknown number of adherents living in a group along the Chillisquaque Creek, the same group reached by deBarth.[17] "I have said mass and preached in one house on the Lord's day when the congregation consisted of 23 poor illiterate Irish & German daily laborers," he reported, but "local inconveniences prevents my opening Easter confessions."

Despite the poverty of Longeran's loosely formed congregation it managed to pay his traveling and lodging expenses and began "with zeal, to contribute to build a Catholic Church" in Northumberland. He asked that Carroll pressure Molyneaux to return the deeds in order to substantiate the Catholics' claim to the property and allow them to acquire additional lots. Longeran's instructions were to achieve results "before Harvest." His efforts were complicated by the grudging toleration accorded Catholics on the frontier. In the same letter Longeran noted the contrasts between those "respectable people of different

15. For the exclusion of the Catholics from the available land allotments, see Bell, *History of Northumberland County*, 518.

16. Patrick Longeran to Bishop John Carroll, May 5, 1796, ABA. See also, Bicentennial Historical Book Committee, *Northumberland Point Township*, 79.

17. Patrick Longeran to Bishop John Carroll, May 5, 1796, ABA.

religious opinions" who supported their efforts to construct a place of worship and those who were not as tolerant, as indicated by his stated need to acquire the additional plots of land "before the proprietors should know it was for a [Catholic] Chapel."[18]

While there is no concrete evidence, there can be little doubt that Longeran and Priestley interacted and discussed religious ideas candidly. Priestley's penchant for theological discussion and his correspondence with other Catholics are both indicators of his willingness to engage in discussions across the religious divide created by the Reformation. Priestley favored universal toleration for all groups; he felt that the social contract promised every citizen protection from religious harassment and he did not hesitate to put his ideas into practice. In England Priestley had been instrumental in gaining tolerance for Catholic dissenters equal to that of Protestant dissenters.[19] Longeran's appointment by John Carroll, the first bishop of Baltimore and himself an avowed advocate of "Enlightenment Catholicism," doubtless led to a similar willingness to an association with such eminent persons as Priestley, especially given that they were neighbors. As an appointee of Carroll, Longeran held very similar beliefs on the role that reason played in the development of a person's religious beliefs. Reason was compatible with revelation, led to an examination of one's conscience, and also promoted toleration and civic responsibility.[20] While Longeran's only reference to Priestley was that he dined with his son while the Reverend was away on one of his trips to Philadelphia and there are no direct references from Priestley on meeting with Longeran, both expressed a desire to engage the other and further the discourse between their religions, and the limited opportunities for interaction with religious figures on the frontier would likely have proven too much to resist for either man.[21]

Longeran's optimism for Catholicism's future in Northumberland was not long-lived. He constantly referred to his desire to move on to Huntington and preach where he felt he had more of a following. During his stay in Northumberland he became involved in a land scheme to settle over a hundred Catholic families on over four thousand acres in a tract twenty miles to the north. But this too fell through.[22] After a year in Northumberland, following a conflict over the lax religious

18. Ibid.

19. Priestley openly supported the English Catholic Relief Act of 1778. His influence helped sway others to support the change in legal toleration of Catholics. See Fitzpatrick, "Toleration and the Enlightenment Movement," 41.

20. Dolan, *In Search of an American Catholicism,* 20–24.

21. Patrick Longeran to Bishop John Carroll, May 5, 1796, ABA.

22. Ibid., November 22, 1796.

convictions of the local Catholics, Longeran moved on to more heavily populated Fayette County and began ministering to its faithful as well as those of neighboring Greene and Washington counties.[23] In 1799 he purchased a plot of ground in Waynesburg with his own money and remained there for two years, where he celebrated Mass in private homes just as he had done in Northumberland. Longeran's departure meant that the only established mission in the county was Saint Joseph's, founded in 1805 at Milton, some twenty miles away. As the only Catholic Church in the entire northern region it served as the mother church for Sunbury, Danville, Northumberland, Lewisburg, Shamokin, and Selinsgrove. Thus the Northumberland and Sunbury Catholics were once again consigned to missionary priests who might happen to pass through the area.

Northumberland's early religious community was a reflection of the broader, national, religious society. The various congregations struggled with organization, the quest to establish a stable membership, erect a "proper" building for worship, and hopefully stake their claims to prominence and dominance. While the distance from the major urban centers and their residency in Pennsylvania forced them into an outward commitment to religious pluralism and legal toleration, they all continued to struggle against the backdrop of competition and theological beliefs of exclusivity. None of them was immune from the effect of population fluidity, lack of access to ministers and resources, or the pull of secular realities. Being unchurched was as much a part of the interior's religious reality as it was elsewhere. The one major difference was that Northumberland was also home to Joseph Priestley. Unitarianism, as an established society of worshippers, was still quite unique in the United States. While well-known and often targeted by many in the ministerial community, the laypeople were less apt to judge by the obtuse theological arguments. The reception that Priestley and his Unitarian followers experienced, therefore, was mixed, and their efforts to combat resistance as well as to make a positive impact on the community varied accordingly.

Northumberland Unitarians

When the Priestleys arrived in Northumberland in 1794, they saw a town that was, in the words of Joseph Priestley Jr., "finely situate at

---

23. Ibid., December 1796–January 1797.

the conflux of the east and west branches of the Susquehanna, one hundred and thirty-three miles from Philadelphia" with Sunbury and Northumberland containing "from one hundred to one hundred and fifty houses each." The land was "very rich but not of any great quantity to be cultivated, as the town is closely surrounded by mountains."[24] The population of the town and the surrounding region was predominantly English and contained less than five people per square mile. The county's population, an area that covered almost a quarter of the present-day state of Pennsylvania, was just over seventeen thousand, of whom four hundred or more lived in Sunbury, the eventual county seat. Another three hundred lived in Northumberland, just across the river.[25] Of the 170 taxpaying residents in 1802, 116 were English; the remaining residents were German or Scots-Irish. Priestley's *Memoirs*, written in 1795 and continued by his son after his death, reveals very little about his perceptions of this new home. What we know about his life in Northumberland and perspectives on the people comes from other sources, including his letters and published writings, and reveals a town that he found to be in religious turmoil, a state that he found alternately agreeable and untenable depending upon the circumstances.[26]

Priestley's sons had preceded him to the United States by eleven months and, with the help of Thomas Cooper, engaged in land speculation.[27] Their goal was to locate a tract of land suitable for settlement by a sizable community of English émigrés. They purchased just such a site several miles to the north of the confluence of the Susquehanna known as the Loyalsock Tract. It offered a promising expanse of fertile

24. Joseph Priestley, Jr., "Observations during a journey from Philadelphia to the Loyalsoc [*sic*] . . . ," in Wansey, *Journal,* 118–19.

25. Northumberland County had 17,161 residents, and Northumberland town (Point Township) had approximately 100 households and a population of around 300 with 170 taxpayers. Northumberland town (Point Township) figures are estimates taken from the 1802 County Tax Collection Records, Northumberland County Public Records, Sunbury, Pennsylvania. Copies of these files are found in JPH, Research File no. 2, "Northumberland Taxes." Northumberland County population density figures are taken from Huffman, *Lutheranism,* 51, 56.

26. Priestley, *Autobiography,* 128–33. The last entry in Priestley's journal is dated March 24, 1795. Only the final page includes any reference to the United States and that is a reference to his landing, journeys, and decision to settle at Northumberland. Six additional pages, written by his son, are appended to the work but primarily provide an account of his father's final illness and death.

27. The move was intended to be a temporary asylum and a profitable one if at all possible. Cooper had plans to stay permanently and was naturalized as an American citizen before Judge Jacob Rush of Northumberland County at Sunbury in November 1795. Cooper was required by law to swear that he had resided in the United States for at least two years and in the Commonwealth for at least one. Northumberland County Records, *Appearance Docket of Northumberland County,* No. 84, November Sessions, 1795, JPH, Research File no. 2.

fields, rolling hillsides, and extensive tributaries. The family planned to stay in Northumberland, the closest town, until the settlement was developed, but it never materialized. Priestley remained in Northumberland and built a house with an extensive library and laboratory. He often praised the town's low cost of living, its climate, and the lack of overcrowding. The solitude of the place provided the necessary hours for reflection required for religious contemplation and writing, as well as for his continued scientific efforts. But the town lacked amenities because of its isolation and the character of the people. In his last decade Priestley often traveled to Philadelphia, sometimes staying up to four months, where he replicated the life of an English gentleman now settled in America.

The most pressing matter of concern for Priestley in his new home was the establishment of a congregation for the propagation of Unitarianism. Priestley, never one to be bothered with the mundane tasks of settlement, turned his attention to the matter of establishing a Unitarian church. "My desire, and I think my duty," Priestley wrote, "is to appear in my proper character, of a minister of the gospel."[28] None of the denominational groups present possessed a church edifice that was anything more than a crude structure, and most, without the services of a regular minister, were forced to worship in private homes. Eventually the Baptists, Lutherans, and the Unitarians, along with others, shared the use of the log schoolhouse located at the corner of Park and Wheatley Avenues, just across the street from the lots Priestley acquired for the purpose of building his house.[29] Eventually the Unitarians moved their services into the homes and parlors of their members, including those of Joseph Jr., Thomas Cooper, and when completed Priestley's own front parlor.

The efforts of the small group of Unitarians matched those of the other denominations in the region. In terms of gathering a congregation, establishing a regular worship service, obtaining the services of a minister, and building a church, no group in Northumberland possessed an advantage over another. The Unitarians lacked something, however, that the other denominations did not—a connection to a larger religious institution and financial support from their brethren in the cities. The efforts of Priestley and his followers thus occurred in relative isolation, with limited financial support, and in the absence of a larger, formalized denominational structure. The budding congregation consisted of

28. Joseph Priestley to John Vaughan, May 6, 1795, Priestley Papers, APS.
29. Bell, *History of Northumberland County*, 538.

Priestley, his immediate family (a total of eleven members), twenty-six fellow émigrés and their families, and a few local residents.[30] These twenty-six settled Unitarians, plus the occasional visitor, were more numerous than several of the other religious groups who were simultaneously in the formative stages and their number, along with Priestley's stature, provided them with a tolerable, if not an open, welcome in the town. Under these conditions Priestley worked hard to establish a disciplined church. He urged consistent and attentive worship in both belief and practice which he thought especially necessary in the challenging environment of the Pennsylvania interior. The small society never felt the need to seek official recognition or to create rules of membership: a charter, such as the one sought by the Philadelphia congregation, was unnecessary on the frontier. "Christian principles soon bring relief, and are capable of converting all sorrow into joy. But this will be in proportion to the strength of our faith, in consequence of the exercise of it, when, according to Hartley, speculative faith is converted into practical," wrote Priestley about the efforts to maintain a structured religious life in Northumberland.[31]

Within weeks of his arrival, Priestley was invited, in the absence of the Reverend Morrison, to preach to the Presbyterians, a task he frequently performed in England. "At present I preach sometimes in the Presbyterian meeting; but then I make a point of doing nothing to offend them. This however, tends to abate prejudice, and will prepare the way for other things. They all know my opinions and in general do not seem to be much shocked at them."[32] The following May he preached a sermon in Sunbury, at the request of the Justices of the State's Supreme Court, presumably in the Presbyterian chapel there, and was saddened though not surprised to learn that some of those in attendance were "much surprised to find that I was a Christian."[33] Priestley's sermons

30. Bakewell, "Some Particulars," 394. Those who were known to attend services included Priestley; his wife Mary (until her death in 1796); their three sons, Joseph, William, and Harry (until the latter's death in 1795); Joseph's wife; and their five resident grandchildren, Thomas Cooper, William Bakewell, John Binns, Hugh Bellas and his family of three, William Christie, John Taggart and his wife, Hannah, and Charles Gale and his family of four. An ideal way to develop this list with more accuracy and certainty would be to compare the list of taxable residents in 1802 with the *Samson*'s passenger manifest. But the latter record has been lost. See also George Frick, "Names of Persons Constituting the Colony Brought over from England by Dr. Jos. Priestley in the year 17__," Joseph Priestley Manuscript Collection, folder #19C504 Priestley 2, DC.

31. Priestley to Theophilus Lindsey, July 3, 1802, in Ware, *Views of Christian Truth*, lxvi.

32. Priestley to Theophilus Lindsey, Northumberland, August 24, 1794, APS, Lindsey Collection, box 21.

33. Priestley to Theophilus Lindsey, May 1795, in *Works*, vol. 1, pt. 2, p. 304.

highlighted his previously mentioned personal affinity for the Presbyterians that stemmed from his experiences in England. He reminded his new listeners that he was not alone in his association of the two on the basis of their common principles. In fact, he recounted the tale of how both groups had been targets of the Birmingham riots; scrawled upon a wall in the city were the words "DAMN PRIESTLEY; DAMN THE PRESBYTERIANS."[34] While Priestley was offended at the violence these words brought forth, he assured his listeners that the implied association was not, to him, an unwelcome one.

But something must have gone wrong, or Priestley must have underestimated the resistance he faced. "I told you that when I came hither I was asked to preach at the Presbyterian meeting-house," he wrote to England. "But though I am sure I said nothing which could give any Christian just offense, they never asked me again." In fact, while some parishioners within the Presbyterian congregation were willing to hear Priestley preach, their minister was not. When the Reverend Morrison returned from attending to his duties in the other districts of his ministry, he was so shocked to learn of his congregation's invitation to Priestley that he threatened to quit if they ever allowed him to ascend the pulpit again.[35] Unwilling to provoke a public battle, Priestley never pushed the issue. The rejection, however, was a significant blow to his hopes for an ecumenical spirit among the people. Though he never again preached to the congregation, he did have one more occasion to use their chapel in October 1794, when "the officer of a company of soldiers who are passing this way requested me to preach to them, and they got the use of the meeting-house." According to his account "some of the people of the place attended" which served notice that not all Presbyterians were willing to reject his ministerial talents or shun him for his theological differences.[36] Soon, however, a prevailing spirit of competition and exclusion emerged. The Presbyterians and the Baptists were soon said to be "terrified" of Priestley, several Baptists even cautioning William Bakewell to "beware of his heresy, lest I should be taken in." Bakewell went on to note that "even some of the English at Northumberland partook of the same fearful apprehension."[37]

34. Priestley, *Appeal to the Public*, pts. 1 and 2.

35. Hugh Bellas, "Joseph Priestley, LL.D., 1794–1805," in Sprague, *Annals of the American Pulpit*, 8:298–308.

36. Wilkinson, "Mr. Davy's Diary," 123–41; 267–68. See also, Joseph Priestley, quoted in Ware, *Views of Christian Truth*, lvii.

37. Bakewell, "Some Particulars," 394.

Priestley did not let this opposition keep him from the principal work of church building in Northumberland. Nor did he rest on the laurels accorded him by his friends and supporters. Priestley spent the remainder of his years writing religious tracts, setting up a school, teaching local youth, and preaching every Sunday. His sermons gained him a reputation and attracted numerous travelers whose presence swelled the numbers of those who regularly heard him preach.[38] His efforts in Northumberland gave him great satisfaction and resulted in the intended outcomes, so much that even he could not resist referring to them with great optimism. "I have a service every Lord's day at my son's house; and several persons, the most respectable in the place, have desired to attend, and even, I hear, talk of building a place of worship for me. [I] shall feel most happy in being so employed, and in instructing such young persons as will attend me."[39] This success and potential for great gains in the backcountry served as further justification for his decision to forgo the seemingly greater opportunities of Philadelphia. "I see so great a certainty of planting Unitarianism on this continent," he wrote, that "I shall be, on the whole of as much use in propagating Unitarianism [here] as if I resided constantly there."[40]

Though they tried not to show it in their actions, Priestley and his followers remained wary about their acceptance among the Northumberland denominations. Priestley often reiterated his doctrines to all in the town who would listen. Unitarians, as reformers, considered themselves Christian dissenters, whereas many Christians considered them heretics. This was as true in the United States as it had been in England and was a problem that plagued the faithful for more than half a century. Rectifying this issue was one of Priestley's primary objectives and determined the course of his subsequent public pronouncements and private practices. Unitarianism, he argued, went beyond theology and constituted a social as well as ethical foundation for one's life. On these grounds Priestley was able to level a social critique against trinitarian beliefs and practices, which, shaped by cultural influences, were steeped in error and corrupted by social interactions and un-Christian violations of charity, openness, and regard for fellow

38. For visitation accounts, see ibid., 393–97, 505–8, 564–67, 622–25; Bellas, "Joseph Priestley," 305–8; Watson, *Memoirs of Elkanah Watson*; Hill, "Journey on Horseback," 189–98; Miller, "Journal of an Unknown Englishman," 36, 45; and Wilkinson, "Mr. Davy's Diary," 123–41; 258–79.

39. Priestley, quoted in Ware, *Views of Christian Truth*, lix; Priestley to Theophilus Lindsey, December 20, 1794, and Priestley to Mr. Spurrell, July 12, 1795, in *Works*, vol. 1, pt. 2, pp. 283–85, 308–9.

40. Priestley to Lindsey, June 24, 1794, in Belsham, *Memoirs*, 414.

humans. Priestley hoped that his claim to the legacy of the original, primitive Christians would establish the Unitarians within the tradition of the town's other Christian reformers.

In Northumberland, however, this effort took a different direction than in Philadelphia. Given the nature of the town and surrounding region, Priestley found himself as concerned about the general state of indifference to all religious ideas and the growing numbers of the disaffected or unchurched as he was about opposition to his ideas. "I pay no attention whatever to the Orthodox, and confine myself to the unbelievers, as by much the more formidable enemy of the two," he wrote in his *Observations* concerning his views on American religion.[41] He was very concerned that the demands of daily, worldly life and the inattentiveness to religious matters could lead to a withering away of the faith in the lives of the people. Even among the Presbyterians, the largest group of believers in the region, communion occurred only once a quarter and high holy occasions with even less frequency.[42] With these new realities ever present, Priestley turned his attention to the increase in infidelity and the establishment of a religious calendar.

Confronting Religious Indifference

"In America," wrote Priestley, "I find nothing but the extremes of infidelity and bigoted orthodoxy." Bigotry he could accept, or as was his preference, overcome: "It was of no long continuance in those minds who could so far surmount their prejudices as to submit patiently to hear him," as many increasingly did.[43] But infidelity was another matter. "The great number of unbelievers here will keep up my attention to the evidences of revelation," Priestley wrote, as he formulated a plan to deal with the problem.[44]

During his stay in New York Priestley had argued that the prevailing sense of infidelity within the city was a consequence of the people's focus on political and commercial matters, as well as the want of good ministers. He found a similar pattern repeated in Philadelphia as a result of the people's quest for civic and social prominence, whence

41. Priestley, "On the Duty of Mutual Exhortation," in *Discourses on Various Subjects*, 3; Ware, *Views of Christian Truth*, lx.

42. Wilkinson, "Mr. Davy's Diary," 259.

43. Bakewell, "Some Particulars," 394.

44. Priestley to Thomas Belsham, December 14, 1794, and Priestley to Theophilus Lindsey, December 20, 1794, in *Works*, vol. 1, pt. 2, pp. 283, 284.

he noted that "the greatest difficulty arises from the indifference of liberal-minded men as to religion in general; they are so much occupied with commerce and politics."[45] And he also found infidelity in Northumberland, where the temptations of society were not as great, but their want for religion more severe. When writing to Lindsey, he called the infidels the "luke-warm, the ill-informed, or the worldly-minded." His protégé William Bakewell further detailed the classifications of religious infidels as those who simply overlooked religion, those who rejected it, those who accepted religion but only as a necessary consequence of the political economy, and the unscrupulous.[46] No matter where one turned, religious indifference reigned.

Priestley was convinced that Unitarianism provided the answer to infidelity, partly as a consequence of its dissenting heritage, but also because of the nature of its beliefs. Unitarianism countered the spread of unbelief at the same time that it resisted the intolerance of the orthodox establishment. "No other denomination of Christians have stood forth as they have done in the defense of Christianity, especially of late years, when infidelity has reared its head in a manner unknown in former times."[47] One had to actively seek to understand the Unitarian religion. The struggle to ward off corruption required constant vigilance. Priestley preached that Unitarianism's discipline and reason countered such attitudes in men and therefore brought more people into the Christian tradition.[48] Scriptural rationalism was also instrumental in making religion relevant to the everyday lives of men. Priestley considered his six-volume *General History of the Christian Church,* the final two volumes of which he completed in Pennsylvania, the definitive "clarification of pure (Unitarian) Christianity that would commend it to the would-be faithful and inhibit further attack upon Christianity from infidels and Deists."[49] His central point, after exploring the history of Christianity from the birth of Christ to the present day, was that "whatever is true and right will finally prevail; that is, when sufficient time has been given to the exhibition of it, rational Christianity will,

45. Priestley to Lindsey, June 15, 1794, in Belsham, *Memoirs,* 411.

46. Priestley to Theophilus Lindsey, July 1794 and December 6, 1795, in *Works,* vol. 1, pt. 2, pp. 257, 325; Bakewell, "Some Particulars," 622–23.

47. Priestley, *Address to the Unitarian Congregation at Philadelphia,* 9.

48. See Priestley, *Free Address to Protestant Dissenters, on the Subject of Church Discipline* and *Discourses on Various Subjects,* in which the first sermon, "The Proper Constitution of a Christian Church, with a Preface on the present state of those who are called Rational Dissenters," details how the dissenters represented a better church polity and remained more true to the nature of a Church as outlined by Christ.

49. George H. Williams, "Joseph Priestley: Minister, Citizen, Church Historian," in Schwartz and McEvoy, *Motion Toward Perfection,* 104.

in due time, be the religion of the whole world. In the prophetical language of our Savior, he will draw all men unto him."[50] Thus, in his own way, Priestley set the prophetic tone for the history of the Unitarians in Pennsylvania.[51]

Priestley's *On the Duty of Mutual Exhortation,* written as an instructive to American Unitarians, noted that *"good and faithful servants"* of God needed to engage in three actions: reading of the scriptures, regular public worship, and habitual private prayer. Those who neglected such a pattern of faith were only Christian in name; "they cannot feel the influence of its doctrines, its precepts, or its motives, when they give no attention to them."[52] He echoed sentiments that he had expressed more than a quarter of a century earlier in *Institutes of Natural and Revealed Religion;* sound religious knowledge was the sole foundation of a respectable life and the only path to salvation, virtuous conduct was a product of a comprehensive understanding of Christ's precepts. In all matters, the only proper authority in matters of faith was scripture.[53] But the only way to show all of this was through worship. According to Priestley, one reason that rational believers were so often attacked was their failure to worship. "We have sufficient proof in the conduct of rational Dissenters that persons easily fall into the habit of neglecting the service entirely."[54] As a culmination of his consideration of infidelity, this sermon also served as justification of Priestley's focus on the need for continuous practice of communion, which was a part of his design for public worship.

Celebrating communion was a common practice of the Unitarians, and Priestley performed the rite weekly among the Northumberland society; all proper Unitarians "consider it as the most proper and public declaration of our being Christians."[55] Priestley's celebrations and teachings concerning communion enjoyed widespread support in

50. Priestley, *General History of the Christian Church,* 6:5

51. In support of Priestley, Lindsey wrote, "We owe lasting obligations to those, who in times of great corruption of the truth, and in the midst of dangers and difficult trials have stood up for it." In England, "from the very beginning of the reign of Elizabeth to our own days, we are presented continually as we pass along, with the edifying spectacle of a number of conscientious Christians, growing by degrees into a large body; dissatisfied with the mode of religion prescribed by the State, and refusing to conform to it, not withstanding severe persecution and sufferings . . . boldly asserting the right of judging for themselves in such matters, and of worshipping God according to the dictates of conscience, in opposition to arbitrary and unjust laws." Lindsey, *Historical View,* 442, 446–47.

52. Priestley, "On the Duty of Mutual Exhortation," in *Discourses on Various Subjects,* 27, 26, 26–29.

53. Priestley, *Institutes of Natural and Revealed Religion,* 1:iii–ix.

54. Priestley, "Of the Lord's Supper," in *Works,* 22:493–95.

55. Ibid., 487–98. See also Eliot, *Heralds of a Liberal Faith,* 65.

his congregation, and long after his death several of his former pupils, family members, and guests were nostalgic about his communion services.[56] Priestley's justification of communion was just one part of his suggested order of service, which provides clear evidence of his efforts to formalize Unitarianism, if not among the wider community, then at least among the believers themselves. Regular services included a congregational prayer, a reading of the psalms and scriptures, the recitation of the "Our Father," as well as the singing of hymns. He frequently wrote the hymns himself, so that they might be "peculiarly suited to the purpose . . . with respect to the present life of trial and discipline, and to a future happy state to which it leads." In fact, Priestley made it a point to keep his service relevant to the lives and conditions of his followers. "His discourses were usually practical, easy to be understood, and reducible to common life . . . his faith seemed simply fixed upon the infinite placability of God."[57] This is how he promoted Unitarianism among the religiously indifferent. As the leader of American Unitarianism, Priestley tried to follow the example of Christ, to worship God with conviction, and to instruct the youth in Christian values.

Priestley's view of communion challenged the commonly accepted practice of excluding children from the celebration. He advocated administering communion to children. Failure to incorporate youth into one of the most meaningful parts of a service was, to his way of thinking, disastrous for the community of religious believers and contributed to religious infidelity. While he admitted that most children were "incapable of understanding what is said and done," nevertheless the more important accomplishment is that "their attention is excited, [and] a general idea of reverence and respect for religious ordinances is impressed, and in due time they will enter into them with understanding." As with the teaching of all things to children, conduct had to come before understanding, and a lapse in conduct was a greater danger to the efforts of Unitarians.[58] Priestley saw communion as "an opportunity of impressing our minds with a sense of the great objects and value of Christianity. These ideas I have therefore kept in view in the forms that I have drawn up for its administration."[59] As he had explained in *Institutes of Natural and Revealed Religion,* Jesus was a special person to whom God had given a special purpose. As the foundation

---

56. See Bellas, "Joseph Priestley," 298–308, and Bakewell, "Some Particulars," 394–95.
57. Bakewell, "Some Particulars," 395.
58. Priestley, "Of the Lord's Supper," in *Works,* 22:22, 493–95.
59. Ibid., 488–89.

of all Christian belief, the Bible gave direction to celebrate the actions of the prophets, of whom Jesus was the foremost. Priestley pointed to the acceptance of Jesus among the Unitarian believers, and the special position he occupied in their theology as well as the "unanswerable evidence of his divine mission."[60] He often cited 1 Corinthians 9:23 in support of his actions: "I do all this for the sake of the gospel, that I may share in its blessings." All communicants, in Priestley's opinion, were in agreement on this point.

In the final year of his life, after a decade of working toward establishing Unitarianism in the United States, Priestley wrote a letter to the Reverend Joseph Berington, a Catholic priest and longtime friend, and to the Reverend William White, the first Episcopal bishop of Pennsylvania. His connection with these two men was more than just an affinity between men of the same occupation. Berington was a kindred spirit. He was adored by parishioners for his ministry, and yet his career in the Catholic Church was marked by constant inner turmoil over matters of doctrine and practice. He was particularly noted for his charity to the poor and the respect he earned from all who knew him. Berington's actions and writings, however, often provoked his bishop to take disciplinary action, such as happened in response to his denunciation of Episcopalianism and his call for free and open religious inquiry. While the two men had been religious opponents, exchanging charges and counter-charges on the issue of materialism, Priestley and Berington were also close companions and often socialized while the two resided in Staffordshire. Priestley even invited Berington to preach to his Unitarian congregation.[61]

When White, rector of Christ Church and St. Peter's Church, and chaplain to the Second Constitutional Congress as well as the United States Senate, was still Pennsylvania's bishop-elect, he received a letter from Bishop Provoost of New York, who wrote that "the doctrine of the Trinity has been a bone of contention since the first ages of Christianity, and will be to the end of the world." As for those who held "a truly liberal spirit" on the matter, Provoost noted that "we ought to learn no other lesson from the diversity of their opinions except that of

60. Priestley, *Institutes of Natural and Revealed Religion*; Priestley to Theophilus Lindsey, September 19, 1796, in *Works*, 15:355.

61. Schofield, *The Enlightened Joseph Priestley*, 61; *Biographical Dictionary of English Catholics*, vol. 1 (Joseph Gillow, 1885). Priestley listed *Berington's Account of English Catholics and his other Smaller Tracts* (1787) in his inventory of works destroyed during the Birmingham Riots, for which he sought compensation from the government. Joseph Priestley, "Birmingham Inventory," 1791, 42, line 4, JPH, Research File no. 1.

perfect moderation and good will toward all those who happen to differ from ourselves."[62] White was obviously connected to Priestley through mutually shared political ideas and their support for the American Revolution. Despite the two men's vastly different beliefs concerning church polity and authority, they often corresponded and shared religious concerns.

Each of them shared the others' views on free inquiry and open discourse on matters of religion. The letter can be read as one of Priestley's final efforts to legitimize Unitarian doctrine, justify his claims to Christianity, and ensure the survival of the growing numbers of adherents through institutionalization. His motivations were also partly personal. Since 1801 his health had been failing; his strength was severely limited; and he frequently expressed his suspicions that his time on this earth, in which to debate such matters, was growing short. The letter was anything but supplicating, however. His style was direct, sometimes provocative, and meticulous in the construction of his arguments—traits that had earned him the nicknames of "honest heretic" from his supporters and "Gunpowder Joe" from his detractors.[63] Never one to shy away from honest differences, Priestley reiterated the distinctions that separated the three men and explained how his belief in the unity of God was only one aspect of a multifaceted theology. "Though few persons have written more than myself to controvert the established principles of each of your churches, I consider the articles in which we all agree as of infinitely more moment than those with respect to which we differ." After all, he noted, "the being, the perfections, the universal providence, and the righteous moral government of God" and of Jesus' teachings were "obligatory on all." These were the universal lessons and the connections that all Christians professed and enjoyed, leading Priestley to end the epistle with a call for unity.

62. Bishop Samuel Provoost to Rev. William White, 1787, as quoted in Foote, *Annals of King's Chapel*, 374.

. 63. Franklin called Priestley an "honest soul" and specifically referred to him in a letter to Benjamin Vaughan as "the honest heretic Dr. Priestley." His letter went on to clarify the assigned title when he wrote, "'tis his honesty that has brought upon him the character of heretic." See Benjamin Franklin to Joseph Priestley, June 7, 1782, and also Franklin to Benjamin Vaughan, October 24, 1788, in Franklin, *Writings*, 1048, 1169. As for his detractors, they picked up on a line from Priestley's sermon "The Importance and Extent of Free Inquiry in Matters of Religion" (November 5, 1785), in which he stated that he and his fellow rationalists were "laying gunpowder, grain by grain, under the old building of error" of the established Christian faiths in order to correct the corruptions heaped on the faiths by centuries of erroneous practices. Subsequently, several cartoonists and essayists caricatured Priestley as "Gunpowder Joe." See Martin Fitzpatrick, "Priestley Caricatured," in Schwartz and McEvoy, *Motion Toward Perfection*, 161–67 and 178.

Our gratitude for the communication of knowledge of such infinite importance must be common to us all, and such as should lead to a cheerful obedience to all the commands of God. I know that the creeds of both of your established churches doom me. . . . But whatever may be your opinion with respect to me, which I know will be as favorable as you can make it, I have no doubt but, if I ever do get to heaven I shall meet with both of you there. In that state . . . the bigotry which has contributed so much to the miseries of this life, but which has, at the same time been a valuable exercise of Christian candor, will no longer exist.[64]

The growing body of Unitarians in America had endured bigotry and false witness, yet they remained true to their principles while striving for religious acceptance. The societies, though few and small, sought nothing more than to be left alone to worship as they chose and to be accepted on their own terms. The initial religious prejudice against Unitarianism, cataloged in Priestley's personal writings and the reflections of many other Americans, was slowly counteracted, at least to the extent that the Unitarians were able to succeed in the face of unfavorable odds. The persistent affirmation that they adhered to the religious and philosophical ideals of the nation was at the core of this defense. Priestley even invoked the name of Charles Chauncy, whose advocacy of reason, scriptural analysis, and the unity of God at the height of the Great Awakening he considered to be in concert with his own Unitarian precepts. Throughout his life Priestley made it clear that he sought fellowship as well as theological truth and that he never saw it as his role to emphasize the distinctions between believers. "Had I been permitted to officiate in either of your meeting houses," he wrote to the Presbyterians of Northumberland, "you would never have heard from me anything but the principles of our common Christianity."[65]

His opponents, however, focused on the extremes of Unitarian theology and the distinctions that barred them from Christian fellowship. Though civil when required they eagerly and vehemently challenged its ideas from their pulpits and in the press. Unitarianism, they noted, was intended "to unsettle the faith, and to break up the constitution of

64. Priestley to Reverend Joseph Berington (England) and Reverend William White (United States), Northumberland, 1804, quoted in *The National Gazette* (Philadelphia), November 13, 1833, 2.
65. Priestley, *Letters to the Inhabitants of Northumberland,* 72.

every ecclesiastical establishment in Christendom."[66] Fearful of Unitarianism's spread and success in America, opposing ministers labeled its beliefs as heresy and the work of corrupted thinking, and they characterized Priestley's efforts inconsequential, irrelevant, and out of touch with the religious needs and civic ideals of the nation and its citizens. In support of their views, they cited the few adherents who followed in his path. They noted that rationalism was not sufficient to meet the changing needs of the people or help them withstand the challenges of the changing nation. They painted his theology as quintessentially European, the product of excess and error.

In truth, however, his efforts, while slow, deliberate, and even numerically minimal, were anything but inconsequential when viewed in the context of the beginning stages of the development of a denomination. Priestley astutely noted that the changing American experience begged for a religion with the simplicity, logical consistency, and tolerance of Unitarianism. He repeatedly wrote to Lindsey of the need for patience and the prospects for a future in America based on these principles.[67] The extent to which Unitarianism took root in Northumberland can be measured by its lasting influence. The model that Priestley had established for a proper religious society remained long after his death. As the believers dispersed, they also spread the rites and denominational structure that Priestley had nurtured them in.[68] Likewise, his writings continued to be popular. Many of them, especially his catechism for children and notes on the scriptures, were repeatedly published in the years following his death and became staple reading for those who were studying for the ministry among many different faiths.[69] The firm conviction, which Priestley instilled in all who followed his teachings, that "religious belief was a private decision with public consequences," meant that their methods for spreading the faith would not attract large numbers of adherents.[70] Because their methods did not result in

66. Samuel Horsley, quoted in Joseph Priestley, in *Works*, 18:47. Horsley, the son of a dissenter, was the archdeacon of St. Albans who engaged Priestley in an eight-year debate over Christ's divinity.

67. Priestley to Theophilus Lindsey, July 5, 1795, in *Works*, vol. 1, pt. 2, pp. 268–70.

68. Toulmin in Kentucky was an ardent follower of Priestley's structure as was Gales in South Carolina.

69. Priestley's works continued to be read at Harvard and the University of Pennsylvania with frequency. See Wright, *Liberal Christians*, 26, and Cooke, *Unitarianism in America*, 79. For Priestley's influence at Princeton, see Mark Noll, *Princeton and the Republic, 1768–1822: The Search for a Christian Enlightenment in the Era of Samuel Stanhope Smith*, 125–56.

70. Frost, *Perfect Freedom*, 74.

widespread adherence, the slow growth of the groups has been incorrectly interpreted as inactivity, weakness in membership, an inability to secure leadership, untenable theology, and even the cessation of their particular beliefs.

But as has been shown, all of these characterizations are false. In response to the circumstances in which they found themselves, the Northumberland Unitarians contested the old established boundaries and created new margins when it came to their religious beliefs and practices. Under Priestley's direct guidance they sought entry into the local society by challenging the false accusations about their religion and by connecting themselves to the general principles of the republic. They defended themselves as the "true Christians" adhering to the uncorrupted teachings of Christ, professing the ideas of the original followers of Jesus supported by the Bible. Though they generally remained quiet, when they found sufficient cause they were never inactive in matters of social principles and Christian charity. Although they remained targets of the religious mainstream, even within Pennsylvania's "mixed multitude" of religious groups and well-established heritage of religious freedom, the Unitarians were viewed with "holy horror" precisely because of their continued adherence to the English system of theology.[71] Despite their failure to keep pace with the other denominations in congregational formation and institutionalization they grudgingly earned a measure of respect and legal toleration, and when faced with a reception that was less than civil, they stood strong in the face of the challenge and demonstrated their "carefully nurtured sense of a separate identity . . . to expose the shabbiness and arrogance of the culture surrounding them" and contribute to the future progress and success of the society to which they fled seeking protection and acceptance.[72]

With Priestley's death the Northumberland Unitarians did not go away. For a time they retained William Christie and after his departure continued to rely upon the method of lay preaching advocated by their founder, maintained connections with the society in Philadelphia, and kept up correspondence with fellow Unitarians in England. While their influence and stature declined without the presence of English

71. The phrase "mixed multitude" comes from Sally Schwartz, *A Mixed Multitude: The Struggle for Toleration in Colonial Pennsylvania*. She applies the phrase and the idea of a struggle within this multitude to the colonial era, but leaves open the expansion and its future applicability to the periods to follow. For "holy horror," see Kemble, *Records of Later Life*, 403.

72. Moore, *Religious Outsiders*, xi–xii.

and American Unitarianism's leading figure, they were bolstered in their confidence, and eventually their efforts, by the immigration of several other leading English Unitarian ministers to the United States, including Harry Toulmin, James Taylor, Robert Little, John Campbell, James Kay, William Wells, John Hobson, Thomas Porter, Thomas Rees, and Theophilus Harris.[73] Rather than shape themselves to fit the prevailing religious culture, they stayed their own course and secured their future prospects.

Unitarianism's Expansion

The effects of Priestley's efforts were felt throughout the United States and both ensured the adherence among many of the societies and individuals who had already adopted Unitarianism's tenets and practices and inspired the formation of several new groups. Building on the example and success of Priestley and the two Unitarian societies in Pennsylvania, new groups emerged in areas that were religiously diverse.

In western New York two Unitarian societies were formed, one in the village of Oldenbarneveld, later known as Trenton Village, near present-day Trenton Falls, fifteen miles from Utica, and the other at Canandaigua, just west of the Finger Lakes region, two years later. Apart from a brief mention in *The Panopolist*, little is known of the Canandaigua group's development and history.[74] Nobody involved with the society thought to record the progress of their efforts, and their presence in the region that would soon be known as the Burned-over District likely had something to do with their society being disbanded and its membership unaccounted for in subsequent histories of the region and Unitarianism. Oldenbarneveld, however, thrived. Named in honor of John Oldenbarnevelt, a Dutchman who was beheaded in the seventeenth century for being too favorable to religious toleration and liberty of conscience—the very traits that English and American Unitarianism sought to uphold—the utopian community was established with the financial backing of the Holland Land Company. By the time of Priestley's arrival in the United States, the settlement was

73. Hill, "Robert Little, John Campbell, and James Kay."

74. See Morse, "Review of American Unitarianism," 16. Morse mentions that this group came into existence two years after the group at Oldenbarneveld and that the minister was ordained "in its vicinity . . . a year or two since in the neighborhood." Beyond this little is revealed about this group, and they do not appear in any Unitarian histories or congregational records.

under the leadership of Colonel Adam G. Mappa, a Dutch Socinian "gentleman of a truly respectable character, and of considerable property and influence," and two ministers, the Reverend Frederic Adrian Vanderkemp, "a learned and pious emigrant . . . whose zeal for the doctrine of the Divine Unity" was inspired by Priestley, and the Reverend John Sherman, a former Congregationalist minister.[75] Of the two, Vanderkemp was the initial force in the establishment of Unitarianism in the village, but it was Sherman who formalized and established the society's practices and tenets along the lines of those espoused by Priestley and who, following Priestley's death, corresponded and maintained contact with both Jefferson and Channing, bridging the extremes of antitrinitarianism in America.

In 1805, before his association with Oldenbarneveld, Sherman had taken up the banner of Unitarianism and published *One God in One Person Only*, defending his beliefs against trinitarian opposition, ideas that were echoed in his 1826 *View of Ecclesiastical Proceedings*. In this writing Sherman declared that "the best orthodoxy is a faithful observance of the sacred precepts of that one God, whom you profess and acknowledge."[76] His views on the Trinity resulted in some difficulties and conflicts with the local ministerial consociation, eventually leading to his removal. The Association of Ministers of Windham County, the group responsible for the action, took care to note that he was a minister "in regular standing" and of "fair moral character," and that they held highly "favorable sentiments of his ministerial gifts, and do recommend him to the kind reception of such churches as may see fit to employ him." They removed him only after they were fully made aware of his "peculiar phraseology, or circumstantial differences of sentiment, on the subject of the Trinity," making it very clear that there were few churches that they felt would "see fit" to enlist his services.[77] Sherman, however, was still well liked by his former church, which offered to reappoint him as their minister despite the consociation's decision, proving that the ministers were far more conservative in their views and proactive in rooting out what they considered to be dangerous heresies than the people themselves. In the meantime, he had found a new home in Oldenbarneveld and gracefully declined his former congregation's offer.

Vanderkemp and Mappa had originally formed a congregation known as the United Protestant Religious Society of Trenton, whose

75. Thomas, *Trenton Falls*, 2–3.
76. Sherman, *Ecclesiastical Proceedings*, quoted in Thomas, *Trenton Falls*, 2–3.
77. Sprague, *Annals of the American Pulpit*, 8:327–28.

views were not in line with any particular denomination then in America. But their exposure to Unitarianism led to the group's decision to drop their independence in favor of an association with Priestley's efforts. They became an avowed Unitarian society, an action that was instrumental in Sherman's decision to become their preacher. The presence of Sherman's brother-in-law, Joshua Storrs, who was a member of the altered congregation, also had much to do with his decision.

When Sherman declined his former congregation's offer of reinstatement, he noted that he was happily settled in New York among a more promising situation for the flowering of Unitarianism and the free expression of his views. His reply stands as an important message and universal statement of Unitarian practice then current in America: "Surely you ought to know whether you are to be the worshipers of Three Gods, or of One God only," he noted. "I wish you may be duly impressed with the importance of openly avowing it, and appearing as its advocates; that as you rise into public life you will never be ashamed of the interesting truth, but boldly and faithfully stand in its defense, though the multitude should be against you," he stated, echoing Priestley's comments to the Philadelphia Unitarians. "Above all," Sherman pleaded with the Windham County Congregationalists, "always remember that the best orthodoxy is a faithful observance of the sacred precepts of that One God."[78]

Sherman was installed as the pastor of the Church at Oldenbarneveld on March 9, 1806, just two years after Priestley's death. He required that no doctrinal test be set for membership and that the Unitarian theology be the guiding force in the rites and practices. The church was renamed the Reformed Christian Church, drawing on the continued insistence that Unitarians were Christians who sought to reform the faith and correct its errors. A committee was assembled to draw up the new church's Articles of Association and commit their beliefs to paper. Article 3 defined free and unfettered religious inquiry, assuring the congregants that "liberty of conscience shall be persevered inviolate" and "every member shall be maintained in his right of free inquiry into the doctrines of Scripture; in publishing what he believes the Scriptures to contain, and in practicing according to his understanding of his duty. This liberty shall not be abridged as to his understanding and practice respecting the ceremonies, ordinances, or positive institutions of Christianity."[79] While Priestley was not the only advocate of

78. Belsham, *Memoirs*, 201n.
79. Reformed Christian Church, Articles of Association, 1806, quoted in Thomas, *Trenton Falls*, 5.

these ideas, the English Unitarian influence upon Sherman and the Oldenbarneveld society is unquestionable. In a series of missives to Thomas Belsham, Sherman had noted that he accepted Unitarianism out of conscience to himself and to God but was inspired by Priestley and Lindsey. It was "in consequence of an attentive perusal" to their works that he had become "a sincere and zealous convert to the doctrine of the proper Unity and sole Supremacy of God, to the simple humanity of Jesus Christ, and to the appropriation of religious worship to the Father only," noted Belsham a decade later. His convictions of the doctrine's importance and wide-spread rejection led him to openly avow and teach its tenets.[80]

The congregation at Oldenbarneveld thrived for several years, maturing in the early years of the nineteenth-century, following Priestley's death, to the great joy of all involved. Sherman even started to undertake itinerant journeys to spread the news of Oldenbarneveld's success. "He preaches in the week twenty miles round, and is sanguine in his expectations that he shall form another society twelve miles from hence," wrote Vanderkemp in 1809. "Few weeks are passing in which some one or other of the vicinity do not join our church, and those by far the most respectable among them."[81] What had begun as a small group of only fourteen members led by a Dutch immigrant was now the foundation for the full-fledged expansion of Unitarianism in New York. The congregation at Oldenbarneveld "was so increased . . . at the present time numbering by hundreds what was originally less than a score," noted one observer at the halfway point of the nineteenth century.[82] Vanderkemp attributed the growth of the congregation to increased contact with Unitarians in Philadelphia and Northumberland. "[Sherman's] ministerial labours are not in vain. Well supplied with a tolerable library, he has seen it enlarged, by Mr. J. Priestley [Jr.] and Mr. J[ames] Taylor from Philadelphia, by some valuable additions."[83]

But Sherman's ministry was also short-lived. In 1810, financial hardship compelled him to resign. In March, Sherman left Oldenbarneveld to focus on his teaching, which was much more lucrative than preaching.

---

80. Belsham, *Memoirs*, 191–92. Sherman's ideas were published in *One God in One Person Only* (1805) and led to his dismissal from his church, not by the request of his congregation, who accepted his right to private judgment, but rather by a consocation agreement of the local clergy, who judged him unfit. Sherman wrote that the local ministers sought "to destroy my ministerial and christian standing" (192n). See also letter of Abiel Abbot to William Sprague, in Sprague, *Annals of the American Pulpit*, 8:329.

81. Belsham, *Memoirs*, 202.

82. Willis, *Trenton Falls, Picturesque and Descriptive*, 8.

83. Belsham, *Memoirs*, 203.

The group was left to fend for themselves, and as did the congregation in Philadelphia, they engaged several lay members as readers. Nevertheless, their convictions were strong, and Vanderkemp was able to write that the group remained vital and steadfast in their Unitarian worship, even erecting a chapel in 1811. Once ensconced in their new house of worship they read sermons by the most notable Unitarians in England and America, "so that we are edified sometimes by Clarke and Tillotson, sometimes by Blair, and sometimes by Lindsey, Priestley, Price, and Toulmin."[84] They eventually folded into the Unitarian church of the New England Arians, following the shift of sentiment begun 1819, but the early years of their efforts and the founding influence clearly stemmed from another source, and the group never disavowed their connections to Priestley and English Unitarianism.

As has been so ably documented by John Allen Macauley in his recent *Unitarianism in the Antebellum South,* the English Unitarian influence was also felt in the states below the Mason-Dixon line. While other influences pulled at those with liberal leanings throughout the South, some notable English Unitarians played a role in the efforts to secure liberalism against the tide of the Episcopal, Catholic, and Baptist strongholds.[85] Harry Toulmin, son of the English minister Joshua Toulmin, sailed to America and traveled throughout the South before settling in Kentucky in 1793. Toulmin, who was personally acquainted with Priestley and well-versed in his writings, had felt pressured to leave England as a result of his Unitarian ideas even before Priestley. In anticipation of his departure, he published three tracts advocating emigration to America. Many of the ideas expressed by Toulmin in *Thoughts on Emigration* had a great effect on Priestley, his sons, and other Englishmen, leading the way for many to leave England.[86] So important were Toulmin's ideas that they became the backbone of the emigration movement that followed. His ideas occupied a central place in Priestley's sermon, *The Case of the Poor Emigrants Recommended,* and also in the charter of the Society of St. George. Priestley even asked Toulmin to come to Pennsylvania, to serve as a minister and a teacher in the college being constructed. But Toulmin was in such a good position that he respectfully declined Priestley's invitation. Although he was much better known for his legal work, he did not neglect his spiritual leanings. In 1803, he sponsored a reprint of Thomas Emlyn's writings in support of a Socinian

84. Ibid., 203–4.
85. Macaulay, *Unitarianism in the Antebellum South,* 1–14.
86. Toulmin, *Thoughts on Emigration.*

Unitarian theology, by a Frankfort publisher, to coincide with a revived effort to do the same in Boston.[87] Toulmin's efforts in Kentucky yielded little in the way of congregational formation, but did have an effect in Alabama, where he later migrated and was instrumental in the formation of a congregation in the 1830s led by his brother.[88]

Many of the New England ministers who had earlier openly turned toward English Unitarianism continued to profess their beliefs and support an open association. Though their efforts often went unnoticed as a consequence of their geographic location, the limitations of religious tolerance in the United States, and the resurgence of revivalism, they were not without effect. Surrounded by New England liberals, James Freeman of Boston nevertheless remained faithful to the tenets of English Unitarianism, expressing his desire that the King's Chapel congregants would one day be fully enlightened Unitarians. While Priestley was still alive, Freeman had written to Belsham with an air of optimism, that "the Unitarian doctrine appears to be still upon the increase," owing much to the Englishman's presence and his distribution of revised versions of his religious tracts. He also spoke of his continuing acquaintance with a number of ministers who continued along the same path as he was then following, and leading their congregations toward the same conclusions.[89]

Early on in Priestley's stewardship, hinting of things to come, Freeman cautioned that there were signs that the Socinians were vulnerable to the confusion and pressures arising from the resurgence of Arianism among the liberal wing of the Congregationalists. "It is possible that Unitarianism may be losing ground in one quarter while it is gaining in another, and that I may not perceive or may not attend to the former. Indeed, I confess and lament that the opinion is scarcely known in the largest part of this vast republic." Though the liberals had, in the words of Conrad Wright, considered the questions of Christ's divinity "far removed from problems of practical Christianity which concerned them much more—that is to say, the problem of the redemption of human nature and the salvation of human souls," their increasing dissatisfaction with the congregational standing order and the occupancy of the Socinian Unitarians in the antitrinitarian seat forced them to

87. Emlyn, *Humble Enquiry*. This is the same work that was promoted by William Hazlitt in 1783–84 during his travels throughout New England in support of Socinianism and later championed by James Freeman of King's Chapel.

88. Frank, "'I Shall Never Be Intimidated,'" 28–29.

89. James Freeman to Thomas Belsham, May 24, 1796, in Belsham, *Memoirs*, 189–90.

reassert their Arian views as a means of distinction.[90] However, Freeman recognized that these issues were far from settled and where English Unitarianism was established it was growing, and he expected much from the presence of Priestley.[91] As his own efforts attest, he was not disappointed. Even among the Unitarian churches of the late eighteenth century, King's Chapel was heralded for its willingness to be among the first to proclaim its adherence to the basic unitarian idea. Freeman was emboldened in January 1809 when he was, at the behest of his congregation, joined by the Reverend Samuel Cary, an English Unitarian, to serve as associate pastor. The relationship between Freeman, Cary, and King's Chapel continued for some years.[92] By 1811, it seems as though his hopes had come true. "Dr. Freeman has himself lived to see his own prediction verified. In a new edition of the Boston Liturgy [1811] . . . nothing is to be found which is inconsistent with the purest principles of Unitarian worship as such."[93]

Elsewhere, the news was just as favorable for the Unitarians. In 1810, several congregants accused the Reverend Abiel Abbot, pastor of the First Church in Coventry, Connecticut, of Socinian heresy. The Consociation was convened and demanded that Abbot answer to the charge that he "does neither preach nor believe the doctrine of the sacred Trinity;—that he does neither preach nor believe the divinity of Jesus Christ;—that he does neither preach nor believe the doctrine of the atonement by the blood of Christ, nor of justification by his imputed righteousness." At this moment Abbot became an unrepentant Unitarian; he answered their charges forthrightly and allied himself with the English Unitarians. Not surprisingly, the consociation declared Abbot to be a "subversive of the Christian's faith."[94] So great was their power over local religious affairs that he was dismissed from his post in April 1811, a separation effected with great prejudice and disdain for his ministry. Though the cause of his dismissal was obviously his Unitarian beliefs, Abbot also raised the question of the authority of ecclesiastical councils, resulting from his acceptance of the Unitarian beliefs in free inquiry and ministerial freedom. By June, Abbot gathered his own council to challenge the Consociation; but in a move that surprised

90. Conrad Wright, unpublished manuscript, 14. I am grateful to the author for sharing portions of his unpublished writings with me. For similarly expressed views, see also Wright, *Beginnings*.

91. Freeman to Belsham, May 24, 1796, in Belsham, *Memoirs*, 190.

92. Sprague, *Annals of the American Pulpit*, 13:174.

93. See Freeman to Lindsey, July 7, 1786, in Belsham, *Memoirs*, 179n.

94. Belsham, *Memoirs*, 199–200.

virtually all parties involved, this new council agreed that while the authority of the ecclesiastical council was dubious, the separation was nonetheless warranted.[95]

Clearly, English Unitarianism had taken root in America and was having an effect on the direction of religious discourse. The Unitarians were building churches and formal organizations. Despite their small numbers and their lack of a central national or international governing body, they had taken their place among the collection of American religious denominations.[96] Their success was noted in England and reflected back into the U.S. landscape in 1812 with the English edition of Belsham's life of Theophilus Lindsey, which provided testimony from a variety of Unitarian believers, practitioners, and even begrudging opponents, that the fruits of Priestley's labors in America were evident. Belsham's was not the only acknowledgment. In 1824 the magazine *Unitarian Miscellany*, published in Baltimore by Jared Sparks, gave Priestley credit for much that had occurred in the course of Unitarianism's development in America. "It seems to us," Sparks professed, "that if there is one man to whom, more than to any other, Unitarianism can look with confidence, and point with pride, as the honest, zealous, pious, unwearied, distinguished champion of their principles, Dr. Priestley is that man."[97] But the contest was just beginning.

95. For the details of Abbot's case, see *The Panopolist* (Boston), August 1812, 1–18, LOC, Rare Book Collection, Misc. Pamphlets, v. 1074, no. 9.

96. Macaulay, *Unitarianism in the Antebellum South*, 18–19.

97. Greenwood, "Dr. Channing's Sermon," 208.

FIVE

Socinianism, Arianism, and the Quest for Unitarian Identity

Upon my arrival in the United States, the religious aspect of the country was the first
thing that struck my attention; and the longer I stayed there the more did I perceive
the great political consequences resulting from this state of things. . . . Religion in
America takes no direct part in the government of society, but nevertheless it must
be regarded as the foremost political of the institutions of that country; for if it does
not impart a taste for freedom, it facilitates the use of free institutions.

—ALEXIS DE TOCQUEVILLE, *Democracy in America*

Throughout much of the eighteenth century Unitarianism was, for
most Americans, merely one theological interpretation among many,
not the defining identity of any congregation and certainly not the
most notable religious precept of a denomination. But Priestley's presence changed all that. Within a quarter of a century Americans had
witnessed the formation of no fewer than twenty openly Unitarian
congregations with well-established practices, a growing recognition of
their place within the wider religious community, and a denominational identity—albeit an informal one.

As successful as they were, however, they had not succeeded to the
point of certainty and religious liberalism was still contested ground
from both within and without. Priestley's death resulted in an opportunity for orthodox opponents of, and the liberal competitors for the
mantle of, religious liberalism to attack Socinianism and denounce
Priestley's influence. His death left a significant void, one that the Unitarians in America were hard pressed to fill, and without the presence
of such a commanding figure the Unitarians became easy prey. The
defense of the faith reverted back to those in England who were in a
stronger position to speak with both theological and institutional
authority. Despite the formal, political separation between the two
nations, the religious and social transmissions continued unabated. It
was, in fact, a book published in England, celebrating the life of Lindsey,
and published in the United States in 1815, that sought to preserve

the legacy of Priestley's efforts in the nation and sparked a conflict that would redefine Unitarianism in America. As a result of Thomas Belsham's *Memoirs of the Late Reverend Theophilus Lindsey,* Unitarians on both sides of the Atlantic were soon embroiled in a conflict over the degree of Christ's divinity and Unitarian identity.

Socinians were pitted against Arians in a heavily contested dispute over ownership of the Unitarian name, the parameters of theological liberalism, and the very identity of Unitarianism itself. Congregationalists and other trinitarians were only too happy to fan the flames and watch the two competing groups rend liberal religion asunder. When it was all over, the Socinian Unitarians had lost the right to the Unitarian name, now claimed by the New England liberals, in a series of transformations that were completely effected by 1825. How the English Unitarians were shoved aside and lost acceptance as the Unitarian denomination and what happened to the theology of Priestley and the achievements of the Pennsylvania Unitarians is the crux of this story. Scholars who have studied Unitarianism have long dismissed Priestley and English Unitarianism as uninfluential, irrelevant, or even trivial. The English version of Unitarianism, they claim, never held sway in the United States and was not part of the story of the faith as it passed through its various stages on its way to becoming modern-day Unitarianism.[1] But as we shall see, such a view comes only if one accepts the arguments of those whose best interests were served in the early nineteenth century to dismiss and deny the English Unitarian legacy in the United States.

Delineating the Religious Landscape

Numerous individuals and organizations sought to chronicle the religious history of the young nation almost from its very outset. The numbers of religious encyclopedias that appeared throughout the early national and antebellum periods are a testament not only to the extent to which religion pervaded all levels of American society but also to the degree of diversity, presenting historical and theological accounts of the various religious denominations and societies as they had emerged and developed. Organized in very similar ways, these works often grouped denominations together by their position in American society—established or sectarian, Christian or non-Christian—

---

1. See Wright, "American Unitarianism in 1805," and Robinson, *Unitarians and Universalists,* 1–21. These are just two of the works that accord Priestley and English Unitarianism brief coverage and conclude that English Unitarianism was irrelevant.

and explored the nuances of their theologies. And, as subsequent volumes were published, new groups appeared, old groups were reclassified according to the most recent developments, and some groups disappeared. Taken together and looked at over time, the collective body of this genre can provide significant insight into America's religious development. When looked to for what they reveal about the history of Unitarianism, these books clearly establish the early successes of the English Unitarians and reveal the subsequent developments that eventually led to their eclipse.

Hannah Adams was among the first to undertake the task of defining, classifying, and giving credence to the various religious groups. Begun in 1784 and organized alphabetically, Adams's *Dictionary of All Religions and Religious Denominations* was a comprehensive—both in terms of the groups covered and its history from the ancient to the modern period—reference guide that documented each group's number of adherents, congregations and missions, religious doctrines, and acceptance by others. Her earliest editions made it clear that English Unitarians had laid substantial foundations in America.[2] She defined Socinianism as a "denomination" whose central beliefs were those found in Priestley's writings, from which she directly lifted her entry, and cross-referenced them in entries under the headings of "Anti-Trinitarians," "Humanists," and "Humanitarians." The last was, she wrote, "a term applied to those modern Socinians who maintain with Dr. Priestley the *simple humanity* of Christ" and a denial of his preexistence and was essentially an alternate name for "Unitarians." In all of these entries Adams noted that the chief articles in the religious system were Socinian, and she liberally cited Priestley in support, drawing heavily from his *Defense of Unitarianism* and *General History of the Christian Church*.

By the time of its fourth printing in 1817, however, the tone of Adams's entries had begun to shift in response to the progressively voluminous writings concerning competing views of the Unitarian presence. She also came to take note of the increasing arguments for a broader coverage of groups who occupied the religiously liberal end of the spectrum. Now Unitarianism was covered in no fewer than six entries. She now included an entry, broadly defined, under "Anti-Trinitarians," which was, she noted, the "general name given to all those who deny the doctrine of the Trinity, and particularly to the Arians and Socinians" and which gave her sufficient grounds to reject Priestley's assertion, made in his *History of Early Opinions concerning Jesus Christ*,

2. Adams, *Dictionary of All Religions*, 295.

that only Socinians are entitled to be called Unitarians. Adams no longer saw Unitarianism as a distinct term referring to one particular group, noting that "Arians, Humanitarians, and all Anti-Trinitarians have an equal right to the denomination."[3] Still two years away from the first formal call for the New England liberals' acceptance of the name and eight from its formal association, Adams's shifts already reflected the arguments in the growing dispute.

Writing in 1811, James Mease included the Unitarians in his account of religious societies then worshipping in Philadelphia and found no version of Unitarianism other than that formed under the influence of Priestley. Focusing only on Philadelphia, Mease was able to document the numbers of a group's adherents, the location of their churches, and the specific tenets and practices of each society. Mease categorized the Unitarians as a "religious society" that was "formed in this country soon after the arrival of the amiable, the pious, the venerable Dr. Priestley" and formed around his theological authority. He also refers to Quakers, Free Quakers, Episcopalians, and even Catholics as religious societies. The implication is that he considered the Unitarians then meeting in a space along Church Alley full-fledged members of the city's standing religious community.

An 1830s entrant into the genre, John Hayward's *Religious Creeds and Statistics of Every Christian Denomination in the United States* fully documents the complexity of Unitarianism's history. It also introduces the Transcendentalist challenge and the effect that it had on Unitarian adherents and the course of American religious belief. In two separate entries Hayward distinguishes Unitarianism from Socinianism and stresses the New England conceptions as the foundation of the denomination, completely dismissing Socinianism, claiming that Arianism was "indiscriminately applied" and thus meaningless as a term of distinction or characterization.[4] According to Hayward, Socinians were a sect "who own that the name of God is given in the Holy Scriptures to Jesus Christ, but contend that it is only a deputed title . . . and say that Christ only preached the truth to mankind, set before them in himself an example of heroic virtue." He set Socinians apart from the Unitarians by virtue of their doctrine, especially since the former "deny the doctrines of satisfaction and imputed righteousness." Furthermore, Hayward noted, Socinians viewed original sin and absolute predestination as "scholastic

---

3. Ibid., 26 and 118. See also the entries on Arians, Humanists, Humanitarians, and Socinians.

4. Hayward, *Religious Creeds and Statistics*, 5.

chimeras." But Hayward was not above entering into the fray and misrepresented the central tenets of Socinianism in order to achieve separation. The most distinguishing characteristic was, he wrote in an attempt to hang one idea around the necks of all, that Socinians "maintain the sleep of the soul, which, they say, becomes insensible at death, and is raised again with the body at the resurrection."[5]

In comparison, he labeled Unitarians "a class of Christians . . . who believe there is but one God, [who] are opposed to the Trinitarian theology . . . that Christ descended to this earth, from a state of pre-existent dignity [and] believe that the history of our Savior, as given in the New Testament, and the events of his life and ministry, answer best to the opinion of the superiority of his nature." The only substantive difference of this definition from the one Hayward provided for the Congregationalists, or for that matter, for any other Christian group, was their position on Christ's divinity. Hayward went to great lengths to show that the Unitarians of the 1830s had not altered their beliefs from those they held before 1800, when they were considered liberal Christians well within the Congregationalist fold.[6] But Hayward's qualifying notes at the end of the entry on Unitarianism further reveal the distinctions that had taken center stage as New England Unitarians sought to disavow English Socinians and their historical influence. Unwilling to assert that Unitarianism was indigenous to America, as William Ellery Channing and others had, Hayward instead acknowledged the broad nature of liberalism and its promotion of free inquiry by noting that "there is another class of liberal Christians, who, whilst they reject [the Trinity] are yet unable to pass a definite judgment on the various systems, which prevail, as to the nature and rank of Christ," and yet still "another class, who believe the simple humanity of Jesus Christ; but these form a small proportion of the great body of Unitarians in the United States."[7] In the appendix, Hayward went even further into the historical link between Priestley's Socinianism and the Arianism of the New Englanders. In a nod to the history of the latter's attempts to avoid the Unitarian title, Hayward noted that there were still "other large bodies of Christians in the United States who adopt the sentiments of the Unitarians, without their distinctive name." He recorded that there had always been a group of English Unitarians who professed the faith and were at one time its leading advocates in

5. Ibid., 105.
6. Ibid., 110.
7. Ibid., 111.

the United States. For their views he turned to Belsham and Lindsey, laid out their creeds, and referred the reader back to the entries on both Socinianism and Humanism.[8]

Hayward was not the lone voice to attempt to clarify the complex, historical connections between the English and American versions of Unitarianism. Daniel Rupp and Robert Baird, both writing in 1844, provided historical and theological accounts of American Unitarianism near the middle of the century. Baird's work separated Christian denominations into two groups: evangelical and non-evangelical, the latter including Unitarians.[9] Rupp, on the other hand, did not categorize the denominations by theological tenets or practices; instead he turned to more than fifty eminent clerical and lay authors, each associated with a faith, and allowed them to describe their denominations.[10] Despite the differences in their approach, both Baird and Rupp concluded that Unitarianism in the mid-nineteenth century was not the Unitarianism of its English antecedents, nor was it in full agreement with its earlier historical manifestation in the United States.

Baird's entry on the Unitarians helped to rewrite the past. After having taken on the Unitarian name two decades after it first came to the United States, nineteenth-century Unitarians had dropped all vestiges of Priestley and the English version of the faith and inserted their own beliefs, which Baird accepted uncritically for his purposes of classification. His personal predilection to identify a "homogeneous character" to American religion caused him to overly stress the period in which the New England liberals existed "silently and without controversy" as Congregationalists, and he placed nineteenth-century American Unitarians near the center of religious respectability because of their Congregationalist past.[11] In his view, the former liberals were the true Unitarians, and Baird saw any association with Priestley as slander. "The greater part of those who are now claimed as having then belonged to the 'liberal' party were only Arminians . . . some of them were decided Calvinists," he noted, being certain to keep them within the Christian fold. Baird dismissed the efforts of the followers of English Unitarianism. Sherman, he noted, "lost his character" for

---

8. Ibid., 150.

9. Baird, *Religion in the United States*.

10. Rupp, *He Pasa Ekklesia*. This work was subsequently amended and reedited for publication under a different title.

11. Whether or not this was fair is another issue. "Except for Catholics and Unitarians, to whom Baird tried hard without success to be fair, he located all the non-Evangelicals on the fringes of American respectability," writes R. Laurence Moore. See *Religious Outsiders*, 6.

his efforts, and Abbott's actions "called forth many expressions of disapprobation." He rejected James Freeman's efforts at King's Chapel as little more than a "convenient medium of communication between [the leading Unitarians in England] and the secret adherents of the same doctrine in America." By accusing the English adherents of keeping their efforts secret, Baird transformed the facts. In what is an otherwise thorough account of the development of Unitarianism in America, he completely ignored Priestley's efforts in Pennsylvania and the prominence of his ideas, making the two groups distinct.[12]

There was widespread and general dissatisfaction with the accuracy of the religious histories of the United States. Rupp compiled a revised version of his work and gave it a new title to correct the situation and address the "injustices" and "numerous complaints" launched against the earlier *He Pasa Ekklesia.* His solution to the problem of bias—to have a representative of each sect contribute its own "truthful history"—had exactly the opposite effect, despite his warning to the reader to make all due allowance for "glowing language." The entry "Unitarian Congregationalists" is a case in point. It was written by the Reverend Alvan Lamson of Dedham, Massachusetts, and was marked by an etched portrait of William Ellery Channing, clearly indicating the entry's leanings. Through careful omission and misrepresentation, Lamson did his best to erase Priestley, the English Unitarians, and all hint of Socinian thought from the history of the denomination.[13]

"In Death the Contest Begins"

A great deal changed following the death of Priestley, that much is clear. His passing was marked by numerous memorial sermons, some delivered as late as five years after the fact, all paying homage to his life and legacy. After word of his death reached England, Belsham delivered a memorial sermon at Hackney in tribute to the deceased's "disinterested love of truth, indefatigable zeal in the pursuit of it, and resolution to adhere to it when found, at all hazards."[14] Belsham spoke at length about Priestley's optimism and honored him as an apostle of the universal Christian faith. Belsham preached from Acts 20:24, amplifying the ministries of Jesus and Paul with the life and teachings

---

12. Baird, *Religion in the United States,* 625–27.
13. Rupp, *Religious Denominations,* 593, 3.
14. Belsham, *Discourse delivered at Hackney,* 17.

of Priestley, and went on to reaffirm Priestley's theology—the gospel of the full and unconditional saving grace of God, the perseverance of a ministry opposed with zeal and persecution, and the consolation and "joy" of a theology and belief that is tied to fidelity and unconditional acceptance of the message of God—and spoke of his glorious accomplishments in establishing Unitarianism on both sides of the Atlantic.[15]

William Wood, minister to Mill Hill Chapel in Leeds, one of Priestley's former congregations, also delivered a eulogy, drawing on John 5:35, "He was a burning and shining light; and for a season ye rejoiced in his light," to set the tone for his oration.[16] Wood focused on the "plain and practical" Priestley, a minister whose approach to faith was methodical and driven by the desire to correct the wrongs that were so often committed in its name. He noted Priestley's undying commitment to the scriptures and his "quest to address all matters that stemmed from their words." But he also mentioned Priestley the man honest to a fault, as did Belsham, in ways that made his role as a Christian even more important. Wood's Priestley was fallible, unguarded in his language, and sometimes too stubborn. Yet he persevered against great opposition, possessed one of the keenest minds of his day, and left behind a legacy, in both England and America, that would survive the ages.[17] Such words were echoed over the coming years, keeping Priestley's efforts in the public eye, but doing very little to compensate for his absence.

The immediate graveside service held at the Friends Burial Ground in Northumberland and attended by a "numerous concourse of respectable citizens," despite the bitter February cold, was delivered by William Christie.[18] Christie proclaimed with certainty that Priestley "will always live and be celebrated, while Religion, Science, and Learning continue to be held in veneration by mortals," owing to his eminent contributions in philosophical, religious, and humanistic pursuits. "Though he might have shone in the national establishment of the Church of England, and acquired lucrative preferments and ecclesiastical distinction, he preferred the humbler line of a *dissenting minister*, where he could

---

15. Ibid.

16. Wood, *A Sermon, preached April 22, 1804*. There appear to be a total of thirty-seven memorial addresses delivered and published on the death of Priestley. There were addresses in France, England, Germany, the United States, and Ireland. The address commissioned by the American Philosophical Society, and delivered by Dr. Benjamin Smith Barton on January 3, 1805, unfortunately remains lost. It was scheduled to be published in the Society's *Transactions* but was pulled for revisions and never again seen. See Smith, *Priestley in America*, 166–73.

17. Wood, *A Sermon, preached April 22, 1804*, 43–45.

18. Christie, *Speech*, 3.

pursue his religious enquiries unfettered by subscription to human articles of faith; and while he performed the ordinary functions of a Christian." As such, the lessons derived from his life and teachings were not to be confined to one group, for Priestley was truly "pastor to the congregation at large," pastor to the world.[19] Christie chose to ignore most of Priestley's more controversial traits and trials and instead focused on his ideas of universal tolerance, religious freedom, and generosity of spirit, thereby concentrating on Priestley the "reformer" and frequently mentioning the man who sought to restore harmony and truth to Christianity through his never-ending inquiries and challenges.

Christie's words, and subsequent attempts to step into the leadership role did little to reduce the impact of Priestley's absence. The Philadelphia and Northumberland congregations were left without a spiritual leader, and Unitarianism was deprived of its most prolific defender, resulting in a prolonged period of uncertainty and inactivity. The loss of the founding figure was always a time of trial for emerging denominations, all too often resulting in a period of precipitous decline, and in many cases eventually leading to the death of the group itself. Even among the Philadelphia society, who had handled its own ministerial matters even when Priestley was alive, his absence created a void in leadership that few others were capable of filling. The Northumberland congregation, which consisted of family and friends, was hit harder. They lost a father and grandfather, a close friend and teacher, who had helped change the town from a backcountry outpost to a potential contender for the state capital and whose presence assured them of religious acceptance. He was their regular minister, and there was nobody who could remotely take his place. Lacking a minister of Priestley's stature, the two congregations turned inward and sought to ensure their own survival, more interested in securing their personal worship and much less so in the theological implications of their beliefs or in defending their standing among the mainstream traditions in the wider religious landscape. Only later was either group able to construct a chapel and acquire the leadership of an established minister.[20]

19. Ibid., 4, 8–9.
20. Belsham passed judgment on the whole of Priestley's efforts as successful yet limited. "Dr. Priestley's personal ministry in the United States was attended with very little apparent success. In Northumberland, where he resided, he collected but a few proselytes; and in Philadelphia, where the chapel in which he preached was at first crowded with the principal characters in the United States, he was afterwards for some reason or other almost deserted. Yet here his labors were not wholly ineffectual. Since Dr. Priestley's decease a small but highly

But the transatlantic connections so inherent in American Unitarianism at this time provided some glimmer of hope that things might turn out positively for Unitarians. England also lacked someone who could defend Unitarianism's tenets with as much vigor and understanding as Priestley. Belsham, who saw himself as "nothing more than a humble disciple in the school of Lardner, of Lindsey, and of Priestley," was unwilling to simply surrender to the opposition or to abandon his brethren in America. Hoping to assist the American Unitarians in their quest to remain viable, and perhaps even give them a boost to continue in their more public prospects, Belsham invoked both Lindsey and Priestley in his efforts to create a wider fellowship of Unitarians, bringing the New England liberals into the fold, and enact the institutionalization of Unitarianism that Priestley had desired but failed to secure.[21] As fervent a Socinian as Priestley, Belsham reasserted the theology's fundamental tenets and sought to establish them as the grounds for the group's continued characterization. "Before [Priestley] led the way, we were all much in confusion, and had no distinct ideas concerning that great corruption of the gospel, and of genuine Christianity," wrote Belsham.[22] But Priestley's efforts had clarified matters. Belsham believed that any rational, thinking person could not help but be swayed by Priestley, and he held up the Pennsylvania congregations as proof as put forth in *American Unitarianism; or a Brief History of the Progress and Present State of the Unitarian Churches in America.* Drawn from his biography of Theophilus Lindsey, letters from James Freeman, and correspondence with William Wells Jr., Belsham's history was the most confrontational Unitarian work since Priestley's *Importance and Extent of Free Inquiry in Matters of Religion,* and provoked a renewed and strengthened attack from the opposition. These efforts, assisted by some key figures in the United States, however, resulted in a "warm, not to say angry controversy on the other side of the Atlantic," and an outcome vastly different from the one they imagined.[23]

In his work, Priestley had drawn the ire of many trinitarians when he noted that "Unitarian principles are gaining ground every day. We are, as it were, laying gunpowder, grain by grain, under the old building

---

respectable congregation has been formed, in which, till a regular minister can be procured, a few of the most intelligent and best informed members conduct the service by turns; and the society, upon the whole, is increasing, though some who once professed zeal in the cause have turned their backs upon it." See Belsham, *Memoirs*, 191.

21. Ibid., 209.
22. Belsham, *Vindication*, 99n.
23. Belsham, *Memoirs*, 209.

of error and superstition, which a single spark may hereafter inflame, so as to produce an instantaneous explosion," earning Priestley the nickname "Gunpowder Joe" and the eternal enmity of trinitarians everywhere.[24] In response to the outcry Priestley attempted to clarify his intent and renew his calls for universal toleration. He implored his critics to consider that "the means we propose to employ are not *force*, but *persuasion*. The *gunpowder* which we are so assiduously laying . . . is not composed of saltpeter, charcoal, and sulphur, but consists of *arguments*."[25] However, the damage was done, and his opponents ignored his efforts to assuage them. This hostility was carried over to and at the core of the opposition in America as well. Aware of this, Priestley issued corrections and additions in his American edition of the sermon, which included a letter he had written to Belsham in 1794, when he had first arrived. The American blessings of liberty and tolerance were so different from what existed in England that Americans "should have no apprehension of . . . metaphorical gunpowder [being mistaken] for real."[26] Though Priestley had hoped to show how confident he was in the prospects for tolerance and liberty in a nation built on religious freedom, his efforts to eliminate the trinitarians' fear fell short; most considered the original sentiments to be the true expression of his intentions.

Belsham, however, had grown weary of the criticisms heaped upon his convictions from the trinitarians and the repeated supplications designed to alleviate their opposition. He also tired of the Arians' attempts to hide their true unitarian leanings, for they had been allowed to remain above the fray and retain Christian fellowship for too long without being called to account for their distinct theology. They neither proselytized enough nor held true to Priestley's legacy; most important, they refused to concede that their theological differences with Socinians still put them in closer fellowship with the Socinians than with trinitarians. He lamented that Lindsey's predictions of "the evil done . . . in the use of the terms, *Arian*, [and] *Socinian*," had come to pass in America and "will not soon or easily be repaired," as it created a false divide within liberal religion.[27] Belsham believed that one could only fully commit to the principle of God's unity and that all who believed accordingly should join together under one, common body. Likewise, in the years following Priestley's death Belsham seemed to lose his patience at the slow yet solid growth of the various Unitarian

24. Priestley, *Free Inquiry*, 4.
25. Priestley, *Letter to the Right Honourable William Pitt*, 21–22.
26. Priestley to Thomas Belsham, August 27, 1794, PSU.
27. Lindsey, *Historical View*, xi.

congregations in America. The Pennsylvania groups had turned inward. The congregations in New York and New England seemed to be doing the same, or worse, as they transformed themselves into liberal churches without continuing their association with English Unitarianism. The time had come for a concerted action, and the most fruitful venue seemed to be New England.

Capitalizing on the groundwork laid by Priestley, Belsham baited the New England liberals by invoking the Bible, recounting the history of English Unitarianism in America, and used their reluctance to separate from Congregationalism against them. First, he accused them of hiding their true beliefs. Their continual denials of association with Priestley and their English forbearers were particularly galling, especially since the record of events was so clear. "This hypothesis, the invention of the eighteenth century, which has never yet had a public advocate, but which is known to be the private opinion of some respectable individuals, falls within the limits of Unitarianism, even according to its most restricted definition." He claimed that the New England liberals' persistent and selective denial of incorporating Socinian ideas into their theology, and thus becoming Unitarians, placed them in an untenable situation and resulted in a situation where they were more engaged in arguing with like-minded believers than they were in countering the arguments of trinitarians. "It would surely better become them to repel arguments which affect the vitals of their system, than to amuse themselves with verbal controversies about the word Unitarian," he argued. Arguments over semantics did nothing but distort the real intent of one's belief, allowing Unitarianism to "be made to include the highest Trinitarian, or to exclude even the lowest Arian, excepting those modern theologians who limit themselves to the belief of the simple pre-existence of Christ."[28]

Belsham further called upon them to recognize the passage of events in England and their connections to America. By the time he was writing there were more than two hundred Unitarian chapels in England, testifying to its influence in a society with a religious establishment not known for its tolerance.[29] This was proof enough for Belsham that the real Unitarianism was found in the views of its English adherents and those in America who adopted the faith from England, not in the modifications of the New England liberals. Therefore, he called upon

28. Belsham, *Vindication*, 99n.
29. Smith, *The Unitarians*, 78.

the New England believers to profess their full faith in the unitarian idea and to follow the lead of those congregations formed under Priestley's influence, who upheld creeds that were "strictly *Unitarian*," and rejected "the *Arian* idea of the pre-existence of Christ's human soul, or that he originally possessed a super-angelic nature; or that his suffering and death were in any sense to be considered as *propitiatory*, or that divine honors were due to him." He concluded that "the *English* Unitarians reject these opinions as absurd, and maintain the *simple humanity* of Jesus. Of this is the character of *Unitarianism*."[30] The Unitarian creed was quite explicit, yet it was being hidden by the theological contortions of those less zealous than Unitarianism deserved.[31] Belsham thus sought to expose the New England Arians, force them to face the truth, and ensure that the achievements of the Unitarians in America could not be ignored. The prolonged existence of several Unitarian congregations, some in New England, was incontrovertible proof. Correspondence with William Wells, who sent him articles published in *The Monthly Anthology, The General Repository,* and *The Christian Disciple,* all detailing the growing number of Unitarians throughout the United States and the influence of English Unitarianism on them, served as further proof.[32]

Belsham turned to Priestley's *Appeal to the Public on the Subject of the Riots at Birmingham* to justify his call to commitment. "It is only in trying circumstances that the full force of religious principle is felt, and that its real energy can show itself," Priestley had reminded both supporters and detractors. He had reiterated these principles in his *Letters to the Inhabitants of Northumberland,* when he and the Unitarians had once again found themselves under suspicion.[33] Belsham believed, as did Priestley when he was living in the United States, that the time had long since passed for the New England liberals to openly avow their principles and confront the trials that would surely follow, as opposed to remaining hidden for fear of repercussions. But this was not just Priestley's position; others held it as well. Francis Parkman Sr., a liberal New England minister, and John Grundy, an Englishman, both held a favorable view of Unitarianism and agreed that the denomination needed the open support of all Christians. As a result of their belief in the need for universal toleration, both men also expressed their

---

30. Belsham, *Vindication,* 10.
31. Belsham, *Memoirs,* 191.
32. Ibid., 205.
33. Priestley, *Appeal to the Public,* in *Works,* 19:422.

dismay that the New England liberals were reluctant to support those who held very similar beliefs and whose open avowal of the ideas was already established.[34]

The old habits of discord, they believed, were failing Unitarianism in the changing religious environment of the day. The reluctance of the Arians to fully rationalize their beliefs and rid them of the vestiges of corruption remained troubling. Arianism was much less consistent and harder to maintain than Socinianism. In 1784, Priestley had anonymously authored a series of essays published in the *Theological Repository* that addressed the Arian and Socinian doctrines. He tackled the issue in stages, first handling a query on the Arian doctrine, then moving on to recount the history of the controversy over its tenets, and finally, in the penultimate essay, showing how Arians were not Unitarians. He began his assault with the same approach that he used when he sought to counter the corruptions of the trinitarians—tracing the historical development of the theological idea and showing with great certainty that it was a product of men long after the time of Jesus and the apostles. "The Arian opinion appears to have had its origin with the *learned,* and philosophizing christians," he wrote, "as much as that of the personification of the Logos." Labeling the Arian beliefs "an interpretation," he placed them on the same footing as those who had adopted the notions of three-in-one in the later councils of men and labeled their beliefs unscriptural.[35] Having publicly asked for others to prove him wrong, and finding no takers, at least to his satisfaction, he set out some months later to share the fullness of his research into the matter.

Priestley recognized that he had to contend with Arianism's "orthodox" stamp of approval. But he did so by demonstrating that the Arian conception of Jesus was merely a derivative of the early Gnostic idea, itself one of three competing "systems of christianity, or rather three opinions concerning the person of Christ." He gave primacy to the unitarian system, owing to its existence at the time of Jesus and among the apostles, and also showed how the other two were developed in later eras. In discussing the major articles of the Arian creed, Priestley was quick to point out how they were both logically inconsistent and seen as heresy. Arianism was, he said, a creed full of "novelty" and "confounding" in its design. He further turned to the criticisms of those whom he labeled as orthodox to put the Arian matter into

---

34. See Parkman, *A Survey of God's providence,* and Grundy, *Evangelical Christianity Considered.* See also, Grundy, *Christianity: An Intellectual and Individual Religion.*

35. Priestley, "Query relating to the Rise of the Arian Doctrine," 71.

perspective. Arianism, he wrote, has always been "considered as a *new heresy*, and Unitarianism as an old one." There was no viable claim to "high antiquity" and their claims of a scriptural foundation were nothing but latter-day, favorable, and misconstrued interpretations.[36] He ended his essay with an acknowledgment that his investigation was into the historical origins and manifestations of the Arian ideas; and yet he was also able to show how the Arians of his day continued to accept the foundational premises, failed to draw their interpretations from an understanding of the original sources, and was the product of an intellectual and learned class who refused to allow the common people their own investigations.

"It is very common at this day for persons to pass from Athanasianism to Arianism, and then from Arianism to proper Unitarianism," wrote Priestley in a moment of consideration for the contemporary justi-fication of his ideas.[37] Thus he set out to show in his final letter that Arians were not Unitarians. This last epistle was in response to the author Moderatus, who did write in defense of the Arian doctrine. It documented why, in Priestley's opinion, Socinians were the only proper Unitarians and the only ones who had a right to the appellation. He called Arians polytheistic, potentially, if one would press them on their beliefs, to the point of being unable to limit their number of gods to even the three that they claimed. Taking the literal definition of the term—belief in one god—then only those who rejected all but one divine presence had the right to call themselves Unitarians.[38]

The ideas at the core of this series of essays, though written in 1784, remained the central ideas at the core of Belsham and Channing's dis-pute. By this time, Belsham had seen and read enough of the movement in America to assert that the liberal Christians were, in fact, moving past their Arian beliefs and toward the more proper Socinian Unitarianism.

Building upon Priestley's earlier arguments, Belsham expressed the belief that the New England liberals' reluctance to shed the errors led to a division that was as unnecessary and unwarranted as it was un-Christian. "I have found such unaccountable prejudices against those whom they call the Socinians in more than one of those who call themselves Arians, so as hardly to allow the former to be [considered] Christians, and to have a total reluctance to join with them in the same worship."[39] Belsham

36. Priestley, "History of the Arian Controversy," 320–21, 330–31.
37. Ibid., 336.
38. See Priestley, "Attempt to shew that Arians are not Unitarians."
39. Theophilus Lindsey to William Tayleur, July 24, 1782, in Lindsey, *Letters of Theophilus Lindsey,* 37.

pointed out that New England Unitarians were not as far removed from English Unitarians and Socinianism as they professed, especially in their continued and widespread use of the liturgical work edited by Freeman and based upon the earlier works by Priestley and Lindsey. Likewise, many of the New England religious educational efforts employed the writings of Priestley and Lindsey. One of Priestley's last major American writings, though not of the same philosophical character as most of his other works, was the more practical and useful *Notes on All the Books of Scripture, for the use of the Pulpit and Private Families*. Completed in late 1803, it reflected the nature of Priestley's ministerial efforts in the United States by putting the order for Unitarian rites and scriptural commentary in the hands of the laity and found a wide audience as an instructional tool.

Belsham's arguments did not go unanswered and there was no shortage of willing and able opponents. John Pye Smith, who is best known for his efforts to reconcile science and the Bible, led the opposition in England with a pamphlet titled *Letters to the Rev. Thomas Belsham*. Smith's *Letters* specifically targeted Belsham's funeral discourse rather than the work that was the spark of the immediate controversy, hoping to clarify the present dispute by turning to the original impetus, the man and the ideas Belsham had eulogized. Throughout the work Smith accepted Belsham's contention that Socinianism and Unitarianism were the same, and he used the terms interchangeably, adding to the sweeping scope of his critique and tackling the broadest possible swath of religious liberalism.[40] By questioning Priestley and his theological tenets, and working his way though the entire canon of Socinian writings, Smith felt that if he could disprove the central tenets the rest would all collapse under their own weight.[41]

In his first entry Smith accused Priestley of being too flexible with his definitions and standards when applied to his own views and too rigid with respect to Calvinism. But the real assault came in Letter IV, where Smith attacked Priestley's judgment on religious history as laid out in *History of the Corruptions of Christianity*. Smith rejected Priestley's views on the early Christians and the humanity of Jesus. Those whom Priestley labeled "primitive Christians" were, in the eyes of Smith, the Jewish accusers of Christ. If Priestley considered Jews the foundation of the Church, there was no reason to accept any of his subsequent

---

40. John Pye Smith, *Letters to the Rev. Thomas Belsham*. Smith constantly noted the predominance of Socinianism as the foundation of Unitarian theology in both the United States and England; see especially 58, 61, 91, and 92.

41. Ibid., 143–44.

interpretations because his fundamental idea was itself corrupt.[42] In this Smith surely had the support of all trinitarians.

Smith's *Letters to the Rev. Thomas Belsham* first appeared in serial form, in the *Eclectic Review* (1804). The first American edition appeared in 1809, but found very few readers. Smith, though he must be credited with one of the more significant and notable defenses of the Trinity against the unitarian error, was better known for his ephemeral conflicts, a reputation which often colored the reception of his writings and led many to overlook his string of endless attacks published in the *Eclectic Review*.[43] Smith also chose poorly in his choice of positions to attack Priestley, often using many of Priestley's preliminary statements about Calvinism and Protestantism, those that Priestley had made before subjecting them to careful refutation, as the basis for his own arguments, as when he accused Priestley of hypocrisy for claiming that he found the principles of Calvinism as "generally favorable to that leading virtue, devotion," yet seeking to reject it as a system worthy of adherence.[44] Beyond Smith's personal weaknesses, attacking Priestley was no longer in vogue. Even many of the most ardent critics considered it "unseasonable" to go after Priestley. Critics saw his death as the potential end of Socinianism and feared that such strident attacks could possibly reinvigorate his followers and call renewed attention to his Socinian-Unitarian ideas, as Smith himself admitted in his introduction.[45]

Still, Smith was among those who saw this as the best moment to attack Priestley, justifying their views on the basis of Belsham's renewed efforts and their own self-interested reasons for seeing such matters made public. Congregationalists wished to expose the connections, however tenuous, between Arians and Priestley, Socinianism, and the English Unitarians in order to force the liberals out of their churches. The Baptists and Methodists, both steeped in emotional religion, wished to expose rationalism's disinterestedness and inability to deal with the religious needs of the people. As in any religious contest all parties looked to the possible positive outcomes of spreading their message and expanding their membership at the expense of others.

Jedidiah Morse, Congregationalist minister, founder of the Andover Theological Seminary and constant opponent of liberalism, began the

---

42. Ibid., 144.

43. Smith's most significant contribution was *Scripture Testimony to the Messiah*, which was notable not only for its ability to counter various unitarian scriptural uses, but also its solid restatement of the entire trinitarian position.

44. Smith, *Letters to the Rev. Thomas Belsham*, 58.

45. Ibid., 14–15.

American assault with an 1815 reprinting of Belsham's *American Unitarianism* in Boston. Morse was motivated to this course of action by the prolonged conflict and general discontent over religious control of Harvard, but also by what he considered the perilous decline in trinitarian beliefs.[46] Like Smith, Morse's personal and religious agendas were best served by tacit support for and acceptance of Belsham's arguments; Morse too decried the Arians' reluctance to declare themselves Unitarians, but for reasons entirely his own. Morse believed that the ideas of the New England liberals were more aligned with the ideas of Priestley and the English Unitarians than they admitted, but he did not view the association favorably. The reluctance of the Arians to fully admit their opposition to trinitarian views was proof of their guilt over their association with the English believers. These emotions manifested themselves in deception, inwardly signifying both greed and a lapse in religious principles. Morse lauded an anonymous minister's portrayal of the liberals as "a body . . . nursed in the lap of ease and affluence, and placed in a station of such high secular consideration and comfort" who were reluctant "to come forward and by an open profession of unpopular truth voluntarily risk the loss of all their temporal dignity and comfort, and incur the contempt and enmity of many who are now their warmest admirers and friends."[47] If they were unable to discern the truth for themselves, he argued, then they were not fit to act as members of religious society. Morse's real objective was not to aid the English Unitarians' expansion, but rather to exclude the liberals from sharing in the benefits of religious power in the Massachusetts establishment. Unitarians no matter where they came from or what slight variation of belief they might hold, he concluded, were not Christians and were thus easily grouped together.

Morse's personal views were announced in a review of Belsham's work published in the *Panoplist and Missionary Magazine* and advanced the orthodox agenda by focusing on extracts of letters that Belsham had exchanged with William Wells and James Freeman. Belsham intended his missives to expose support for the English version of the faith in America; Morse used them to show that the actions of Freeman and

---

46. The dispute at Harvard began in 1803 over the issue of an imposed declaration, by the faculty, of an institutional creed. This resulted in a dispute over the selection of faculty who would accept the creed. The Arians (liberals) denounced the Trinitarian (orthodox) attempts to impose a creed and in so doing exposed the degree of dissent that existed within the Congregational denomination. This split was an early sign of the schism that later was codified with the declaration of Unitarianism in 1819, and the subsequent formation of the AUA in 1825. See Robinson, *Unitarians and Universalists,* 33–35.

47. Belsham, *Memoirs,* 208ff.

Wells deceptively seduced unwitting Christians into a false religion. "Defection [into Unitarianism] has gradually increased; has silently and covertly extended itself into a considerable number of congregations in the vicinity; and has been, in a few instances, openly avowed," he wrote, but had not happened innocently or as the result of a fairly conducted exercise in religious choice. Rather, "from a great variety of anonymous publications it has been evident, that the defection has proceeded in the downward course to the lowest degrees of Socinianism, and to the very borders of open infidelity," destroying the Christian character of its followers.[48]

In 1815 an unknown benefactor subsidized the reprinting of Richard Price's *Sermons on the Christian Doctrine as Received by the Different Denominations of Christians* because it offered a more balanced perspective on the issues at the core of this dispute. The first sermon described the common beliefs of all Christians, what Price called the "grand facts" held by the broadly defined categories of Calvinists, Arminians, unitarians, trinitarians, papists, Protestants, and dissenters. The commonalities rested on the idea of one God (without discussing multiple persons) and Christ's teachings as revealed in the Gospels. The points of disagreement—including the humanity of Christ, the state of mortality, the gospel of works, and the resurrection of man—were theologically of lesser importance, so much so that even if one did not agree with Unitarianism the concession had to be made that it nevertheless "maintain[ed] all that we need to be anxious about in Christianity; and that consequently the prejudices against it have no just foundation."[49] Price considered Unitarianism in its broadest possible terms, assigning no animus or giving no preference to any particular derivations beyond the simple rejection of the fullness of the Trinity. "An *Unitarian*, therefore, may or may not be a believer in Christ's preexistence." All who rejected him as God's coequal were Unitarian, and Price set about to ensure that no single faction of liberal antitrinitarian had any more right to this appellation than another.[50] But the dispute surrounding the claim to the name "Unitarian" would not end so simply.

It was at this point that William Ellery Channing, as a result of his public and private exchanges on this very subjects, emerged as the leading liberal spokesman, although not everyone on the liberal side acknowledged his leadership or agreed with his views. Samuel Worcester, the

48. Morse, "Review of American Unitarianism."
49. Price, *Sermons on the Christian Doctrine*, Sermon I, 6–13 and Sermon III, 38.
50. Ibid., Sermon III, 37.

minister at Salem's Tabernacle Church, who would not live to see the outcome of the disagreement between the various sides, advocated that the liberals should remain as they were, within Congregationalism. In a brief pamphlet rebutting Channing, Worcester cautioned his associate against any declaration of separation, suggesting that it would subject the liberals' theological shortcomings to even greater scrutiny, which he doubted would be to their benefit. Such exposure, Worcester argued, was more likely to diminish their stature in the religious arena of New England.[51]

Channing, who took several bold steps toward assuming the title of Unitarian, believed that he could do so while ridding the name of its association with the efforts of the Pennsylvania Unitarians, Priestley, Belsham, and the English Unitarian tradition. This all came to light in a series of exchanges with the Reverend Samuel Thacher. Channing's contention was that fellowship between the Socinians and Arian-Arminian liberals was intolerable, and had been made all the more so when trinitarian Congregationalist Jedidiah Morse reissued Belsham's pamphlet in an attempt to brand the New England liberals as Socinians and force them into the fringes of religious society normally reserved for non-Christians. In rebuttal Channing declared that "*Unitarianism*, as denoting opposition to Trinitarianism, undoubtedly expresses the character of a considerable part of the ministers. . . . But we both of us know that their Unitarianism is of a very different kind from that of Mr. Belsham."[52] The most significant difference, he noted, was the "prevailing sentiment" that Jesus was more than man and was pre-existent, clearly held by the New England ministers and laity.[53] He went on to reject any attempts to link Unitarians with any other class of liberal Christians who held differing views on the divine nature of Jesus, specifically Socinians. The latter, he argued, "form a small proportion of the great body of Unitarians in this part of the country," and cast doubt that any held the full complement of theological views as adopted and professed by English Unitarians. "In giving to the *whole* collection the name *Unitarianism*, and in exhibiting this to the world as the creed of the Liberal Christians in this region, is perhaps as criminal an instance of unfairness as is to be found in the records of theological controversy."[54] He left little doubt; he wanted nothing to do with English

---

51. See Worcester, *Letter to the Rev. William E. Channing*.
52. William Ellery Channing to Rev. Samuel C. Thacher, June 20, 1815, in Channing, *The Life of William Ellery Channing*, 196; italics in the original.
53. Ibid.
54. Ibid., italics in the original.

Unitarians or their Socinian theology. Their standing as the recognized Unitarians, however, proved a significant impediment to his plans.

Like all people, Channing was the product of his education. This was particularly true in the case of his unitarian beliefs. His studies at Harvard, notes one historian, were "strangely lacking in evangelical and orthodox writers. Judging by the charging lists of the college library . . . nothing by Edwards or Hopkins seems to have attracted him. Instead he was reading English and Scottish writers, of a rationalistic and even at times Socinian temper," a list that included Thomas Belsham, Richard Price, and Joseph Priestley, English Unitarians all.[55] He also spent a period of eighteen months reading Priestley's philosophical and theological writings while living with the family of Edmund Randolph in Virginia. He even wrote a letter in which he revealed that his theological studies closely followed the path of Priestley and other English Unitarians—from the evidences of Christianity to the history of religious corruption.[56] But reading them did not convince him of their wisdom.

Struggling to find an appropriate appellation for his beliefs, Channing at first adopted the name "Liberal Christian," a term that he defended in an explanatory footnote. But he also began laying the groundwork for taking up the name "Unitarian." Throughout the letter, which Channing wrote with the intention of public dissemination, he repeatedly refers to his use of the word "Unitarian" with the clarifying phrases "in the proper sense of that word," or "in the proper meaning of that word,"[57] replicating the phraseology used by Priestley in order to employ its intentions to the benefit of his cause and reject the calls for a broader, more inclusive understanding of Unitarianism put forth by Belsham.

Channing's proper meaning meant Arianism and it was clear that he felt forced by the looming controversy to establish that his unitarianism was a theological position, used only to indicate his rejection of the Trinity, but in no way was it to be construed (yet) as being part and parcel of a denominational appellation or as one aspect of a complex and multifaceted theology. Ironically, he also spent a great deal of time in his writings defining Liberal Christianity as a belief system that permitted theological openness and was against exclusivity.[58]

55. Wright, *Liberal Christians*, 26. There is additional evidence that the works of Priestley, which were donated to Harvard by Theophilus Lindsey, were popular not just with Channing, but were widely circulated and in demand as accepted reading for many undergraduates. See Cooke, *Unitarianism in America*, 79.

56. Channing, *Memoirs*, 1:122–23.

57. Ibid., 198.

58. Ibid., 195–96. For the Priestley quotation, see Price, *Sermons on the Christian Doctrine*, Notes, 105.

A Convoluted Faith

Channing fully planned, at the height of the Unitarian controversy, to claim the Unitarian mantle for Liberal Christianity while rejecting any connection with English Unitarianism. "With Dr. Priestley, a good and great man," he wrote, "I have less sympathy than with the 'Orthodox.'" Channing's statements on Priestley were always qualified, although toward the end of his life they became less zealous in their critical tone and carefully calculated to rid Unitarianism of Priestley's influence.[59] John Pierpont summarized the objectives of Channing and those who joined with him when he said: "We have and must have the Unitarian name."[60] Taking the name and eliminating Priestley's influence were not easily accomplished, as Channing himself lamented in 1839. "This system was, at its recent revival, a protest of the understanding against absurd dogmas, rather than the work of deep religious principles, and was early paralyzed by the mixture of a material philosophy, and fell too much into the hands of scholars and political reformers," he noted in a thinly veiled reference to Priestley and English Socinianism. "And the consequence is a want of vitality and force which gives us little hope of its accomplishing much under its present auspices, or in its present form."[61]

Channing began by tackling the arguments of his Congregationalist brethren. In his response to Jedidiah Morse's accusations that Unitarianism was everywhere and an ever-present danger, Channing acknowledged the existence of many versions of Unitarianism. Morse was correct, he wrote, if Unitarianism was defined as nothing more than "opposition to Trinitarianism."[62] But wise to the methods of his opponents, who often used such sweeping definitions to cast aspersions on all liberals, Channing argued that critiques were only valid if they were confined to the specific and narrower view of Unitarianism of the Boston liberals. To further deflect his critics, he claimed no need to read Priestley's errant writings and said that if being a Unitarian was defined according to Priestley's terms, then he was, in fact, not a Unitarian.[63] Channing's tactic was to acknowledge the multitude of views stemming from the unitarian idea, but to redirect all criticisms onto the more radical Socinianism. In the end, he hoped to prove that the efforts of the

59. Channing, *The Works of William Ellery Channing*, 407.
60. John Pierpont, quoted in Lyttle, *Freedom Moves West*, 22.
61. Channing, *Memoir*, 2:404.
62. Channing, *Letter to the Rev. Samuel C. Thacher*, 6.
63. See Channing, *Memoir*, 2:379–80, 390, and 444.

orthodox to attach a single label to multiple groups were untenable and obscured the distinctions among them.

The culminating elucidation of the "new" Unitarianism, or what one later adherent has called "the Pentecost of American Unitarianism," and "the distinguishing circumstance of them all," came on May 5, 1819, when Channing delivered the sermon "Unitarian Christianity" at the First Unitarian Church of Baltimore at the installation of Jared Sparks as their first minister.[64] The ideas he outlined in his sermon became the platform of the denomination that followed, openly joining unitarianism with Congregationalist polity and identity (many of the churches, in fact, retained their former names), moralism, and religious rites. To do so, Channing was forced to employ a "system of exclusion and denunciation," ridding his beliefs of all associations with many of the earlier manifestations of Unitarianism and denouncing the liberals' past reluctance to assume an independent identity.[65] This was a complicated task. The Baltimore society had been formed as a result of James Freeman's influence much as the Philadelphia society had emerged as a result of Priestley's. Freeman preached in Baltimore three times in 1816, drawing ever larger crowds. The church was started when a group of local men were inspired by Freeman and met at the house of Henry Payson the following year with the intention of starting their own religious society. Construction on the chapel was begun and completed in 1818 and dedicated on November 29. Though Freeman was geographically distant from the society, he remained their theological inspiration and returned to deliver the chapel's dedication sermon in ceremonies presided over by the Reverend Henry Coleman of Hingham, another minister who was a follower of Priestley.[66]

The task of delivering the installation sermon fell to Channing almost naturally. At the time of the Baltimore sermon he had already served as the minister to the congregation of the Federal Street Church in Boston for sixteen years, a position he held until his death in 1842. Though a controversial figure, his intellectual stature was unquestioned. His role

64. Lyttle, quoting Dr. Burnap, in *Pentecost of American Unitarianism*, 3. See Channing, *Unitarian Christianity*.

65. Conrad Wright, "Institutional Reconstruction in the Unitarian Controversy," in Wright, *American Unitarianism, 1805–1865*, 3–4. Wright is most concerned with the impact of the conflict on the "ecclesiastical institutions of New England." Accordingly, he dismisses the need for any further investigation into the "theological adjustment to enlightenment currents of thought," which he claims, somewhat ironically, were responsible for the "intellectual capital on which the liberal Christians drew" throughout the early period of development.

66. Sprague, *Annals of the American Pulpit*, 8:xvi.

in the dispute over control of Harvard proved that he was the equal of virtually any other religious figure. Channing specifically chose the Baltimore installation to reveal his views. Seeking to eliminate the Socinian legacy, his decision to reveal a new version of the faith in Baltimore was a clear message to all sides in the conflict. He not only sought to end the controversy but to pull the Baltimore flock into his sphere of influence.[67] Channing selectively recounted the history of the Baltimore congregation in order to help effect his desired change. He maintained that the Unitarian congregation's existence in Baltimore signified the appeal of his theological position across regional boundaries, strengthening his claim to speak for all American Unitarians and ignored the connections to Priestley and Freeman. In fact, Sparks asked Channing to account for the diversity of Unitarian views, knowing that the entrenched Unitarian identity was actually Socinian. Such a request called for "the presence of some gentlemen who are remote from Boston, to prove to our southern brethren that our peculiarities are not confined to this town," noted Channing in a letter inviting a fellow minister from Maine to attend.[68] The New England intellectual and theological leaders turned out in force. Present among the assembly were the president of Harvard Divinity School, John T. Kirkland, young John Gorham Palfrey, and Henry Ware Sr., a man of great importance in his own right.[69] Ware had been at the center of the Harvard controversy when his appointment as the Hollis Professor of Divinity at the college in 1805 had been quite contentious. Many considered it the first public expression of liberal and Unitarian sentiment among New England Calvinists. Palfrey, one of the younger generation of emerging leaders, was instrumental in the movement to give Unitarianism a more traditional denominational structure.

Although Channing sometimes wavered on the issue of institutionalization, Palfrey and others never did. Their much publicized appearance at the Channing sermon signaled that this group of liberal Congregationalists intended to make a bold statement and that the heretofore internal theological controversy was about to be made very public. In Baltimore the growing need for a formal theological declaration and the building of an institutionalized structure took definitive shape for

67. See Lyttle, *Pentecost of American Unitarianism*, 3.

68. Channing to unknown , May 15, 1815, Archives of the First Unitarian Church at Baltimore, Maryland; quoted in Ahlstrom and Carey, *American Reformation*, 90.

69. See ibid., 90–91, for their introductory remarks on the occasion of the sermon and those who were present. See Robinson, *Unitarians and Universalists*, 33–38, for a concise history on the development of Unitarian religious institutions.

those who held that the Trinity was a logical impossibility. Intending to make Unitarians out of the unitarians, Channing selected 1 Thessalonians 21, "Prove all things; hold fast that which is good," to set the tone. He opened by calling upon Unitarianism's opponents to give him a fair hearing before passing judgment. "The principles adopted by the class of *Christians* in whose name I speak, need to be explained, because they are often misunderstood." Building upon these ideas he undertook an exploration of the areas shared with the orthodox. First, he looked at the Bible. "Our leading principle in interpreting Scripture is this," he claimed, "the Bible is a book written for men, in the language of men, and that its meaning is to be sought in the same manner as that of other books," that is, through reason and interpretation. Without such tools of the mind, he argued, all Christians were powerless to understand the word of God, which God himself through Jesus had promised man would be able to comprehend. He contended that "the existence and veracity of God, and the divine origin of Christianity, are conclusions of reason, and must stand or fall with it."[70]

Channing presented his five central tenets of Unitarianism. First was the belief that "the doctrine of God's UNITY, or that there is one God, and one only," which, based on scripture, led him to insist on the humanity of Christ. "We worship the Father, as the only living and true God."[71] The second doctrine, the rejection of the divinity of Jesus, was the most important and the one most likely to give offense to other Christians. Confident in his theology, Channing confronted the issue directly. "We complain of the doctrine of the Trinity, that, not satisfied with making God three beings, it makes Jesus Christ two beings; and thus introduces infinite confusion into our conceptions of his character. This corruption of Christianity, alike repugnant to common sense and to the general strain of Scripture, is a remarkable proof of the power of a false philosophy in disfiguring the simple truth of Jesus."[72] Such views led him to amplify the idea of corruption upon which Unitarianism had long staked its birthright, "that Christianity is, at this moment, dishonored by gross and cherished corruptions."[73] In describing the remaining three points, Channing detailed the evidences for the moral perfection of God, the spiritual mission of Christ, and the basis of morality. New England liberal Christians believed that both social and moral evils were created by human beings, not imposed by God,

70. Channing, *Unitarian Christianity*, 7.
71. Ibid., 9.
72. Ibid., 17.
73. Ibid., 24.

and therefore could be remedied by human efforts. Even in these early years, before their denominational formation, Unitarian believers were closely identified with social and political reform, the basis of which was their view of the mission of Christ.

Channing's position was calculated to separate his followers from the Congregationalists and other trinitarians, who were not simply going to concede ground to the New England liberals without careful examination. By stressing the significance of reason within Unitarianism, particularly as it applied to the Trinity, he had challenged the core of their faith. "We are particularly accused of making an unwarrantable use of reason in the interpretation of scripture," he noted, and of using it as the basis for all derivative doctrines and practices.[74] But reason was not something to be feared. It was crucial in the justifications for any religion. According to Channing the central beliefs of Unitarians and orthodox were similar, if not identical: the moral perfection of God, the spiritual mission of Christ, and morality. All that set them apart were the ideas of God's unity and the unity of Jesus. Channing acknowledged that these latter principles constituted significant religious differences, but he emphasized, not ones that undermined common ground. Channing believed that a public profession would correct the misperceptions that endangered their association. Trinitarian fears of the "godless Unitarians" in the midst of a pious nation might "give a degree of influence to principles which they deem false and injurious." But it was preferable to have such views out in the open and subject to debate. Channing assured the trinitarians that a public forum was the ideal occasion to accept or reject any doctrines.[75]

When the sermon had concluded, his listeners were well aware that they had just witnessed the first open declaration in which Channing dropped the "Liberal Christian" title and claimed the Unitarian name for his beliefs. Within six years Channing would move to institutionalize his efforts and spread his version of Unitarian beliefs through the formation of the American Unitarian Association.

Denouncing Priestley

Channing's sermon gave the New England Arians a theological structure and a means to proactively propagate their beliefs instead of merely

74. Ibid., 4.
75. Ibid., 3.

reacting to the challenges of others. The sermon's heavy emphasis on theology came at a time in America's history when religion was becoming increasingly individualistic, charismatic, and emotional. Its disregard for Priestley's legacy was an attempt to cast Unitarianism in terms that trinitarians might find acceptable and that the New England Arians could identify with. He hoped this would allow his fellow believers to slip quietly into their new name without an uproar.

Channing's sermon, however, failed to put any of the controversies surrounding Unitarianism to rest.[76] First to speak out were those who viewed Channing's efforts as an attempt to quell the tide of emotionalism. In the year following "Unitarian Christianity," Samuel Miller, a Presbyterian and professor of ecclesiastical history and church government at Princeton Theological Seminary, made a trip, echoing Channing's, to Baltimore to deliver an ordination sermon. Miller's visit was an attempt to retake the theological and moral ground from the Unitarians. In his discourse, "God in the Flesh: Letters on Unitarianism," he contended that Unitarians had no right to call themselves Christians and that it was impossible to derive unitarian foundations from the teachings of Christ. As a result, Miller argued, Unitarians were not entitled to the tolerance accorded to the variety of other denominations underneath the umbrella of the Christian tradition. Miller's homily sought to expose the "evils of Unitarianism" and the deceptions behind free inquiry. His task was to depict rationalism as an attempt to undermine all faiths, so that "orthodox Christians can guard against the inroads of Unitarian errors."[77] Miller went even further in his second sermon and labeled Unitarians "nonbelievers," and defended Calvinism while rejecting all claims of affinity and association between Unitarianism and orthodoxy.[78] Andover Seminary's Moses Stuart joined the fray by coming to Channing's defense on the issue of the right of free inquiry and asserting that Unitarians adhered

76. Over the course of the next several years Channing authored additional sermons as measures of clarification and in response to further challenges from the orthodox opposition. Among them were *The Moral Argument Against Calvinism* (1820), *Likeness to God* (1828), and *Self Culture* (1838).

77. Miller, *God in the Flesh*, 3. Miller was a long-time opponent of Unitarianism having engaged Jefferson in a dialogue concerning his religious views while the latter was president. Miller felt that Jefferson's stance on fast days, and his refusal to call for one, was a sign of his godlessness. Jefferson's reply stands as one of the standards of interpretation on the First Amendment and the free exercise clause. See Jefferson to Rev. Samuel Miller, January 23, 1808, in *The Writings of Thomas Jefferson*, 1186–87.

78. Miller continued his writings against such errors in *Letters on the Eternal Sonship of Christ*. Miller's reply to his critics is attached to this work as a "Letter to the Editor," which was originally printed in the *Unitarian Miscellany*.

to fundamental Christian values. But he rejected the prominence assigned to rationalism in Unitarianism's theological system and extended the critiques against its views on salvation. He was joined in his efforts by fellow Andover professor Leonard Woods. In his reply to Channing's "Unitarian Christianity," Woods thought it necessary to distinguish, repeatedly, between the Unitarianism that sprang up in New England and that which Priestley had brought to the United States from England, even as he critiqued them on the basis of their commonalities—most centrally their rejection of the Trinity. Numerous other opponents employed similar rhetorical and divisive tactics.[79] Though Miller, Stuart, and Woods all professed many of the same religious principles, Stuart represented the more tolerant wing of the orthodox believers and was far more forgiving of the Unitarian errors. In the end, Stuart still rejected Channing's conclusions but at least it was not for the lack of giving them a fair hearing.[80] These attacks by various trinitarians, many of whom had earlier been in fellowship with the liberal Congregationalists, exposed a weakness in Channing's plan. As some of the detractors within his own body of liberals had feared, there was no possible theological foundation for Unitarianism that the trinitarian majority would find tenable. Nonetheless, within his own network of believers his efforts were ultimately a success and gave New England liberals the leadership of Unitarianism.

As Channing wove his theological design, he was conscious of the legacy passed down to the New England liberals from the collective theology of European free-thinkers as well as the liberal heritage of American Protestantism. "When Channing came to announce the new reading of the gospel of peace, he did not bring any new thing to the ears of the people, or declare to them an unknown God," reflected George Batchelor some years later.[81] But Channing did promote a different theology when he assumed the old name. When he put forward the Arian vision of Christ, that he was divine and more special than man but not one with God, as a replacement for the Socinian Unitarian theology, he was advocating a drastic shift in understanding. Channing was well aware of the prevalence of Socinian ideas throughout the Middle Atlantic states and the South and could not easily have ignored Freeman's acceptance of most of its tenets. Nonetheless, he stayed with the more familiar concepts, including the Arian conception of

79. Woods, *Letters to Unitarians*. See his specific comparisons and differentiations on pages 5, 131, 134, 149, 152.
80. See Stuart, *Letters to the Rev. Wm. E. Channing*.
81. Batchelor, *Social Equilibrium*, 273.

Christ, because, in his words and in his mind, "only a small minority believed in the simple humanity of Jesus."[82] These believers were to be excluded from his newly defined Unitarianism. He was not seeking to establish an all-inclusive Unitarianism, but rather, to represent the views of those in New England who professed his version of the unitarian idea.

Channing was aware, however, that no matter how much he desired to distance himself from the legacy of English Unitarianism and Socinianism, he would never be completely free of an association with it. And it was an association that continued to haunt him right up until his own death. "I have felt that that [Socinian] doctrine, with its natural connections, was a millstone around the neck of Unitarianism in England," he wrote in 1839 a full twenty years after his initial declaration. "I have always lamented that Dr. Priestley's authority had fastened this doctrine on his followers," noting especially how it had hampered efforts to espouse a rational doctrine and still remain a part of Congregationalism and the Protestant community among the liberals in the United States.[83] Two years later Channing openly attacked Priestley in a letter to New York College's George Bush, by outlining his own objections to the Trinity and denouncing Priestley's efforts to establish Unitarianism in America as he had done in England. "In saying this, I do not speak as a Unitarian, but as an Independent Christian," he related to Bush. "I have little or no interest in Unitarians *as a sect*. I hardly have anything to do with them. I can endure no sectarian bonds. With Dr. Priestley, a good and great man, who had most to do in producing the late Unitarian movement, I have less sympathy than with many of the 'Orthodox.'"[84] He ended his letter by hinting at an upcoming address he had scheduled to deliver to the Philadelphia Unitarians, in which he planned to detail his reasoning behind his aversion to Priestley's Unitarianism.

In the final years of his life, English Unitarianism continued to eat away at Channing's sense of proper Unitarian dignity, theology, and acceptance. He returned again and again to the topic of Priestley, championing him as a person, but denying his value as a formative theological influence. In a letter to the Englishman William Trevilcock, Channing was unable to reconcile his earlier professions of "the cause of *religious liberty*. To vindicate the rights of the mind, to maintain intellectual freedom, to withstand intolerance . . . this has been nearer my

82. Channing, *Unitarian Christianity*, 112.

83. William Ellery Channing to Rev. James Martineau, November 29, 1839, in Channing, *The Life of William Ellery Channing*, 447.

84. William Ellery Channing to Professor George Bush, May 8, 1841, in Channing, *The Life of William Ellery Channing, D.D.*, 427.

heart than to secure a triumph to any distinguishing doctrine of a sect," an idea that he often repeated, demanding that his followers abandon the sectarian strife so often found in other denominations.[85] Instead he now found himself once again denouncing Priestley; if being associated with Priestley was what it meant to be a Unitarian in America, he wrote Trevilcock, then "I am little of a Unitarian; [I hold] little sympathy with the system of Priestley and Belsham, and stand aloof from all but those who strive and pray for a clearer light."[86]

The publication of his sermon delivered in Philadelphia before the First Unitarian Church revealed the depth and fervor of his lasting opposition. The symbolism of his decision to deliver a sermon to the Pennsylvania congregation at such a late stage of his life should not be overlooked. In the sermon Channing was respectful of Priestley's character yet denounced his theology and never once mentioned Priestley by name when it came time to attack the theological ideas he abhorred. It was a well practiced tactic, one that he had tried out in a letter two years earlier to James Martineau, one of Priestley's English disciples. In the letter to Martineau Channing noted that many people had accused him of "using *patronizing* language towards Dr. Priestley," but such was not his intent. "I must be strangely wanting in humility," he wrote, "if I did not feel my great inferiority to that extraordinary man, or if I could think of him as needing my patronage. The truth is," he noted, as he turned the subject toward their theological differences, "that I could never speak of him without qualification, in consequence of my deep conviction of injury done to the cause of truth by his speculations on the moral nature of man, reaching, as they must do, to the moral nature of God."[87] The qualifications always included Priestley's theological drift into Socinianism and his insistence on the materialism of the soul.

In his sermon, Channing went right to the heart of his disagreement with Priestley, the nature of Jesus' divinity, and reaffirmed his own belief and standing among Christians. "There *is* one grand all-comprehending church," he preached, "and as I am a Christian I belong to it, and no man can shut me out of it. You may exclude me from your Roman church, your Episcopal church, and your Calvinistic church, on account of supposed defects in my creed or my sect, and I am content to be

85. Channing, *Memoirs*, 2:369, 373.
86. William Ellery Channing to Mr. W. Trevilcock, August 29, 1841, in Channing, *The Life of William Ellery Channing*, 427.
87. Channing to Martineau, November 29, 1839, in ibid., 447.

excluded. But I will not be severed from the great body of Christ."[88] Priestley, on the other hand, had done just that. Channing continued to hold that Jesus was divine, miraculous, and separate from other men. Equally, Priestley's denial of Christ's divinity and claims to Socinian exclusivity meant a denial of his freedom from sin and moral evil, and a rejection of his creation in the perfect image of God. He had trouble seeing, then, how the authority of Jesus and the scriptures could be upheld if so many of these preconditions were rejected.[89] Yet Channing did not dismiss Priestley's lesser theological contributions to religious inquiry and was charitable to him by name. His appeal for God to "over- turn the strong-holds of spiritual usurpation" in order that "the con- spiracy of ages against the liberty of Christians may be brought to an end," was taken straight from the annals of English Unitarianism.[90] Since the liberal Christians had hidden behind the mantle of Congre- gationalism and it had not experienced such attacks, Channing was forced to adopt one of Priestley's central arguments, that Christianity had experienced centuries of distortion and must be corrected. This was a keystone of Priestley's theological argumentation.[91] He did, however, downplay the latter's contributions toward furthering such ideas and practices in the Enlightened age. "Individuals are better than their creed; and amidst gross error and the inculcation of a narrow spirit noble virtues spring up, and eminent Christians are formed . . . in the Anti-trinitarian church, John Milton, John Locke, Samuel Clarke, Price and Priestley. To repeat these names does the heart good," he shared with the congregation. Yet he blamed Priestley and others for their sec- tarian impulses. "With the churches of which they were pillars or chief ornaments, I have many sympathies," provided that those sympathies were expressed with equal scorn for their "spirit of sectarianism . . . shutting up God in any denomination" and for thinking that theirs was the one true word.[92]

The continuous association between the new Unitarianism and Priestley's Unitarianism signaled a weakness that Channing was anxious to overcome. It allowed the orthodox a wider basis from which they could continue to challenge and oppose the liberals. Channing knew

88. William Ellery Channing, *The Church*, 26.

89. William Ellery Channing to Miss E. P. Peabody, July 6, 1841, in Channing, *The Life of William Ellery Channing*, 449–51.

90. Channing, *The Church*, 12.

91. Priestley, *History of the Corruptions of Christianity*.

92. Channing, *The Church*, 32–34.

well the story of the development of Unitarianism in Pennsylvania and lamented that his actions would take a toll on the conception of a broad liberal religious fellowship. But the strength of the orthodoxy, in numbers, power, and presence, brought him to the more immediate realization that his proposal for adopting the Unitarian name could only be accomplished by a dissociation. The prominence of the revivalist spirit in the nation and the lasting legacies of a Congregationalist-inspired establishment did not allow him and his followers the luxury of embracing all manifestations and expressions of rationalist thought. He played a very complex game in his quest. "Traditional Calvinist doctrines could be skirted or suppressed by the early liberals, and at the same time an evangelical temper [could] be communicated to the congregation." Continuing to walk the tightrope of being unitarian in sentiment and avowing oneself Christian meant that the liberals would have to be "temperamentally inclined towards this kind of accommo-dation."[93] It was an uneasy transformation that he hoped to effect and a multifaceted Unitarianism might lead to even greater resistance from the New England establishment. Most dangerous of all, noted Channing, was the potential outcomes of Priestley's rationalism, an outcome that undermined Channing's constant attempts to remain an important and established partner in the American Christian com-munity. Priestley had once written that "should free inquiry lead to the destruction of Christianity itself, it ought not on that account be discontinued. For we can only wish for the prevalence of Christianity on the supposition of its being true; and if it falls before the influence of free inquiry, it can only do so in consequence of its not being true."[94] Channing was adamantly opposed to a course of thought that would allow rationalism to relegate Christianity to irrelevance. He argued that rationalism would lose its purpose once it was at a crossroads with Christianity, and that those who took it to such extremes were not true Christians. Christians needed to ward off rationalist extremes.[95] Finally, Channing was no more inclined to accept Socinianism as part and parcel of his collective than Priestley had been willing to accept Arianism. William Sprague, who chronicled the first century of American religious groups reflected on these developments when he noted that Channing's efforts resulted in Unitarianism becoming "much more decided in its manifestations, and the line between the two parties," Socinian and

93. Wright, *Liberal Christians*, 30.
94. Ibid., 23.
95. Channing, *Unitarian Christianity*, 112.

Arian, "which had before been faint and scarcely discernable, began to take a form of decided visibility."[96]

The continuous existence of groups adhering to Priestley's legacy and theology, however, made Channing's task all the more difficult. The Socinian Unitarians represented a visible and viable competing group, at least in terms of attention paid to them by the orthodox, who pointed to them to demonstrate that liberalism was unable to clearly define itself, and in the energy expended by liberals themselves to clarify the distinctions. The Priestleyan societies possessed a theological integrity—especially in the areas of rationalism, moralism, and the foundations of revealed religion—maintained an established identity, and actively sustained a link to the increasingly important Unitarian denomination in England.[97] These Unitarians, who had held claim to the title for almost a quarter of a century adhering to Priestley's fundamental ideas, had gained a measure of acceptance. Though they were not part of the traditional religious establishment in the United States, they nonetheless held an accepted position. For their part, they continued to publicly pronounce that Priestley was a central figure in all Unitarian and liberal theological systems, further arguing that the central tenets of Priestley's ministry were the same as those of Channing's proposed ministry, and highlighting the foundational nature of reason, revelation, and inquiry to all forms of liberal Christianity. Though their earlier efforts at institutionalization progressed slowly, they were stable, for as those who independently chronicled America's religious developments have shown, English Unitarianism held its own. Priestley's efforts were equally focused on developing the faith of Unitarianism as a denomination and for the benefit of the individual. Those who point to his decision to decline ministerial positions in both New York and Philadelphia overlook that he had equally optimistic hopes for a full-fledged English émigré settlement in the Susquehanna Valley, where it was anticipated that he would be of more value in firmly establishing the faith.[98] That he could not know that this settlement would fail cannot be used to demonstrate that he had no interest in setting up an institutionalized religion. But Priestley was equally aware that he was living at a time when one's religion could not always be ascertained by or secured through the structures of a formal denomination. His plans always accounted for this, both for himself and his followers. "Whatever men

---

96. Sprague, *Annals of the American Pulpit*, 8:xvi.
97. Robinson, *Unitarians and the Universalists*, 9–10.
98. Ibid., 23.

may intend, or execute, all their designs, and all their actions, are subject
to the secret influence and guidance of one who is necessarily the best
judge of what will most promote his own excellent purposes," he wrote
in 1777. According to Priestley, God's excellent purposes were those
that were most consistent and rational and produced the best effect
within each individual. A denominational organization was not always
in God's plans.[99]

The new Unitarians also had to contend with the continuing presence
of a very vocal and involved English Unitarian community. Though the
numbers of English Unitarian émigrés that Priestley had been holding
out for never materialized, there was a constant influx of ministers and
lay people who sustained the links between the two nations. Furthermore, Belsham, who had for all intents and purposes instigated much
of the controversy and set in motion the events that led to Channing's
actions, continued in his role as spokesman for the Unitarians. One
year after Channing's sermon, Belsham revised his *Memoirs of the Late
Reverend Theophilus Lindsey* to serve as a response. Updating his remarks
on the history of Unitarianism in America and focusing on the newly
highlighted attempts to treat Arianism as if it were the only unitarian-
inspired theology, Belsham set out to preserve Priestley's legacy and
predict Channing's failure.

> Dr. Priestley and others descended from the heights of ortho-
> doxy to the plains of Unitarianism through the medium of
> Arianism. I am therefore very far from intending the slightest
> disparagement to those who hold the Arian doctrine, as I
> myself for many years very honestly did, with perhaps a slight
> modification of what is now called the indwelling scheme,
> *in whatever language I may now think it right to enter my protest
> against it.* . . . [M]odern Arianism . . . is polytheism in its
> strictest sense. But modern Arians, as if they were determined
> to recede as far as possible from the letter of Scripture, having
> thus defined their Lord and Master, and raised him into the
> situation of a substitute for the Supreme Being, strangely, and
> in direct opposition to the dictates of common sense and to
> the plainest language of Scripture, deny him the worship and
> homage due to the rank and character to which they have
> elevated him. . . . It is indeed astonishing that so many wise
> and good men should be so blind to the plain consequences of

99. Priestley, *Disquisitions,* 450.

their own opinions, and should fancy that they are Unitarians, when they believe not only in two, but in two hundred thousand gods. But as Dr. Price says, we are apt to wonder at one another: and it is almost impossible to make sufficient allowance for the strength of early prejudice and the influence of fixed principles. But at least I think it would be allowed me that, while I entertain these sentiments of the Arian hypothesis, I cannot very consistently class Arians with Unitarians.[100]

Belsham denounced Channing's attempts to recast the history and theology of American Unitarianism in such new terms. While he conceded that Channing's actions were likely to "redeem the liberal theologians in America from the censure of concealing what they believe to be the truth," they were equally unlikely to bring them into fellowship with the real Unitarians.[101]

Belsham, however, did not fully appreciate the importance of Channing's numerical advantage and how the concept of majoritarianism was fast becoming a staple of American affairs, religious or otherwise. Channing also had the advantage of operating in a religious atmosphere conducive to his ideas. Though not in total accord with it, the standing religious order in America was more tolerant of a religion that maintained ties with emotionalism and whose criticisms of the Trinity only went so far. Many trinitarians were able to accept the new Unitarianism because its principles were familiar to them; their congregations had long debated such questions. Belsham was at a greater disadvantage, given the distance—both physical and theological. He faced American suspicion of the English, and he wrote from the perspective of an English Unitarianism that was itself undergoing a religious transformation.[102]

Nonetheless, Channing's inability to completely effect the adoption of his views, the nagging accusations as to the irrationality of his theology, his attempts to please both the liberals and the orthodox within Congregationalism, his use of several key ideas that were promulgated by those whom he declared as adversaries, and his forfeiture of an association with the Unitarians already in existence resulted in greater confusion

100. Belsham, *Memoirs*, 209–12.
101. Ibid., 214.
102. This transformation was effected by Robert Aspland, who took over the pulpit of the New Gravel Pit Chapel at Hackney, once occupied by Price, Priestley, and Belsham. Aspland, beginning in 1805, effected a transition within the faith, pressing for institutionalization, the establishment of more formal organizations and religious orders and rites. He eventually brought the Unitarians in England their religious and civil liberties as well as their first national structure. Aspland was a strong follower of Priestley's teachings.

than he could have ever anticipated. While many liberals rallied to his cause, the movement was not universally adopted, and confusion and competition continued to develop over the course of the nineteenth century, leading to the need for continuous refinement of Unitarian views. Other challenges quickly emerged as well. These challenges, most notable among them the humanism of Transcendentalism, required a response, and one of the best answers was to be found in Priestley's legacy and his followers. The unique theological thread followed by Priestley and the Pennsylvania Unitarians was cut, but it would be repaired.

The American Unitarian Association and Joseph Priestley

In 1835, Henry Ware Jr., having just completed his term as secretary of the American Unitarian Association (AUA), called for a reevaluation of the Socinian controversy and the legacy of Joseph Priestley in the development of Unitarianism. His primary objective was to stay the tide of the denomination's slide into unfettered rationalism. Though Transcendentalism had yet to emerge by name, the strains of "excess" it represented already presented a formidable challenge to Unitarianism. It threatened to make all Unitarians infidels in the eyes of the trinitarians, thus confirming the greatest fears of both Priestley and Channing and giving credence to the orthodox critiques of the decades past. As one part of a very complex response, Ware felt that the battle against infidelity required a return to some of the more temperate ideas behind Priestley's theology. Ware's objective, however, was complicated by the fact that Socinianism still carried considerable opprobrium and separating out the most unacceptable elements was no easy task.

The dialogue on Socinianism remained ever-present despite the absence of an even respectable minority to promulgate its ideas. Indeed, the Unitarians, after they had taken to accepting the term and calling themselves by that name, were constantly engaged in discussions concerning the presence of Socinian ideas. The pages of the *Unitarian Miscellany* reflected this tendency; every edition included references to Socinianism's legacy, both positive and negative, throughout the editorial reign of both Jared Sparks and F.W.P. Greenwood. The same holds true for Priestley, as his name was constantly invoked in order to establish or refute select theological opinions.[103] One volume, that

---

103. Priestley was a constant source of reference on the matter of conversion of the Jews. See Sparks, "Notes on Priestley," 222–36.

of February 1823, contained a letter to the editor titled "Dialogue on Unitarianism," in which two gentlemen traveling on a steamboat exchanged views on religious developments in the United States. The exchange characterized Unitarianism as being full of misrepresentations, prejudice, and ignorance, especially when the "Elderly Gentleman" involved in the conversation to discuss the Unitarians in New York as Socinian. Clearly, substantial animus toward Priestley and English Socinianism remained.[104]

Ware sought to disarm the historical and theological objections by arguing that rationalist-inspired infidelity was a greater danger to Unitarianism than Priestley's legacy and theology. He claimed that the passage of time had erased the distinctions emphasized by Channing and that now Socinianism was a counter to greater dangers. "The commotion has been extensive, the tossing has been fearful, the alarm and bustle of those exposed to the spray has been loud and earnest. At length the height of the swell seems to have passed . . . and it is time to look about us, and see what is the result . . . what use is to be made of the losses and the acquisitions of the contest."[105] Ware, the son of the renowned professor and a notable minister in his own right, specifically pointed to the period of Socinian dominance as a defining moment in Unitarianism's past, providing lessons for the ongoing transition from "inwardness" to "orthodoxy" that continued to plague Unitarianism.[106]

Ware hoped to redirect the denomination's course and rescue the Socinian influences from the obscurity into which they had been pushed by an important and influential group of ministers and laymen. English Unitarianism and its related ideas did not fare so well in the reformulation of Unitarianism following 1819. The New England adherents had gained the upper hand as a result of their substantial numbers, the retention of the established houses of worship, and continued connections to the political and cultural establishments. They then moved the faith in a different direction and were reluctant to identify with Priestley's Socinianism. The shift was such that intense animosity was not hard to find. "The Athanasiuses, the Cyrils, the Appllonariuses, the Jerieus, the Priestleys, the Topladys, &c, are not considered as the men who have most promoted the knowledge of the Bible. They made a great noise in their age, and now they are dead and almost forgotten," wrote one Unitarian commentator. "Peace to their ashes, I

104. "Dialogue on Unitarianism. To the Editor," 37–44.
105. Ware, *Sober Thoughts*, 1–2.
106. James, *Varieties of Religious Experience*, 369.

say, and peace to all the souls they have ever disturbed. I hope they will all die—just as soon as God pleases."[107]

Others on both sides of the Atlantic copied Ware's attempt to safeguard Priestley's legacy. Not all of the new Unitarians were willing to simply forget the lessons learned from the earlier crises, nor were they all at ease with the Arian-focused theology Channing had advocated. Priestley's Unitarianism continued to thrive in England, and the transatlantic exchange assured that its contributions to liberal religion would not simply disappear. Priestley's theology still formed the core of English Unitarian thought and his liturgy was still the form of worship practiced throughout that nation. English Unitarians remained in touch with their American cousins and were well informed about the course of events surrounding the religion and the English commentaries on American Unitarianism's development were both provocative and influential. Furthermore, many English believers still honored Priestley for bearing the initial burdens of religious dissent and forcing the realm to accept alternatives to the established church.

The American Unitarians interested in parts of Priestley's theology, and in a resurrection of the English Socinian foundations, were a varied group. Ware, James Freeman Clarke, and George Batchelor, all invoked Priestley throughout the nineteenth century, and were all, at various times, secretaries of the AUA.[108] This continued interest in Priestley and a great many, though not all, of his theological writings were facilitated by the confusion and dissent that seemed inherent within Unitarianism. Externally, the denomination was divided by the critical social issues of the day, especially slavery and women's rights. Internally Unitarianism was consumed by disputes over the development of a national church organization, as a follow-up to the formation of the AUA. By mid-century the American Unitarians had formed the National Conference of Unitarian Christians, which was an attempt to drive out both theological and social extremists. Within just a few years, however, controversy and schism again resulted in an internal conflict, and many Unitarians walked away from the National Conference in favor of the more liberal Free Religious Association. Concurrent with those challenges was a series of theological-intellectual shifts, most notably in the form of the Transcendentalist movement. The transcendental idea threatened to move Unitarianism away from religious faith entirely

---

107. Old Experience, *Final Tendency*, 15.

108. Henry Ware Jr. served as secretary from 1829 to 1834, Clarke from 1859 to 1861, and Batchelor from 1894 to 1898. AUA (AHTL) bMS 571.

and into extreme humanistic rationalism.[109] Led by Ralph Waldo Emerson and Henry David Thoureau, the Transcendentalists discounted the religion of revelation and replaced it with the idea of an individual, spiritual deity, similar to the Quaker idea of a light within. A humanitarian-rationalism also emerged as a challenge in 1841 when Theodore Parker predicted that all denominations and theology would pass away in favor of the simple, direct, and moral teachings of Jesus the prophet. Parker's ideas resurrected Jefferson's nascent unitarian beliefs, as delineated in the latter's reformulated Bible, which omitted all miracles and focused instead on moral teachings.[110] Early in the twentieth century the debate over the personal faculties of individuals again surfaced and most of the denomination's adherents moved permanently away from its Christian roots.[111]

Over the course of these controversies Priestley's reformist, Christian-based principles appealed to those Unitarians who sought to return to the Christian foundations of their Congregationalist heritage, as well as to those who were interested in resisting the new trends. Though these two groups remained in the minority, they supported the efforts to reincorporate Priestley's theology. A third group, the English Unitarians, also championed the efforts to bring back Priestley, but simultaneously challenged the Americans' efforts to selectively pick apart or adopt Priestley's theology in a piecemeal fashion. While the American denomination needed Priestley, the British argued, they should and could only employ his legacy if they accepted it in its entirety. Some Americans argued a similar point—that a mixed theology would only result in continued confusion and renewed trinitarian opposition. But for most Americans Priestley's basic ideas and character were sufficient. Indeed, adopting Priestley's theology in its entirety would have been difficult, since they rejected many of its rationalist excesses. Nevertheless, many Unitarians were willing to turn to Priestley and his Socinianism, in spite of what they perceived as its errors, because it was far more tolerable than the modern errors that confronted them directly.

Thus Priestleyan Unitarians had one more moment of significance in Unitarian history. The transatlantic resurrection of Priestley resulted in a complex series of events as his legacy was manipulated and made acceptable to people who had once rejected it, as the AUA invoked Priestley to enhance the Unitarian position in the wider Christian world. These

---

109. For a summary of these conflicts, see Robinson, *Unitarians and the Universalists*, 3–8.
110. Jefferson, *Jefferson Bible*.
111. See Robinson, *Unitarians and Universalists*, 75–142.

transformations resulted in a new outlook on Socinianism and the moral example of Priestley. In the words of one revisionist of the day, Priestley and the English Unitarians had gone from heresy to saintliness.[112]

Sustaining Socinianism

Henry Ware sensed that Unitarianism was moving away from its Christian foundations, and he feared the potential implications of such a change. His worries were shared by a significant portion of Unitarian believers; and even if they did not fully agree with his efforts to reintroduce Priestley's theology, within Unitarian circles his proposed solution held credence. For more than four years his writings on the subject prepared like-minded thinkers for the oncoming challenges and presented an array of suggestions for meeting them.[113]

As part of his plan to counter the effects of extreme rationalism Ware published a compilation of Priestley's writings under the title *Views of Christian Truth, Piety, and Morality, Selected from the Writings of Dr. Priestley*, to which he also added a brief biography of Priestley, all in an effort to reassure the Christian community of the wisdom behind accepting Priestley's legacy.[114] According to Ware, Priestley was the premier figure in the history of liberal thought and deserved credit for establishing the Unitarian denomination in the United States. He was also one of the most maligned Unitarian figures, and his enemies had gone to great lengths to misrepresent his ideas. "They put a wrong construction [on them] . . . culling from his works a quantity of his hasty and rash expressions, and publishing them to the world. . . . These citations from his works, not very numerous after all, have been copied from one writer to another, till they have become a sort of stock-in-trade in controversy, and may be expected to appear as a matter of course." The time had come, however, for an end to such manipulations. The times called for a renewed effort to "instruct and animate religious readers, and do something toward vindicating the character of an injured man" and his religious views.[115] Ware even went so far as to attend the general

---

112. Everett, *Immortality*, 98.

113. The earliest work by Ware on this subject was *On the Foundation of the Christian Character*, written in 1831. Over the course of the next four years he wrote several other tracts on the subject, including *Sober Thoughts* and *Views of Christian Truth*.

114. The copy of this work in the collections of the American Philosophical Society was presented to John Vaughan by Henry Ware Jr. and signed. Vaughan then donated the work to the Society in May 1837.

115. Ware, *Views of Christian Truth*, lxxii.

meeting of the British and Foreign Unitarian Association in June 1829. In recognition of his presence, the British issued a proclamation that championed their "Trans-atlantic Brethren; and that the meeting indulges the hope and expectation that this is 'the commencement of a series of acts of fraternal recognition on both sides, which shall be serviceable to the common cause of Christian Truth and righteousness in both the United States of America and Great Britain.'"[116] This tone of affinity and affiliation carried over into subsequent correspondence and facilitated the exchange of religious tracts that were considered to be of mutual interest, including twelve copies of Belsham's *Translation and Exposition of Paul's Epistles* sent that September by John Bowring, secretary of the British and Foreign Unitarian Association.[117]

As American Unitarianism matured, its foes changed. The competition between opposing, liberal theologies, all attached to the unitarian belief, and once considered the most significant challenge, was now seen in a different light. "It is astonishing how far away [Priestley] often seems," lamented Charles Carroll Everett. But his ideas were suddenly more tolerable and an integral part of the Unitarian identity. Given this transition, Everett wrote, "we realize how the intellectual world has changed." Indeed, "there has been a change in the thought that is called Unitarianism."[118] The theological differences between the New England liberals and those who still followed Priestley's ideas were less important in face of the challenge posed by Transcendentalism. Priestley's fight against infidelity, usually directed against outsiders, was now directed against the internal challenge of the Transcendentalists and the external need to remain within the Christian community.[119] Such was the case made by the Reverend James de Normandie, who included Priestley on the roll of those who had assured the triumph of liberal faith in America—a list that also included Channing, Furness, Emerson, Bellows, and Parker.[120] Thus Priestley was recast into a more mainstream role in the contemporary Unitarian theological debate. Those who

---

116. John Bowring to Ezra Stiles Gannett, June 16, 1829, AUA (AHTL), bMS 571/9.

117. Bowring to Gannett, September 18, 1829, AUA (AHTL), bMS 571/9. Thomas Rees of Kensington noted "the zeal and judgment with which the friends and advocates of our common cause are labouring among you." F. B. Wright wrote that he was "pleased to find that pure and undefiled religion prospers so well and is making such rapid strides on your side of the water." See Rees to Gannett, December 4, 1828, Kensington, AUA (AHTL), bMS 571/7, and F. B. Wright to Gannett, March 19, 1829, ibid.

118. Everett, *Immortality*, 98, 103–4, 124.

119. See Norton, *Discourse on the Latest Form of Infidelity*, which he identified as Transcendentalism.

120. Normandie, "Sermon."

wished to see Priestley's ideas utilized in defense of Christian Unitarianism commended his writings and depicted him as an essential figure in the development of the faith. Considerable attempts were made to link his ideas, even some of the more extreme ones, to those promoted by more modern, leading religious thinkers from other Christian and Protestant denominations. Priestley's doctrines on materialism were compared to those professed by Richard Whately, the archbishop of Dublin, and Reginald Courtenay, the bishop of Kingston, both devout Anglicans. The arguments concerning the soul and moral perfectionism expressed by Whately in his *Essays* compared favorably to Priestley's writings in *Disquisitions on Matter and Spirit*. More and more of Priestley's ideas were held and espoused by Anglicans and other Christian groups without challenge and accepted as rational elements consistent with their overall theology. Such connections were vital to the Unitarians, who needed proof of their Christian standing in the face of accusations to the contrary and needed to prove their position from all possible corners of liberalism's history and espoused creeds. Additional connections were established through Priestley's explorations of the roots and rationales of his ideas in contrast with Hinduism and Judaism and in consensus with Catholicism, Presbyterianism, and Methodism. Having derived his proofs from Christian scripture, Priestley argued from a Christian viewpoint, and those who sought to incorporate these arguments into contemporary refutations against infidelity and Transcendentalism hoped that Priestley's legacy would help pull Unitarianism back to its Christian foundations.[121]

Priestley's message also appealed to Unitarians as they struggled to build the denomination, not just define its theology. His commentary and actions with respect to the organizational structures of a religious denomination held significant lessons for the future of Unitarianism, then in the throes of a second organizational conflict. This time the competition was between the structure and authority upheld by the AUA in contrast to the alternatives offered by the National Conference of Unitarian Christians and, subsequently, the Free Religious Association. While Priestley believed in the authority of the laity, he did not necessarily agree with the free forms of worship and structure that were now advocated by the Free Association or the upstart Transcendentalists. Even Channing, prior to his death, had once professed Priestley to be "next to Lardner, the most laborious advocate of Christianity against the attack of infidels" and in his "vindication of our common [Christian]

---

121. Huxley, "Joseph Priestley," in *Collected Essays,* 24–26.

faith."[122] Later advocates of Priestley's ideas also sought to use his call for simplicity as a counter to the recent developments. As Unitarianism suffered under the weight of a new schism, and attempted to remedy its own contradictions, it seemed as though the religion and its adherents were more burdened by its complexities than relieved. The philosopher John Dewey noted how few "beliefs, practices and modes of organization that have accrued to and been loaded upon the religious elements" were actually resolved by the alterations and new manifestations in Unitarianism and religion in general. The only way for religion to reach a state of intellectual and emotional effectiveness was "for emancipation of the religious quality from accretions that have grown up about it and that limit the credibility and the influence," thus assigning meaning for those to whom it mattered.[123]

By the middle of the nineteenth century Unitarianism was attempting to become more centralized and unified, and to move toward a common creed. This flurry of conformist activity blurred Unitarianism's more tumultuous and uncertain past and glossed over significant distinctions within the membership and their multitude of beliefs. Granted, some distinctions were allowed to remain, but only those that were unlikely to spark controversy—free thought, candor, the insistence on individual reason, and others—elements that were so universal that they were never distinctly Unitarian at all.[124]

But none of this should be mistaken for a complete watering down of Priestley's ideas, even the most controversial. Socinianism was not totally cast aside, as indicated by Jared Sparks's decision to include Priestley as a defining personage in the history of the religion attests. "Several theologians of the greatest piety and learning have been led by their inquiries to results, which have not accorded in all respects with the opinions of the multitude, and hence they have been proscribed by the popular voice, either as unsound in faith, or erroneous in their principles." Priestley was foremost among these theologians. Just the opposite was true of Priestley, whose theological writings were of the character of those that "strengthen the faith of Christians in the divine origin and authority of their religion—to diffuse a critical

---

122. Channing, *The Life of William Ellery Channing*, 407.

123. Dewey, *A Common Faith*, 6–8, 84–85.

124. Manschreck, "Critical Appraisal," 227. Manschreck links Priestley's insistence on individual reason with the earlier ideas of Chauncy and Mayhew and the later ideas of John Murray, James Freeman, Thomas Jefferson, William Emerson, and William Ellery Channing. See also Lambert, *Founding Fathers*, 288–96, and Wolfe, *Transformation of American Religion*, 1–5.

knowledge of the scriptures—to exhibit rational and consistent views of the Christian scheme—to inculcate principles of religious liberty and toleration—to encourage the exercise of piety and charity—and to secure obedience to the laws of Christ," wrote Sparks.[125] Given many of the latter elements raised, we can clearly see how Priestley was a natural choice. His philosophical, political, and religious writings were all in accord with ideas of piety, liberty, education, and attacks against infidelity. But Sparks also raised the issue of divine origin and authority of the faith. These ideas required an exposition of Socinian belief and the process by which Priestley's personal rationalism had led him to such views.

Jared Sparks was one of the earliest figures to contend that such an exposition was necessary. His association with the Baltimore congregation, though brief, had brought him into direct contact with Priestley's beliefs, and in 1822 he proposed a compilation of essays on Unitarian subjects that he deemed vital for the religious practitioner that included a biography of Priestley and an examination of his theology.[126] Sparks mailed the proposal to John Vaughan, then a lay leader of the Philadelphia congregation, with a brief letter commending the series to Vaughan in the hope that it would meet with his approval. Sparks called Vaughan's attention to his focus on "rational views of theology . . . estimated for their excellence" as consistent with the prevailing theology among the Philadelphia society.[127]

English Socinianism clearly left a lasting mark on the religious thinking of many Americans. Those who were sympathetic, such as Thomas Cooper, Thomas Jefferson, and the Vaughan brothers, continued to support ideas first set down by Priestley and practiced by the Pennsylvania congregations. In June 1822, Jefferson wrote to Benjamin Waterhouse concerning the corruptions that had invaded American Christianity, using Priestley's *History of the Corruptions of Christianity* as the foundation for his argument in favor of excising many objectionable aspects from religious belief and practice. Jefferson noted that the followers of Calvin and the Protestant denominations were "mere usurpers of the Christian name, teaching a counter-religion made up of the *deliria* of crazy imaginations, as foreign from Christianity as is that of Mahomet. Their blasphemies have driven thinking men into infidelity."[128] Instead

---

125. Sparks, *Proposals for publishing by subscription*, APS.
126. Ibid.
127. Sparks to John Vaughan, Baltimore, July 8, 1822, APS.
128. Thomas Jefferson to Dr. Benjamin Waterhouse, June 26, 1822, in Jefferson, *Writings*, 1458.

of succumbing to infidelity, Priestley had held true to the most fundamental of all Christian beliefs. "Had the doctrines of Jesus been preached always as pure as they came from his lips, the whole, civilized world would now have been Christian," wrote Jefferson. "I rejoice that in this blessed country of free inquiry and belief, which has surrendered its creed and conscience to neither kings nor priests, the genuine doctrine of one only God is reviving."[129] For his part, Cooper carried the ideas with him to South Carolina, where he was united with Joseph Gales, a former member of the Philadelphia congregation, and the two became leading figures in the spread and survival of Unitarianism in the South.[130]

In May 1823 a like-minded group of ministers from Boston and the surrounding area put forward three questions that later served as the operating principles of the AUA. They asked themselves where Unitarian societies might be formed to best serve the movement and where Unitarian ministers could be heard and where books "containing just notions of religion and duty" could be sent to the greatest effect.[131] The group, as a result of what has been called their "nationally minded" sense of duty, then established subcommittees to establish and maintain communication with Unitarians throughout the nation; assigned to the Middle Atlantic states were Henry Ware, a Mr. Bond, and John Ware.[132]

This approach was not universally applauded, and not everyone who participated even believed that the AUA was capable of achieving its objectives. As the idea of the association progressed, John Aikin noted that Unitarianism's "religious systems are still, indeed, full of error, and are little, if at all, mended in their principles," despite the changes promised.[133] Several leading Unitarians of the day feared that the creation of the Association would lead to the establishment of a sect that would in turn seek to impose its will upon other free-thinking, liberal Christians. Even Channing cautioned that "among Unitarians the aversion to sectarianism is so strong that there seems to be growing up among us a party against a party, a sect to suppress sects."[134] The Boston *Recorder and Telegraph* added their vote for caution (while simultaneously warning Calvinists): "To those who have been accustomed

---

129. Ibid., 1458–59.
130. Macaulay, *Unitarianism in the Antebellum South,* 18–19.
131. Graves, "Adventure of Faith," AUA (AHTL), bMS 11180.
132. Ibid., 24–25.
133. Aikin, *Memoir of John Aikin,* 312.
134. William Ellery Channing, quoted in Graves, "Adventure of Faith," 53, AUA (AHTL), bMS 11180.

to hear the outcries of Unitarians against consociations and Presbyterianism, as if such things were wholly incompatible with Christian liberty, it may be a little interesting to know that an 'American Unitarian Association' has been recently formed."[135]

The AUA was not formally established until 1825, and even then it was merely a voluntary ministerial organization, six years after Channing's initial appeal for an association. Despite the group's potential promise, its earliest activities were limited to effecting a widespread conversion to Channing's adaptations of Unitarianism. Though it was clear that the prevailing forces of New England liberalism were in agreement, not all parties were immediately swayed into the new camp, and there was open opposition, often using Priestley's ideas as a counterforce to the potential of the newly proposed, monolithic Unitarianism—rejecting the premise of the AUA as the one association that could ensure a true definition of Unitarianism and effectively oppose attempts to marginalize liberalism's theological diversity.

Having sparked this latest controversy, Thomas Belsham could not help but observe the course of events with a measure of both satisfaction and dismay. "I am happy to learn that the ministers both of the Arian and Unitarian persuasions are now in the habit of openly professing the doctrines which they believe," he wrote, and at the same time he noted that the implications of such a new direction were endless. "I do not wonder that, in consequence of this fearless integrity in a land of perfect religious liberty, Christian truth is flashing like lightning through that highly favored empire, from Boston to Baltimore, and from Philadelphia to the Illinois."[136] But he also believed that Channing had not completed the task set before him. He had not gone far enough in incorporating Priestley and English Unitarianism. A more fundamental effort was still required. Belsham echoed the words of Aikin and expressed his disappointment that Channing and his successors had failed in these efforts.[137] Predictably, Belsham's additional comments and the reissue of his *Memoirs* caused a furor among all parties concerned.

The need to revitalize the Christian component of Unitarianism became apparent in the mid 1830s when Alexis de Tocqueville expressed

135. *Recorder and Telegraph,* quoted in ibid., 54–55.

136. Belsham, *Memoirs,* 214.

137. Belsham's most important work was a translation and exposition of the *Epistles of Paul the Apostle Translated.* His defense of English Unitarianism was most solidly presented in *Extracts from the writings of eminent divines of the Church of England* and subsequent responses to challenges in the pages of the *Quarterly Review* and *Gentleman's Magazine* of the early nineteenth century. Belsham was considered by many to be the ablest defender of the faith, excluding Priestley to whom Belsham always offered deference.

highly critical views of the denomination in his reflections on the United States.[138] The first thing that struck Tocqueville, a Catholic, was the religious atmosphere of America and the liberty that accompanied worship. He was very critical of the lack of a recognized authority in American religious matters, perhaps a natural response from one who accepted the authority of the Holy See. The proliferation of sects that claimed authority was particularly troublesome, mitigated only by the fact that there remained a prevailing sense of established religious practices and beliefs. Similarly, he decried the proliferation of rationalism among American denominations. Accordingly, he impugned the motives of the Unitarians. He suggested that their claim to Christianity masked their true beliefs. "They aim so far as possible to resemble on the surface the Christian sects. So no kind of ridicule attaches to them; no party spirit pushes them or arrests them." If the test of a true religion was its use of the scripture, Tocqueville found the Unitarians wanting in this respect as well. He considered any attempt by the Unitarians to invoke the Bible in support of their beliefs as self-serving. They only spoke of the scriptures "because they do not wish to shock public opinion, still entirely *Christian*, too deeply." As a result, he relegated Unitarianism to cult status, a group "on the confines of Protestantism" and, despite their rhetoric, "a sect which is Christian only in name."[139] Tocqueville thus revealed the fragile and uncertain nature of the Unitarian movement, and the continued confusion over the central tenets of its theology and social foundations. The union that Channing had hoped to achieve was not yet a reality, and hence Tocqueville found not one class of Unitarians, but many. There were those "who deny the Trinity and recognize only one God, there are some who see in Jesus Christ only an angel, others a prophet, others, lastly, a philosopher like Socrates."[140] It seemed as if each generation of Unitarians offered something new and different and as a consequence no generation was able to adhere to the same ideas. Such perceptions also prevailed among the general public, as they witnessed the slide of Unitarianism away from Christianity into Transcendentalism.

Though the AUA had captured the Unitarian name and depicted themselves as the sole agents of unitarian rationalism, it was clear that their identity as such was not as widely accepted as they wished to

---

138. See Alexis de Tocqueville, *Democracy in America* and "Essay on American Government and Religion."

139. Alexis de Tocqueville, "Essay on American Government and Religion," excerpted from Pierson, *Tocqueville in America*, 156.

140. Ibid., 156–57.

believe. Their claims remained contested and resulted in a lengthy period of uncertainty despite pretensions to the contrary. "As the religion of a sect, Unitarianism is feeble—feebler, relatively than it was in the days of Kippis and Priestley . . . it is widely diffused," wrote George Ellis fifty years after the controversies had first surfaced.[141] With Channing gone, men like Henry Ware Jr. and Andrews Norton stepped forward, but even they were unable to come to an agreement as to the foundations and direction of the faith. Ware favored a personal religion based entirely on experiential aspects, while Norton supported a reliance on scripture, including miracles and Jesus as prophet.[142] While such men argued over theology, others were more concerned about the institutionalization of the religion, yet each was heavily dependent on the other in ways that they could not or did not recognize, just as earlier Unitarians had failed to see similar connections.

Two works, one focused entirely on Unitarianism and the other a religious encyclopedia, brought the contest over creed, structure, and history into sharp relief. They were Samuel Wood's *Present State and the Prospects of Unitarian Christianity in the United States of North America* and John Hayward's *Religious Creeds and Statistics of Every Christian Denomination in the United States and British Provinces.* In 1837, when the English minister Samuel Wood had visited the United States and published an account of his journey, he demonstrated the inseparable link between a coherent theology and a structured denomination. It was clear that the Unitarians of the age possessed neither. Wood's work differed remarkably from earlier writings precisely because there were now so many more options to consider. He had started his investigation in Boston, the center of nineteenth-century Unitarianism, where he was received by the secretary of the Unitarian Association and given assistance in his task. During this visit he compiled a list of Unitarian churches and societies belonging to "the Unitarian Congregationalist denomination in the United States."[143] His use of the Congregationalist notation, a full decade after the creation of the AUA, attested to the continued internal divisions and the lasting legacy of English Socinianism. The old characterizations were still important, and the distinct theologies had not yet lost their relevance. Wood's list of churches included 221 congregations, with 150 in Massachusetts, 2 each in Pennsylvania and New York, and the rest scattered across the South and West, including

141. Ellis, *Unitarian Controversy*, 317.
142. Robinson, *Unitarians and the Universalists*, 59–61.
143. Wood, *Present State*, 4. Originally published in *The Christian Reformer*, September 1837. APS

Maryland, Virginia, South Carolina, Kentucky, Ohio, and Missouri. In order to arrive at such an extensive list, however, the net had to be extended well beyond the groups that held the Arian theology.

Wood rejected both a narrow theological definition and the newly formed denominational identity in favor of the broadest belief in the simple unitarian idea. This allowed Wood to claim over 2,500 unitarian-leaning congregations throughout the United States. His estimate included the Pennsylvania Socinians, the Universalists, the Hicksite Friends, and groups "considered in the main to hold the same sentiments." This also included some congregations that were identified as Lutherans and Campbellite Baptists, yet almost all of these groups denied any association with the Unitarians.[144]

John Hayward used a more restrictive definition of Unitarianism in *Religious Creeds and Statistics*. While his estimate of congregations that used the Unitarian name was similar to Wood's, the grand total of those who were in accord with its sentiments was significantly different. According to Hayward there were only 174 Unitarian Congregationalist ministers in the United States and "about thirty more congregations and churches, than stated ministers." Hayward's figures, based on the narrower interpretation of denominational membership, excluded those he classified as Socinian and Humanitarian.[145] Later encyclopedias, however, found ways to overlook the distinctions made by Hayward on the grounds that what creed did exist in Unitarianism was centered on the leading doctrine, but permitted deviation in other areas. Citing "little reverence for human creeds, having no common standard but the Bible, and allowing, in the fullest extent, freedom of thought and the liberty of every Christian," future encyclopedic works found Hayward's limits out of touch with the changes taking place.[146]

---

144. Ibid., 10–11. Wood provided a breakdown of each group considered to be unitarian in thought:

Unitarians	221
Christians	1200
Universalists	718
Hicksites	367
Total	2506

These congregations were formed from an American population of only 15 million, in contrast to the significantly larger English population (including Ireland and Great Britain) of almost 26 million which held only a little more than three hundred congregations.

145. Hayward, *Religious Creeds and Statistics*, 150.

146. Rupp, *He Pasa Ekklesia*, 704; See also Baird, *Religion in the United States*, 625–27.

For his part, Priestley had favored the broadest theological definition of Unitarianism. Still, his position on infidelity would have placed him in opposition to Transcendentalism. Priestley did not consider himself in opposition to the trinitarian churches, but rather a reformer who wanted to incorporate many different denominations into one broadly defined church. His theology included a broad spectrum of rationalist ideas, but was still contained in a Christian framework. As a result, during the early years of the Transcendentalist challenge, the adoption of Priestley's ideas grew.

The Reverend James Taylor of Philadelphia, who was elected to be a vice-president in the AUA at the initial meeting in 1825 and then reelected every subsequent year until 1844, remained in contact with the English Unitarians and spent almost seven months in England and Scotland, much of it in Liverpool.[147] Upon his return home he promoted a transatlantic association. "The present impression in England appears to me to be in favour of such a society as was lately formed at Boston, from a persuasion that it is better to concentrate strength & influence than to divide these," he wrote, then unaware of the developments in that direction that had taken place. "When in England last summer, I had much intercourse with many prominent Unitarians, & particularly with the minister of that denomination. It was pleasing to find, both from their publick declarations & from their private communications, that a lively & generous interest is felt in the welfare of the American Unitarians, & in the success of their exertions to promote the knowledge & practice of true religion." After praising the central tenets of Unitarian worship and public discourse, Taylor spoke of the potential for sustained discourse via the *Monthly Repository,* the *Christian Reformer,* and the efforts of transatlantic missionaries. Taylor also went on to describe the happy state of Unitarianism he found in Scotland during a two-month residence. While Unitarianism was not flourishing—a direct parallel with the situation in the United States—it was at least finding a degree of tolerance and acceptance that allowed its adherents to live happily and in peace.[148] Taylor also spoke of the mutual regard that existed between Philadelphia and the two congregations in central Pennsylvania—Northumberland and Harrisburg. He noted that the Philadelphia congregation decided to raise funds for the Harrisburg

147. Other Pennsylvania Unitarians who held elected positions in the AUA included Martin Hurlburt from 1832 to 1837, then again from 1840 to 1842; Benjamin Bakewell in 1838–43; and Harm Jan Huidkoper in 1840.

148. James Taylor to Ezra Stiles Gannett, December 21, 1825, AUA (AHTL), bMS 571/2.

chapel, independent of the Association in Boston, noting that they had purposely decided not to involve Boston in such matters.[149]

Taylor also sought to engage the Bostonians in the matter of defining themselves and their relationship to English Unitarians. He first inquired if those who identified themselves as Liberal Christians might drop the term "liberal" on the grounds that it was too easily attacked by outsiders and more often seen as an affront by insiders. This, he noted, was similar to a matter that once confronted those in England who had sought to employ the term "rational" as an identifying trait. "The force of prejudice is strong & early opinions take root," he stressed, adding urgency to their need to address such concerns. He then presented estimable proof of the usefulness in engaging in a concerted effort to promote Unitarianism on both sides of the Atlantic. "You will rejoice to hear that the memory of Dr. Priestley is held in increasing veneration, not only among those of similar religious views, but that he has recently been spoken of in the most respectful manner by distinguished ministers in the ranks of orthodoxy." Lamenting that a recent article in the *Christian Examiner* took the opposite tack and was exceedingly *derogatory* in its remarks about Priestley, Taylor proposed that such open hostility only served to damage the potential for a more cooperative relationship.[150] Taylor continued to use English Unitarianism as a bellwether of American Unitarian success. He lamented that Boston often used the rationale of small numbers of adherents as the cause of so few numbers of chapels or as the indicator of theological conformity. He noted that just four churches in Boston could hold all of London's Unitarians and yet in all of England there were more than four hundred congregations. He also highlighted the class and status differences between English and American Unitarians. "[English] Unitarianism finds little favor among the rich, the fashionable, & those who are immersed in the concerns of an extensive business; it has much greater attractions for persons in comparatively humble life, & of unpretending manners, who love to cultivate their understandings, preferring the improvement of the mind to the gratification of the senses, & regarding this world as a place of preparation for a better & higher state." There was little doubt that he considered both the Brahmin status and professed theological exclusivity professed by the AUA leadership as obstacles to the continued growth of Unitarianism.[151]

149. James Taylor to Stephen Higginson, January 25, 1826, AUA (AHTL), bMS 571/2.
150. James Taylor to Henry Ware, May 11, 1826, Philadelphia, AUA (AHTL), bMS 571/2. Taylor referenced an article on page 65 of the January/February edition.
151. James Taylor to Ezra Stiles Gannett, June 4, 1828, Philadelphia, AUA (AHTL), bMS 571/6.

Harriet Martineau, the British author and social critic, also called attention to Priestley's work and legacy as a fundamental part of Unitarian identity in both England and the United States. Following the publication of several articles in the *Monthly Repository* and the release of her *Illustrations of Political Economy* in 1832 on the status of English society and religion, Martineau decided to visit the United States and examine its religious societies.[152] While in America, she made a pilgrimage to Northumberland that resulted in a chapter in her travel memoir that served as both a defense of Priestley and an attack on the self-serving attempts to misinterpret his theology. "Before I went to America I was aware that the Unitarians there, who ought to know every thing about the apostle of their faith who took refuge in their country, were so far in the dark about him," she contended, "that they misapprehended his philosophy, and misrepresented its tendencies in a way and to a degree which seemed irreconcilable with the means of information within their reach."[153] She was particularly incensed about Channing's seemingly unending efforts to cast Priestley's contributions in an errant light, reflecting that their efforts to create conformity resulted in "the tendency of this sect in America to lean upon authority—with some other causes—[that] must indispose them to do justice to Priestley."[154] She was well aware of the need to adapt Priestley's ideas in response to Transcendentalism, a point echoed by Ware, who expressed his mortification that the necessity of the moment was neither enough to overcome animosity toward Priestley nor give him credit for his extensive theological contributions.[155]

But Martineau was not prone to condone what she considered to be an equally inappropriate use of Priestley's ideas, justified purely on the basis of expediency, to stave off the challenges of the Transcendentalists and others while ignoring the truth of his theology. She took both Channing and Ware to task for their equally patronizing, yet distinctly apologetic stances toward Priestley and his contributions, accusing them of trying to profit off of Priestley on their own terms, not his. "Such facts show that the character and mission of the man are not understood."[156] The combination of ignorance and manipulation of the Priestleyan heritage was particularly troublesome to Martineau, who then argued

152. Martineau, *Harriet Martineau's Autobiography.*
153. Martineau, *Retrospect of Western Travel,* 1:186.
154. Ibid., 187.
155. Ware, *Sober Thoughts,* lxxii.
156. Martineau, *Retrospect of Western Travel,* 187.

that the men undertaking such activities were ill equipped to undertake such a complex and dangerous theological effort.

> Those who, like the Americans, are unprepared for—alienated from—his philosophy . . . cannot possibly sympathize with Priestley's convictions; and a full appreciation of him ought not be expected of them. But they had better, in such a position of circumstances, let his works alone. . . . In the transition which the religious and philosophical society of America has to make . . . the philosopher may or may not yet become an apostle to them. In their present condition, he cannot be so . . . no presumptuous hand should offer to endorse his merits, or push claims to partial approbation of one who was created to command reverent discipleship; reverent discipleship in the pursuit of truth, if not in the reception of doctrine.[157]

Martineau's views were dismissed by the American Unitarians as the product of a woman with a character equal in its failings to the man she praised. James Freeman Clarke denounced "her tone of dogmatism, and her *ex cathedra* judgments, which, as we have before hinted, are among the defects of her qualities." But these were also qualities that made her a notable writer. "Every article or book which she has printed was a blow delivered against some flagrant wrong, or what she believed as such—in defense of some struggling truth, or something supposed to be the truth. She might be mistaken, but her purposes through life were, in the main, noble, generous, and good."[158]

Clarke's challenge was not surprising; as a defender of the new Unitarianism and its Christian traditions, he sought any means to preserve its legacy. He took exception to Martineau's effort to label the ministers and laity of the age as craven and reminded readers of the great divines who served in such a capacity. Though he did not count Priestley as one of the central figures of the American Unitarian past, Clarke included Priestleyan ideas in his own theological writings. Paramount among these, Clarke accepted the probable perfectibility of man and the role of a man's personal character in the formation of religious belief.[159]

157. Ibid., 187.
158. Clarke, "Harriet Martineau," 441, 437.
159. Ibid., 450; Clarke, *Vexed Questions in Theology*, 10–16.

Martineau was correct in accusing the American Unitarians of self-interested manipulation of Priestley. Despite her best efforts, however, the needs of the Americans outweighed the objections of the English. Martineau's arguments were no match for the peril to the religion should the infidel Transcendentalists emerge victorious or the orthodox move the nation completely toward its camp. Otis Skinner noted that he "was almost daily assailed" by both the revivalist force or emotionalism and the excesses of pure rationalism. The attacks were conducted "in a personal and exceedingly abusive manner" in which liberal Christians were "denounced as infidels, and doomed to hell."[160] Few Americans were thus interested in sustaining the transatlantic connections and the theological integrity that many of the English believed were important. The selective use of Priestley's theology, albeit in a very simplified manner, continued unabated. Ware went so far as to admit that Martineau's critique was correct but shortsighted. When it came to Priestley, he wrote, "it is not the *error* . . . which is admired; it is the virtue which is seen to exist in the midst of and in spite of the error."[161]

Therein lay the effective use of Priestley's legacy. The Americans came to accept Priestley because they needed to in order to fend off new challenges. But the English Unitarians, like Martineau, thought that they continued to abuse his memory. Channing's rejection of Priestley's Socinian theology, on the one hand, and his need to use many of Priestley's arguments, on the other, was proof of the contradiction within the Arian attempts to transform Unitarianism in America.

160. Skinner, *Letters*, preface.
161. Ware, *Views of Christian Truth*, iv.

SIX

"Respecting the Good Cause in Our Neighborhood": James Kay and Pennsylvania Unitarianism in the Nineteenth Century

Dr. Priestley is not by all of us abandoned to be trodden under foot.

—ROBERT ASPLAND

In 1823 John Aikin declared Priestley a failure. "If [Priestley] had any sanguine hopes of diffusing his religious principles over the new continent; or if his friends expected that the brilliancy of his philosophical reputation should place him in a highly conspicuous light among a people yet in the infancy of mental culture, such expectations were certainly disappointed."[1] The Unitarianism he had helped establish and the congregations that followed were centered on an untenable theology corrupted by human error, just as they had claimed others had been corrupted by history, Aikin remarked, and thus all ties were severed between the New England liberals, who by this time were prepared to take on the Unitarian name, and the immigrant Socinians. Aikin was only too happy to downplay Priestley's influence and success, for there was much to gain by dismissing Socinianism's presence and importance.

But Aikin's assessment was behind the times. His certainty that Channing's new Unitarianism had emerged as the unquestionable representation of Unitarianism in America failed to take into account the continuing migration of English Unitarians to the United States. Furthermore, it remained tied to the premises that liberalism's only need was to defend itself from trinitarian opposition, that a broad-based theological constituency was a weakness not a strength, and that Priestley's theological system centered around just a few ideas that were wholly unacceptable in a Christian-dominated nation.

---

1. Aikin, *Memoir of John Aikin*, 387.

As events would show, although Priestley's legacy had undeniably suffered a setback and had been severely challenged, it was not completely eradicated. Channing's attempts to sever all ties to the Socinians were shortsighted and unsuccessful. Furthermore, with the arrival of James Kay, an English Socinian, at Northumberland in 1822, Priestley's ideas found a new and most vocal defender. Over the course of the next two decades Kay secured Priestley's legacy, not just in Northumberland, but throughout the United States, through his own itinerant travels, public writings, connections with a cohort of like-minded Unitarian ministers and laypeople, and his association with the Western Unitarian Association. Kay also realized that despite their many differences in theological conclusions, an association with the newly formed AUA after 1825 was important, so long as his ideals were not compromised. This dualistic approach—maintaining the legacy and accommodating the revisionists— resulted in almost as many setbacks as successes for Kay, but in the end was central to the preservation of Priestley's American legacy.

Northumberland, 1804–1822

After Priestley's death the Unitarian mantle in Northumberland immediately passed to William Christie. Christie, who had been in the town since 1801, had already been serving as a minister in Priestley's stead. Thomas Cooper, better known for his political activities, was also in Northumberland and had lived with Priestley and his family for a period of time. Though Cooper had published "Argument for Unitarianism" in England, which was later reprinted in the United States in the *Christian Reformer or Evangelical Miscellany,* the leadership of the Northumberland society fell to Christie.[2] Christie's attention to the needs of the growing congregation included his continuation of the services under the order set down by Priestley, an emphasis on staving off the effects of infidelity among the rest of the population, and continuing the religious instruction of Unitarian children. Christie's initial education classes were held in a log schoolhouse on North Way, the occasional location of the Unitarian services, directly opposite the Priestley home. In 1803, attesting to the increased respect for Christie, the protégé became the teacher of record at the Northumberland Academy, the new college that Priestley had supported since his arrival, infusing and

---

2. Cooper's article was printed in 1819 under the title "Summary of Unitarian Arguments."

framing the secular education of the children with religious principles. The state government had granted the college a charter only after Priestley had pledged both his personal financial backing and his library. There Christie taught more than fifty students over three years.[3]

The last conversation between Christie and Priestley took place five days before Priestley died. Christie recounted the conversation, one he characterized as being typical, in his eulogy. The subjects were wide-ranging—this one in particular concerned the state of dying, the degree to which pain during death was desirable, the state of Priestley's writings, and Priestley's sentiments on the apocalypse—and the tenor of the conversation was stimulating and engaging. Ever the devil's advocate, Priestley had probed Christie's ideas and countered several of his positions, forcing the latter to strengthen his arguments and fortify his defenses of his theology. "God bless you," Priestley intoned upon Christie's departure, to which Christie replied, "the Lord be with you, Doctor."[4] Christie remained in Northumberland for another three years. But it is clear that his efforts, owing to financial considerations and the dwindling numbers of adherents as a result of Priestley's death, were more focused on the Academy and the search for a more settled ministry.[5] With the departure of both Christie and Cooper the group was forced to rely upon lay leadership and steel themselves for the foreseeable future against the inevitable decline that was to come.

From 1806 until 1822 the Northumberland society, now down to a few remaining family members and truly committed adherents, continued and survived under the leadership of various lay members who continued Priestley's practice of reading sermons.[6] There is little question that their existence as a group was threatened. Several of Priestley's family members returned to England, and the lack of a prominent leader, one with the reputation of Priestley in both the pulpit and in print, made them much more vulnerable to the attacks of the opposition. With Christie's departure they lost control over the Academy, the first overt sign of the strength and depth of the opposition. Isaac Grier, the local Presbyterian minister, was called to serve as head of the school in 1805. "This school needed a Presbyterian to make it go. Dr. Priestley was a Unitarian. That faith was not acceptable in the West Branch," the Northumberland Presbytery claimed in its records

3. Wickersham, *History of Education in Pennsylvania*, 480. See also Gutelius, *Northumberland*, 10–14.
4. Christie, *Speech*, 19.
5. Ibid., 9.
6. Bell, *History of Northumberland County*, 536–37.

some years later.[7] The Presbyterians certainly enjoyed a strong hold on the religious affairs of the town. They were the only denomination in Northumberland to have their own permanent house of worship and settled minister, dating back to 1787 and were, even when Priestley was alive, the most vocal in their opposition. Furthermore, the decline in membership once again forced the Unitarians to worship in private homes; they were no longer a large enough collective to warrant or afford the use of more public buildings.

The Unitarians in Northumberland continued in this manner for nearly fifteen years, giving rise to the New England position that the congregation was defunct and Priestley's legacy eradicated. But events in 1817 show that such a view was more a product of wishful thinking and Northumberland's relative isolation than of reality. In 1817 the local Episcopal, Lutheran, and German Reformed congregations broke ground for a chapel. The association of these three groups was an oddity given the latter two groups' German origins and theological differences with the former. Nonetheless, they banded together to raise the funds for construction of the chapel, which they would jointly share for several decades. Their fundraising efforts, however, fell short. Six years after the chapel was built the parishioners still owed money to the contractor, who in turn sued the congregations and placed a lien against the property and structure. Hugh Bellas, a Unitarian and former pupil of Priestley's but also the lawyer for the chapel's congregations, arranged with the groups to purchase the property and have the legal suit against the congregations dismissed, but only on the condition that he could donate three-quarters' ownership of the property to the three congregations and reserve the final quarter for the Unitarians, which would entitle them to the use of the structure one Sunday a month.[8] The acceptance of this arrangement led to the shared structure's new name as the "Union Church," which it remained for the next eleven years.[9]

7. Finney, *History of the Chillisquaque Church*, 34.
8. Gutelius, "Churches," 144.
9. The church was originally named St. John's and no doubt kept that name among the original congregations, but publicly it was always referred to as the Union Church, which itself was a common name throughout the Pennsylvania countryside. The sharing of houses of worship was both a necessity and a practicality at this time. The evidence for Bellas's donation remains questionable. One independent scholar, H. L. Dufour Woolfley has found that Bellas actually sold a portion of the chapel to William Lloyd for one dollar. Lloyd's family connections, by way of marriage, had left him with ties to the Episcopalian and Lutheran congregations. See Woolfley, *Susquehanna Squire*, 90.

The religious landscape of the town was changing dramatically. Since Priestley's day, the number of religious groups had doubled and included the more established groups as well as several that were more fleeting and sectarian in their outlook. The new groups often grew from "a few converts to an expanding organization . . . in large part the work of a dedicated corps of charismatic leaders . . . [who] standardized what once had been spontaneous" and were responsible for the creation of "new institutional forms" of worship and church polity, thus reflecting the very similar process that Unitarianism had gone through.[10] Unitarianism's lasting presence now gave it a cachet that these others were striving for.

The Ministry of Reverend James Kay

When Kay arrived in Northumberland, he set about attempting to reestablish a strong congregation, both spiritually and financially, and re-create the active Sunday school program so vital to the continuation of the faith. Three years later, when asked by the Reverend Ezra S. Gannett to relate the details of his Northumberland ministry's beginnings, Kay explained how much he had had to do to achieve his goals. "When I arrived in this town, not quite four years ago, the number of Unitarians was very small indeed. I commenced my labors under the most inauspicious circumstances, and had to contend, from the very first, with the most marked and concentrated opposition." He remarked that he encountered almost the same level of hostility that Priestley had three decades earlier. "The Orthodox were inclined with sectarian feelings against us," he wrote, and "the cry of heresy was instantly raised." He related that the most notable of these efforts came when "a popular neighboring minister" publicly demanded that Kay make an open and unequivocal statement of his intentions and beliefs so that his errors might be exposed. This request, coming as it did from a minister who shared the Union Chapel pulpit with Kay signaled a distinct change of heart on behalf of the town's Christian community. "In this discourse, he attempted to establish the doctrine of the Trinity—pointed out its vast importance—denounced the Unitarians by name—representing them as Deists in disguise—as sapping the foundations of Xtianity— and teaching doctrines destructive of the souls of men," lamented Kay

10. Mathews, "Second Great Awakening," 30.

in his letter to Boston. Most appalling was that "he dared to slander the venerated name of Priestley, and associated him with the worst and most inveterate enemies of Xtianity." Kay viewed this exchange as one in which "the Orthodox had thrown down the gauntlet."[11] In response he and his congregation took a vote to begin collecting funds to raise their own chapel and separate themselves from their current shared pulpit agreement.

In 1827 Kay would again write to Gannett about "a controversy on the leading points of the Xtian doctrine" that he had been engaged in for nearly nine months with a local Presbyterian minister. The conflict centered on the historical foundations of the nature of the Trinity and was fought in the pages of one of the local county newspapers. "This has greatly increased my labours, yet I am abundantly satisfied that it has contributed to excite a spirit of inquiry in numbers who would not otherwise have heard of our views," concluded Kay.[12]

If the town's "orthodox" thought that this would end the Unitarian efforts, they misjudged both Kay's resolve and the strength of a group that had been quiet for so many years only because they lacked leadership. Kay's response was to increase his efforts to reach out to the Unitarians and to respond to the challenges head on. By these measures he was able to affect a resurgence of Unitarianism and a renewed appreciation for Priestley's legacy. Kay was asked to preach in several other towns once word had spread, some of which had never previously expressed a desire to hear a Unitarian minister. He concluded, "We have much reason to rejoice in the good that has been done. Several avowed unbelievers have received and rejoice in our views—many have left the ranks of the Orthodox and united with us—and a spirit of inquiry, liberality, and candour has been extensively promoted."[13]

Kay also responded by taking his ministry on the trails of the Pennsylvania interior, serving as an itinerant minister over an area that spanned hundreds of miles, a religious territory that he once referred to as his "diocese." Going wherever he found people in need of his message, Kay extended his ministry by preaching in such nearby places as Lewisburg, Milton, and Bloomsburg, and going much farther afield to minister to those in the towns of Harrisburg, Carlisle, and Liverpool.[14] In November of 1825 in a letter designed to introduce the Boston Unitarians to the breadth and scope of his successes, Kay sent Gannett a table of the towns

11. James Kay to Ezra Gannett, March 11, 1825, AUA (AHTL), bMS 571/1.
12. James Kay to Ezra Gannett, May 23, 1827, AUA (AHTL), bMS 571/4.
13. Ibid.
14. "Unitarianism in Northumberland," 199.

in which he had preached and where he had introduced Unitarianism.[15] The chart listed twenty-four different towns, the distance required for travel to each from Northumberland, the general number of people present at his services, the probable number of Unitarians among the larger group, the frequency of services, and where he was able to preach in each town. His schedule was such that Kay preached in Northumberland three out of four Sundays a month, on average, and used the fourth Sunday for alternating visits to the towns of Sunbury, Chillisquaque, Lewisburg, Milton, Harrisburg, Pennsborough, Hewsburg, and Goosetown; these were the towns he noted as places of frequent visits (at least once every month, six weeks, or in circuit every three months). The remaining fifteen towns were served only occasionally as time, travel, and health permitted.[16] Kay's regular circuit of preaching thus took him as far as seventy miles distant from Northumberland. In several subsequent letters Kay also mentioned his interactions with Unitarians in Pittsburgh and Lancaster, though it is certain, despite his stated desire to do so, that he never preached in either place.[17]

The most interesting component of Kay's chart is the numerical estimates he provides of the number of people who attended his sermons and the portion of those whom he considered "probable" Unitarians. For Northumberland Kay listed that he routinely attracted between seventy and one hundred people, thirty-five of whom were actual Unitarians. Judging by his numbers, Lewisburg (at 100 to 150), Harrisburg (100 to 300), Washington (100 to 150), Williamsport and Berwick (both at 150), there was no shortage of attentive people and attractive places for his efforts.[18] Harrisburg's interest, he later noted, was at its apex when the state legislature was in session.[19] When Kay traveled to these towns to preach he did so in a wide array of places. In Northumberland, Lewisburg, Pennsborough, Washington, and Berwick he was afforded the use of a church. As in Northumberland, the churches he was permitted to use were "free to all" or union churches. In five towns he was permitted to use the local courthouse while ten

15. James Kay to Ezra Gannett, November 3, 1825, AUA (AHTL), bMS 571/2.

16. The fifteen additional towns mentioned were Mount Lewis, Elk Lands, Jersey Town, Washington, Moresburg, Danville, Catawissa, Bloomsburg, Berwic[k], New Berlin, Williamsport, Loyalsock, Millersburg, Liverpool, and Carlisle. See Kay to Gannett, November 3, 1825, and James Kay to James Freeman Clarke, April 1, 1846, AUA (AHTL), bMS 571/2 and bMS 571/65.

17. James Kay to Ezra Gannett, December 31, 1825, and May 23, 1827, AUA (AHTL), bMS 571/2 and 571/4.

18. Kay to Gannett, November 3, 1825, AUA (AHTL), bMS 571/2.

19. Kay to Gannett, December 31, 1825, AUA (AHTL), bMS 571/2.

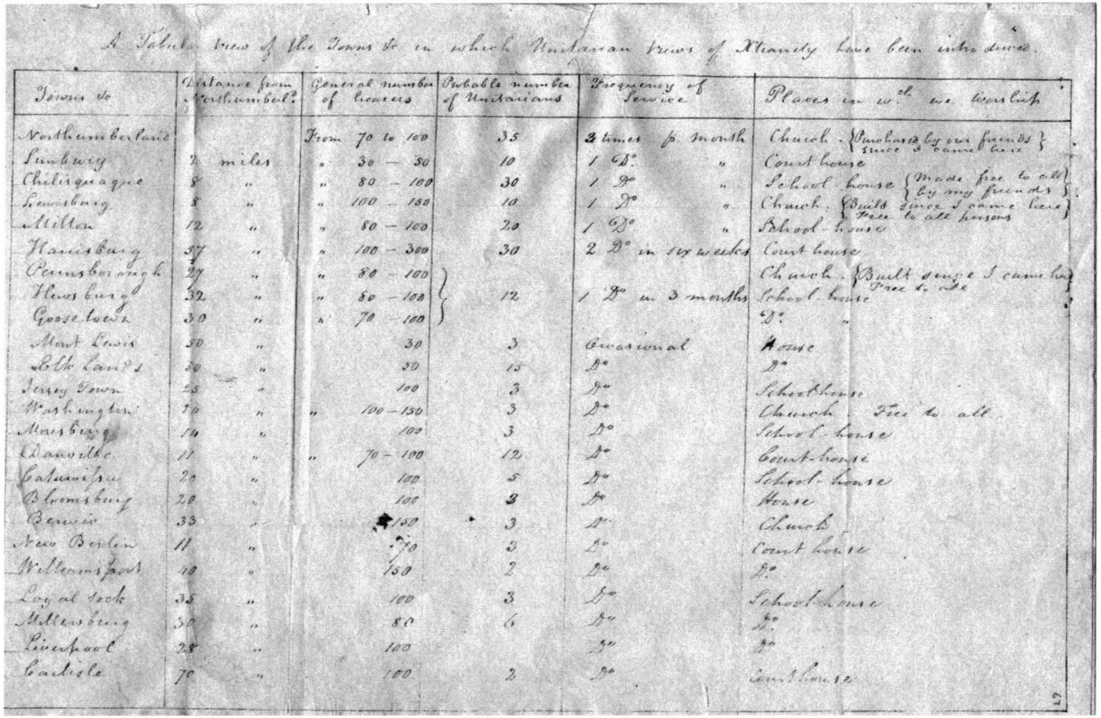

A Tabular view of the Towns &c in which Unitarian views of Xtianity have been introduced.

Towns &c	Distance from Northumberl.d	General number of hearers	Probable number of Unitarians	Frequency of Service	Places in w.ch we worship
Northumberland		From 70 to 100	35	3 times p. month	Church {Purchased by our friends since I came here}
Sunbury	2 miles	" 30 — 50	10	1 D° "	Court house
Chilisquaque	8 "	" 80 — 100	30	1 D° "	School-house {Made free to all by my friends}
Lewisburg	8 "	" 100 — 150	10	1 D° "	Church {Built since I came here. Free to all persons}
Milton	12 "	" 80 — 100	20	1 D° "	School-house
Harrisburg	57 "	" 100 — 300	30	2 D° in six weeks	Court house
Pennsborough	27 "	" 80 — 100	} 12	1 D° in 3 months	Church {Built since I came here Free to all}
Hewsburg	32 "	" 80 — 100			School house
Goosetown	30 "	" 70 — 100			D° "
Mount Lewis	30 "	30	3	Occasional	House
Elk Lands	30 "	50	15	D°	D°
Jersey Town	25 "	100	3	D°	School house
Washington	20 "	" 100 — 150	3	D°	Church Free to all
Marsburg	14 "	100	3	D°	School-house
Danville	11 "	" 70 - 100	12	D°	Court-house
Catawissa	20 "	100	5	D°	School-house
Bloomsburg	20 "	100	3	D°	House
Berwick	33 "	150	3	D°	Church
New Berlin	11 "	70	3	D°	Court house
Williamsport	40 "	150	2	D°	D°
Loyal Sock	35 "	100	3	D°	School house
Millersburg	30 "	80	6	D°	D°
Liverpool	28 "	100		D°	D°
Carlisle	70 "	100	2	D°	Court house

Fig. 3 Itinerant travels chart from a letter by James Kay. Letters from various Unitarian ministers, American Unitarian Association, Letterbooks, 1822–1902, bMS 571. Published by permission from Andover-Harvard Theological Library, Harvard Divinity School, Harvard University.

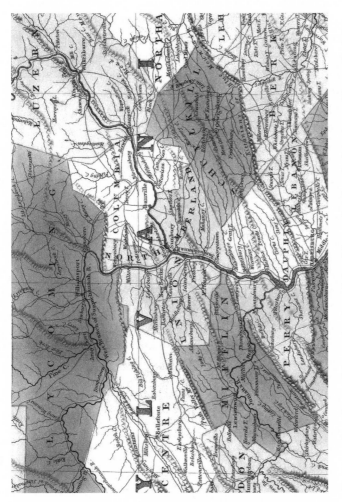

Fig. 4   Map of central Pennsylvania and detail inset, showing the locations of James Kay's ministry. Detail, Anthony Finley 1826 map of Pennsylvania, New Jersey, and Delaware. Courtesy of David Rumsey Map Collection, www.davidrumsey.com, and Cartography Associates.

towns opened up their schoolhouses, much like Northumberland had done for Priestley three decades earlier. Only in three towns did he have to conduct his services in private homes.[20]

These efforts resulted in a very successful ministry for Kay and promising prospects for Unitarianism. Despite all this success, however, Kay was alone in central Pennsylvania, not just as an avowed Unitarian, but as a minister of any liberal stance whatsoever, which was the very reason for his exchanges with prominent ministers in Boston. In a religious landscape filled with Presbyterians, Methodists, and numerous Reform groups, there were few ministers who offered a tolerant and inquisitive approach to matters of faith and religion. In 1846, toward the end of his ministerial career and life, Kay wrote a letter to James Freeman Clarke that summarized his perceptions of the history of Unitarianism in Northumberland. Priestley and Christie had resulted in "a few" embracing the Unitarian doctrines, and Christie's departure had further taken its toll on even that small number. "When I settled here, there was no preaching . . . there were only 3 or 4 Unitarians in this town," remarked Kay. But his efforts soon transformed the situation, allowing him to claim that "My congregation is more than a hundred . . . they are most of them mechanics and labourers. Had we more frequent preaching both in town and the surrounding country, I think our congregation would soon be doubled."[21]

Wishing to see for themselves the accuracy of the reports from the interior, the newly formed AUA sent Moses Thomas on their behalf to investigate the spread of Unitarianism and its worth in places distant from Boston. Thomas first stopped in Philadelphia for four days, where he met with Henry Furness, James Taylor, and John Vaughan. He then traveled to Harrisburg where he met and dined with Henry Alward (a bank teller), took tea with William Grimshaw, and visited Mr. Magennes (a lawyer and surveyor). When he arrived in Northumberland on April 25, 1826, he immediately called upon Kay, who was also being visited by his son Samuel from Lancaster, and he took the time to travel across the river into Sunbury and visit with Hugh Bellas. Obviously not very taken with the town, Thomas noted that "I know of nothing but pure zeal, and the grave of Priestley, that can induce him to remain here." But, as to the state of Unitarianism, Thomas saw more promise, especially as judged by the condition of their worship in comparison

---

20. Kay to Gannett, November 3, 1825, AUA (AHTL), bMS 571/2.
21. Kay to Clarke, April 1, 1846, AUA (AHTL), bMS 571/65.

to the other denominations present. Still, this was no Boston and Thomas remained somewhat critical of Kay's attachment to Priestley.[22]

The relationship between the AUA and Kay thus got off to a difficult start and would never fully recover. Kay first greeted the news of the formation of the AUA with excited anticipation, noting that it would serve to unite and strengthen the cause of liberal religion and proposed that both Harrisburg and Northumberland would unite with the association.[23] But he quickly came to view the Boston association as out of touch with Unitarians who were not in their immediate geographic radius, and the AUA never felt that Kay ever attempted to bring his actions and beliefs fully into line with their expectations. At the formative meeting of the Anonymous Association, the precursor to the AUA, the third central purpose of association was "to produce a unity of purpose and effort among Unitarian Christians" in effecting true religion, disclaiming sectarianism, and promoting social virtue, ideas that were all carried over into the formal declarations of the AUA.[24] But the two parties, the leadership of the AUA and James Kay, never fully agreed on how this tenet of association was to be defined.

In early May 1826, Gannett invited Kay to travel to Boston in order to attend the first annual meeting of the AUA. Kay declined the invitation, citing both ill health and financial limitations. The initial annual report of the AUA Executive Committee issued from the meeting, called Kay "a valuable minister . . . a worthy man, and one peculiarly fitted to increase the friends of Unitarian Christianity in that part of the country," and discussed the situation in Pennsylvania in very favorable terms, praising those "correspondents [who] have furnished the Committee with ample details respecting the history and conditions of Unitarians in Pennsylvania" and made positive mention of the correspondence with congregants and ministers from the Northumberland, Philadelphia, Harrisburg, Meadville, and Pittsburgh churches. The Treasurer's Report further revealed two disbursements of $100 each, one in 1825 to Kay in support of his ministry and the second in 1826 to the Harrisburg congregation in support of their efforts to construct a chapel.[25] The report also talked about opening a formal dialogue with

22. Moses Thomas to Ezra Gannett, April 25, 1826, AUA (AHTL), bMS 571/1.

23. James Kay to Ezra Gannett, September 27, 1825, AUA (AHTL), bMS 571/1.

24. This meeting took place on February 25, 1822, at the house of William Ellery Channing in Cambridge. See Graves, "Adventure of Faith," AUA (AHTL), bMS 11180, especially pp. 18–20.

25. AUA, *First Annual Report*, 9, 10, 12, and 21.

English Unitarians as "the thoughts of the committee have been turned to their brethren in other lands." The report went on to acknowledge the entirely coincidental, simultaneous formation of the British and Foreign Unitarian Association and the American Unitarian Association on the same day in 1825. "A constant communication will be preserved between the two Associations . . . [to] beneficial effect . . . making us better acquainted with one another . . . by the influence we shall mutually exert, and by the strength which will be given to our separate, or it may be, to our united efforts."[26]

Kay's correspondence with Boston frequently included requests for additional financial assistance and asking that numerous religious tracts be sent to him for distribution. In one of his earliest letters Kay noted that he had, within his first three years, already distributed four thousand Unitarian tracts. In December 1825 he requested another twelve hundred tracts (always noting that the cheaper the price, the more successful his efforts would be in terms of being able to sell them to the people) for distribution along his circuit. Kay estimated that at least one-third of the tracts would be used in Northumberland and the immediate vicinity, while the remainder would be taken to Harrisburg and points farther south and west. In a notation made upon the letter in handwriting other than Kay's (presumably Gannett's) it is noted that only sixty of each were sent for a total of one hundred eighty. The tract most often requested and distributed during the first few years of Kay's travels was *Dissertations on the Offices of Christianity* by Henry Ware Jr.[27]

But all was not well between Kay and the nascent AUA, as a close reading of the subsequent exchanges reveals. Kay's letter declining the invitation mentioned the continuing gulf that existed between his beliefs and concern for Priestley's legacy and those views being espoused by the leading figures of the AUA. Although Kay donated one dollar toward the efforts of the association and expressed support for their planned missionary efforts in India and other parts of the world, his words were tinged with skepticism.[28] While the polity of the Unitarian Church has always been congregational, the AUA and its associated conferences sought to suppress what it believed to be the errors in practice and thought of congregations not in compliance with the New England–based majority. Correspondence between Kay and Boston was soon filled with overt and covert references to the tensions which existed

---

26. Ibid., 16.
27. Kay to Gannett, December 31, 1825, and June 1, 1826, AUA (AHTL), bMS 571/2.
28. James Kay to Ezra Gannett, May 21, 1826, AUA (AHTL), bMS 571/2.

as a result. Channing promulgated such a view in 1829 during his speech given on the occasion of the fourth anniversary of the founding of the AUA, continuing with his attacks on Priestley and Socinianism despite his continuous decrying of the "injurious treatment" that Unitarians received from those who stood in opposition to them.[29]

Recognition of Kay's efforts and the presence of Unitarians who were of a different theological bent were sporadic. In 1825 Kay noted that the Unitarian Tract Society of Northumberland had thirty members, clearly one of the more numerous and active such groups, and he also noted the efforts to establish a similar group in Harrisburg. The membership in Northumberland (which most likely included several members from Sunbury as well as the other nearby towns) warranted consideration, as it stayed roughly the same size for the next twenty years. Yet, the *Auxiliaries to the American Unitarian Association,* which recorded the efforts and success of the tract societies throughout the country up to 1832, does not list either, although it does list both the Philadelphia and New York societies.[30] In 1834, a decade after Northumberland's society was formed, Philadelphia, Pittsburgh, and Peterborough, New Hampshire, could each only boast of fifty, twenty-three, and thirty-four Tract Society members respectively; Baltimore, only twenty. In the same year Furness lamented the absence of a Unitarian bookseller in Philadelphia, while George W. Burnap spoke of the situation in Baltimore, where Channing had delivered his famous address, as having "no very flattering prospects" for the spread of Unitarianism, "as such and by name," he added.[31]

Affairs between Kay and the AUA came to a head in 1826 when the AUA leadership ordered him to Harrisburg, thus beginning Kay's only official hiatus from his ministry in Northumberland. As the new state capital, it was believed that Harrisburg would yield a much stronger congregation than Northumberland and give the Unitarians a foothold among the political leadership and economic elites who resided there. Kay's early contact with the Harrisburg Unitarians, reaching back to 1823 and the fact that he routinely traveled the fifty-seven miles to preach in the city Courthouse every two Sundays out of eight, led them to conclude that his efforts would best be spent there. His

29. AUA, *Unitarianism in America*, 11.

30. Kay to Gannett, September 27, 1825, AUA (AHTL), bMS 571/1, and *Auxiliaries to American Unitarian Association,* AUA (AHTL), bMS 193/1/5.

31. E. G. Lakeman to Alexander Young, October 1, 1832; W. H. Furness to Jason Whitman, May 13, 1834; Abiel Abbot to Jason Whitman, May 14, 1834; G. W. Burnap to Jason Whitman, May 24, 1834. AUA (AHTL), bMS 571/13 and 15.

letters served as testimony in favor of a permanent ministry farther south, where the state's population was more numerous and prospects seemed more certain. "I have lately had letters from my friends in Harrisburg and in the neighboring town of Carlisle, which give me every reason to cherish the most sanguine hopes of the triumph of pure views of truth, over error, superstition, and intolerance. In the latter mentioned town, which is much larger than Harrisburg, we have every reason to hope that in a year or two, a temple will be raised," he noted. "I shall not only preach regularly in Harrisburg and Carlisle, but occasionally in the city of Lancaster, where I understand our cause is silently gaining ground, and in several of the large villages which exist in this section of the country."[32] Nonetheless, Kay's response to the AUA's request was tempered by his reservations and suspicions concerning their motives. Though he was satisfied that it was his duty to remove himself to Harrisburg and, to be fair, he even cherished the new opportunities it might provide, he also made it very clear to Gannett that he thought that the request was designed to stamp out the Northumberland congregation and end Priestley's legacy. If that were indeed the case, he wanted Gannett to know that such a move was as unwise as it was unprincipled.[33] Yet, at this stage he still held out hope that his goodwill gesture and constant stream of details sent to Boston would result in more ministerial help and that he would then be able to sustain the Northumberland congregation from afar, just as he had done with Harrisburg.

Kay's move to Harrisburg was also precipitated by a letter from Henry Alward to Boston in April 1825, detailing the history of the congregation's development and Kay's substantial efforts. He noted that Kay had begun preaching in Harrisburg more than eighteen months earlier to a group of "but two unitarians and those marked out by personal attacks from the pulpit, as well as in private by the prominent advocates of orthodoxy." On each successive visit Kay's sermons drew increasing crowds of those seeking pure and undefiled religion, attracting anywhere between sixty to five hundred persons. By September of that same year the group claimed a membership of close to one hundred. In response the Committee of Boston Appropriate Ministers, under the leadership of Henry Ware Jr., Alexander Young, and Gannett, raised $220 to be sent and solicited additional donations from other prominent Unitarians, including Lewis Tappan, Edward Everett, Samuel

---

32. Kay to Gannett, May 23, 1827, AUA (AHTL), bMS 571/4.
33. Ibid.

Eliot, Francis Parkman, Jared Sparks, and Andrews Norton. They also hatched their plans to request Kay's relocation.[34] Subsequent events saw Charles G. Appleton of Baltimore appealing directly to Channing, promoting the cause of Harrisburg and detailing the amount the Baltimore congregation had already sent in support.[35]

Such vitality carried over into the public sphere, as the Harrisburg Unitarians quickly found themselves under attack from Harrisburg's Presbyterian minister. "A few months ago the Calvinists republished in this borough a pamphlet, that was first published, I believe, in your state, entitled *An Exhibition of Unitarianism*, hoping thereby to put a stop to the further progress of 'heresy' as the[y] call our cause; but it has not had the desired effect, but rather the contrary. *We* have now in progress, and will shortly publish, *An Exhibition of Calvinism*." Alward then wrote Gannett and requested additional help by means of two "tracts containing our views," specifically asking for copies of *The Faith Once Delivered to the Saints* and *The Unitarians' Answer*, two Unitarian tracts then circulating in Boston and Philadelphia. He also asked for a catalog listing of all the tracts published in Boston so the group in Harrisburg could select those that would have the greatest impact in their city.[36]

With such a large membership, the backing of the AUA, and the commitments from other congregations throughout the country, the Harrisburg Unitarians were able to raise sufficient funds to construct their own chapel within two years. The church opened to great fanfare in February 1827, with sermons by the Reverends James Walker of Charlestown, Massachusetts, and William Furness of Philadelphia. Walker, who was touring the major cities of the East Coast and made the detour to Harrisburg for the dedication, preached the morning service, followed by Furness in the evening. Walker's sermon text was derived from Numbers 4, "If Balak would give me his houseful of silver and gold" and asked that the congregation not just bask in the glory of their building but also seek to maintain their individual faith. Just as Priestley had received a positive reception among the members of the U.S. government when he first preached in Philadelphia, Walker noted that "the members of the legislature were present in considerable

34. Henry Alward to AUA, April 13, 1825, Harrisburg, subscription request, AUA (AHTL), bMS 571/1; for the final tally of members, see Henry Alward to William G. Appleton, September 26, 1825, AUA (AHTL), bMS 571/1.

35. Charles Appleton to William E. Channing, September 28, 1825, Baltimore, AUA (AHTL), bMS 571/1.

36. Henry Alward to Ezra Gannett, December 26, 1826, Harrisburg, AUA (AHTL), bMS 571/3.

numbers, & it is understood that several experience much satisfaction in the new doctrines."[37]

But the optimism of the society was as short-lived. Even with a newly constructed chapel, settled minister, and the growing prominence of Harrisburg, the congregation did not last very long. Part of this had to do with a subsequent decision reached by Kay in 1828. Citing personal and health reasons, Kay informed the AUA of his intentions to return to Northumberland and to spend the rest of his days with the congregation he considered to be his true responsibility.[38] Kay's departure was also facilitated by the fact that the Harrisburg congregation, though numerous, was unable or unwilling to financially commit to the obligations of both a chapel and minister, while just the opposite was true in Northumberland where the congregation was "better able to support his ministry" through their financial and personal commitments. The nascent AUA, having lost the struggle to keep Kay out of Priestley's seat, was subsequently unable to fill the Harrisburg vacancy created by his departure and the congregation disbanded in 1829, still owing on the initial $500 loan they had taken to secure construction of the chapel.[39]

Not wishing to abandon the group in their time of need, Kay continued to request assistance, both pecuniary and pastoral, from Boston. Past experience had taught him, however, not to expect a positive response. In 1829, frustrated with the lack of attention given to his most important request for assistance Kay took it upon himself to attempt to recruit John Scholfield of Philadelphia to the Harrisburg pulpit. Kay also leaned on his friendship with Henry Alward and Silas Marsh of the Harrisburg congregation, asking them to do the same. The response was not what they hoped. "Tho' I should have been pleased if you had carried on my little work, or commenced another under a different title; yet I acquiesce in your reasons," replied Kay to Scholfield's letter of rejection. Not to be totally disappointed, he offered a counterproposal, asking if Scholfield could at least agree to a plan whereby he could travel to Harrisburg and "give them three Sunday's in a row" so that the congregation did not languish. This too, we know from Kay's later remarks concerning the absence of any services in the

---

37. James Walker to Ezra Gannett, February 21, 1827, Harrisburg, AUA (AHTL), bMS 571/5.

38. AUA, *Unitarianism in America*, 11.

39. The Unitarian Church of Harrisburg, "UCH History," http://www.paonline.com/uchuua/UCHHIST.htm/; accessed Februay 20, 2003.

city led by an official minister, failed.[40] The state's capital would thus remain without a Unitarian congregation for the next fifty years.

Despite central Pennsylvania's distance, both physical and spiritual, from Boston, Kay had ample evidence to believe that the region was fertile ground for the propagation and spread of Christian Unitarianism. In support of these views he cited his extensive travels and the numbers of people he encountered at his services. Nevertheless, "in the centre of the most populous part of Pennsylvania, exclusive of Philadelphia, I stand alone," Kay noted. "But alas! I fear that field is too large both for my abilities and strength . . . I stand alone, without a single co-adjutator. How I should rejoice, if I had but one brother in the ministry. Here is a field for half a dozen ministers." Without such assistance, Kay was the dominant figure responsible for the spread and propagation of Unitarianism throughout central Pennsylvania, especially Northumberland, Snyder, Union, and Dauphin counties. "I humbly do what I can, and have abundant reason to rejoice in what has been affected, and look forward with hope to the future. The cause is good, and it must prevail, and is prevailing," he communicated back to Boston in response to one of their many requests for information.[41] One of the most significant divisions between Kay and the AUA was over this very issue—ministerial presence. Repeated requests by Kay for help, bolstered by the glowing reports of his success, were met by absolute silence from Boston. Kay interpreted this response as testimony to the extent to which the new Unitarians would go to ensure that Priestley's legacy, and those who sought to perpetuate it, withered on the vine. The gulf between the two opposing convictions remained ever-present.

Despite the differences between the two groups, the central concern for Kay was not the adoption of a common unitarian theology, but rather a liberal alliance that brought all parties to the table. Once that was accomplished, a process which Kay had initially believed had begun with the Anonymous Association prior to 1825 and carried on under the AUA after that year, the distinctions would slowly diminish. It was evident that Kay needed the assistance, both financial and spiritual, of the AUA in order to succeed in his efforts at spreading "the exclusive worship of the One Jehovah, the God and Father of our Lord Jesus Christ."[42] In return for such support, Kay's letters were filled with

40. Henry Alward and Silas March to John Scholfield, June 29, 1829, and James Kay to John Scholfield, April 20, 1829, AUA (AHTL), bMS 571/9.
41. Kay to Gannett, May 23, 1827, AUA (AHTL), bMS 571/4.
42. Ibid.

expressions of support for the activities of the AUA and even requests for copies of the annual reports or meeting agendas of the organization.

The Northumberland congregation under Kay's leadership was able to accept membership within the AUA because of their willingness to see beyond particular distinctions of theology, as Priestley had preached, and join together under the cause of liberal religion. One cannot be too quick to dismiss the fact that Priestley also clearly denounced the Arian theology as incomplete and error-laden. His spirit of liberal ecumenism was replete with the notion that the truth would eventually win out and all liberals would come to see the Socinian position's truth. Thus it is easy to understand why, as the situation warranted, the AUA engaged in numerous and assorted attempts to discredit Priestley's legacy. The most notable was their decision to remove Kay from Northumberland, whose pulpit they intentionally left vacant during that time. Their actions removed him from a vibrant congregation, and he returned against the stated desires of Ezra Stiles Gannett, the first secretary of the AUA and the other members of the executive committee, including Henry Ware, whom Kay held in high regard.[43] The AUA's inability to replace Kay in Harrisburg resulted in that society's collapse. Given the tenuous situation in Harrisburg, it is interesting that Kay even agreed to follow the directive, but his decision to return home to Northumberland, where he lived out his days in Priestley's former home, served notice that the Socinian conflict was not over.[44]

Yet one must balance this against evidence of subtle support. Clearly the AUA financially propped up Kay's efforts to the extent permitted by their own financial limitations and certainly in proportion to the numbers he claimed against those attended to throughout Massachusetts. Kay began his November 3, 1825, letter to Gannett by thanking him (and requesting he pass along his sentiments to the AUA Executive Committee) for sending him $99.00 to support his ministry.[45] Kay's letters to the AUA reveal continued consideration of Kay's situation by the association or at least some of its individual members, and numerous statements of Kay's willing engagement with the group.[46]

43. First Records of the AUA Executive Committee May 1825–1847, Miscellaneous Collections, bMS 800/5. See also Kay to Gannett, March 11, 1825, AUA (AHTL), bMS 571/1.

44. Kay's residence in Northumberland, in the Priestley home where he lived with his wife and nine children, was of a much longer duration than Priestley's. In fact, the home was more commonly known as "the old Kay House" for most of its history. See Gutelius, *Northumberland*, 12.

45. Kay to Gannett, November 3, 1825, AUA (AHTL), bMS 571/2.

46. Kay to Gannett, December 31, 1825, and May 23, 1827, AUA (AHTL), bMS 571/2 and 571/4.

Emboldened by his return to Northumberland, Kay undertook his only major foray into publication in 1832 when his *Twenty Questions to Trinitarians. With Answers from Scripture* was printed as a tract by the AUA. The pamphlet consisted of eighteen pages of text and sold for two cents, five thousand copies of which were printed for distribution.[47] In an age when booksellers' profits were directly tied to the market they served, and they could easily be put out of business if they sold works that raised the religious ire of the population, few publishers outside Boston were willing to risk their livelihoods for the sake of Unitarianism. Kay's format for the tract was to pose a question, provide scriptural passages that answered the question, and then give his personal conclusions. The work was both a restatement of Unitarian principles for trinitarians and a reassertion of the Socinian views of Jesus' divine nature. The questions focused on issues of Christ's connections with God and his actions during his life. "It is demonstrably true," wrote Kay in response to the fifteenth question, concerning the nature of Christ, "that Jesus was *in all things made like unto his brethren.* If then he possessed a *divine nature,* it will follow beyond a doubt that all believers possess the same." Since human beings are not divine, it follows that Jesus was not divine either.[48] Perhaps precisely because of such an ambivalent and sometimes contradictory relationship between Kay and the Boston leadership, Northumberland was further marginalized. The records of the AUA indicate that they sent a steady supply of circulars to James Taylor and William Furness as well as John Vaughan in Philadelphia, James Kay and Hugh Bellas in Northumberland, Henry Alward and William Grimshaw of Harrisburg, and Benjamin Bakewell in Pittsburgh. But when they voted to establish depositories at twenty-four locations, including Philadelphia, Harrisburg (despite the fact that the congregation there was already defunct), Baltimore, Washington and Charleston, Northumberland was one of the more prominent locations of Unitarian activity excluded.[49]

Kay's return to Northumberland also resulted in a major success for the Northumberland congregation in 1834. His three-year absence had both abated the trinitarian opposition and sapped support for the movement in Northumberland. Among the pressing matters that were dropped was the fund for the construction of an independent chapel. After recovering from the three-year hiatus, the group responded with

47. Kay, *Twenty Questions.*
48. Ibid., 14–15 (AUA Tract pages, 178–79).
49. AUA Circular Book, October 25, 1825, AHTL, bMS 193/1 (4).

renewed vigor to the cause so that sufficient funds were on hand by 1834. A familiar name, Joseph Priestley, reappears in the records of the society at this time, but this was Joseph R. Priestley, a grandson, who was instrumental in helping Kay assemble the financial support for the project. The land was purchased from John and Hannah Taggart in February and construction rapidly followed. Among the trustees named on the deed of purchase was Priestley's grandson, then the treasurer for the Northumberland National Bank; Hugh Bellas, Priestley's former student; John Gaston; and John Taggart.[50] These latter two men were the grandson and son, respectively, of members of Priestley's original congregation in Northumberland.[51] When the brick chapel, which still stands as the oldest existing religious edifice in the town, was completed, it stood two stories high with a footprint of almost nine hundred square feet and far outshown the Presbyterian and Baptist churches which were then still wood, unpainted, and each only sixteen by eighteen feet.[52] Kay dedicated the chapel to Priestley's "earnest flock of hearers" (its dedication in Priestley's name would not take place for almost a hundred years) "who have never yet allowed the fire of his spirit to die out upon the altar which his hands raised . . . [may] his descendants strive to carry on the labor which he began," serving as a testament to Priestley's call to Unitarian worship, no matter what the secular circumstances.[53]

As Kay's health and ministerial prowess declined, he took it upon himself to find assistance and make certain that the Northumberland congregation would not be left without leadership should his ability to serve end altogether. In a series of letters addressed to the AUA, Kay informed them of his decision to hire a local minister from Lewisburg, the Reverend John Sutton, to preach in Northumberland on half of the Sundays of each month. "Till lately I had no prospect of gaining any help in this neighborhood," he wrote to James Freeman Clarke. But after a meeting with Sutton he was convinced, if the proper sum could

50. Bellas's close association with Priestley led to his drafting of comments about the Reverend and his own Unitarian beliefs, which was included in Sprague's *Annals of the American Pulpit*. Bellas was instrumental in keeping the Northumberland congregation alive, and his association with the group did not cause his public career to suffer. In 1809, Bellas was appointed to be Prothonotary of Northumberland County, replacing Daniel Levy. See *Luzern County Federalist*, January 20, 1809.

51. Gutelius, "Churches," 136. See also 1802 Northumberland County Tax Collection Records, JPH Research File no. 2, for a list of residents of the town while Priestley actively preached.

52. Bell, *History of Northumberland County*, 538–45.

53. Helen T. Clark, "Chapel Dedication," in *Public Press* (Northumberland, Pa.), May 16, 1881, JPH.

be secured, that Sutton could take over not only two out of four Sundays a month at the Northumberland Chapel, but also assume many of his other, more taxing, missionary duties. "I am extremely anxious to preserve the congregation we have, and if possible to increase it; which I think is very probable if we can secure Mr. Sutton's assistance in the way he proposes."[54] Sutton, a former Methodist, was then serving as the pastor of the Christian Chapel in Lewisburg, some twelve miles away, the successor to George Richmond, who had assumed the position in 1825 as the congregation's first permanent pastor.

Sutton's church was situated on Fourth Street, between the existing churches of St. John and St. Anthony, and was begun in 1822 when a local businessman, Elijah Bacon, began a series of meetings to formally gather and establish the congregation leading up to the chapel's opening service on Sunday, September 14, 1823.[55] The initial Sabbath service was led by Kay, who delivered the day's sermon. On the occasion of the chapel's consecration the *Miltonian*, the region's leading newspaper published five miles north of Lewisburg, noted that "it will be gratifying to the friends of religious liberty and free inquiry to learn that this church has been built upon the most liberal principles, and is intended to accommodate all those who acknowledge the divine mission of our Lord Jesus Christ."[56] John Blair Linn, in his history of Lewisburg and the surrounding area, further noted that the group was inclined "mainly against the discipline of the orthodox, and the church was open to all persons for free discussion of religious tenets."[57] While Lewisburg contained almost fifteen other congregations, it was, like so many other towns in the central Susquehanna River valley, deeply integrated into a wider religious community, with townspeople routinely attending services in Selinsgrove, New Berlin, Buffalo Township, Northumberland, and Mifflinburg, depending upon their denominational affiliation and the availability of regular ministers.

Sutton's ecumenical tendencies were well known. In 1845 he was one of four preachers who helped the town celebrate Independence Day at the local religious camp in Brown's Woods. With over seven hundred young Sunday school children present Sutton, along with the Reverends Crever, Harbaugh, and Zeller, spoke to the youth about

54. James Kay to James Freeman Clarke, March 9, 1846, AUA (AHTL), bMS 571/46.
55. Linn, *Annals of Buffalo Valley*, 460. In 1855, the chapel was moved to Third Street below Market Street.
56. *The Miltonian* (Milton, Pa.), September 14, 1823, 2. As quoted in Linn, *Annals of Buffalo Valley*, 460.
57. Linn, *Annals of Buffalo Valley*, 460. See also p. 441.

both their civic and religious obligations.[58] Kay included this information in his letters to Boston: "Mr. Sutton is a married man with a family of three children. He is about 35 years of age. He is a worthy and excellent man. He has preached occasionally to my Congregation with acceptance; and I believe is well fitted for usefulness in the country."[59] When he received no official response, Kay assumed that his actions were acceptable.

Expanding Unitarianism's Reach

Although Kay was increasingly unable to make his missionary rounds as he once did and could no longer preach to the congregation in Northumberland more than a few times a year, he remained active in efforts to overcome the adversities of isolation and opposition. To the end he remained a staunch advocate of Priestleyan Unitarianism and appealed to the officers and influential members of the AUA to recognize the contributions of Priestley and English Unitarianism in America. Finding that his petitions were often ignored, Kay decided to capitalize on his common associations with those Unitarians who were also distant from Boston and who also believed that association with the AUA was more a matter of convenience than a shared and common identity.

Kay's efforts to reach out began with Robert Little, a Unitarian minister in Washington, D.C., and an English immigrant who also harbored many affinities for the teachings and legacy of Priestley. Little had come to the United States in 1819 and was invited to deliver the morning sermon for Jared Sparks's Baltimore ordination. Given the plans that Channing had for the occasion, Little's presence provided a clear reminder of the multiple theological influences on the Baltimore congregation and a visible link to the English Socinians.[60] Once settled in the United States, Little continued to preach Priestleyan Unitarianism while maintaining connections with New England and associating with members of the government.[61]

As with Priestley in Philadelphia, the associated group of Unitarians already in Washington, D.C., where Little had chosen to settle, hoped that his presence would prove the catalyst to solidify their congregational

58. Ibid., 544.
59. Kay to Clarke, April 1, 1846, AUA (AHTL), bMS 571/65.
60. See Channing, *Memoir*, 2:162.
61. Little, *Religious Liberty and Unitarianism Vindicated*, 10.

presence. They consisted of roughly a dozen members and held services, which were attended by no more than forty souls, in a rented room. Little was properly elected as their minister in November 1821, and they then set out to formally organize themselves into the First Unitarian Church, Washington. Among the founders of the church were John Quincy Adams and John C. Calhoun. Right before his election he delivered the sermon "The Mystery of Christ," a refutation of the "late attack upon the system of Unitarianism by Mr. [Anthony] Kohlmann, and also upon the violent unchristian-like abuse heaped on us every Sunday from certain pulpits in this neighborhood"; on that topic Kay was able to share some of his own experiences.[62] But troubles with the orthodox and the vehemence of their opposition were to be expected. Little's major concern, as expressed in a letter to Gannett upon learning the news about the formation of the AUA, was a broader liberal fellowship that by its very nature could help quiet the opposition. "I rejoice that our New England friends have at length assumed decision enough to avow & patronize such an unpopular name. I am sure we shall not be backward to unite ourselves in such a good work," he wrote, making an overture of accommodation and seeking the same from Boston. "Union is strength," he continued, pushing the AUA to consider opening their fellowship to all believers, "and if a spirit of frank & unreserved cooperation should exist among all the Churches of our Denomination in the Atlantic States, it will not be long before the triumphs of Unitarianism (i.e. of true Religion, as opposed to all falsehood & [unknown]) are spread over the whole Union."[63] But events quickly proved such optimism to be premature, so that five months later his correspondence with Gannett was much more reserved yet still cordial in tone. Little's subsequent letters to Boston reveal his continuing concerns over their disregard for theological diversity as evidenced in the tone and content of their pamphlets, the contradiction between their expressions of widespread concern and actions that were Boston-centered, and their lack of regard for the continuing efforts of those not in their immediate circle of influence. He, like Kay, openly lamented that he had been "obliged for six years to stand isolated and almost alone" in the work of spreading Unitarianism among the residents and visitors to the capital city.[64]

62. Little, "Mystery of Christ," 2–3.
63. Robert Little to Ezra Gannett, July 8, 1825, AUA (AHTL), bMS 571/1.
64. Robert Little to Ezra Gannett, November 24, 1825, and May 20, 1827, AUA (AHTL), bMS 571/2.

By 1826 the First Unitarian Church, Washington, had amassed sufficient funds to build a church with seventy-five pews and claimed almost thirty families as members and regular attendees. Like Kay, Little declined the invitations to attend the annual AUA meetings on the grounds that his presence was required in Washington, and there were none who could fill in during such a prolonged absence. Little, however, also made clear that he would not feel completely welcome, knowing that his views on Unitarianism would not be shared by most others in attendance. His words reflected clarity of thought and the writings of Priestley. "Respecting the progress of pure Christian truth in the hands of Unitarianism—the more we approximate to that initial simplicity of manner, character, social feelings, and high toned morality, which characterized the first Christian teachers, the greater our success will be. . . . Our grand distinctive character should be—Liberty of opinion & holiness."[65]

Little's presence in the capital once again put English Unitarianism in the seat of the nation's government, and he made the most of it, even delivering a sermon before the House of Representatives titled "Religious Liberty and Unitarianism Vindicated." The sermon was both provocative and defensive.[66] His two main arguments positioned Unitarianism within the larger religious framework of the United States. First, he noted "the advantages our system possesses in this country from the absence of a national religion," and then he tackled the thornier proposition: "the impossibility of our opponents overthrowing that cause in which we are embarked," a cause designed to promote Christian rationalism.[67] Here again, Priestley served as the central support. Little praised Priestley's contention that liberal rationalism could exist in concert with Christian principles and an intense belief in the Christian religion. Little's sermon was all the more notable given his own religious transformation. As an Englishman brought up within the Methodist movement, Little had once thundered against "the poisonous heresies of Socinians and Universalists."[68] By 1810, Little moved away from the religion of his youth, sparked by a series of rebuffs from independent churches in England and changes in his personal views of established practices such as infant baptism, the role of the minister, and congregational practices that relied on English

65. Robert Little to Ezra Gannett, May 21, 1827, Washington, D.C., AUA (AHTL), bMS 571/4.
66. Little, *Religious Liberty and Unitarianism Vindicated*, 3–4.
67. Ibid., 10.
68. Little, "Ordination Sermon," 4.

notions of status.[69] By 1814 he was a Unitarian, owing to a long association with the Toulmin family and the Reverend John Campbell.

The ties with Kay were more than a coincidental alignment of ideals. The two were of a like mind given their similar readings, experiences, and personal exchanges. In August 1827 Little and his family traveled to Harrisburg to visit Kay and his family. The two men were seeking to boost each other's spirits, and Little was seeking rest. But the illness from which Little was seeking to recover got the best of him, and he died that same month. Perhaps Little had requested it, or perhaps it was something Kay decided on his own, in consultation with Little's family, but whatever the case, Little's body was taken upriver to Northumberland and buried alongside Priestley's. After settling their affairs in Washington, Little's family returned to Pennsylvania to take up residence.[70] But the pulpit in Washington would not stay empty. Even the AUA saw the wisdom of maintaining such an important post, as Charles Bullfinch reminded them in a letter, "we consider our station as an important one for diffusing the principles we profess."[71]

John Campbell, who had brought Little to Unitarianism, had also been friends with James Kay back in Europe. The two were reunited when Campbell eventually settled in Pittsburgh where he became a leading figure in Unitarianism's progress in the western region of Pennsylvania. Like Kay, Campbell was originally a Baptist minister whose conversion took place sometime in the winter of 1811. Just as Kay was vacating his Unitarian Baptist pulpit in Kendal, Westmoreland County, Campbell was called to take over at the Market Place Chapel, of the old English Presbyterian foundation. After Kay's departure, the two congregations merged under Campbell's leadership, where he remained until 1820. It was Campbell's daughter Jean Armour and her husband Joseph who encouraged the minister to migrate to Pittsburgh and to set up a Unitarian chapel where none then existed. With the substantial financial assistance of Benjamin Bakewell a chapel was constructed, with an additional room for a school, and dedicated on October 19, 1823. Although the extant letters of Kay do not speak to his journey to Pittsburgh for this event, it was reported in the *Unitarian Miscellany* of 1824 that he preached the dedication sermon, taking his text from John 4:24, "The hour cometh, and now is when the true

---

69. See Hill, "Robert Little, John Campbell, and James Kay," 6–7.

70. Christopher P. Cranch to Gannett, March 3, 1831, AUA (AHTL), bMS 571/12.

71. Charles Bullfinch to Stephen Higgenson, December 3, 1827, AUA (AHTL), bMS 571/5.

worshippers shall worship the Father in spirit and in truth." The article made it a point to mention the "very numerous and respectable audience which attended, and the desire of great numbers to hear, who could not gain admittance for want of room," statements that were later echoed during the similar events in Harrisburg and Northumberland.[72] The congregation flourished over the next several decades, outgrowing their original chapel. Eventually, the congregation joined with the ministers of nearby Meadville in the formation of the Western Conference of Unitarians, a group which was more reflective of the unique social and theological needs of those Unitarians, who were, increasingly, geographically and religiously distant from Boston.

Campbell himself, however, died the year after the opening of the chapel. Kay had earlier noted the dichotomy between Campbell's ministerial prospects and his increasingly poor health, which failed on July 20, 1824. "His piety to God, his benevolence to man, his patience under suffering, his resignation to the Divine will, his perfect disinterestedness, and his ardent love of truth, have rarely been equaled," wrote one chronicler of his life and legacy.[73] For a brief time, here too, Kay had established substantive contact with a minister who came to the United States heavily influenced by English Unitarianism.

Kay's position on the "frontier" of rationalism—both with respect to his isolation from Boston and as one of the few Unitarian ministers in central Pennsylvania—was alleviated with the emergence of Jan Huidekoper and the Meadville Seminary to the west. Encouraged by the work being done in Pittsburgh, Kay had seen his own prospects greatly enhanced by the presence of this new organization. He immediately saw the new seminary as providing an important and lacking resource—trained ministers—even going so far as to let those in Boston know that he was disappointed in their neglect and that he was turning to Meadville in order to fill the ministerial vacancies in the region.[74] With this in mind he first wrote to J. H. Huidekoper, the founder of the theological school at Meadville, praising his articles in the *Western Messenger*, thus establishing an intellectual and theological contact that would sustain him throughout his final days.[75]

---

72. Jared Sparks, "Editor's Note," *Unitarian Miscellany and Christian Monitor* (Baltimore), November 1823, 120.

73. F.W.P. Greenwood, "Dr. Channing's Sermon at the Ordination of a Colleague," *Unitarian Miscellany and Christian Monitor* (Baltimore), October 1824, 218–23.

74. James Kay to Ezra Stiles Gannett, August 3, 1829, Northumberland, AUA (AHTL), bMS 571/9.

75. James Kay to J. H. Huidekoper, December 4, 1840, MLTS.

Turning to Meadville was more than a matter of expedience. Kay suggested that the Bostonians' insistence that ministers be trained in the classical languages was both unnecessary and limiting and designed to limit the spread of Unitarianism elsewhere in the country. Many who went through such a program of study had acquired such a sense of themselves and the status of a minister that they only considered parishes and ministerial positions capable of offering comfortable stipends. What the interior and frontier regions required was a man who was willing to live on less, endure personal hardship, meet religious challenges head on, and never resolve to accept only a settled pulpit. In the end Kay's despair and exasperation showed through: "But I suppose, that for a minister to take the whole charge amongst us, we must ultimately look to Meadville, where, I hope and pray, many useful men will be prepared, to proclaim 'the unsearchable riches of Christ.'"[76] It was at this time that Kay also turned away from the *Christian Register* as the medium of choice for his communication with other Unitarians and opted, instead, for the newly devised *Western Messenger,* which, though under the editorship of transplanted New Englanders, was much broader in its outlook and appeal than the journals that remained based in New England.[77]

The quest to ensure the future of Unitarianism in central Pennsylvania under Kay's leadership continued right into the final year of his life, even after his own ministerial efforts had all but ended. Huidekoper wrote to Kay inquiring about the feasibility of sending a young minister trained at Meadville to resume Kay's itinerant ministerial efforts and take over the Harrisburg post. But this time, for the first time, Kay was not receptive; the request came too late and seemed too little. What precisely weighed on this decision is unknown. Kay felt that it was unwise for the Reverend Billings, whom Huidekoper had suggested as appropriate for the kind of ministerial work required in the region, to move into central Pennsylvania, perhaps due to his marital status or the lack of compensation that awaited him. Kay did note that there were no vacant pulpits and that those with whom he had discussed the idea were "not disposed to encourage it."[78] Foremost in Kay's mind, no doubt, was the lack of support from Boston over the preceding quarter of a century. Kay deflected Huidekoper's suggestion

76. Kay to Clarke, April 1, 1846, AUA (AHTL), bMS 571/65.
77. James Kay to Ezra Stiles Gannett, February 25, 1835 (letter forwarded by Gannett to Jason Whitman), AUA (AHTL), bMS 571/17.
78. James Kay to J. H. Huidekoper, May 30, 1846, MLTS.

by noting, as he had so frequently to the AUA leadership in the past, that no ministry in the central Pennsylvania region was destined to be feasible unless those, like Huidekoper, "who have influence with the Boston Societies," could convince them to see beyond their own boundaries. Only then would a Unitarian minister in central Pennsylvania have the capacity to effectively compete against the other growing denominations and find a fruitful ministerial existence. Nonetheless, Kay lauded the establishment of the Meadville Seminary, noting that it was sure to produce well-trained young men who would extend "the knowledge of primitive Christianity."[79] Neither man would have overlooked or misunderstood this statement as anything other than a thinly veiled reference to Priestleyan theology. That same year Kay sent Huidekoper a copy of the *Christian Register* (no doubt an unnecessary gesture given Huidekoper's own connections with New England and his role in publishing his own Unitarian weekly) in which he had published Priestley's sermon "Divine Influence" along with his personal commentary on its passages. The Northumberland minister asked Huidekoper to consider republishing the sermon in the *Western Messenger* on the grounds that it "would probably give rise to some discussion [and] might be of service to our young speculators" and secure the denomination within Christianity.[80]

Kay's letters also hint at a subject that was becoming increasingly important to all Unitarians, the birth and growth of Transcendentalism. While Kay would not live long enough to fully see its effects, he was well aware of its initial impacts, and he did not like what he saw. He called Transcendentalism an "intuitive religion" and equated it with "darkness itself." His reactions were taken straight from the writings of Priestley, and he reasserted Priestley's legacy as a man who never wavered from the belief that Unitarians were Christians. Transcendentalism threatened to destroy all of that. "The Transcendental Philosophy," Kay wrote Huidekoper, "if I am not greatly mistaken, will corrupt the beautiful system of Christianity as exhibited in Unitarianism; if it does not subvert, in the minds of some, Christianity itself." Kay then went on to express his full support for any and all attempts taken at Meadville in the education of new ministers or the publication of new writings to marshal all the forces of Unitarianism against this encroachment.[81]

79. James Kay to J. H. Huidekoper, September 6, 1844, MLTS.
80. Ibid.
81. Ibid.

Interspersed among this flurry of new and newly directed correspondence and writings was a series of final letters to the AUA, letters that reveal the continuing tensions between Kay and the Boston leadership. Kay's constant requests for assistance and their rejection had taken a heavy toll on his spirit. But he never tired of reminding Boston of the legacy he was trying to sustain. Reflecting on his mortality, he wrote that "it would be a painful thought to me, and I have no doubt, to all the friends of Unitarianism, if the neat church in [Northumberland] should be closed, for want of a minister. Let it be recollected that this is the place where the late Dr. Priestley (the father of Modern Unitarianism) lived—labored—and died, and where he is buried." It was a request and a reminder that he was sure they could not ignore. "Will you then, my dear sir," he implored James Freeman Clarke, "interest yourself on this subject?"[82]

The Congregation Evolves

The Northumberland ministry that Kay had secured lasted, with a succession of eight ministers. But over the years, the membership steadily dwindled, as these successors had neither Kay's interminable energy nor the talents and stature of Priestley, and there were interludes of inactivity, such as the one between 1853 with the death of Thomas Lathrop and 1869 when there was no settled minister until the arrival of David H. Clark. Furthermore, Kay was the last English Unitarian to occupy the pulpit of the Northumberland Chapel; all who followed him, including his immediate successor Lathrop, were American and came to Northumberland following their training in Boston under the influence of the AUA. The membership's shift was partly in response to the theological shifts within Unitarianism, the drag of Transcendentalism, and growing disregard for their own legacy as one of the first Unitarian societies in the nation. Only one of the successors, Hasket Derby Catlin, who was married to Hannah Taggart Priestley, one of Priestley's great-great-granddaughters was able to bring a renewed sense of purpose to the congregation. Catlin preached at Northumberland from 1873 to 1877 and would return to minister there again starting in 1910, but during his first years of service it was the family ties that served to bind only the descendents of Priestley to the society,

82. Kay to Clarke, March 9, 1846, AUA (AHTL), bMS 571/64.

a group who needed no such impetus, and he spent the height of his ministerial career attending to more lucrative and stable churches in New York, New Hampshire, and Maine.

The extent of New England's efforts to bury the history and legacy of Priestley and the Socinians can be seen through a careful reading of *The Unitarian Annual Register* and its reports over the years. The 1846 *Register* published what purported to be a comprehensive list of "Churches and Societies with their Pastors" throughout the country. The *Register* listed only two congregations in Pennsylvania, the one in Philadelphia under the leadership of William Furness and the Meadville congregation led by Rufus Stebbins. Neither the Northumberland nor the Harrisburg congregations were included or even mentioned, although the defunct Washington, D.C., congregation was. The only recognition given was a mention of Kay among the "Clergymen Without Parishes" category, which included "aged men, who have resigned their charge; others, invalids unable to preach or labor."[83] The records of the *Register* are also a testimony to the passage of the most prominent ministers who were heavily influenced by Priestley and theological supporters, listing the entire cadre of deceased Unitarian ministers, including Abiel Abbot, William Bentley, James Freeman, and John Prince, but not Priestley himself. These sentiments were further revealed in the encapsulated denominational history appended to the records. Intended to inform those who were either not knowledgeable about Unitarianism or had only a cursory understanding, the history begins in 1805, excluding any mention of the earlier English-inspired societies, and only narrating the transformation of the Congregationalist liberals into Liberal Christians, and ultimately their claims to the Unitarian name.

Perhaps someone called these glaring omissions to the attention of the editors or implored the leadership of the AUA to more fully account for all of the contributing impulses, for in the following year's *Register,* Kay, though now deceased, and the Northumberland congregation are both included.[84] Furthermore, in another section of the work, "Ministry at Large," English ministers make the 1847 list, while they did not make it in 1846, including those who were then occupying Priestley's

83. AUA, *Unitarian Annual Register for the Year 1846,* 19, 20–21; henceforth cited as "*Register*" with the year in parentheses. The Harrisburg congregation is not mentioned or listed in any *Register* following that of 1829. In the *Monthly Journal* of July 1865 the Executive Report included a reference to financial support to Washington, D.C., and other "feeble societies." See *Monthly Journal* (Boston), Boston, July 1865, 309.

84. AUA, *Register* (1847), 21.

old pulpits.[85] In this edition the editors even went so far as to include a report from England, drafted by Mary Carpenter of Bristol, detailing the affairs of the English churches.[86] There is no explanation for this shift in attention or rationale for the editorial changes. And though this is an interesting twist to the recognition accorded the English Unitarians, there was still no mention of Priestley, Socinianism, or the efforts of the early Unitarians in America. Socinianism was entirely omitted from a subsection of the work "The Name of 'Unitarian,'" which laid out the theology behind the denomination and provided an account of the origin of the name and how it came to be adopted in New England. Any reference to Christ's full humanity was also excluded, even in historical terms, from the accompanying entry "The Brief Statement of Unitarian Belief."[87] The subsequent *Registers* all follow suit.

Had the *Register* been accounting for the Northumberland society, they would have been able to document a significant transition in 1878 when it lost its minister and, unable to find a replacement, was led by lay members, most notably three of Priestley's great-great-granddaughters, until well after the turn of the century. Services now consisted of readings from preprinted sermons, frequently from the *Christian Register*, organ music, and messages centered on the role of charity and civic responsibility among believers. The family served as caretakers for the property and continued the Unitarian presence in Northumberland. Shortly before 1900, however, even these services ceased, and the building was placed in the service of the township, temporarily ending its role as a chapel.[88]

But the society was not completely defunct, and they still continued to focus on doctrinal issues, especially the ones that often separated them from the prevailing sentiments.[89] In 1910, the remaining Northumberland Unitarians, led by descendents of Priestley and John Taggart, called the Reverend Hasket Derby Catlin to serve, once again, as their minister. Under Catlin's leadership, the congregation rededicated the chapel, giving it the name of the Joseph Priestley Memorial Chapel, and subsequently deeded the property to the AUA, with whom Catlin had been affiliated for his entire ministerial career. Along with the

---

85. AUA, *Register* (1846), 19, and (1847), 22.
86. AUA, *Register* (1847), 44–46.
87. Ibid., 49–50, 55–60.
88. Gutelius, "Churches," 136.
89. Thomas Lathrop to James Freeman Clarke, September 24, 1849, AUA (AHTL), bMS 571/83.

property went a small fund, which was established as a trust to be used in support of the structure's maintenance. The AUA agreed to the transfer and on October 24, 1910, affirmed the rededication in Priestley's name and initiated the Joseph Priestley Unitarian Conference. The Reverend Dr. Samuel A. Eliot, president of the AUA, delivered the event's sermon, "The Administrative Ideals of a Free Church," speaking to the relationship between groups that had come to the same association through different paths.[90] The schism between the AUA and Priestley's congregation was ended as the congregation found peace as a part of the larger, national organization and were overjoyed by the reincorporation of his ideas into the theological and denominational accounts and future of the faith.

Catlin's earlier service to the Northumberland congregation was just a brief stop among many in his fifty-year ministerial career and had left little impact on the society. His second term of service was quite different. Those who honored him upon his death in 1917 noted that he had given "devoted service . . . to this church of sacred inspiration and memories."[91] The Reverend Albert J. Coleman came to Northumberland from Germantown to conduct the service, and was joined by both the local Methodist and Presbyterian ministers. Catlin's death, noted one, "has taken from the town one who, though he had but a small church and congregation, was a pastor-at-large in the community," and no death in the town was "more keenly felt."[92] But Catlin's rejuvenated congregation did not survive for very long after his death, and until the 1930s languished as they once had. For their part, Boston would not invest much in the group or even put much effort into maintaining the chapel, only committing to having a minister make a once-a-year journey to deliver an address and check on the property. Since that day the executive committee of the Board of Trustees of the AUA has determined the fate of the church and Priestley's memory, doling out the necessary funds to keep the edifice intact and reformulating the congregation in the 1950s.

90. Sarah C. Taggart to Samuel A. Eliot, February 20, 1911, AUA (AHTL), bMS 496/40 (9). Today the Joseph Priestley District of the Unitarian Universalist Congregations serves central and eastern Pennsylvania, southern New Jersey, Delaware, Maryland, District of Columbia, and northern Virginia. Of these, only Virginia was not part of the original Conference.

91. Rev. Albert J. Coleman, "Address . . . at the Funeral Service of the Rev. Hasket Derby Catlin, Northumberland, PA, June 6, 1917" (Northumberland: Public Press Print, 1917), AUA (AHTL), bMS 01446/27.

92. Unknown, "Rev. Hasket Derby Catlin," [obituary, 1917], AUA (AHTL), bMS 01446/27.

As the Northumberland Unitarians progressively matured, experienced the ebb and flow of congregational success and failure, and endured the constant shifts of the nation's prevailing religious sentiments marked by revivalism, emotionalism, and rationalism, they were joined in common purpose by the AUA. Both groups saw the advantage of moving away from the particularities underlying the various manifestations of Unitarian beliefs, seeking to finally live up to the spirit of free inquiry and tolerance that both Channing and Priestley had advocated, albeit each from his own perspective. In the course of these developments Priestley's reputation and contributions enjoyed a renaissance of sorts, as his ideas about being a Unitarian Christian were once invoked by the Unitarian leadership in order to counter "the transformation of Unitarianism from a Christocentric religion to a pragmatic, humanistic theism, retaining the Christian name but actually being Christian only in the sense of recognizing its dependence upon the religious patterns of Western culture."[93] Thomas Huxley pointed to the central distinction that had originally expelled Priestley from the Unitarian religion in 1819, noting that it was less about theology than politics. "He was the steadfast champion of that hypothesis respecting the Divine nature which is termed Unitarianism by its friends and Socinianism by its foes" but made it clear that such was the case no more.[94]

An exchange between Hasket Catlin and Samuel Eliot, one of the leaders of the AUA in 1915, effectively sums up the foundations of the long-standing mutual suspicion between Unitarians in Northumberland and those in Boston as well as the later shifts toward the end of the nineteenth century. Catlin wrote to Eliot asking for "distinct assurance that the Association will never during its long existence suffer the Joseph Priestley Memorial Church to die." Both Catlin and Sarah Taggart had seen enough of Boston's continuing indifference to bring into question the commitment of the AUA to sustaining the reemergence of the Chapel Society.[95] Eliot took more than just a little offense at the accusation that he was not committed to supporting the Priestley Society. Such a request was, he noted at first, "beyond my power" to assure. But, he further noted, that "it is impossible to believe that the fellowship of churches of which this Association is simply the agent will ever let the Priestley Memorial become merely a name. It seems to me that

93. Persons, *Free Religion*, 154.
94. Huxley, "Joseph Priestley," in *Collected Essays*, 3:1.
95. Hasket D. Catlin to Samuel Eliot, October 22, 1915, AUA (AHTL), bMS 496/40 (9).

we can rest with reasonable assurance upon the historic sense of our communion and its appreciation of what has been done at Northumberland and what is being done there now. . . . A body of churches that would let the Priestley Memorial go out of existence would not deserve to live at all, and probably would not continue to exist."[96] The tone and contents of the original letter from Catlin were subsequently explained away by Jean Priestley as she related to Eliot the details of Catlin's deteriorating mental and physical health. Nonetheless, the ideas expressed by Catlin were quite similar to ideas expressed by others who had been involved with the Chapel throughout its history and who constantly found the support of the AUA lacking.

96. Samuel Eliot to Hasket D. Catlin, October 28, 1915, AUA (AHTL), bMS 496/40 (9).

CONCLUSION: THE DEATH AND
RESURRECTION OF ENGLISH UNITARIANISM?

> Let us agree, then, that Religion, occupying herself with personal destinies and
> keeping thus in contact with the only absolute realities which we know, must
> necessarily play an eternal part in human history. The next thing to decide is what
> she reveals about those destinies, or whether indeed she reveals anything distinct
> enough to be considered a general message to mankind.
>
> —WILLIAM JAMES, *The Varieties of Religious Experience*

May 1900 marked the seventy-fifth anniversary of the founding of the
AUA, the organization having declared May 25, 1825, to be "taken as
the birthday of the Unitarian denomination in America." The organizers
invited twelve foreign associations to send delegates, foremost among
them the British and Foreign Unitarian Association, and scheduled
plenary sessions for the event to discuss the denomination's past and
plan for its future.[1] In planning for these sessions the organizers cast a
wide net, looking to include a multitude of liberal Christians who could
help account for the breadth of liberal principles in America. While
William Ellery Channing was clearly the central figure in American
Unitarianism's past, the organizers understood that the passage of events
over the previous seventy-five years had involved Priestley's ideas on
Christianity's corruptions, denominational foundations, the inseparable
nature of Christianity and especially his stance on Jesus' humanity. His
theology had been vital to the continuing life of the denomination, and
its proponents could point to a history of repeated engagement with
Priestley; thus he was included among those to be honored.

In the course of the century since his death, Joseph Priestley had been
fully reformed into a major underlying influence of Unitarianism, often
being touted as a "defender of the [Christian] faith with unbelievers."[2]

---

1. AUA, "Seventy-fifth Anniversary of the American Unitarian Association," February
1900, AUA (AHTL), bMS 11092/1. This announcement was really a solicitation for financial
support. It was not the first or last time that the AUA solicited funds from its members and
supporters. In fact, the entire file cited herein is filled with solicitations beginning in 1854
and going right to the end of the period covered by the collection.

2. Ware, *Sober Thoughts*, lxxii.

But he had also stood as a major influence on his own terms, propagating English Unitarianism and calling America's liberal Christians to openly avow their sentiments. As the needs of religious liberals changed, so too did their perspective, and as the history of America became more complex, the fullness of his religious influence and debate was further revealed.

On the eve of the American Civil War, William Sprague, in his multivolume work *Annals of the American Pulpit,* established Priestley as the figure of Unitarianism's early years against which all others were to be measured. Although Priestley had once represented an extreme on the Unitarian spectrum, the situation had changed to such a degree that such a classification no longer applied, and his ideas were now fully accepted as an important part of the denomination's past.[3] In the face of the changes wrought within the denomination and its engagement with the larger American religious community, Priestley had come to occupy a central place, as George Ellis wrote in 1857, when he noted that "the open profession of Socinianism is a very harmless affair."[4] In 1879, following a trip to the United States, the Englishman Dean Stanley reflected on the intertwined history of English and American Unitarianism in much the same light. "We meet from time to time with instances which reveal to us as with a lightning flash, the need of higher inspirations," he stated. "We now all acknowledge that the mob was wrong, and that the few who would have tolerated Priestley were right . . . [both] in the institutes of our great English towns, as in the United States of America."[5] At the end of the century, in his sermon "Unitarian Principles" delivered at the Unitarian Church of Troy, New York, on May 16, 1897, the Reverend Joseph Henry Crooker spoke of the value of the "very large degree of liberty of thought respecting all matters pertaining to religion" as enjoyed by Unitarians. "We are in religious organization 'independents,' in that glorious company with Milton and Cromwell, Vane and Williams, Locke and Priestley, by whom the great principles of the modern state respecting religious freedom and religious equality were wrought out and made fundamental in government."[6] Over the course of the last half of the nineteenth century Priestley and Socinianism were revitalized in countless numbers of religious pamphlets, journal articles, sermons, and speeches, and each

---

3. Sprague, *Annals of the American Pulpit,* 8:ix.

4. Ellis, *Unitarian Controversy,* 317.

5. Stanley, "Historical Aspect," 267.

6. Rev. Joseph Henry Crooker, *Unitarian Principles,* Unitarian Church, Troy, N.Y., May 16, 1897, AUA (AHTL), bMS 14018/1.

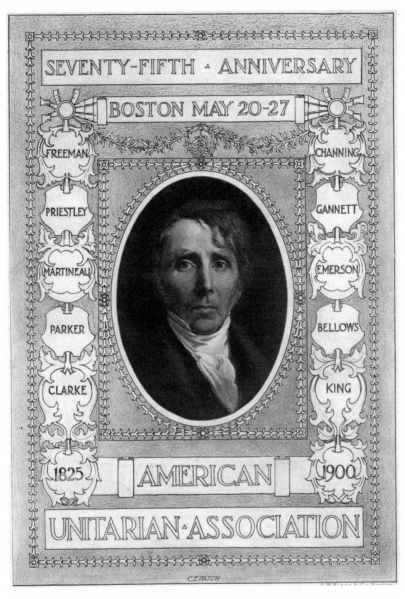

Fig. 5 Postcard announcing the seventy-fifth anniversary of the American Unitarian Association. American Unitarian Association, Central Administrative Subject Files, 1851–1962, bMS 11092, box 1, general, 1876–1900. Published by permission from the Andover-Harvard Theological Library, Harvard Divinity School, Harvard University.

successive mention seemed to heighten the praise. One author went so far as to call Priestley "the hero of the eighteenth century."[7]

That is not to say that the praise and recognition were universal. If the story of Joseph Priestley in America can teach us anything, it is that religious developments are hotly contested and the process of defining and redefining history is fraught with peril and opposition. Such was made clear in 1865 when the Reverend Samuel Osgood of New York delivered an address at the fortieth anniversary of the founding of the AUA in which he renounced Priestley's legacy. He rejected the pre-1819 characterizations of liberal New Englander ministers as being "on the verge of sinking into the shallow and unchristian speculations"; to do so, he remarked, unjustly grouped Channing and others with those "theological bunglers, Priestley and Belsham," who, he continued, "are of no account with us now; and neither of them, if now living, would be accepted as a sufficiently evangelical preacher in our most radical churches." He ended his critique with the claim that a sermon by either Priestley or Belsham was simultaneously unacceptable to the transcendental Theists as well as those he categorized as "ultraists."[8]

But men like Osgood were increasingly in the minority, and the AUA became less tolerant toward similarly uncharitable and ahistorical characterizations. When the eminent and renowned William Henry Furness visited the Northumberland congregation in the early spring of 1867, he delivered a sermon that carefully honored the religious and historical sensibilities of those who traced their religious lineage to Priestley. Furness was not a Socinian, but he willingly allowed for a divergence of opinion and theological ideas, and paid homage to all who professed their beliefs, no matter how different from his own. His message, delivered under the title "The Authority of Jesus," ascribed to Jesus the simple "being of man," still allowing for possible divine manifestations, but stating with certainty that any other manifestation were "an error," such as making him God's coequal. "Hitherto the inspiration of his personality has been greatly obstructed by the fact that his name has for a long period ceased to stand for his person, and been made representative of one or another system or fixed form of thought. At best it has stood for the Teacher and the Wonder-worker, and not for what is greater than both, the Man." As he concluded the sermon, he addressed the audience in blunt terms. Not until "the positive side of the life of Jesus comes to be known, will the two divisions

---

7. "A Few Words About the Eighteenth Century," 73.
8. Osgood, "Address."

of the Liberal body be entirely harmonized," he prophesied.[9] Furness, who played an active role in the AUA and sustained correspondence with ministers of all stripes, was likewise well aware of the heritage and legacy of Priestley that existed in his own congregation, as well as all those others that were inspired by Priestley. In broadening the foundations of Unitarian theology he opened up its ability to accommodate and respond to the shifting ground of American religious faith. He had hit the nail on the head; those who helped form the AUA on the basis of a sectarian theological creed, exclusive to one faction of religious liberals had destroyed any potential harmony and fostered continuing dissension.

Furness's sentiments were echoed during the 1900 annual meeting of the AUA, when a resolution was adopted to survey the 459 churches then in fellowship with the AUA in an effort to collect and compile an account of the multitude of church covenants and statements of faith. The report revealed that the Unitarian churches were rather evenly divided on their acceptance of congregation-specific covenants and the Spring Garden Covenant of 1899. They were also divided on the definition of the meaning of the word "church," as well as the proper governance and authority for the local church, and, perhaps most telling, admission into fellowship based on one's personal beliefs and definite membership criteria.[10]

In *The Varieties of Religious Experience,* William James documented the process of religious development among Christian groups. James observed that virtually all beliefs, on their way toward coalescing into a denomination's collective theology, undergo an initial period of development, which he called "the day of inwardness." This early period is tumultuous and complex, marked by competing beliefs. Slowly, one version emerges as the most dominant and visible set of beliefs. This transitional period is coupled with confusing perceptions of the group, as outsiders attempt to sort through the competing sets of ideas and the groups behind them. Eventually, however, one group and one set of beliefs prevail and the period of inwardness draws to a close. The denomination then emerges and begins to evolve toward, in James's words, "orthodoxy." The process does not end at that moment, however, for the denominational transformation cannot be seen as complete until all vestiges of the past confusion, turmoil, and competitions are expunged. Accordingly, the denomination adopts a selective history of

9. Furness, *Authority of Jesus,* 12–13, 21.
10. AUA, *Report of the Committee,* 3.

its origins and early development and sets out to establish that history as the one true version of their group's origins. The subjective interpretation of past events is a "protective action" taken in order to stave off resurgent or future movements that might draw inspiration from the past conflicts, and to align itself with other "orthodox" denominations. Later, the dissenting ideas of the early developmental period are erased altogether.[11]

The early history of American Unitarianism matches James's description of religious development almost perfectly. Unitarianism emerged in the United States through several different channels, yet the multiple versions of the religion were and are often denied or discredited.[12] The version that eventually prevailed emerged from within Congregationalism and quickly aligned with already established denominations—it formed a ministerial association matching those of other denominations, was established through legal channels, and professed to be in accord with the theological ideas held by the majority of American Christians. This is the Unitarianism that members speak about, historians have written about, and those who study religion learn about.

As the triumphant proponents of Unitarianism tried to secure their place in the nation's pantheon of religious denominations, they cast aside the early theological tendencies and beliefs counter to their own. They refrained from acknowledging earlier theological contests in an effort to present their group as a cohesive and historically homogeneous denomination. Mid-nineteenth century Unitarians, influenced by the emotionally charged religious atmosphere of the nation, believed that "a settled denominational life . . . without antagonism . . . and without a constant assertion of the things that rendered it distinct, was taken as sufficient indication that a group was central to God's providential scheme and would endure."[13] Thus, by the time of the late nineteenth century, there had emerged an origin story that ignored the period of inwardness and the very real, established presence of Unitarianism as imported from England and presented Unitarianism instead as an outgrowth of New England Calvinism.

11. James, *Varieties of Religious Experience*, 369.
12. See Robinson, *Unitarians and the Universalists*, 3–5, 9–23, and Macaulay, *Unitarianism in the Antebellum South*, 1–12.
13. Moore, *Religious Outsiders*, 13. Moore goes on to explain that the unsettled periods and those who challenged the dominant wing's authority were viewed "condescendingly or with open contempt." Nor did later generations inquire about the earlier eras, for "to have placed those questions and points in the foreground would have been to suggest that God made mistakes."

From the 1820s through the end of the century New England Unitarians maintained that their theological ideas derived from adaptations entirely internal to their existence over a century and a half, stretching back to the original Puritan founders. The stringent demands of Puritanism, the story held, yielded over time to rational reservations about the Trinity and its theological underpinnings. Without departing from the authority or structure of Congregationalism, an internal distinction emerged as a sizable minority rejected Christ's equal status to God. This minority eventually became known as the liberal wing of the Congregationalists—liberal in their acceptance of rationalist ideas but Congregationalist in all other elements. They denied original sin, denounced the concept of the election of saints, and supported free will. They rejected the Trinity on the grounds that Christ was subordinate to God. Their theology rejected Calvinism and was contemporaneous with, but not influenced by, Arminianism.[14]

There is little doubt that the liberal Congregationalists adopted their unitarian theology as a result of their unique and independent situation, but this is not the whole story.[15] In fact, noted R. Laurence Moore in his examination of religious outsiders, "in stressing the continuity that has marked many histories of American religion, we have neglected important counter tendencies."[16] It is precisely toward the early counter tendency in American Unitarianism that this work has gravitated.

What became the Unitarian denomination in America in the early nineteenth century did not get its start in the Unitarian congregations of the late eighteenth century. Nor were the earliest liberal Congregationalists considered to be Unitarians. Instead, these earliest believers labored under the influences of Arian-Arminianism, a movement with links to Europe and the Great Awakening, inherited from the Puritan legacy of religious dissent. This ensured that the unitarian idea remained as a doctrine surrounded by many other ideas, encased in a traditional Protestant framework. Although many were moving in the direction of the unitarian idea, "none of these may truly be called Unitarian (although this has often been done), for while they had clearly ceased to hold the doctrine of the Trinity, they should not be considered more than Arian."[17]

14. Wright, *Beginnings,* 6.
15. The liberal Congregationalists acknowledged that unitarianism had a history that stretched back to the third century, was passed down through Europe, and influenced their religious forefathers. See Wilbur, *History of Unitarianism,* 2:379–400.
16. Moore, *Religious Outsiders,* 17.
17. Wilbur, *History of Unitarianism,* 2:389. Arianism viewed Christ as neither coequal nor coeternal with God, but still affirmed his likeness to God and assigned him a special

The competing version was on the periphery of the nation's religious groups. As a product of Enlightenment rationalism, in opposition to Protestant practices and many Christian ideas, Socinianism was considered to be unacceptable. The development of denominational Unitarianism—which placed unitarianism at the core of a broader Socinian-inspired doctrine—began in England. By the middle of the 1770s the leading unitarian believers in England, under the leadership of Theophilus Lindsey and Joseph Priestley, established a formal Unitarian church and placed their Socinian beliefs at the center of its religious tenets. Although Socinians arrived in America as early as 1738, the ideas did not really take hold or emerge publicly until the 1780s. Though not as numerous in America and lagging in the development of a formal church, the Socinians, who differed in their beliefs from the Arians in important ways, held the Unitarian appellation and were the only ones to profess their views openly.[18]

Under the leadership of Joseph Priestley this Socinian faction of unitarian believers brought the tenets of a budding Unitarian church to America and laid claim to the name. Priestley's leadership generated a great deal of attention, both positive and negative, and attracted an important following in American liberal circles. His supporters spanned the country—from Boston to the Carolinas, and Pennsylvania to Kentucky—though not in any great number, and negotiated their way into American religious circles. Following Priestley's arrival in 1794 the believers developed a permanent presence in America following much the same course that it had taken in England and elsewhere in Europe.[19]

For a time, then, the unitarian idea was present in two distinct, yet intertwined paths. One group, the liberal or Arian wing of the Congre-

---

divine status. Arians could, and most often did, remain within the confines of established churches while altering their theology on this single point.

18. Socinianism was grounded in antitrinitarianism and backed by the use of reason. Socinians rejected religious mysticism but accepted limited revelation where it could be proved by reason. They believed that Christ was solely human and altered their entire theological belief system in response, rejecting the message and historical developments of the established churches. Ibid., 185–235.

19. A unitarian was a person who rejected the divinity of Christ. It was a theological idea but not the foundation for a new denomination. A Unitarian was a member of the denomination and accepted a broad theology, with unitarianism at its core. Before 1819 American Unitarians followed the teachings of Priestley. Congregations emerged in Pennsylvania, Kentucky, Maine, South Carolina, and Massachusetts. After 1819 both groups laid claim to Unitarianism as a denominational title, creating confusion and controversy. For a detailed history of the development and progression of Unitarianism abroad, see Wilbur, History of Unitarianism, 2:129–95.

gationalists, accepted the unitarian idea within the existing framework of their religion. The other group, the Socinians, saw it as the foundation for a restructuring of the prevailing religious convictions of Protestantism and as a way to return to apostolic Christianity. When the latter grew in prominence and presented a credible threat to the former, competition developed. Throughout the early course of this conflict the New England liberals were content to coexist within the Congregationalist framework and refused to call themselves Unitarians. Instead they painted their adversaries as extremists, unrelated to their own cause, and used them as the perfect lightning rod to bear the brunt of the trinitarian opposition. Though they were unitarian, the liberal wing of New England Congregationalism chose to avoid the Unitarian name— and the animus that went with it. Therefore, the initial identity of the Unitarian religion fell to those willing to assume the name much earlier.

In the end, however, the New England version became dominant. They subsumed the ideas of English Unitarianism and took the name entirely unto themselves. The history of Priestley and his followers, before William Ellery Channing and his fellow New England liberals emerged and excluded competing ideas, has not been explained adequately by historians. Moreover, the Priestley faction influenced the development of Unitarianism in America to a greater extent than is currently understood. Dismissing this early contest has been so complete that present-day Unitarians and religious scholars have all come to accept the version as it has been passed down by those who won.

Historical accounts of Unitarianism's development in America almost always exclude the period of Priestley and English Unitarianism's influence on the religion's development and neglect the complex and multifaceted period of inwardness that they represent. Religious scholars, including those who have most recently written about Unitarianism, continue to claim an absolute New England provenance for American Unitarianism despite evidence to the contrary. The most "important accomplishment of the new scholarship [is] to show that American Unitarianism was indigenous to New England," notes Conrad E. Wright.[20] His position merely echoes the arguments presented by other histories of Unitarianism, most of which have continued to overlook the early conflicts and to reject the presence of influential elements coming from abroad or anywhere outside New England.[21]

20. Wright, *American Unitarianism*, viii.
21. See ibid. Wright claims that the history of the Unitarian denomination places it "squarely within the tradition of American Puritanism . . . an outgrowth of seventeenth-century preparationist teachings and the rise of the Arminian wing within the Standing

Try as they might, however, the new Unitarians were never able to completely eradicate Priestley's legacy or abandon his ideas. The two congregations he had started continued a transatlantic exchange that nourished the early American Socinians, transcending the political and social barriers created by the Revolution that remained unhealed until the second decade of the nineteenth century. Priestley's influence was felt throughout the new nation, ranging from Boston to Charleston, Philadelphia to Louisville. The Socinians reached out, across denominational lines, with their use of common Protestant practices and rhetoric. In comparison to the longevity of the New England Unitarians, the success of the Priestleyan Unitarians was short-lived. Their ideas and actions were influential for a period of roughly twenty years, they were eventually supplanted, and attempts were made to discard their legacy. But the Priestleyan believers heavily contested such actions, forcing an accommodation with their ideas.

Previous scholars, and many Unitarians, have claimed that Priestley's efforts are immaterial in the course of Unitarian history. By noting that Priestley's Socinianism was theologically distinct from the Arianism that later flourished, and that Priestley's religion was not sustained over time, they have been able to dismiss the link between the Unitarianism of the pre-1819 era and the religion as it emerged under Channing's leadership. But such criteria are often selectively applied. The claims that the history of Unitarianism has remained unchanged from William Ellery Channing to the present, or that the ideas of the Socinians totally disappeared from the religion, and even that Priestley's efforts were irrelevant to the course of Unitarianism's development throughout time, are simply incorrect.

If measured by their objective—to capture the entire theological ground of Unitarianism—both the Socinians and Arians failed in the end. Neither faction produced a religion that survived much beyond the immediate influence of their founding figures—at least not without some significant and lasting revisions. Even while Channing was alive, Unitarianism came under attack and changed in response to Transcendentalism. Within thirty years of Channing's efforts and fifty years of Priestley's arrival, Unitarianism became sharply divided. One wing, which gained the most notoriety, was distinctly non-Christian and openly creedless, something that both Priestley and Channing had abhorred and feared, while the other, led by prominent figures

---

order of Massachusetts." See also Wilbur, *History of Unitarianism,* 2:380, and Robinson, *Unitarians and the Universalists,* 9–22.

such as Theodore Parker, tried to retain its Christian identity in the face of growing humanism. Later developments increasingly marginalized those who sought to retain the religion's Christian elements and by the turn of the twentieth century humanism had entirely won out. Unitarians had become Socinian in their conceptions of Jesus, abandoning Channing's beliefs, but they had also stepped away from the veneration of Jesus that Priestley and Ware had promoted. Unitarianism's association in 1961 with Universalism resulted in a lasting transition to a religion that neither man could have agreed with, in principle or practice. Though this official transition did not take place until well over a century after each had died, similar transitions that did take place during their lives were unwelcome.

Those who have relegated Priestley, English Unitarianism, and the Socinian-inspired congregations to the dustbin of history, have been misguided. Like Channing, they have put forward a history of the denomination that has failed to accurately account for the multiple and lasting influences upon its development, both before the New England liberals took over and as it faced significant challenges in the nineteenth century. The yardstick of institutionalization used to support such a view is both artificial and insufficient. Not only does it unduly favor the standing order, with its constructed churches and written regulations, but it also overlooks the developmental process that occurs with all faiths. Chronicling the history of a denomination only according to its most visible and "successful" versions is not sufficient to explain its importance in history or accurately depict its pattern of development.[22] Priestley and the English Unitarians were the first in America to proclaim their ideas, to champion a faith based on reason in an age of enthusiasm, and to seek salvation on their own terms as members of the Unitarian religion. They were not always at the forefront of American Unitarianism, but the theology, polity, and structure that they promoted were instrumental, though by no means singularly determinant, in the changes that took place.

"American religious culture never belonged exclusively to any side," argues R. Laurence Moore in justifying the need to see beyond a monolithic view of religious history; but when such claims are made, it is almost always from "groups that presume to uphold norms" and those are the ones with the economic, legal, social, and political power to do so. But this should not lead us to ignore or overlook the groups that get pushed aside in such contests. Moore notes that religious contests

22. Stokes, *Church and State,* 1:720–21.

"have to do with the perceptions, even the frictions, that competitors create; and perceptions obscure and sometimes, in effect, reverse insider and outsider roles. . . . Those who play the role of outsiders can wield enormous public influence that the alleged insiders are powerless to block. They can also determine in crucial ways the outlook and behavior of the insiders."[23] Moore's sensitivity to the potential for obscured reality, as competing groups vie for dominance, fits the Unitarian example quite well. For a time Priestley and the English Unitarians were the dominant force in American Unitarianism. When people spoke of Unitarianism, they spoke of the ideas and practices set down by Priestley and his followers. Unitarianism was not what the liberal New Englanders professed, but rather, something completely different. And for a time, Priestley and his followers occupied the rational ground in the American religious landscape, challenged the provisions of religious freedom, issued challenges to the theological and social foundations of other denominations, and found them as wanting in their principles and practices as these same groups judged others to be wanting. Only later did the New England liberals reverse the positions of the two groups, cast the former aside, and establish themselves as the denomination. By the end of the nineteenth century, the Unitarians had "always claimed to be orthodox," and nothing else.[24] Such perceptions left them, and those who studied them, to make historical and theological determinations based on an obfuscated account of the past. It is time to set these matters right. A correct account of the past is vital to a proper understanding of Unitarianism, not to mention the history of American religion, and has implications for the present day.

Today, Unitarians are no longer Christians, given how the term is defined in the common domain of American religion. It should be pointed out, however, that this is only true so far as it is applied to the denomination at large, for there are many individuals who attend Unitarian services who do consider themselves Christian. On the whole, however, the Unitarians no longer profess a creed as much as they do an idea, and they dismiss the need for an articulated, church-wide, common theology. There is an accepted language that Unitarians use to discuss religious matters and for the most part this discourse excludes a discussion of virtually all matters divine. There are, however, a few contemporary Unitarian thinkers who contest this point. In 2002 the Reverend William Sinkford, president of the Unitarian Universalist

---

23. Moore, *Religious Outsiders*, xiii.
24. Batchelor, *Social Equilibrium*, 259.

Association, called upon his followers to reassert God as a part of their religious terminology that refers to the divine, what he calls a "vocabulary of reverence" in the daily discourse of the church.[25] While Sinkford does not advocate a complete reversal of all theological distinctions that make up the Unitarian-Universalist belief system, his call is one step closer to restoring the religion to a form recognizable as a Christian faith, something of which Priestley would certainly approve.

There are others who even hope to bring back Priestley's theology. They see Socinianism as a potentially important and shaping force in the (re)creation of a new Unitarian theology, one that returns to the old principles and teachings. Anthony Buzzard has been a leading Unitarian proponent in arguing for a return to Christian traditions. Joined by other theologians, including Charles F. Hunting, Buzzard has written numerous "evangelical" works (from a Unitarian standpoint), that argue for a return to a belief in Jesus as the Messiah. This model is a return to the beliefs expressed by Priestley, when he argued for the restoration of biblical faith, hoped for an increased fellowship with Christians, and at the same time, argued from scripture against the doctrine of the Trinity.[26] Clearly the religious ideas and contributions of Joseph Priestley continue to resonate within the American religious landscape. His story and the impact of his ideas need to be included if modern-day Unitarians and religious Americans hope to understand the fullness of the nation's religious heritage and to be able to evaluate and make plain the process of denominational change.

25. Eckstrom, "Unitarian leader wants 'God' back in church dialogue," 10.
26. Buzzard, *Who Is Jesus?* See also Buzzard and Hunting, *Doctrine of the Trinity.*

BIBLIOGRAPHY

Primary Sources

Manuscript Sources

American Philosophical Library
    General Collection
    Thomas Paine Papers
    Vaughan Family Papers
Archives of the Archdiocese of Baltimore. Baltimore, Md.
Historical Society of Pennsylvania. Philadelphia, Pa.
Joseph Priestley House and Museum, Pennsylvania Historical and Museum Commission. Northumberland, Pa.
Library of Congress, Rare Book and Manuscript Collection. Washington, D.C.
Library Company of Philadelphia. Philadelphia, Pa.
Meadville/Lombard Theological School. Chicago, Ill.
Northumberland County Historical Society. Sunbury, Pa.
Northumberland County, Pennsylvania, Records and Papers. Sunbury, Pa.
Pennsylvania State University, University Park, Pennsylvania. Bertrand Library, Rare Book and Manuscript Division, Joseph Priestley Papers. College Park, Pa.

Books, Pamphlets, Sermons, etc.

Adams, Hannah. *A Dictionary of All Religions and Religious Denominations: Jewish, Heathen, Mahometan, and Christian, Ancient and Modern. With an appendix containing a sketch of the present state of the world, as to population, religion, toleration, missions, etc., and the articles in which all Christian denominations agree.* Fourth edition. New York: J. Eastburn, 1817.

Adams, John Quincy. *The Writings of John Quincy Adams.* Edited by Worthington Chauncy Ford. Seven volumes. New York: Macmillan, 1913–17.

Aikin, Lucy. *Memoir of John Aikin, M.D.: With a Selection of his Miscellaneous Pieces, Biographical, Moral, and Critical.* London: Baldwin, Cradock, and Joy, 1823.

American Unitarian Association. *First Annual Report of the Executive Committee of the American Unitarian Association.* Boston: Isaac R. Butts, printers to the AUA, 1826.

———. *Report of the Committee to Collect and Codify the Covenants and Statements of Faith in Use in Unitarian Churches.* Boston: American Unitarian Association, 1901.

————. "Seventy-fifth Anniversary of the American Unitarian Association," February 1900, AUA (AHTL), General Manuscripts, 1876–1904, bMS 11092/1.

————. *The Unitarian Annual Register for the Year 1846*. Boston: Wm Crosby and H. P. Nichols, 1846.

————. *The Unitarian Annual Register for the Year 1847*. Boston: Wm Crosby and H. P. Nichols, 1847.

————. *Unitarianism in America: A Report of the Speeches Delivered at the Fourth Anniversary of the Unitarian Association, Held at Boston, May 26, 1829*. Liverpool: F. B. Wright, 1829.

————. *Unitarianism: Its Origin and History: A Course of Sixteen Lectures Delivered in Channing Hall, Boston, 1888–1889*. Boston: American Unitarian Association, 1889.

Baird, Robert. *Religion in the United States of America. Or, An Account of the Origin, Progress, Relations to the State, and Present Condition of the Evangelical Churches in the United States. With Notices on Unevangelical Denominations*. Glasgow and Edinburgh: Blackie and Son, 1844.

Bakewell, William. "Some Particulars of Dr. Priestley's Residence at Northumberland, America." *The Monthly Repository of Theology and General Literature* (London), vol. 1, no. 8 (August 1806).

Batchelor, George. *Social Equilibrium and Other Problems Ethical and Religious*. Boston: G. H. Ellis, 1887.

Bellamy, Joseph. *Jesus Christ the Only God; Being a Defense of that Fundamental Doctrine of the Christian religion, against Arianism and Socinianism. Addressed to the Reverend Dr. Priestley, with some observations on his Letters to the members of the New Church, signified by the New Jerusalem in the Revelations*. London, 1792.

Bellows, Henry W. *Restatements of Christian Doctrine in Twenty-five Sermons*. New York, 1860.

Belsham, Thomas. *American Unitarianism; or a Brief History of the Progress and Present State of the Unitarian Churches in America. Compiled from Documents and Information Communicated by the Rev. James Freeman, D.D. and William Wells Jun. Esq. of Boston, and from other Unitarian Gentlemen in this Country*. Second edition. Boston: Nathaniel Willis, 1815.

————. *A Discourse delivered at Hackney, April 8, 1804, on occasion of the death of the Rev. Joseph Priestley. . . .* London: J. Johnson, 1804.

————. *Epistles of Paul the Apostle Translated*. London: R. Hunter, 1822.

————. *Extracts from the writings of eminent divines of the Church of England*. London: R. Hunter, 1824.

————. *Memoirs of the Late Reverend Theophilus Lindsey, M.A., including a brief analysis of his works; together with anecdotes and letters of eminent persons, his friends and correspondents: Also a general view of the progress of the Unitarian Doctrine in England and America*. Revised second edition. London: R. Hunter, 1820.

————. *A Vindication of Certain Passages in a Discourse, On Occasion of the Death of Dr. Priestley; and a Defense of Dr. Priestley's Character and Writings, in Reply to the Animadversions of the Rev. John Pye Smith. In Letters to a Friend*. London: C. Stower, 1805.

Benson, Joseph. *A Demonstration of the Want of Common Sense in the New Testament Writers, On the Supposition of their Believing and Teaching the abovementioned Doctrine: In a Series of Letters to the Rev. Mr. Wesley*. Birmingham: E. Jones, 1791.

Bentley, William. *The Diary of William Bentley, D.D.* Salem, Mass., 1905–14.

Biddle, John. *The Apostolical and true opinion concerning the Holy Trinity, revived and asserted partly by twelve arguments levied against the traditional and flase opinion about the Godhead of the Holy Spirit, partly by a confession of faith touching the three persons . . . : with testimonies of the fathers, and of others.* London, 1691.

Branagan, Thomas. *A Concise View of the Principal Religious Denominations in the United States of America.* Philadelphia, 1811.

Briggs, Charles A. *The Authority of Holy Scripture: An Inaugural Address.* New York: Charles Scribner's Sons, 1891.

Burgess, Tristam. *Extracts from Rev. Mr. Burgess, in the Divinity of Christ: in answer to Dr. Priestley.* Philadelphia: Francis and Robert Bailey, 1796. Earlham College Archives.

Carey, Mathew. *Proposals . . . for publishing by subscription, Dr. Priestley's History of the Christian church to the present time.* Philadelphia: Printed by the author, 1801.

Channing, William Ellery. *The Church: A Discourse delivered in the First Congregational Unitarian Church of Philadelphia, Sunday, May 30th, 1841.* Philadelphia: J. Crissy, 1841.

———. *The Complete Works of William Ellery Channing D.D., including "The Perfect Life," and containing a copious General Index and a Table of Scripture References.* London: Christian Life, 1884.

———. *A Letter to the Rev. Samuel C. Thacher, on the Aspersions contained in a Late Number of the "Panoplist," on the Ministers of Boston and the Vicinity.* Third edition. Boston: Wells and Lilly, 1815.

———. *The Life of William Ellery Channing, D.D. The Centenary Memorial Edition.* By his nephew William Henry Channing. Boston: American Unitarian Association, 1882.

———. *Memoir of William Ellery Channing, with Extracts from his Correspondence and Manuscripts, in three volumes.* Boston: W. Crosby and H. P. Nichols, 1848.

———. *Unitarian Christianity.* 1819. Boston: American Unitarian Association, 1919.

———. *The Works of William Ellery Channing.* Boston: American Unitarian Association, 1875.

Chapman, Jedediah. "A Synodical Discourse." In *The American Preacher, or a Collection of Sermons,* ed. David Austin. Volume 2. Elizabethtown, N.J.: Kollock, 1793.

Charter for the first society of Unitarian Christians in . . . Philadelphia. [S.1.], 1814. American Philosophical Society, Pamphlet, v. 1032, no. 10.

Christie, William. *Dissertations on the Unity of God in the Person of the Father, and on the Messiahship of Jesus with Proofs and Illustrations from Holy Scripture and Ecclesiastical Antiquity.* Philadelphia: Abel Dickinson, 1808.

———. *Remarks on the Constitution, framed by Three Leading Members, and lately Adopted by a Majority of the Society of Unitarian Christians, Who Assemble in Church Alley; &c.* Philadelphia, 1807.

———. *A Speech Delivered at the Grave of the Revd. Joseph Priestley.* Northumberland: Andrew Kennedy, 1804.

Clarke, James Freeman. "Harriet Martineau." *The North American Review* (Cedar Falls, Iowa), vol. 124, no. 256 (May 1877).

———. *Vexed Questions in Theology.* Boston: American Unitarian Association, 1886.

Clarke, Samuel. *A Collection of the Promises of Scripture.* London: Printed for J. Murgatroyd, 1790.

——. *The Works of Samuel Clarke, D.D. . . .: in four volumes.* London, 1738. Reprint. New York: Garland, 1978.

Cobbett, William ["Peter Porcupine"]. *Observations on the Emigration of Dr. Joseph Priestley: To Which is Added, A Comprehensive Story of a Farmer's Bull.* Philadelphia, 1794.

Constitution of the First Society of Unitarian Christians. See First Society of Unitarian Christians.

"Dialogue on Unitarianism. To the Editor." *Unitarian Miscellany and Christian Monitor* (Baltimore), February 1823, 37–44.

Dwight, Timothy. *The Nature and Danger of Infidel Philosophy: Exhibited in two discourses, addressed to the candidates for the baccalaureate, in Yale College.* New Haven: George Bunce, 1799.

Eddowes, Ralph. *On the Early Treatment of Children: A Discourse delivered at the place of worship of The First Unitarian Society in Philadelphia, April 9th, 1809.* Philadelphia: Thomas Dobson, 1809. APS, General Collection, 288 Pam., vol. 1, no. 1.

——. "Proceedings on Laying the first Corner-Stone of the New Unitarian Church, 10th fronting on Locust Street, Philadelphia, 25th March, 1828, With a Brief Account of the Rise and Progress of the Society." Philadelphia, 1828. APS, General Collection, 200 Pam., vol. 4, no. 1.

——. *Remarks of a Paragraph and Note, which appeared in the Christian's Magazine for September, 1810.* New York: n.p. 1810.

——. *The right, duty and importance of free inquiry in matters of religion; a discourse delivered at the evening lecture instituted by the First Society of Unitarian Christians in . . . Philadelphia, Nov.1, 1807, by a member of the society.* Philadelphia: Bartram and Reynolds for Thomas Dobson, 1807.

——. *The Unity of God and the Worship that is due to HIM Alone. A Discourse Delivered at the Opening of the Church Erected by the First Society of Unitarian Christians in the City of Philadelphia, on the 14th February, 1813.* Philadelphia: Thomas Dobson, 1813.

Edwards, John. *Some Thoughts Concerning the Several Causes and Occasions of Atheism, especially in the Present Age. With some brief reflections on Socinianism: and on a late book entitled The Reasonableness of Christianity as deliver'd in the Scriptures.* London: J. Robinson and J. Wyat, 1695.

——. *Socinianism Unmask'd. A Discourse shewing the Unreasonableness of a late Writer's Opinion concerning the Necessity of only One Article of Christian Faith; and of his other Assertions in his late book, entitled, The Reasonableness of Christianity as deliver'd in the Scriptures, and in his Vindication of it, with a brief reply to another (professed) Socinian Writer.* London: J. Robinson and J. Wyat, 1696.

Edwards, Jonathan, Jr. *The Necessity of the Belief of Christianity by the Citizens of the Sate, in order to preserve our Political Prosperity.* Hartford: Hudson and Goodwin, 1794.

Emlyn, Thomas. *An Humble Enquiry into the Scripture Account of Jesus Christ: or a Short Argument Concerning His Deity and Glory, According to the Gospel.* Frankfurt, Ky.: James M. Bradford, 1803.

Everett, Charles Carroll. *Immortality and Other Essays.* Boston: American Unitarian Association, 1902.

Everett, S. *Sermons by the Late Rev. Abiel Abbott, D.D., of Beverly, Mass., with a Memoir of his Life.* Boston: Wait, Green, 1831.

Finney, William Gardner. *The History of the Chillisquaque Church.* Selinsgrove, Pa.: privately printed, 1926.

First Society of Unitarian Christians, in the City of Philadelphia. "Charter of 1814." APS, Pamphlet, v. 1032, no. 10.

———. *A Collection of Pieces and Tracts, chiefly intended to establish the doctrine of the Unity of God, and the salvation of sinners by his free grace in The Gospel.* Philadelphia: Thomas Dobson, 1810. APS, General Collection, 288 Pam., vol. 1, no. 1.

———. *Constitution of the First Society of Unitarian Christians, in the City of Philadelphia; Adopted, August 23, 1807. With Explanatory Observations.* Philadelphia: Bartram and Reynolds, 1807.

Fletcher, John. *Socinianism unscriptural, or the Prophets and Apostles Vindicated from the charge of holding the doctrine of Christ's mere humanity: Being the Second Part of a Vindication of his Divinity, inscribed to the Rev. Dr. Priestley.* Birmingham: E. Jones, 1791.

———. *Vindication of the Catholic Faith of the Trinity: Being the first part of a Vindication of Christ's Divinity, inscribed to the Rev. Dr. Priestley.* Hull and London: G. Prince, 1788.

Franklin, Benjamin. *Benjamin Franklin: Writings.* Edited by J. A. Leo Lemay. New York: Library of America, 1987.

———. *Dissertation on Liberty and Necessity, Pleasure and Pain* (1725). In *Benjamin Franklin: Writings,* ed. J. A. Leo Lemay. New York: Library of America, 1987.

Freeman, James. *A Liturgy, Collected Principally from the Book of Common Prayer, for the use of the first Episcopal Church in Boston; together with the Psalter, or Psalms of David.* Boston: Peter Edes in State Street, 1785.

Furness, William H. *The Authority of Jesus: A Discourse Delivered before a Conference of Liberal Christians, held in Northumberland, PA., April 10, 1867.* Philadelphia: King and Baird, Printers, 1867.

———. *A Discourse, Delivered on the Occasion of the Death of John Vaughan, in the First Congregational Unitarian Church, Sunday, Jan. 16, 1842. With the Services at the Funeral.* Philadelphia: J. Crissy, 1842.

———. *Discourse on the Occasion of the Fiftieth Anniversary of His Ordination, January 12, 1875.* Philadelphia, 1875.

Greenwood, F.W.P. "Dr. Channing's Sermon at the Ordination of a Colleague." *Unitarian Miscellany and Christian Monitor* (Baltimore), October 1824, 208–11.

———. *History of King's Chapel in Boston: The first Episcopal church in New England: comprising notices of the introduction of Episcopacy into the northern colonies.* Boston: Carter, Hendee, 1833.

Grundy, John. *Christianity: An Intellectual and Individual Religion, a discourse delivered in Renshaw Street, Liverpool, October 20th, 1811, in a chapel opened on that day for the worship of the one undivided God.* Liverpool: E. Smith, 1811.

———. *Evangelical Christianity Considered: And shewn to be synonymous with Unitarianism, in a course of lectures on some of the most controverted points of Christian doctrine addressed to Trinitarians.* London: C. Stower, 1813.

Hayward, John. *The Religious Creeds and Statistics of Every Christian Denomination in the United States and British Provinces. With Some Account of the Religious Sentiments of the Jews, American Indians, Deists, Mahometans, & c., Alphabetically Arranged.* Boston: J. Hayward, 1836.

Jefferson, Thomas. *The Jefferson Bible*. Edited by F. Forrester Church and Jaroslav Pelikan. Boston: Beacon Press, 1989.

———. *The Writings of Thomas Jefferson*. Edited by Merrill Peterson. New York: Library of America, 1984.

Jeremy, David John. *See* Wansey, Henry.

Jones, William. *The Catholic Doctrine of a Trinity, proved by above a hundred short and clear arguments expressed in terms of the Holy Scripture . . . to which is added, A Letter to the Common People, in answer to some popular arguments against the Trinity*. Second edition. London: J. Rivington, Robinson and Roberts, and S. Folingsby, 1767.

———. "A Preservative against the Publications Dispersed by Modern Socinians." In *Theological and Miscellaneous Works of the Rev. William Jones*, 2:223–47. London: F. C. and J. Rivington, 1810.

Kay, James. *Twenty Questions to Trinitarians. With Answers from Scripture*. Boston: Gray and Bowen, 1832. LOC Rare Books and Manuscripts, Pamphlet Collection.

Kemble, Francis Ann. *Records of Later Life*. New York, 1883.

Lindsey, Theophilus. *The Apology of Theophilus Lindsey, M.A., on Resigning the Vicarage of Catterick, Yorkshire*. Dublin: T. Walker 1775.

———. *The Catechist*. London, 1781.

———. *A Discourse: Address to the Congregation at the Chapel in Essex Street Strand, on Resigning the Pastoral Office Among Them*. London 1773. APS, General Collection.

———. *Farewell Address to the Parishioners of Catterick*. London: J. Johnson, 1774.

———. *An Historical View of the State of the Unitarian Doctrines and Worship from the Reformation to our Own Time, with some Account of the Obstructions it has met with at Different Periods*. London: J. Johnson, 1783.

———. *Letters of Theophilus Lindsey*. Edited by Herbert McLachlan. London: Manchester at the University Press, 1920.

———. *A Sermon preached at the Opening of the New Chapel at Essex-Street, Strand, on Sunday, March 29, 1778*. London, 1778.

———. *A Sermon preached at the Opening of the New Chapel in Essex-House, Essex-Street, in the Strand, on Sunday, April 17, 1774*. Second edition. London: J. Johnson, 1774.

———. *Two Dissertations on the Introduction to St. John's Gospel, and the Lawfulness of Praying to Christ*. London, 1779.

———. *Vindiciae Priestleianae: An Address to the Students of Oxford and Cambridge*. Two volumes. London: Printed for J. Johnson, 1788. APS, General Collection.

Linn, John Blair. *Annals of Buffalo Valley Pennsylvania, 1755–1855*. Harrisburg, Pa.: L.S. Hart, printer and binder, 1877.

Little, Robert. "The Mystery of Christ: A Sermon delivered in the City of Washington, October 7, 1821, with notes, chiefly in reference to a publication by the Rev. Anthony Kohlmann." Washington, D.C.: W. Cooper, 1821. *Sermons*, LOC, General Collection, 3

———. "Ordination Sermon." Reprinted in Alexander Gordon, *Christian Life* (Washington, D.C.), June 23, 1923.

———. *Religious Liberty and Unitarianism Vindicated. A Sermon preached in the Hall of the House of Representatives of the United States, Washington City, Sunday, April 28, 1822*. Washington: Pishey Thompson, 1822.

Locke, John. *A paraphrase and notes on the Epistle of St. Paul to the Galatians*. London: Printed for Awnsham and John Churchil, 1705.

————. *The Reasonableness of Christianity as Delivered in the Scriptures.* London: Printed for Awnsham and J. Churchil, 1695.

Macgowan, John. *Infernal Conference; or dialogues of devils: on the many vices which abound in the civil and religious world, to which is added a looking glass for the professors of religion; together with Discourses on the Book of Ruth, likewise Socinianism brought to the test; . . . also the Arians' and Socinians' Monitor.* London: Richard Evans, 1816.

————. *Socinianism brought to the test: or Jesus Christ proved to be either the adorable God, or a notorious imposter: in a series of letters to the Reverend Doctor Priestley, in which it appears, that if Jesus Christ is not a divine person, the Mohammedan is, in all respects, preferable to the Christian religion.* London: G. Keith, J. Johnson, A. Bell, and J. Matthews, 1773.

Martineau, Harriet. *Harriet Martineau's Autobiography.* Edited by Maria Weston Chapman. Boston: J. R. Osgood, 1877.

————. *Retrospect of Western Travel.* Three volumes. London: Saunders and Otley, 1838.

McLachlan, Herbert. *Letters of Theophilus Lindsey.* London: Manchester at the University Press, 1920.

Mease, James. *The Picture of Philadelphia, Giving an Account of its Origin, Increase and Improvements in Arts, Sciences, Manufactures, Commerce and Revenue, with a Compensious View of its Societies, Literary, Benevolent, Patriotic, & Religious. Its Police—the Public Buildings—The Prison and Penitentiary System—Institutions, Monied and Civil—Museum.* Philadelphia: B. and T. Kite, 1811.

Miller, Samuel. *God in the Flesh: Letters on Unitarianism.* Princeton, 1821.

————. *Letters on the Eternal Sonship of Christ: Addressed to the Rev. Professor Stuart, of Andover.* Princeton, 1823.

————, ed. *Memoir of the Rev. Charles Nisbet, D.D., Late President of Dickinson College, Carlisle.* New York: Robert Carter, 1840.

Morse, Jedidiah. "Review of American Unitarianism." *The Panoplist and Missionary Magazine* (Boston), vol. 11, no. 6 (June 1815). LOC, Rare Book collection, Misc. Pamphlets, v. 1074, no. 12.

Newton, Isaac. *An Historical Account of the Two Notable Corruptions of the Scriptures, in a Letter to a Friend.* 1690. Reprint. London: J. Greene, 1894.

Normandie, James de. "Sermon." In *Seventy-fifth Anniversary and Reconsecration of the First Independent Christ's Church, Baltimore, MD.* Baltimore: Jon. Williams, 1893.

Norton, Andrews. *A Discourse on the Latest Form of Infidelity.* Cambridge, Mass., 1839.

Old Experience. *The Final Tendency of the Religious Disputes of the Present Day, Impartially Considered.* Boston, 1829.

Osgood, Samuel. "Address." *Unitarianism in America: A Report of the Speeches Delivered at the Fourth Anniversary of the Unitarian Association, Held at Boston, May 26, 1829.* Liverpool: F. B. Wright, 1829.

Parkman, Francis, Sr. *A Survey of God's providence in the establishment of the churches in New England.* Boston: John Eliot, 1814.

Price, Richard. *Sermons of the Christian Doctrine as Received by the Different Denominations of Christians, with an appendix, occasioned by Dr. Priestley's letters to the author.* Boston: Wells and Lilly, 1815.

Priestley, Joseph. *An Account of a Society for Encouraging the Industrious Poor.* Birmingham, 1787.

———. *An Address to Protestant Dissenters.* London: J. Johnson, 1773.

———. *An Address to the Unitarian Congregation at Philadelphia, Delivered on Sunday, March 5, 1797.* Philadelphia: Joseph Gales, 1797.

———. *An Appeal to the Public on the Subject of the Riots at Birmingham.* London, 1791.

———. *An Appeal to the Serious and Candid Professors of Christianity. To Which are Added, A Concise History of the Rise of those Doctrines: And the Triumph of Truth; Being an Account of the Trial of Mr. E. Elwall, for Heresy and Blasphemy, at Stafford Assizes.* Philadelphia: Robert Bell, 1784.

——— [Photinus, pseud.]. "An Attempt to shew that Arians are not Unitarians." *Theological Repository* 4 (1784): 338–44.

———. *The Autobiography of Dr. Joseph Priestley (written by himself) with a Journal of his Travels.* Edited by Jack Lindsay. Teaneck, N.J.: Fairleigh Dickinson University Press, 1979.

———. *The Case of the Poor Emigrants Recommended, in a Discourse Delivered at the University Hall in Philadelphia, On Sunday, February 19, 1797.* Philadelphia: Joseph Gales, 1979.

———. *A Catechism for Children and Young Persons.* Salem, Mass., 1785.

———. *Discourses on Various Subjects.* Northumberland, Pa.: John Binns, 1805.

———. *Discourses Relating to the Evidences of Revealed Religion.* Philadelphia: Dobson, 1796.

———. *Disquisitions Relating to Matter and Spirit.* London: Wilkie, 1777.

———. *Forms of Prayer, and Other Offices for the Use of Unitarian Societies.* Birmingham: Printed by Pearson and Rollason, for J. Johnson, 1783.

———. [A Dissenter]. *A Free Address to Protestant Dissenters, on the Subject of Church Discipline.* London: J. Johnson, 1771.

———. *A General History of the Christian Church.* 3 vols. Northumberland, Pa.: John Binns, Printer, 1803.

———. *A General View of the Arguments for the Unity of God; and against the divinity and preexistence of Christ, from Reason—and from the Scriptures—and from History.* Philadelphia: Thomas Dobson, 1794.

———. *A General View of the Arguments for the Unity of God; From Reason, From the Scriptures, and From History.* Philadelphia: Robert Bell, 1784.

——— [Beryllus, pseud.]. "The History of the Arian Controversy." *Theological Repository* 4 (1784): 306–37.

———. *History of the Corruptions of Christianity.* London: Wilkie, 1778.

———. *The Importance and Extent of Free Inquiry in Matters of Religion.* London: J. Johnson, 1787.

———. *Institutes of Natural and Revealed Religion.* Two volumes. London: J. Johnson, 1772.

———. *Lectures on History and General Policy.* Birmingham, 1788.

———. *A Letter to a layman, on the subject of Rev. Mr. Lindsey's proposal for a reformed English church, upon the plan of the late Dr. Samuel Clarke.* London: Wilkie, 1774.

———. *A Letter to the Right Honourable William Pitt . . . on the Subjects of Toleration and Church Establishments.* Second edition. London: J. Johnson, 1787.

———. *Letters to Dr. Horsley in Answer to his Animadversions on the History of the Corruptions of Christianity: with additional evidence that the primitive Christian church was Unitarian.* Birmingham: Printed by Pearson and Rollason, for J. Johnson, 1783.

————. *Letters to the Inhabitants of Northumberland and Its Neighborhood, on subjects interesting to the Author and Them.* Two volumes. Northumberland, Pa.: John Binns, 1799.

————. *A Letter to the Right Honourable William Pitt . . . on the Subjects of Toleration and Church Establishments.* Second edition. London: J. Johnson, 1787.

————. *Memoirs, with a Journal of his Travels.* Northumberland, Pa.: John Binns, 1805.

————. *The Proper Objects of Education in the Present State of the World: Represented in a Discourse, Delivered on Wednesday, the 27th of April, 1791, at the Meeting-House in the Old-Jewry, London; to the Supporters of the New College at Hackney.* London: J. Johnson, 1791.

———— [Beryllus, pseud.]. "A Query relating to the Rise of the Arian Doctrine." *Theological Repository* 4 (1784): 70–72.

————. *A scripture catechism: consisting of a series of questions, with references to the scriptures instead of answers.* London: J. Johnson, 1781.

————. *The Theological and Miscellaneous Works of Joseph Priestley, 1817–1832.* Edited by John Towill Rutt. Bristol: Thoemmes Press, 1999.

————. *Unitarianism Explained and Defended: In a Discourse Delivered in the Church of the Universalists, at Philadelphia, 1796.* Philadelphia: Printed by John Thompson, 1796.

Randolph, Francis. *Scriptural Revision of Socinian Arguments in a letter to the Rev. Dr. Priestley.* Bath: R. Cruttwell, for T. Cadell, 1792.

Rupp, I. Daniel. *He Pasa Ekklesia; An Original History of the Religious denominations at Present Existing in the United States . . . Written Expressly for the Work by eminent theological professors, ministers, and lay-members . . . Projected, compiled, and arranged by I. Daniel Rupp.* Philadelphia: J. Y. Humphreys, 1844.

————. *Religious Denominations in the United States: Their past history, present condition, and doctrines, accurately set forth in fifty-three carefully-prepared articles, written by eminent clerical and lay authors connected with the respective persuasions . . . together with . . . statistics, to which is added a historical summary of religious denominations in England and Scotland.* Philadelphia: C. DeSilver, 1861.

Rush, Benjamin. *Letters.* Edited by Lyman H. Butterfield. Volume 2. Princeton: Princeton University Press, 1951.

Schaff, Philip, ed. *A Religious Encyclopedia or Dictionary of Biblical, Historical, Doctrinal, and Practical Theology.* Third edition, revised and enlarged. New York: Funk and Wagnalls.

Sherman, John. *A View of Ecclesiastical Proceedings in the Country of Windham, Connecticut.* Trenton Falls, N.Y., 1826.

Skinner, Otis A. *Letters to Rev. B. Stow, R. H. Neale, and R. W. Cushman on Modern Revivals.* Boston: Abel Tompkins, 1842.

Smith, Adam. *An Inquiry into the Nature and Causes of the Wealth of Nations.* London, 1776.

Smith, John Pye. *Letters to the Rev. Thomas Belsham, on some Important Subjects of Theological Discussion, Referred to in his Discourse on Occasion of the Death of the Rev. Joseph Priestley.* Boston: Farrand, Mallory, 1809.

————. *Scripture Testimony to the Messiah.* Two volumes. London, 1818–21.

Sparks, Jared. *The Comparative Moral Tendency of the Leading Doctrines of Calvinism and the Sentiments of Unitarians.* Baltimore, 1823.

————. "Notes on Priestley." *Unitarian Miscellany and Christian Monitor* (Baltimore), June 1823, 222–36.

————. *Proposals for publishing by subscription, a Collection of essays and disquisitions, by different authors, on various important subjects.* Baltimore, 1822.

Sprague, William B., ed. *Annals of the American Pulpit; or, Commemorative Notices of Distinguished American Clergymen of Various Denominations, from the Early Settlement of the Country to the Close of the Year Eighteen Hundred and Fifty-Five. With Historical Introductions.* Nine volumes. New York: Robert Carter and Brothers, 1857–69.

Stephen, Leslie, and Sidney Lee, eds. *Dictionary of National Biography.* London: Oxford University Press, 1882.

Stuart, Moses. *Letters to the Rev. Wm. E. Channing: Containing remarks on his sermon recently preached and published at Baltimore.* Andover: Flagg and Gould, 1819.

Toulmin, Harry. *Thoughts on Emigration, to which are added, miscellaneous observations relating to the United States of America; and a short account of the State of Kentucky.* London, 1792.

Toulmin, Joshua. *A Review of the Life, Character and Writings of the Rev. John Biddle, M.A. who was Banished to the Isle of Scilly, in the Protectorate of Oliver Cromwell.* London, 1791.

————. *Unitarianism; or The Doctrine of the Trinity Confuted by Scripture.* Philadelphia, 1795.

"Unitarianism in Northumberland." *Unitarian Miscellany and Christian Monitor* (Baltimore), May 1823.

Wansey, Henry. *The Journal of an Excursion to the United States of North America in the Summer of 1794.* Salisbury: J. Easton, 1796. Reprinted as *Henry Wansey and His American Journal, 1794,* ed. David John Jeremy (Philadelphia: APS, 1970).

Ware, Henry, Jr. *Sober Thoughts on the State of the Times, Addressed to the Unitarian Community.* Boston: American Unitarian Association Tracts, first series, no. 99, 1835.

————. *Views of Christian Truth, Piety, and Morality, Selected from the Writings of Dr. Priestley, with a Memoir of his life.* Cambridge, Mass.: Munroe, 1834.

Watson, Elkanah. *Memoirs of Elkanah Watson, Including Journals of Travels in Europe and America from 1777 to 1842.* Edited by Winslow Watson. New York, 1856.

Watson, Richard. *A Collection of Theological Tracts.* Six volumes. Cambridge, Mass.: Printed by J. Archdeacon, for J. and J. Merrill, T. Evans, and J. and J. Fletcher, 1785.

Webster, Noah. *Letters.* Edited by H. R. Warfel. New York: Library Publishers, 1953.

————. *Ten Letters to Joseph Priestley in Answer to His Letters to the Inhabitants of Northumberland.* New Haven: Read and Morse, 1800.

Wesley, John. *The Death of the Rev. Mr. John Fletcher, Vicar of Madeley, Shropshire* (London, 1785), as transcribed on The Wesley Homepages, Sermon 133, http://gbgm-umc.org/umhistory/wesley/sermons/serm-133.stm, modified June 2, 2000.

Wetherill, Charles. *The divinity of Jesus Christ proved: Being a reply to Dr. Joseph Priestley's "Appeal to the serious and candid professors of Christianity," and, to a pamphlet published by Lewis Nichola, entitled "The divinity of Jesus Christ, considered from Scripture evidences, &c." with some observations upon Arianism.* Philadelphia: Francis Bailey and Thomas Lang, 1792.

————. *History of the Religious Society of Friends, Called by Some The Free Quakers, in the City of Philadelphia.* Philadelphia: Printed for the Society, 1894.

Wharton, Charles Henry. *A Short and Candid Enquiry Into the Proofs of Christ's Divinity; In Which Dr. Priestley's History of Opinions Concerning Christ, Is Occasionally Considered. In a Letter to a Friend.* Wilmington, Del.: Brynberg and Andrews, 1791.

Whately, Richard. *Essays, First Series, on some of the Peculiarities of the Christian Religion.* Fourth edition, revised. London: B. Fellowes, 1837.

Wood, Samuel. *The Present State and the Prospects of Unitarian Christianity in the United States of North America.* Hackney: n.p. and n.d. Originally published in *The Christian Reformer,* September 1837, APS.

Wood, William. *A Sermon, preached April 22, 1804, at Mill-Hill Chapel, in Leeds, on the Death of the Rev. Dr. Priestley, Formerly Minister of that Chapel; published at the request of the Congregation.* Leeds: Edward Baines, 1804.

Worcester, Samuel. *A Letter to the Rev. William E. Channing, on the subject of his letter to the Rev. Samuel C. Thatcher* [sic], *relating to the review in the Panoplist of American Unitarianism.* Boston: Samuel T. Armstrong, 1815.

Secondary Sources

Adams, Herbert Baxter. *The Life and Writings of Jared Sparks.* Cambridge, Mass.: Riverside Press, 1893.

Ahlstrom, Sydney E. *A Religious History of the American People.* New Haven: Yale University Press, 1972.

Ahlstrom, Sydney E., and Jonathan S. Carey, eds. *An American Reformation: A Documentary History of Unitarian Christianity.* Middletown: Wesleyan University Press, 1985.

Allen, Joseph Henry, and Richard Eddy. *A History of Unitarians and Universalists in the United States.* American Church History Series, vol. 10. New York: Christian Literature, 1893–97.

Anderson, Phillip J. "William Linn, 1752–1808: American Revolutionary and Anti-Jeffersonian." *Journal of Presbyterian History* 55 (1977).

Andrews, Dee. *The Methodists and Revolutionary America, 1760–1800: The Shaping of an Evangelical Culture.* Princeton: Princeton University Press, 2000.

Andrews, Stuart. *Unitarian Radicalism: Political Rhetoric, 1770–1814.* New York: Palgrave, 2003.

Armitage, David, and Michael J. Braddick. *The British Atlantic World, 1500–1800.* New York: Palgrave, Macmillan, 2002.

Baseler, Marilyn C. *"Asylum for Mankind": America, 1607–1800.* Ithaca: Cornell University Press, 1998.

Batchelor, George. *Social Equilibrium and Other Problems Ethical and Religious.* Boston: G. H. Ellis, 1887.

Bauman, Richard. *For the Reputation of Truth: Politics, Religion, and Conflict among the Pennsylvania Quakers, 1750–1800.* Baltimore: The Johns Hopkins University Press, 1971.

Baylen, Joseph, and Norbert Gossman, eds. *Biographical Dictionary of Modern British Radicals.* Vol. 1, 1770–1830. Sussex, N.J.: Harvester Press, 1979.

Beeman, Richard, Stephen Botein, and Edward C. Carter II, eds. *Beyond Confederation: Origins of the Constitution and American National Identity.* Chapel Hill: University of North Carolina Press, 1987.

Bell, Herbert C., ed. *History of Northumberland County, Pennsylvania, Including its Aboriginal History; The Colonial and Revolutionary Periods; Early Settlement and Subsequent Growth; Political Organization; Agricultural, Mining, and Manufacturing Interests; Internal Improvements; Religious, Educational, Social, and Military History; Sketches of its Boroughs, Villages, and Townships; Portraits and Biographies of Pioneers and Representative Citizens, Etc., Etc.* Chicago: Brown, Runk, 1891.

Bicentennial Historical Book Committee. *Northumberland Point Township, Pennsylvania: Bicentennial 1772–1972.* Sunbury, Pa.: The Daily Item Publishing Company, 1972.

Bodle, Wayne. "Themes and Directions in Middle Colonies Historiography, 1980–1994." In "Mid-Atlantic Perspectives," ed. Paul G.E. Clemens, special issue, *William and Mary Quarterly,* third series, 51 (July 1994): 355–88.

Bonomi, Patricia. *Under the Cope of Heaven: Religion, Society, and Politics in Colonial America.* New York: Oxford University Press, 1986.

Brigham, David R. *Public Culture in the Early Republic: Peale's Museum and Its Audience.* Washington, D.C.: Smithsonian Institution Press, 1995.

Brock, Peter. *Pioneers of the Peaceable Kingdom: The Quaker Peace Testimony from the Colonial Era to the First World War.* Princeton: Princeton University Press, 1968.

Brooks, Marilyn. "Priestley's Plan for a 'Continually Improving' Translation of the Bible." *Enlightenment and Dissent,* no. 15 (1996): 89–106.

Bureau of the Census. *A Century of Population Growth from the First Census of the United States to the Twelfth.* Washington, D.C.: Office of the Census Agency, 1998.

Burr, Elizabeth. "Review Essay: Inspiring Lunatics: Biographical Portraits of the Lunar Society's Erasmus Darwin, Thomas Day, and Joseph Priestley." *Eighteenth-Century Life* 24 (spring 2000).

Butler, Jon. *Awash in a Sea of Faith: Christianizing the American People.* Cambridge: Harvard University Press, 1990.

Buzzard, Anthony. *Who Is Jesus? A Plea for a Return to Belief in Jesus, the Messiah.* Morrow, Ga.: Atlanta Bible College, 1992.

Buzzard, Anthony, and Charles F. Hunting. *The Doctrine of the Trinity.* Lanham, Md.: International Scholars Publications, 1998.

Chiles, Robert E. *Theological Transition in American Methodism, 1790–1935.* 1965. Reprint. Lanham, Md.: University Press of America, 1983.

Clark, Helen T. "Chapel Dedication." *Public Press.* Northumberland, Pa.: May 16, 1881. JPH.

Clark, John Ruskin. *Joseph Priestley: A Comet in the System.* 1990. Reprint. Northumberland, Pa.: The Friends of the Joseph Priestley House, 1994.

Conkin, Paul. *American Originals: Homemade Varieties of Christianity.* Chapel Hill: University of North Carolina Press, 1997.

Cooke, George. *Unitarianism in America: A History of Its Origins and Development.* Boston: AMS Press, 1971.

Cox, James A. "Nonconformist Joseph Priestley." *Colonial Williamsburg* 21 (autumn 1998).

Crook, Ronald. *A Bibliography of Joseph Priestley, 1733–1804.* London: The Library Association, 1966.

Daniels, Roger. *Coming to America: A History of Immigration and Ethnicity in American Life.* New York: HarperCollins, 1990.

Davie, Donald. *Essays in Dissent: Church, Chapel, and the Unitarian Conspiracy.* Manchester: Carcanet Press, 1995.

Dent, Robert K. *Old and New Birmingham: A History of the Town and Its People.* Birmingham: Houghton and Hammond, 1879–80.

Dewey, John. *A Common Faith.* New Haven: Yale University Press, 1934.

Dolan, Jay. *In Search of an American Catholicism: A History of Religion and Culture in Tension.* New York: Oxford University Press, 2002.

Durey, Michael. *Transatlantic Radicals and the Early American Republic.* Lawrence: University of Kansas Press, 1997.

Ekstrom, Kevin. Religious News Service, "Unitarian Leader Wants 'God' Back in Church Dialogue: Call To Reexamine Beliefs Stirs Furor," *Chicago Tribune* (May 23, 2003).

Eliot, Samuel E., ed. *Heralds of a Liberal Faith: The Prophets.* Boston: American Unitarian Association, 1910.

Elkins, Stanley, and Eric McKitrick. *The Age of Federalism: The Early American Republic, 1788–1800.* New York: Oxford University Press, 1993.

Ellis, George Edward. *A Half Century of the Unitarian Controversy, with Particular Reference to Its Origin, Its Course, and Its Prominent Subjects Among the Congregationalists of Massachusetts. With an Appendix.* Boston: Crosby, Nichols, 1857.

Ferguson, Robert A. *The American Enlightenment, 1750–1820.* Cambridge: Harvard University Press, 1997.

"A Few Words About the Eighteenth Century." From the Nineteenth Century. *Littell's Living Age* (Boston), fifth series, vol. 42, no. 2025, April 14, 1883.

Fithian, Philip Vickers. *Journal.* Princeton: Princeton University Press, 1934.

Fitzpatrick, Martin. "Toleration and the Enlightenment Movement." in *Toleration in Enlightenment Europe,* ed. Ole Peter Grell and Roy Porter. Cambridge: Cambridge University Press, 2000.

Foote, Henry W. *Annals of King's Chapel: From the Puritan Age of New England to the Present Day.* Vol. 2. Boston: Little, Brown, 1896.

———. *James Freeman and King's Chapel, 1782–87. A Chapter in the Early History of the Unitarian Movement in New England.* Boston: Leonard C. Bowles, 1873.

Frank, Willard C. "'I Shall Never Be Intimidated': Harry Toulmin and William Christie in Virginia, 1793–1801." *Transactions of the Unitarian Historical Society,* April 1987, 28–29

Frost, J. William. *A Perfect Freedom: Religious Liberty in Pennsylvania.* University Park: Pennsylvania State University Press, 1993.

Geffen, Elizabeth. *Philadelphia Unitarianism, 1796–1861.* Philadelphia: University of Pennsylvania Press, 1961.

George, Timothy, and Denise George, eds. *Baptist Confessions, Covenant, and Catechisms.* Nashville: Broadman and Holman, 1996.

Graham, Jenny. *Revolutionary in Exile: The Emigration of Joseph Priestley to America, 1794–1804.* In *Transactions of the American Philosophical Society,* vol. 85, pt. 2. Philadelphia: APS, 1995.

Graves, Charles. "An Adventure of Faith: An Account of the Origins and Proceedings of the American Unitarian Association." AUA (AHTL), bMS 1180.

Greenberg, Douglas. "The Middle Colonies in Recent American Historiography." *William and Mary Quarterly,* third series, vol. 36 (July 1979): 551–98.

Greene, Evarts B., and Virginia D. Harrington. *American Population Before the Federal Census of 1790.* 1932. Reprint. Gloucester, Mass., 1966.

Gutelius, C. Warren. "The Churches Which Joseph Priestley Established in Northumberland and Philadelphia." *Northumberland County Historical Society: Proceedings and Addresses* 21 (August 1957).

——. *Northumberland: The Story of an Old Town, 1829–1929.* Northumberland, Pa.: The Susquehanna Press, 1929.

Hatch, Nathan. *The Democratization of American Christianity.* New Haven: Yale University Press, 1989.

Heilman, Samuel. *The People of the Book: Drama, Fellowship, and Religion.* Chicago: University of Chicago Press, 1983.

Hill, Andrew M. "Robert Little, John Campbell, and James Kay: American Unitarian Ministers." 1982. JPH.

Hill, Thomas. "A Journey on Horseback in 1799." *Pennsylvania Magazine of History and Biography,* vol. 19 (1890).

Hillar, Marian. "Laelius and Faustus Socini: Founders of Socinianism: Their Lives and Theology." Center for Socinian Studies. http://www.socinian.org/files/FaustusSocini.pdf/.

Hodge, Charles. *Constitutional History of the Presbyterian Church in the United States,* Vol. 1. Philadelphia: Presbyterian Board of Publication, 1851. Reprint. Philadelphia: American Presbyterian Press, 1978.

Holifield, E. Brooks. *Theology in America: Christian Thought from the Age of the Puritans to the Civil War.* New Haven: Yale University Press, 2003.

Hudson, Winthrop. *Religion in America.* New York: Charles Scribner's Sons, 1965.

Huffman, Morna M. *Lutheranism Takes Root in the Settlement of Pennsylvania, 1682–1982.* Whitney, Pa.: privately printed, 1982.

Hutchinson, William. *Religious Pluralism in America: The Contentious History of a Founding Ideal.* New Haven: Yale University Press, 2003.

Huxley, Thomas. *Collected Essays.* Nine volumes. London, 1893–94.

Ireland, Owen S. *Religion, Ethnicity, and Politics: Ratifying the Constitution in Pennsylvania.* University Park: Pennsylvania State University Press, 1995.

Jacob, W. M. *Lay People and Religion in the Early Eighteenth Century.* Cambridge: Cambridge University Press, 1996.

James, William. *The Varieties of Religious Experience: A Study in Human Nature.* New York: The Modern Library, 1999.

Jeremy, David John, ed. *Henry Wansey and His American Journal.* Philadelphia: APS, 1970.

Kerrison, S. E. "Coventry and the Municipal Corps. Act of 1835." Master's thesis, Birmingham University, 1939.

Kloppenberg, James T. "The Virtues of Liberalism: Christianity, Republicanism, and Ethics in Early American Political Discourse." *Journal of American History* 74 (June 1987).

Kring, Walter D. *Liberals Among the Orthodox.* New York: Oxford University Press, 1976.

Lambert, Frank. *The Founding Fathers and the Place of Religion in America.* Princeton: Princeton University Press, 2003.

Lerner, Ralph. *Revolutions Revisited: Two Faces of the Politics of Enlightenment.* Chapel Hill: University of North Carolina Press, 1994.

Lyttle, Charles. *Freedom Moves West: A History of the Western Unitarian Conference, 1852–1952.* Boston: The Beacon Press, 1952.

————. *The Pentecost of American Unitarianism: Channing's Baltimore Sermon.* Boston: The Beacon Press, 1920.

Macaulay, John. *Unitarianism in the Antebellum South: The Other Invisible Institution.* Tuscaloosa: University of Alabama Press, 2001.

Manschreck, Clyde L. "A Critical Appraisal of Some Consequences Inherent in Socinianism." In *Socinianism and Its Role in the Culture of XVI-th to XVIII-th Centuries,* ed. Lech Szczucki. Warsaw: Polish Academy of Sciences, 1983.

Mathews, Donald G. "The Second Great Awakening as an Organizing Process, 1780–1830." *American Quarterly* 21 (1969).

McFarlane, Anthony. *The British in the Americas, 1480–1815.* New York: Longman, 1994.

McGarvie, Mark. *One Nation Under Law: America's Early National Struggles to Separate Church and State.* DeKalb: Northern Illinois University Press, 2005.

McLachlan, H. John. *Socinianism in Seventeenth-century England.* London: Oxford University Press, 1951.

Miller, E. Lynn, ed. "Journal of an Unknown Englishman Traveling Through Central Pennsylvania, 1794." 1988. PSU.

Miller, Perry. *The New England Mind: From Colony to Province.* Cambridge: Harvard University Press, 1953.

————. *The New England Mind: The Seventeenth Century.* Cambridge: Harvard University Press, 1954.

Miller, Peter, ed. *Joseph Priestley: Political Writings.* Cambridge: Cambridge University Press, 1993.

Miller, Randall M., and William Pencak, eds. *Pennsylvania: A History of the Commonwealth.* University Park: Pennsylvania State University Press, 2002.

Miller, Roy F. "The Presbytery of Northumberland." *Proceedings and Addresses of the Northumberland County Historical Society* 24 (1963): 9–21.

Moore, R. Laurence. *Religious Outsiders and the Making of Americans.* Oxford: Oxford University Press, 1986.

Morgan, John. "The Unitarian Universalist 'Revival' in Northumberland and Environs." Unitarian-Universalists Congregation of the Susquehanna Valley website. http://home.ptd.net/~sjrubin2/uucsv/history.htm (accessed February 20, 2003).

Moser, Gerald. *Seven Essays on Joseph Priestley.* State College, Pa.: privately printed, 1994.

Mullin, Robert B., and Russell E. Richey, eds. *Reimagining Denominationalism: Interpretive Essays.* New York: Oxford University Press, 1994.

Noll, Mark. *Princeton and the Republic, 1768–1822: The Search for a Christian Enlightenment in the Era of Samuel Stanhope Smith.* Princeton: Princeton University Press, 1989.

Payne, Michael. "Priestley, Pantisocracy and the Poets." Pt. 1. *Proceedings and Addresses of the Northumberland County Historical Society* 32 (1994): 25–34.

Pelikan, Jaroslav. *The Christian Tradition: A History of the Development of Doctrine.* Five volumes. Chicago: University of Chicago Press, 1971–89.

————. *Jesus Through the Centuries: His Place in the History of Culture.* New Haven: Yale University Press, 1985.

Pierson, George Wilson. *Tocqueville in America.* Baltimore: Johns Hopkins University Press, 1996.

Pointer, Richard W. *Protestant Pluralism and the New York Experience: A Study of Eighteenth-Century Religious Diversity.* Bloomington: Indiana University Press, 1988.

Powell, John Harvey. *Bring Out Your Dead: The Great Plague of Yellow Fever in Phila-delphia in 1793*. 1949. Reprint. Philadelphia: University of Pennsylvania Press, 1993.

Purvis, Thomas L. "The European Ancestry of the United States Population, 1790." *William and Mary Quarterly* 41 (1984).

———, ed. *Revolutionary America, 1763 to 1800*. New York: Facts On File, 1995.

Richardson, William N. "Joseph Priestley's American Home." Pt. 1. *Proceedings and Addresses of the Northumberland County Historical Society* 32 (1994): 61–70.

Robbins, Caroline. *The Eighteenth-century Commonwealthman*. Cambridge: Harvard University Press, 1961.

Robinson, David. *The Unitarians and the Universalists*. Westport, Conn.: Green-wood Press, 1985.

Scharf, J. Thomas, and Thompson Westcott. *History of Philadelphia, 1609–1884*. Vol. 2. Philadelphia, 1884.

Schnure, William M. *Selinsgrove, Penna. Chronology*. Vol. 1, *1700–1850*. Middle-burg, Pa.: Middleburg Post, 1918.

Schofield, Robert. *The Enlightened Joseph Priestley: A Study of His Life and Works from 1773 to 1804*. University Park: Pennsylvania State University Press, 2004.

———. *The Enlightenment of Joseph Priestley: A Study of His Life and Works from 1733 to 1773*. University Park: Pennsylvania State University Press, 1997.

———. *The Lunar Society of Birmingham: A Social History of Provincial Science and Industry in Eighteenth-Century England*. Oxford: Clarendon Press, 1963.

———. *A Scientific Autobiography of Joseph Priestley, 1733–1804*. Cambridge: MIT University Press, 1966.

Schwartz, A. Truman, and John G. McEvoy, eds. *Motion Toward Perfection: The Achievement of Joseph Priestley*. Boston: Skinner House Books, Unitarian Universalist Association, 1990.

Schwartz, Sally. *A Mixed Multitude: The Struggle for Toleration in Colonial Pennsylva-nia*. New York: New York University Press, 1987.

Shammas, Carole. "The Space Problem in Early United States Cities." *The William and Mary Quarterly*, third series, 57 (July 2000): 505–42.

Smith, Edgar F. *Priestley in America: 1794–1804*. Philadelphia: P. Blakiston's Son, 1920.

Smith, Leonard. *The Unitarians: A Short History*. Cumbria: Lensden Publishing, 2006.

Stanley, Dean. "The Historical Aspect of the United States." *Littell's Living Age* (Boston), fifth series, 25, no. 1807, February 1, 1879.

Staples, William C. *Washington Unitarianism: A Rich Heritage*. Washington, D.C.: All Soul's Church, 1970.

Starbuck, Edwin D. *The Psychology of Religion: An Empirical Study of the Growth of Religious Consciousness*. New York: Charles Scribner's Sons, 1901.

Stephens, W. B., ed. *A History of the County of Warwick*. Vol. 8, *The City and County of Warwick*. London: Published for the Institute of Historical Research by the Oxford University Press, 1969.

Stokes, Anson P. *Church and State in the United States*. Two volumes. New York: Harper and Row, 1950.

Thomas, D. O. *The Honest Mind: The Thought and Work of Richard Price*. Oxford: Clarendon Press, 1977.

Thomas, Howard. *Trenton Falls: Yesterday & Today*. Prospect, N.Y.: Prospect Books, 1951.

Tocqueville, Alexis de. *Democracy in America*. The Henry Reeve text as revised by Francis Bowen, now further corrected and edited with introduction, editorial notes, and bibliographies by Phillips Bradley; introduction by Daniel J. Boorstin. New York: Vintage Books, 1990.

Toulmin, Priestley. "The Descendents of Joseph Priestley, LL.D, F.R.S." Pt. 2. *Proceedings and Addresses of the Northumberland County Historical Society* 32 (1994): 1–126.

U.S. Senate. *Journal of the Senate of the United States of America*. Vol. 3, December 14, 1802. Washington, D.C.: U.S. Government Printing Office, 1802.

Wallace, Dewey D., Jr. "Socinianism, Justification by Faith, and the Sources of John Locke's *The Reasonableness of Christianity*." *Journal of the History of Ideas* 45, no. 1 (1984): 49–66.

Wickersham, James P. *A History of Education in Pennsylvania, Private and Public, Elementary and Higher*. 1885. Reprint. Harrisburg: Pennsylvania Historic and Museum Commission, 1979.

Wilbur, Earl Morse. *A History of Unitarianism in Transylvania, England, and America*. Cambridge: Harvard University Press, 1945 and 1952.

———. *Our Unitarian Heritage*. Second edition. Cambridge: Harvard University Press, 1953.

Wilkinson, Norman, ed. "Mr. Davy's Diary, 1794." *Pennsylvania History* 20 (April 1953).

Williams, George. "Joseph Priestley: A Commemorative Sermon." Pt. 1. *Proceedings and Addresses of the Northumberland County Historical Society* 32 (1994): 1–12.

Williams, George Huntston. *The Radical Reformation*. Philadelphia: Westminster Press, 1962.

Willis, N. Parker, ed. *Trenton Falls, Picturesque and Descriptive: Embracing the Original Essay of John Sherman, the First Proprietor and Resident*. New York: N. Orr, 1868.

Wolfe, Alan. *The Transformation of American Religion: How We Actually Live Our Faith*. New York: The Free Press, 2003.

Woolfley, H. L. Dufour. *Susquehanna Squire: The Story of William Lloyd*. Westminster, Md.: Heritage Books, 2005.

Wright, Conrad. "American Unitarianism in 1805." *Journal of the Unitarian Universalist History* 30 (2005).

———. *The Beginnings of Unitarianism in America*. Boston: Beacon Press, 1955.

———. *The Liberal Christians: Essays on American Unitarian History*. Boston: Beacon Press, 1970.

Wright, Conrad Edick., ed. *American Unitarianism, 1805–1865*. Boston: The Massachusetts Historical Society and Northeastern University Press, 1989.

INDEX

Page numbers in *italics* indicate illustrations.